Instructor's Resource Manual
for
Woolfolk

Educational Psychology
Seventh Edition

Prepared by
A. M. O'Donnell
Rutgers University

Allyn and Bacon
Boston · London · Toronto · Sydney · Tokyo · Singapore

Copyright © 1998, 1995, 1993, 1990, 1987, 1984, 1980 by Allyn and Bacon
A Viacom Company
160 Gould Street
Needham Heights, Massachusetts 02194

Internet: www.abacon.com
America Online: Keyword: College Online

All rights reserved. The contents, or parts thereof, may be reproduced for use with *Educational Psychology*, Seventh Edition, by Anita Woolfolk, provided such reproductions bear copyright notice, but may not be reproduced in any form for any other purpose without written permission from the copyright owner.

ISBN 0-205-26336-4

Printed in the United States of America

10 9 8 7 6 5 4 3 2 1   02 01 00 99 98 97

Contents

Section	Topic	Page
Introduction		3
Chapter 1	Teachers, Teaching, and Educational Psychology	6
	Handouts	16
Chapter 2	The Mind at Work: Cognitive Development and Language	28
	Handouts	40
Chapter 3	Personal, Social, and Emotional Development	52
	Handouts	69
Chapter 4	Learning Abilities and Learning Challenges	81
	Handouts	103
Chapter 5	The Impact of Culture and Community	123
	Handouts	139
Chapter 6	Learning: Behavioral Views	151
	Handouts	165
Chapter 7	Cognitive Approaches to Learning	176
	Handouts	191
Chapter 8	Complex Cognitive Processes	199
	Handouts	213
Chapter 9	Learning and Instruction	220
	Handouts	239
Chapter 10	Motivation: Issues and Explanations	257
	Handouts	272
Chapter 11	Motivation, Teaching, and Learning	282
	Handouts	297
Chapter 12	Creating Learning Environments	304
	Handouts	325
Chapter 13	Teaching for Learning	338
	Handouts	351
Chapter 14	Standardized Testing	359
	Handouts	373
Chapter 15	Classroom Evaluation and Grading	380
	Handouts	395
Research Appendix		408

Introduction

Educational psychology is the study of psychology in education. On the one hand, it involves the application of psychological principles in educational settings and thus requires in-depth knowledge of basic psychological principles. On the other hand, educational psychology is more than simply the application of psychological principles in educational settings. The nature of educational settings demand a consideration of the effects of settings on the psychology of the participants. The field of educational psychology is therefore concerned with the applications of knowledge but also the generation of knowledge.

Courses in educational psychology differ on many dimensions that influence an instructor's needs and priorities in the course. These dimensions include the instructor's prior teaching experience (their experience in teaching the course, teaching philosophies of the instructors), the purpose of the course (it may be part of a teacher education program or it may be part of a general suite of offerings in a psychology department), the students (second year students, juniors, seniors, or graduate students), and whether field experiences accompany the course. Depending on a constellation of factors, the course may be taught quite differently. The instructor's resource manual is developed around the expectation of multiple types of users and the organization of the text is such that the instructor can locate those materials he or she may find useful. The research base for knowledge in educational psychology is important and many activities included here involve research in some fashion. Many activities are described as cooperative activities but could also be done as individual activities.

Activities

The activities in the Instructor's Resource Manual are grouped as follows;
- cooperative activities
- research activities
- using technology

- field experiences
- other teaching activities

Cooperative Activities

Because educational psychology involves complex knowledge (both declarative and procedural knowledge), students may benefit from sharing ideas, comparing products, or generating joint plans. Many of the activities included here are cooperative but could also be done individually (with some exceptions). The activities described would involve mostly in-class work. For instructors who are uncomfortable with group activities or prefer a different style of teaching, activities in other categories may be more appropriate.

Research Activities

The activities included under "research activities" in this manual include a variety of activities. These vary from experiences in which the students' own research skills are developed to ones in which students summarize what is known about a particular topic and critique available research. The goal of these activities is to help the student develop skills as a critical consumer of research and to rely on evidence for teaching practices.

Using Technology

Technology of various sorts is an increasingly important component of learning and instruction. The activities in this category provide students with opportunities to use technology in the service of their own learning in this course. Many activities ask students to locate resources on the World Wide Web that will be helpful to them as teachers.

Field Experiences

The opportunity to observe and participate in classrooms is an important element of the knowledge acquisition desired in an educational psychology class. Activities in this group involve students observing and collecting information in classes, interviewing teachers, and a variety of other kinds of tasks.

Reminders. If you have students working in classrooms, remember to get the appropriate clearances from the school administration. If your students are going to be collecting data of any sort in classrooms or in the college community, you will need to check with your Institutional Review Board for Research with Humans about the necessary precautions and permissions that must be in place <u>before</u> such information can be collected.

Other Teaching Activities

In this group, you will find some additional activities. Teachers who prefer not to rely on groups may find activities here that are more appropriate to their teaching methods. You should remember, however, that most activities can be reconstructed in an alternative format.

Organization of the Instructor's Resource Manual

The manual is organized in fifteen sections corresponding to the fifteen chapters in the text, <u>Educational Psychology</u> by Anita Woolfolk. Within each section, you will find:

- a teaching outline
- activities
- handout masters
- additional resources

The teaching outline provides a detailed outline of the chapter. The activities and handout masters are designed to both give you ideas about activities you might use to enhance your teaching. The handout masters that accompany these activities will provide you with some materials to support your instruction. Finally, the additional resources section will direct you to additional materials.

1

Teachers, Teaching, and Educational Psychology

Teaching Outline

I. What Do You Think? What Would You Do?
II. What Is Good Teaching?
    A. Inside five expert teachers' classrooms.
        1. A bilingual first grade
        2. A suburban sixth grade
        3. An inner-city middle school
        4. Two advanced math classes
    B. Expert knowledge as defined by Lee Shulman (1987)
        1. Academic subjects taught
        2. General teaching strategies
        3. Curriculum materials/programs for their subject area and grade level
        4. Subject-specific knowledge for teaching
        5. Characteristics of learners and their cultural backgrounds
        6. Settings in which student learn
        7. Goals and purposes of education
III. Teaching: Artistry, Technique, And A Lot Of Work
IV. Point/Counterpoint: Whose Classroom Is It, Anyway?
    A. Concerns of beginning teachers
        1. Developing confidence in their teaching skills
        2. Maintaining classroom discipline, motivating and accommodating differences among students
        3. Surviving the real-life situation of the classroom: "reality shock"
    B. What about the students?
V. The Role Of Educational Psychology
    A. Common sense answers and those based on research
        1. Example: Taking turns
        2. Example: Classroom management
        3. Example: Skipping grades
    B. Using research to understand and improve teaching: Types of research
        1. Descriptive research: Describes what is happening in class
            a) Ethnography: Descriptive research about naturally occurring events
            b) Participant observation: The researcher is part of the action

                        c)   Case study: In-depth investigation
              2.   Correlational: Indicates the strength and direction of a relationship between two events/measurements (negative or positive)
              3.   Experimentation: Changes are introduced and results are noted
      C.   Theories for teaching

VI.   The Contents Of This Book
      A.   A quick tour of this book
            1.   Part 1: Human Development
            2.   Part 2: Individual Variations
            3.   Part 3: Learning: Three Approaches to Theory and Practice
            4.   Part 4: Motivation and Management
            5.   Part 5: Teaching
            6.   Part 6: Assessment
      B.   How this book can help you
            1.   Helps build professional knowledge base for teaching
            2.   Enables reader to think critically about teaching
            3.   Helps develop a repertoire of effective principles and practices for first years of teaching

VII.   Summary

VIII.   Key Terms And Concepts

Teachers, Teaching, and Educational Psychology

Learning Activities and Related Research

Chapter 1: ACTIVITIES	HANDOUTS
	1.0 Lecture Outline Concept Map: Expert Teachers
Cooperative Activities	1.1 Concept Map: Expert Teachers
1.1 Creating and Maintaining Groups	1.2 Group Contract
1.2 Characteristics of Influential Teachers	1.3 Best Teacher Competition
	1.4 Most Effective Teacher Competition
	1.5 Summary of Teacher Characteristics
	1.6 Categories of Attributes
Research Activities	
1.3 Survey of Teacher Roles	1.7 Survey of Teacher Roles
1.4 What Research Has To Say	1.8 Journals in Educational Psychology
1.5 Experimental vs. Correlational Research	
Using Technology	
1.6 Search engines on the Internet	1.9 Using search engines
Field Experience	
1.7 Observation: Tasks & Process	1.10 Planning a visit to schools
Other Teaching Activities	
1.8 Contribution of Educational Psychology	

Cooperative Activities

1.1   Creating and Maintaining Groups

Many of the suggestions in this manual involve students working together. Some instructors experience concern about the use of groups in a college class because group discussion can be unfocused, all students may not participate equally or benefit equally, and interpersonal difficulties may emerge. The use of "base groups" (Johnson & Johnson, 1991) can limit many of the problems typically experienced by groups. Your task as an instructor will be to:
- assign students to groups
- provide tasks that are possible to complete within the class
- monitor student progress

Some instructors assign students to groups based on students' previous test grades, maintaining a balance of high and low achievers in each group. If your goal is to use the same groups throughout the semester, however, you may not have access to information which would allow you to do so. Random assignment of students to groups works well.

Maintaining the groups. Prevention is better than cure. Once students have been assigned to a group, ask students to develop a group contract for conduct within the group (**See Handout Master 1.2**). Many problems are eliminated when students make their expectations explicit. From time to time throughout the semester, you should ask students to check how well they are implementing their contract.

Copyright © 1998 by Allyn and Bacon

1.2   Characteristics of Influential Teachers

This activity can be done using **Handout Masters 1.3 to 1.6**. The activity combines some individual work and some group work. First, ask students to complete **Handout Masters 1.3** and **1.4** in which they describe the attributes of their "best" and "most effective" teachers. You should look to see if students actually name the same teacher as both "best" and "most effective." Students should work alone on this part of the activity. Once completed, students should be arranged in groups to discuss their decisions. **Using Handouts 1.5a and 1.5b**, students in groups will summarize the strengths and weaknesses of the teachers mentioned. Students should then complete **Handout 1.6**, which asks them to induce general categories of attributes that might characterize best and most effective teachers. These induced categories might be expected to resemble the areas of professional knowledge proposed by Shulman (see text by Woolfolk).

Research Activities

1.3   Survey of Teacher Roles

Distribute **Handout Master 1.7** and have students ask five teachers to rate each of the "seven roles" of teaching according to the degree of importance and strength in each role (teacher as motivator, manager, instructional expert, counselor, model, leader, and reflective professional). Tabulate and summarize the findings for your sample. Have your students critique the interpretations that might be made of this summary. What could be misleading? Then have your students consider each of the seven roles of teaching in relation to their own perceptions of their teaching goals and abilities. Which areas are the strongest for them? In what ways will they strengthen weak areas?

1.4   What Research Has To Say

Have your students consider the statement "Students should be grouped according to ability." How could they find out if this was true or false. What would it take to convince you of the truth of this statement? Assign students the task of locating an article in the library that addresses this question. The directions should be deliberately ambiguous so that students return with a variety of types of articles (e.g., popular, research) that will provide the basis of a general discussion of what constitutes good evidence.

1.5   Experimental vs. Correlational Research

From Maknosky, V. P., Wittemore, L. G., and Rogers, A. M. (eds.)(1987) *Activity handbook for the teaching of psychology*, Washington, DC.: American Psychological Association.

Teachers, Teaching, and Educational Psychology

Concept: Initially, many students of educational psychology think all research is experimental. The following activity can illustrate for you students the difference between experimental research and descriptive/correlational research.

Instructions: After you have discussed experimental and correlational research in class, have students form into groups of two to four people. Give them the following instructions: Suppose you are hired as a research psychologist by a dental products firm.

1. Outline an experiment in which you are trying to prove that brushing with BEST toothpaste results in fewer cavities. Be sure to describe who your research participants will be and how you will assign them to different conditions or groups. Also identify your independent and dependent variables.

2. Outline a correlational study in which you are trying to determine if there is a relationship between brushing with BEST toothpaste and the number of cavities subjects have. Suppose your correlational study resulted in a correlation coefficient of +.81. How would you interpret this result? How would you interpret a correlation coefficient of -.81? How would you interpret a correlation of +.08?

You may wish to assign half of the class to work on Study 1 and half to work on Study 2. However, the difference between correlational and experimental research is appreciated better if students have experienced both studies.

Discussion: The major emphasis of the discussion should be on: (a) How correlational studies allow us to make predictions but do not demonstrate causation; (b) Why experimental research allows us to talk about causation; and (c) Why replication is important in determining causation.

Using Technology

1.6   Search Engines on the Internet

The Internet is a vast network of computers connected to one another. The World Wide Web allows people to take advantage of this network of computers to locate information about almost any topic. Because of the enormous amount of information available on the World Wide Web, a variety of search engines were developed to assist with searching. Using any browser (e.g., Netscape Navigator, Microsoft Explorer), click on a portion of the screen that says "search." Most browsers provide access to the following search engines:

Alta Vista	Excite	Infoseek	Yahoo
Magellan	Webcrawler	Netguide	Lycos

Teachers, Teaching, and Educational Psychology

Using Handout Master 1.9, ask your students to type the word "Teachers" into the search field of many of these search engines and compare the results provided by the different search engines.

Field Experience

1.7   Observation: Tasks and Process

This activity requires your students to visit a school and articulate their expectations and conclusions about their visit. **Using Handout Master 1.10**, ask your students to plan a visit to a nearby school. The questions in the handout master are divided into three parts: before the visit, at the school, and after they have looked around for a while. They are asked to compare expectations to what they observe. You should ask them to make notes of some initial responses to the questions on the handout. Students will need to contact the school principal for permission to visit.

Other Teaching Activities

1.8   Contributions of Educational Psychology

Berliner, D. and Rosenshine, R. (Eds.) (1987). *Talks to teachers*, NY: Random House.

Eisner, E. W. (1983, January). The art and craft of teaching. Educational Leadership, 413

Gage, N. (1985). Hard gains in soft science. Bloomington, IN: Phi Delta Kappan.

The following quotes can be used as a prompts for a discussion about the value of educational psychology.

I do not believe that with greater specificity or by reducing the whole to its most essential parts we can produce the kind of prescriptions that have made the space shuttle, radar, or laser beam possible. The aspiration to create a prescriptive science of educational practice is, I believe, hopeless." (Eisner, p. 8)

Rather, it (research on the scientific basis of teaching) calls for the same kind of steady effort that improved cures for Hodgkin's disease, surgery for detached retinas, social roles for women, freedom from racial discrimination in employment, equality of educational opportunity, and human longevity. The natural and social sciences have contributed magnificently to these advancements of the human condition. Over the decades, scientific method can do the same for teaching and teacher education. (Gage, pp. 53-59)

You make a great, a very great mistake, if you think psychology, being a science of the mind's laws, is something from which you can deduce definite programs and schemes and methods of instruction for immediate school use. Psychology is a science and teaching as art: And sciences never generate arts directly out of themselves. An intermediary inventive mind must make the application, by using its originality. (William James, from Berliner and Rosenshine).

For a follow-up discussion question, students might consider what aspects of teaching they consider more of an art than a science, i.e. more intuitive than formally learned.

Discussion Questions

1. Should teachers' jobs and salaries depend on how much their students learn? What would happen to curricula, attention to students' differences?

2. Irrespective of length of service or expertise, the job of teaching is often the same. Should this be the case? What changes in a teacher's job might occur as a function of increased experience or expertise?

3. Students often identify teachers as most effective who were not very personable or approachable. Is it possible to be personable, caring, and effective? When would it be a liability to be personable or approachable? When would it be an advantage?

4. Indicate whether each of the studies described below is an experimental or correlational study and what could be learned from them:

- Instructors give three groups of children different types of computer training to determine which type of computer training is most effective in teaching word-processing skills.

- Psychologists give fine-motor tests to a group of boys and girls to determine if there is a relationship between sex and fine-motor dexterity.

- Two groups of athletes begin a fitness program. To determine the impact of nutrition, sports psychologists give one group explicit instructions regarding nutrition while advising the other group to continue eating their regular diet.

5. Define and differentiate purposes of educational psychology. In your opinion, can the study of educational psychology be helpful to teacher candidates and to practicing teachers?

Additional Resources for Teaching This Chapter

REFERENCES

Andre, T. and Hegland, S. (1990). Educational psychology and the reform of teacher education. Educational Psychology, 2, 237-254.

Blumenfeld, P. C., & Anderson, L. (Eds.). (1996). Teaching educational psychology (A special issue of Educational Psychologist, 31. Mahwah, NJ: Lawrence Erlbaum Associates.

Calderhead, J. and Gates, P. (eds.) (1993). Conceptualizing reflection in teacher development. London: Falmer Press.

Killon, J. P. and Todnem, G.R. (1991). A process for personal theory building. Educational Leadership, 48(6), 14-16.

Larke, P., Wiseman, D. and Bradley, C. (1990). The minority mentorship project: Changing attitudes of preservice teachers for diverse classrooms. Action in Teacher Education, 12(3), 5-11.

Johnson, D. W., Johnson, R. T., & Smith, K. A. (1991). Cooperative learning: Increasing college faculty instructional productivity. ASHE-ERIC Higher Educational Report No. 4, Washington, D. C.: The George Washington University, School of Education and Human Development.

Murphy, D. S., Colvin, C. and Morey, A.I. (1990). Helping new teachers to become thoughtful practitioners. Educational Horizons, 68(4), 183-186.

Philips, D. C. (Ed.), (1994). Epistemological perspectives on educational psychology. A special issue of Educational Psychologist, 31. Mahwah, NJ: Lawrence Erlbaum Associates.

Shane, H. G. (1990). Improving education for the 21st century. Educational Horizons, 69(1), 10-15.

Yaxley, B. G. (1991). Developing teachers' theories of teaching: A touchstone approach. London: Falmer Press.

Teachers, Teaching, and Educational Psychology

FILMS, VIDEOTAPES, AND AUDIOCASSETTES

Experiments in human behavior, video, 35 minutes, color. This video illustrates how experiments serve as problem-solving tools. It reviews the steps involved in setting up an experiment, the concepts of an independent variable and researcher bias. Also describes observation, and the use of questionnaires.

In pursuit of the expert pedagogue, 50 min. David C. Berliner and his colleagues in a University of Arizona research project are trying to understand the nature of expertise in pedagogy. Their strategy has been to find and study expert and experienced teachers and to compare them with ordinary or novice teachers in order to discover how they differ in their behavior and their approaches to tasks. Early findings indicate that among the most important differences is problem solving ability, which expert teachers share with experts in such other fields as chess or physics. To purchase: $30 (AERA members), $40 (nonmembers). Order from: AERA Videotape Sales, P.O. Box 19700, Washington, DC 20036.

Sara Lightfoot, video, 30 minutes. Part of Bill Moyer's World of ideas series. According to Sara Lightfoot, a professor of education at Harvard's Graduate School of Education, "The currency of a good teacher is ideas, as conveyed through relationships." Lightfoot describes what makes certain schools good and some teachers memorable. She highlights the problems and promise of American Schools and stresses the need to put learning back into teaching. From PBS.

Standards: National Teacher Certification. 22 min. The video examines the challenges in developing a national certification system. Teachers who serve on the National Board for Professional Teaching Standards answer questions from peers and respond to their concerns. From Insight Media, 2162 Broadway, New York, NY 10024-6620

Teachers make a difference, video, 10 minutes. This emotionally charged video is a morale booster. Developed for ASCD's celebration of 1985 as year of the teacher, this tape consists of testimonials about teachers who have made a difference in the lives of both ordinary and well-known people. From ASCD.

Teacher decision making, film, 30 minutes. This film identifies the most important daily teaching decisions that are the foundation of learning efficiency and effectiveness. (MP 402, Campcut Film Distributors, 1971) To light a fire: Great teachers in America, video, 30 minutes. This video takes you into the classrooms of two teachers who were selected after a nationwide search of America's outstanding educators for those who have demonstrated outstanding success in the classroom. From PBS.

Understanding research, video, 30 minutes, color. This video examines the scientific method and the ways in which data are collected and analyzed in the lab and the field.(Annenberg CPB Collection, 1990)

Understanding the Internet. 30 min. Provides a basic introduction to the Internet. From Insight Media, 2162 Broadway, New York, NY 10024-6620

Handout Master 1.0

Lecture Outline ----- Teachers, Teaching, and Educational Psychology

- What is Good Teaching?

- Teaching: An Art and a Science

- The Role of Educational Psychology

- Research as a Tool for Understanding and Improving Teaching and Learning

Copyright © 1998 by Allyn and Bacon

Handout Master 1.1 Expert Teachers

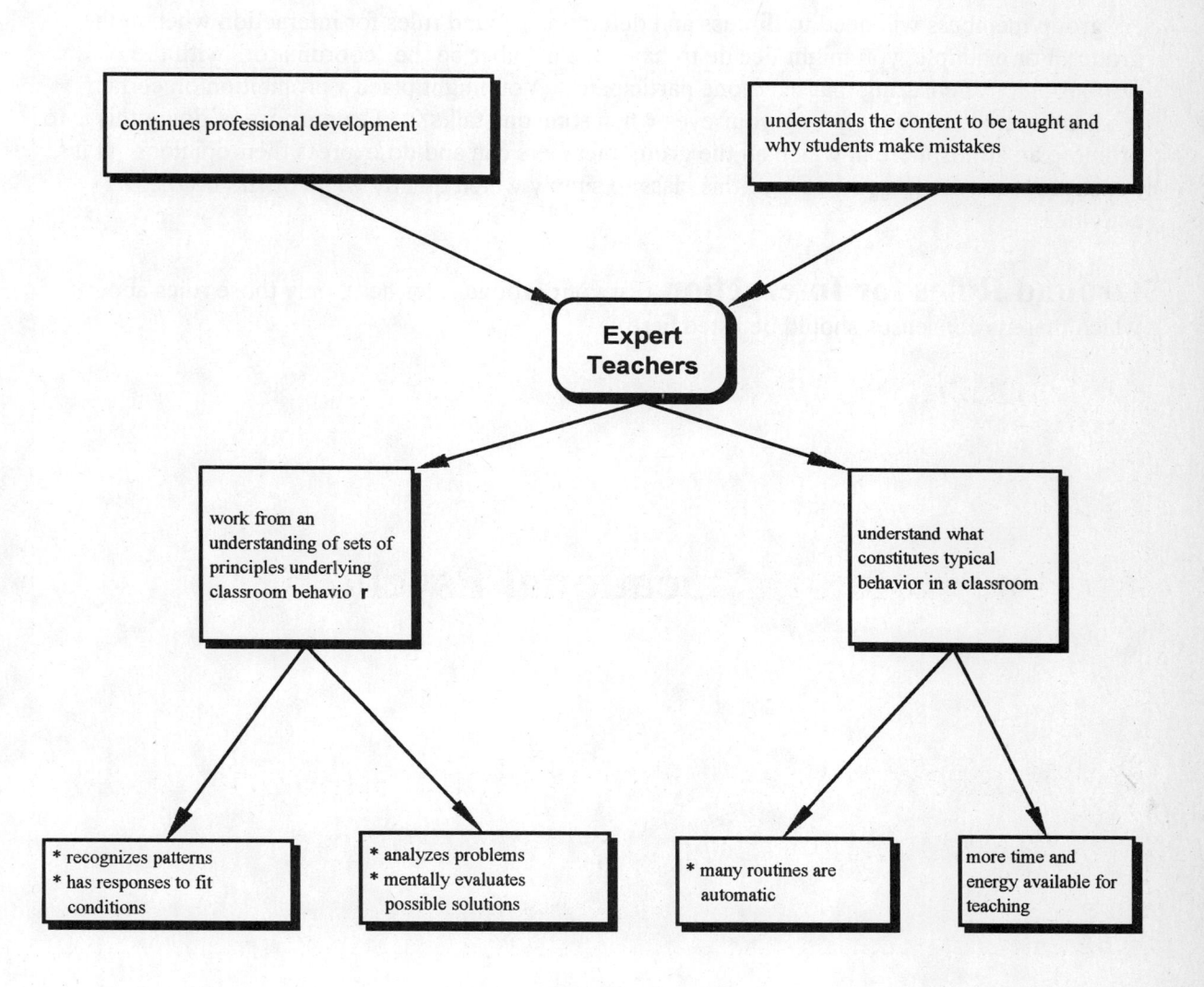

```
continues professional development                    understands the content to be taught and
                                                      why students make mistakes
                              ↘                    ↙
                                 Expert Teachers
                              ↙                    ↘
work from an                                      understand what
understanding of sets of                          constitutes typical
principles underlying                             behavior in a classroom
classroom behavior
     ↙            ↘                                  ↙            ↘
* recognizes      * analyzes problems          * many routines     more time and
  patterns        * mentally evaluates           are automatic     energy available for
* has responses     possible solutions                             teaching
  to fit
  conditions
```

Copyright © 1998 by Allyn and Bacon

Handout Master 1.2

Contract for Group [   ]

All group members will need to discuss and determine ground rules for interaction when in the group. For example, you might decide to have one member be the "coordinator" with the responsibility of ensuring that everyone participates. You might place a prohibition on certain kinds of interaction (e.g., rolling your eyes when someone talks?). The purpose of doing this is to promote an atmosphere in which all the group members can and do express their opinions. It is not appropriate for the purposes of this class to simply watch quietly while others do the activities.

Ground Rules for Interaction (list your ground rules here; only those rules about which there is consensus should be listed here):

Copyright © 1998 by Allyn and Bacon

Handout Master 1.3

Name: **Date:**

BEST TEACHER COMPETITION

You are asked to nominate one of your former teachers for the "Best Teacher of the Year" award. The teacher you nominate can be a teacher you had in either elementary, middle or high school, or a college teacher. In the space provided below, list your nomination and then answer the questions that follow.

Nominee:

Why should this teacher win the award of "Best Teacher of the Year?"

What were the teacher's greatest strengths?

What were the teacher's greatest areas of weakness?

What was the single most important attribute of this teacher?

Copyright © 1998 by Allyn and Bacon

Handout Master 1.4

Name: **Date:**

MOST EFFECTIVE TEACHER COMPETITION

You are asked to nominate one of your former teachers for the award of "Most Effective Teacher of the Year." The teacher you nominate can be a teacher you had in either elementary, middle or high school, or a college teacher. In the space provided below, list your nomination and then answer the questions that follow.

Nominee:

Why should this teacher win the award of "Most Effective Teacher of the Year?"

What were the teacher's greatest strengths?

What were the teacher's greatest areas of weakness?

What was the single most important attribute of this teacher that made him or her effective?

Copyright © 1998 by Allyn and Bacon

Handout Master 1.5 a

BEST TEACHER SUMMARY SHEET

Group [   ]

REASONS	STRENGTHS	WEAKNESSES

Copyright © 1998 by Allyn and Bacon

Handout Master 1.5 b

MOST EFFECTIVE TEACHER SUMMARY SHEET

Group [   ]

REASONS	*STRENGTHS*	*WEAKNESSES*

Copyright © 1998 by Allyn and Bacon

Handout Master 1.6

CATEGORIES OF ATTRIBUTES: Group [   ]

Can the attributes listed for "best" and "most effective" teachers be grouped into a smaller number of categories? List the categories and the attributes that belong to each one.

Copyright © 1998 by Allyn and Bacon

Handout Master 1.7

Survey of Teaching Roles

Please rate each of the roles of teachers listed in the left-hand column according to (a) its importance and (b) your perception of your own strength in that area. A "5" indicates the strongest rating and a "1" indicates the weakest rating. After you rate the items, please briefly answer the questions that follow.

	Teacher Roles (Circle one)	Importance (Circle one)	Strength
1.	Motivator	1 2 3 4 5	1 2 3 4 5
2.	Manager	1 2 3 4 5	1 2 3 4 5
3.	Instructional-Expert	1 2 3 4 5	1 2 3 4 5
4.	Counselor	1 2 3 4 5	1 2 3 4 5
5.	Model	1 2 3 4 5	1 2 3 4 5
6.	Leader	1 2 3 4 5	1 2 3 4 5
7.	Reflective Professional (planning, experimenting, thinking, improving, etc.)	1 2 3 4 5	1 2 3 4 5

8. What is the main reason for your choice of the most important teacher role?

9. What one experience was most important in helping you to identify your area of greatest strengths?

10. In which of your weaker areas do you wish most to improve? What is one step you could take toward that goal?

Handout Master 1.8

Journals in the Educational Psychology Field

Professional education journals discuss current topics in education and often include information about research in educational psychology as well. Here are some examples:

American Journal of Education	*Journal of Education*
Childhood Education	*Journal of Teacher Education*
Contemporary Education Review	*Phi Delta Kappan*
Educational Leadership	*The Review of Education*
Educational Researcher	*Theory into Practice*
Harvard Educational Review	*Young Children*

Other journals specialize in reports of research studies or reviews of several studies on one topic. Here are some examples:

Adolescence	*Journal of Experimental Education*
American Educational Research Journal	*Journal of Learning Disabilities*
American Psychologist	*Journal of Research and Development*
Child Development	*Journal of School Psychology*
Cognition and Instruction	*Learning and Instruction*
Cognitive Psychology	*Monographs of the Society for Research in Child Development*
Computers in Education	*Psychological Bulletin*
Contemporary Educational Psychology	*Psychological Review*
Curriculum Review	*Psychology in the Schools*
Educational and Psychological Measurement	*Review of Educational Research*
Educational Psychology Review	*School Psychology Review*
Elementary School Journal	*Teaching and Teacher Education*
Exceptional Children	
Human Development	
Instructional Science	
International Review of Educational Research	
Journal of Applied Behavior Analysis	
Journal of Applied Developmental Psychology	
Journal of Educational Computing Research	
Journal of Educational Research	
Journal of Experimental Child Psychology	

Copyright © 1998 by Allyn and Bacon

Handout Master 1.9

Using Search Engines

A search engine is a tool for searching the huge amount of information available on the Internet. For the following exercise, you will need to connect to the Internet using your computer and a browser (e.g., Netscape or Internet Explorer). The browsers give you a number of search engines to choose from. Type the word "Teacher" in as many of these search engines as are available to you. In the spaces provided, list the top three "hits" or results of your search.

Search Engine	First	Second	Third
Lycos			
Yahoo			
Infoseek			
Alta Vista			
Magellan			
Excite			
Webcrawler			
Netguide			
Hotbot			
AOLNetfind			

How did the results provided by the different search engines differ?

Which search engine gave you the most useful information? Why?

Copyright © 1998 by Allyn and Bacon

Handout Master 1.10

Planning a Visit to Schools

Part 1: Just before I enter the school:

What are my thoughts and feelings?

What are my predictions of what I will find when I look around?

Part 2: In the school:

What are my thoughts and feelings?

How is this school similar to the schools I went to?

How is this school different from the schools I went to?

Part 3: Now that I have spent some time looking around:

What do I expect of a good teacher at this school? Is this expectation different from what I would normally expect of a good teacher? If so, how, and why?

What do I expect of a teacher who is having problems? Is this expectation different from what I would normally expect? If so, how, and why?

How do the classroom setups differ from what I expect?

What do I expect of a well-disciplined student at this school? Is this expectation different from what I would normally expect of a well-disciplined student? If so, how, and why?

What do I expect a teacher to do if a student does not behave appropriately in this school? Is this expectation different from what I would normally expect? If so, how, and why?

What are my other thoughts and feelings?

From: McNeeley, S. L. (1997). <u>Observing students and teachers through objective strategies</u>. Needham Heights, MA: Allyn & Bacon.

Copyright © 1998 by Allyn and Bacon

Cognitive Development and Language

2

Cognitive Development and Language

Teaching Outline

I. What Do You Think? Overview/What would you do?
II. A definition of development
    A. Orderly, adaptive changes by human and animals between conception and death: physical, personal, social, and cognitive
    B. Influential factors
        1. Maturation--genetically programmed, naturally occurring changes
        2. Environmental interaction
    C. Principles of development
        1. Occurs at different rates
        2. Is relatively orderly
        3. Takes place gradually
    D. The brain and cognitive development
        1. Various parts of the brain are involved with various functions
        2. Two hemispheres of the brain shows lateralized development
        3. Contemporary research connects learning to brain functioning
III. Piaget's Theory Of Cognitive Development
    A. Piaget's basic assumption: Development as "making sense of the world"
    B. Influences on development: Maturation, activity, social transmission
    C. Basic tendencies in thinking
        1. Organization: Tendency to organize thinking processes into psychological structures/schemes
        2. Adaptation: Tendency to adapt to the environment through complementary processes of assimilation and accommodation
        3. Equilibration: A balance among organization, assimilation and accommodation
        4. Disequilibration: Failure of a scheme to produce satisfying a result, so search continues through assimilation and accommodation
    D. Four stages of cognitive development: stage theory broadly defines the unvarying sequence of steps in the development of thinking abilities
        1. Infancy: The sensorimotor stage (approximate ages 0-2)
            a) Development based upon information obtained through the senses or body movements
            b) Development of understanding of object permanence
            c) Development of goal-directed actions and reversible actions
        2. Early childhood to the early elementary years: The preoperational stage (approximate ages 2-7)
            a) Beginning of logical mental actions (operations)

Cognitive Development and Language

3. Difficulty with two principles: Decentering and conservation
4. Egocentrism: Tendency to see world from own view
5. Collective monologue characterizes children's speech (no real interaction takes place)
6. Guidelines: Teaching the Preoperational Child

E. Later elementary to middle school years: The concrete operational stage (approximate ages 7-11)
1. "Hands-on thinking" stage: Recognizes stability of physical world, realizes elements can be changed and retain original characteristics (identity), and is capable of reversible thinking
2. Operations mastered at this stage: Conservation, classification and Seriation
3. Guidelines: Teaching the Concrete Operational Child

F. Junior and senior high: Formal operations (approximate ages 11-15)
1. "Scientific" reasoning stage: Hypothetico-deductive and inductive reasoning
2. This stage not necessary for survival; achieved in areas of interest and experience
3. Do we all reach the fourth stage?
4. Guidelines: Helping Students to Use Formal Operations

IV. Implications of Piaget's theory for teachers
1. Understanding students' thinking
   a) Learning is a constructive process
   b) Determine students' logic/solutions as they solve problems
   c) Look for repeated mistakes or problems
   d) Matching strategies to abilities
   e) Keep disequilibrium "just right" to encourage growth
   f) Ensure students active engagement in learning process
   g) Apply and test principles learned in one situation to a new situation
2. Point/Counterpoint: Can Cognitive Development Be Accelerated?

B. Some Limitations Of Piaget's Theory
1. Children's development does not fit consistently into stages
2. Possible underestimation of younger children's cognitive ability
3. Alternative explanations for performance on conservation tasks
4. Inattention to the effects of children's cultural and social group

V. Vygotsky's Sociocultural Perspective
A. Cognitive development depends on interaction with:
1. the people in the child's world
2. the tools that the culture provides to support thinking

B. The role of language and private speech
1. Allows younger children to guide behavior and thinking
2. Transitions to inner speech--helps solve problems
3. Comparison of Vygotsky and Piaget's views of private speech

Cognitive Development and Language

                4.   Self-talk and learning: Teaches students to use cognitive self-instruction
        C.   The Role of Adults and Peers
              1.   Serve as guides to support cognitive growth, the process of providing guidance is often referred to as scaffolding
              2.   Assisted learning: Provides categories and concepts for thinking
              3.   Most guidance is communicated through language

VI.   Implications of Vygotsky's Theory for Teaching
        A.   Assisted Learning
              1.   requires scaffolding, giving information, prompts, reminders, encouragement
              2.   Examples: Meichenbaum's cognitive self-instruction, cognitive apprenticeship, reciprocal teaching
        B.   The zone of proximal development
              1.   Area where child cannot solve problem alone, but can with "scaffolding"
              2.   Optimal for teaching and learning
              3.   Dynamic assessment or assessment of learning potential

VII.   The Development Of Language

VIII. How Do We Learn Language?
        A.   Universal grammar : A set of specifications and rules that limit the range of language created
        B.   Language is learned like other cognitive activities by active pattern-seeking
        C.   Care-givers may use reward to shape language

IX.   Stages In The Process Of Language Acquisition
        A.   First words
              1.   Holophrases: Single words to express complex ideas
              2.   Overextension: Use of one word to cover a range of concepts
              3.   Underextension: Use of words too specifically
        B.   First sentences
              1.   Telegraphic speech: Nonessentials omitted, as in a telegram
              2.   Sentences are short, but semantics are complex
        C.   Learning grammar
              1.   Overregularization uses rules too extensively
              2.   The order of words in a sentence is simplistically understood
        D.   Learning vocabulary
              1.   Between ages 2 and 4, vocabulary doubles every six months
              2.   By age 5-6: Child masters basics of language; still egocentric with meanings

X.   Language Development In The School Years
        A.   Pronunciation: The distinctive sounds of a language
              1.   By first grade most phonemes mastered
              2.   Intonation: Word emphasis may still cause problems
        B.   Syntax

1. Early elementary -school years: Passive sentences understood but not generally used
           2. Elementary school--Complex grammatical structures first understood, then used
       C. Vocabulary and meaning
           1. Average six year old has a vocabulary of 8,000-14,000 words
           2. From 9-11, 5000 new words added
           3. Abstract words, justice or economy still difficult in early years
       D. Pragmatics: Appropriate use of language in context
           1. Use of simpler sentences to talk to younger children
           2. Ability to argue or contribute to conversations on the same topic
           3. Interest in understanding the perspective of other speakers
           4. Metalinguistic awareness: explicit understanding of language and how it works
XI. Language, Literacy, and Teaching
    A. Literacy includes oral language, reading, and writing
    B. Teachers can help students' language abilities by
        1. focusing on ideas expressed , not usage
        2. planning interactions and conversations with adults to promote word meaning
        3. Reading aloud to promote language
        4. Interacting one-to-one with a student
    C. Partnerships with Families
    D. Guidelines for working with families and communities in literacy programs
XII. Summary
XIII. Key Terms And Concepts
XIV. Teachers' Casebook: What Would They Do?

Cognitive Development and Language

Learning Activities and Related Research

ACTIVITIES	HANDOUTS
Chapter 2	2.0 Lecture Outline
	2.1 Concept map: Piaget's Theory
Cooperative Activities	
2.1 Using the teacher's casebook.	2.2 What is this a case of?
2.2 What develops?	2.3 A day in the life of an elementary school teacher
	2.4 A day in the life of a secondary school teacher
2.3 Children's conception of death	2.5 Children's conception of death
Research Activities	
2.4 Comparison of Vygotsky and Piaget	
Using Technology	
Field Experience	
2.5 Four tasks that assess children's thinking	2.6 Four tasks that assess children's thinking
2.6 Observation of kindergarten	2.7 Observation checklist
Other Teaching Activities	
2.7 Piagetian Concept of Schemes	
2.8 Water levels	2.8 Water Levels
2.9 Cognitive Disequilibrium and responses	2.9 Cognitive Disequilibrium
2.10 Teacher roles in Vygotskian and Piagetian frameworks	2.10 Teacher Roles in the Classroom
	2.11 Concept map: Links to other chapters.

Cooperative Activities

2.1   Using the Teacher's Casebook

The teacher's casebook in the Woolfolk text provides examples of practical situations in which knowledge of educational psychology might be required. Students work in groups (using **Handout Master 2.2**) to decide what the case described on page 26 of the text is a case of? The goal of this activity is to move students beyond a layperson's analysis of a situation to one that involves complex professional knowledge.

2.2   What Develops?

Use **Handout Masters 2.3 and 2.4** that describe a day in the life of an elementary school teacher and a secondary school teacher. Chapter 2 of the Woolfolk text provides information about development and its implications for teaching. Organize students in groups to answer the question "What develops?" based on a comparison of the concerns of the elementary and secondary school teacher.

Cognitive Development and Language

2.3   Children's Conception of Death

From Craig, G. (1986). Human development. Englewood Cliffs, NJ: Prentice Hall, 245.

Other sources: Carey, S. (1985). Conceptual change in childhood. Cambridge, MA: MIT Press.

   Speece and Brent (1984). Children's concept of death: A review of three components of a death concept. Child Development, 55, 1671-1684.

Use **Handout Master 2.5** to stimulate a discussion on children's discussion of death and how their understanding of death is a function of their developmental status.

Research Activity

2.4   Comparison of Vygotsky and Piaget

   Students can apply what they know about Piaget and Vygotsky by comparing and contrasting the two theorists on core issues. For example:
1. What age range of individuals did the theory address?
2. Are theories continuous or discontinuous models?
3. Where did the theorist stand on the nature/nurture issue?
4. How did the theorist explain individual differences?
5. According to the theorist, what stimulates cognitive development?
6. Did the theorist think his model was universal to the rest of the world or was it culture specific?
7. What kind of investigative methods did the theorist use?
8. What kind of special terminology applies to each theorist?

   Have students develop a grid of important activities in the classroom tasks that teachers do (e.g., working in groups, teaching, reading, giving and taking tests). Using the information from the text and additional library resources, have students develop a comparison of the implications of Piagetian and Vygotskian theory for these kinds of tasks. The students should be able to reference appropriate research (rather than commentary) in completing this grid. See also activity 2.10.

Field Experience

2.5   Four Tasks that Assess Children's Thinking

   Give the class **Handout Master 2.6** and discuss the tasks. As a field experience, have the students present the tasks to three school-age children, two of whom are the same age but are functioning at different achievement levels. Students should determine

Cognitive Development and Language

the cognitive level of each child and write a summary paragraph explaining this conclusion.

2.6   Observation of a Kindergarten Class

Additional Resource for this activity: McNeely, S. L. (1997). Observing students and teachers through objective strategies. Needham Heights, MA: Allyn & Bacon.

Have students visit a kindergarten class. The students should spend at least one hour and take notes on what they observe (see **Handout Master 2.7**). In class discussion, they should note characteristics of the class and what evidence they observed of Piagetian principles in action. How is student development supported in the class?

Other Teaching Activities

2.7   Piagetian Concept of Schemes

Makosky, V. P., Wittemore, L. G., and Rogers, A. M. (Eds.) (1987) Activity handbook for the teaching of psychology. Washington, DC: American Psychological Association. Harper, G. F. Activity 28.

This activity contains two exercises, one with lollipops and the other with *gloquexes,* to help students rediscover some of the basic schemas and to relive the exciting prospect of learning about (or trying to equilibrate) a novel object. You will need sugarfree lollipops for everyone in the class and a black box large enough to conceal the *gloquex.*

Instructions:

Exercise 1. Give each student a lollipop to suck on. Lollipops elicit the most basic schemas--sucking, a fact that is loudly apparent. This is an example of how an innate, reflexive behavior is modified through the assimilation of an object.

Exercise 2. Now show the class an imaginary object, the *gloquex* (pronounced glocks), by removing it from the back box and placing it on the table. Presenting an unnamed imaginary object prevents students from prematurely labeling it. As you handle the *gloquex,* create the impression that it was a specific size and weight with certain properties. For example you might "plug in" the *gloquex* to warm it up. Then invite the students to ask questions and answer in ways like the those suggested below:

Q: *What is it called?*
A: A gloquex
Q: *What does it do?*
A: The gloquex counteracts negative electromagnetic waves (i.e. bad vibes often encountered by instructors in classrooms.

Cognitive Development and Language

Q. *How does it work?*
A: An inversely reciprocating frimfram bollixes any waves from entering the aperture.
Q: *What is it made of?*
A: Hyperventilated case hardened mollox.
Q: *Why can't I see it?*
A: You can't? (followed by an incredulous look; or alternatively) It's clear.

After answering student questions, explore how much students really understand about the *gloquex*. Do they understand the principles on how it operates? They will probably have some difficulties. You can then suggest that students have little understanding of the abstract qualities of *gloquexes* and presumably because the *gloquex* fits into no previously existing schemas, their attempts to describe it or talk about it sound mainly like this: "it's a ...." or "it's similar to a ..." or "It's sort of like something I saw once on Star Trek," and so forth. Most of these definitions are enactive (as are a young child's) and clearly reflect attempts to fit a novel object into previously existing schemas (assimilation). Since by definition this cannot occur, students are forced to modify existing schemas or create an entirely new schema (accommodation).

In discussion, you should point out the lollipop exercise involves variations in the pop sucking schema (for example, rolling the lollipop on the tongue, biting, chewing, etc.). Students often comment that the sucking schema may be applied to a variety of other objects or their contents with some adaptive modifications (e.g., pop bottles, straws). These adaptations of course, are the essence of intelligent behavior. Finally, remind students that lollipops are a good mnemonic device for assimilation, because they can be assimilated in both the biologic sense and cognitive sense, a similarity that is consistent with Piaget's notion of the continuity of these processes.

The *gloquex* presents an excellent starting point for discussions on the nature of concepts and how in most cases they are constructed by exposure to a variety of objects belonging to that class. A 25-year-old learning about a *gloquex* is faced with a task similar to an 18-month-old learning about a dog. Both groups are uncertain about the relevant definitional characteristics of the objects. This limited knowledge will undoubtedly cause them to confuse similar objects (e.g., the young child's confusion over similar-looking animals) or to identify two different objects as being the same (e.g., the student's assumption that the gloquex you demonstrated today is the same one you had in class yesterday).

2.8   Water Levels

Ask students to complete **Handout Master 2.8**. How would students assist a student who could not do this task?

Cognitive Development and Language

2.9   Cognitive Disequilibrium and Responses

Ask students to identify when an experience in which they felt something of true significance was learned. Then have students explore the idea of cognitive equilibrium versus cognitive disequilibrium. Were they pushed just a little beyond their current level of learning or was the gap between what they already knew and what was being taught many levels away or conversely very narrow? How did this make them feel--comfortable, uncomfortable? As students reflect, they should speculate on how teachers create this ideal state of optimal level of cognitive disequilibrium.

When a student experiences perturbation or disequilibrium, many responses are possible. Some of these responses result in learning, others do not. Use **Handout Master 2.9** to have students discuss possible responses to disequilibrating events.

2.10   Teacher Roles in Vygotskian and Piagetian Frameworks

Some of the earlier activities (e.g., 2.4) were designed to have students process the information they knew about Vygotsky and Piaget. In this activity (using **Handout Master 2.10**), have students identify roles they anticipate playing in their classrooms (you might want to refer back to the activities with Chapter 1 in connection with this activity). They should describe how Piaget and Vygotsky might have differed on the kinds of advice they might have provided to students about how to play these roles.

Discussion Questions

1. You are on a textbook committee to select the social studies text for eight grade. What kinds of things would you expect to find in a good text for this age group?

2. Do you think it is possible for a teacher to accelerate cognitive development? Explain.

3. Suppose you are teaching the concept "clouds" to a third-grade class and to a tenth grade class. How would your presentations and expectations differ? (Explain in terms of organizational changes and the development of more complex schemes.)

4. Vygotsky's theory that language usage promotes cognitive development has been used to justify extensive use of cooperative learning groups in elementary classrooms. Does working with other students at the same cognitive level supply the scaffolded learning that is necessary for children to grow within a zone of proximal development from assisted to unassisted performance?

5. Based on what you have learned about how spoken language emerges, how do you think deaf children learn sign language?

Cognitive Development and Language

Additional Resources for Teaching This Chapter

REFERENCES

Berk, L. E. (1985, July). Why children talk to themselves. Young Children, 40 (5), 46-52. Offers a readable view of Piaget's and Vygotsky's theories of language and thought as well as related research on the development of private speech.

Duckworth, E. (1987). The having of wonderful ideas and other essays for teaching and learning. New York: Teachers College Press. An examination of teaching ideas in relation to Piaget.

Fischer, K. and Lazerson, A. (1985). Research: Brain spurts and Piagetian periods. Educational Leadership, 41 (5), 70.

Gelman, S. A. and Markman, E. M. (1987). Young children's inductions from natural common names for unfamiliar objects. *Child Development, 55*, 1535-1540. Demonstrates preschooler's sensitivity to the nonperceptual features of natural kind categories thereby indicating that the young child's thought is not as perception-bound as Piaget believed.

Jacob, S. H. (1985). Foundations for Piagetian education. Maryland: University Press of America.

Leitner, K. L. (1989, June). Cognitive and social development in the second year of life: A neo-Piagetian perspective. International Journal of Early Childhood, 21, 43-49.

McLaughlin, B. (1992). Myths and misconceptions about second language: What every teacher needs to unlearn. Center for Applied Linguistics/National Center for Cultural Diversity and Second Language Learning.

Morrow, L. M. (1993). Literacy development in the early years : helping children read and write (2nd ed.). Boston, MA: Allyn & Bacon.

Morrow, L. M. (1995). A survey of family literacy in the United States. Newark, Del. : International Reading Association.

Morrow, L. M. (1995). Family literacy : connections in schools and communities. Newark, Del. : International Reading Association.

Pratt, M. W., Kerig, P., and Cowan, G. P. (1988). Mothers and fathers teaching 3-year-olds: Authoritative parenting and adult scaffolding of young children's learning. Developmental Psychology, 24, 832-839.

Cognitive Development and Language

     Riley, N. J. (1989, August-September). Piagetian cognitive functioning in students with learning disabilities. Journal of Learning Disabilities, 22, 444-451.

FILMS, VIDEOTAPES, AND AUDIOCASSETTES

Adolescent mental development, video, 30 minutes, color. Examines Piaget's formal operational stage and explains adolescent egocentrism, the imaginary audience and the personal fable. (Insight Media, 1988).

Childhood, a series of 7 videos, each 1 hour, color. This in-depth series offers an in-depth documentary on new scientific data and international context on the process of growing up. Twelve families on five continents filmed in their daily lives for over a year form the backbone of the series. Experts add a wealth of recent findings by anthropologists, sociologists, historians, educators, and psychologists. It also offers insights on the ways children and families deal with issues. It reveals new information on the complex learning process of physical development, the role of genes and environment. (Ambrose Video Publishing, Inc., 1290 Avenue of the Americas, Suite 2245, New York, NY, 10104.

Children's private speech, video, 30 minutes, color. A substitute teacher, upon encountering an especially noisy classroom, reflects on the research concerning why children talk to themselves. Research by developmental psychologist Laura Berk is featured in this video. (Produced by Allyn and Bacon and TR Productions, 1988)

Cognitive development, 16 mm, 18 minutes, color. Contrasts Piaget's cognitive developmental theory with behaviorists learning principles and shows how each viewpoint leads to different teaching practices in the classroom for young children. (CRM Films, 1973)

How young children learn to think, video, 19 minutes, color. Provides a discussion with noted early childhood educator Constance Kamii, who examines Piaget's theory. (National Association for the Education of Young Children, 1986)

Language, video, 60 minutes, color. The evolution of language and the special human phenomenon of speech are considered in this video. Viewers learn that there is an innate drive to communicate and that linguistic capacity is present even without speech and hearing. (PBS Series, *The Mind*, 1988)

Language development, video, 30 minutes, color. The development of language and how psychologists hope to discover truths about the human mind, society, and culture by studying how children use language in social communication. (Discovering Psychology, 1989)

Nature and nurture, video, 53 minutes, color. This program, one of the widely acclaimed Human Animal series, looks at identical twins separated at birth and reports some fascinating findings--some 10-15% of children are born with a slight tendency to be very

Cognitive Development and Language

outgoing or very apprehensive; that there may be a chemical predisposition to anger or to seeking high risk. The video concludes that biology is not everything; a supportive environment helps. Films for the Humanities and Sciences, Inc., P. O. Box 2053, Princeton, NJ. 08543. Call 1-800-257-5126, ED-1412.

Out of the mouths of babes: The acquisition of language, video, 28 minutes, color. Language development is described in the context of biological maturation. (Filmmakers' Library, 1977)

Piaget on Piaget, 16 mm, 42 minutes, color. Piaget himself sets forth his ideas on the nature and development of knowledge and illustrates with some classic tasks administered to children. Carefully translated English subtitles accompany Piaget's presentation in French. (Yale University Media Design, 1975)

Preschool mental development, video, 30 minutes, color. Compares Piaget's view of the preschooler with the behaviorist approach to mental development and learning. Visits a Head Start program and the Pacific Oaks School as examples of enriching a child's learning environment to enhance development. (Insight Media, 1983)

The developing child: The crucial early years, video, 26 minutes, color. This program shows how mental growth can be assisted in normal infants and young children. As infants learn to control their environment, they are learning to learn--a task in which parents can provide help by encouraging learning without creating stressful conditions. The program also covers the issues of group behavior and IQ testing. (Humanities and Sciences, Inc.)

The first few years: What to expect, video, 19 minutes, color. The video examines the critical parent/child relationship in the first five years: The effects in adolescence of traits learned in early childhood and the relationship between emotional and social development. Films for the Humanities and Sciences, Inc., P. O. Box 2053, Princeton, NJ. 08543. Call 1-800-257-5126, ED-1412.

Handout Master 2.0

Lecture Outline ----- Cognitive Development and Language

- Defining Development

- Piaget's Theory of Cognitive Development

- Implications of Piaget's Theory for Teachers

- Vygotsky's Alternative to Piaget

- The Development of Language

- Language, Literacy, and Teaching

Copyright © 1998 by Allyn and Bacon

Handout Master 2.1 Piaget's Theory

Influences on Development
- Equilibration
- Biological Maturation
- Activity
- Social Experience

Piaget's Theory of Cognitive Development

Innate Basic Tendencies
- organization
  - adaptation
- equilibration
- assimilation
- accommodation

4 stages of development
- sensorimotor (0-2 years)
- preoperational (2-7 years)
- concrete operations (7-11 years)
- formal operations (11-15 years)

Limitations of Piaget's Theory
* underestimates children's abilities
* use of fixed stages
* does not take the role of culture into account

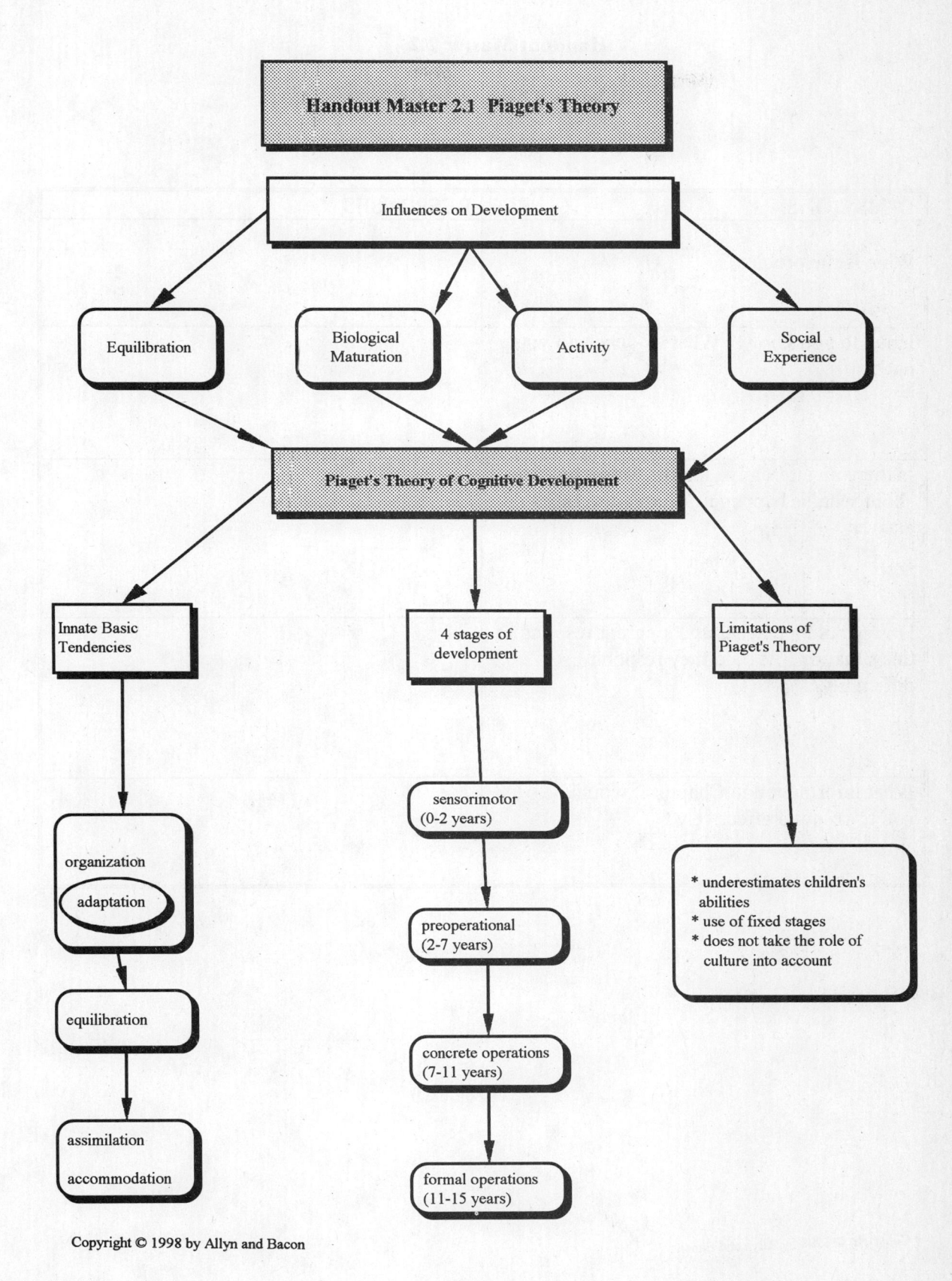

Copyright © 1998 by Allyn and Bacon

Handout Master 2.2

What is This a Case Of?

QUESTIONS	RESPONSES
What is the problem?	
How do you know? What evidence do you have?	
Is there an alternative interpretation possible about what is happening? Explain your answer.	
How would a teacher and a parent respond to this situation? Would they respond differently?	
What information in Chapter 2 would help you to respond effectively?	

Copyright © 1998 by Allyn and Bacon

Handout Master 2.3

A Day in the Life of An Elementary School Teacher

Thoughts before students arrive   *Why do I always begin the day feeling as though I'm behind? I guess it's just part of teaching. Lets see, what really has to be done before the kids get here? I've got to run off those dittoes, get my film order in for next week...and if I don't make it to the teacher's room for coffee, I may not speak to another adult all day! I love the quiet in the halls before the buses unload. I've got to remember to be nice to Jenny-she needs so much love. I've got to ask Andy about the note I sent home. I hope his parents will allow him to see the child study team.*

Morning duties: "No, Susie the books aren't here yet. I just mailed the order in last Friday. Well, you tell your mother that it usually takes about two weeks. Jack, the nurse needs to see you this morning. Oh, thanks for reminding me. Does anyone else have money for the PTA? Alright class. Please take your seats. How many people are buying lunch today?"

Morning lessons: *Language first.* "Jack, please pass out the paper for everyone." *Creative writing-Brainstorm. Some great ideas. What's wrong with Andy again?* "How about If I help you get started? Carl, what are you doing: You're finished already? Let me see. Can you add to this? Tell me more. Come on just try. Heather this is really good. Mary watch those run-ons. Is there anyone else who wants to share? Kelly are you still writing? Yes, I'll let you finish while we do science."

If I can just keep them busy while I get the experiment set up..."Page 65. Jane, would you please read. John, come here. Mr. Kuchta has the equipment I need. Please ask him if we can use it now." "Class these are the groups you'll be in for the experiment. No, you may not choose your own groups. Each group should...It's time to get cleaned up. Jerry Jones stop that right now."

"Please take out your social studies homework." *I wonder what Aaron's excuse will be today?* "Well, Aaron, I'm sorry to hear that, but as I've said before, if you don't have your work done you must stay in at recess time. I'll see you then." *Another short lunch break!* "Who can remember where we left off yesterday? Good, Joe. Today we're going to...Jennifer, please sit down; we're in the middle of a discussion. No, you may not get a drink right now."

Lunch: *Lunch at last. Pizza day! Today's not my day for duty thank goodness!*

Afternoon lessons   *After lunch we need to switch to homogeneous group for reading and math. Today math is at the end of the day. I hope I didn't plan for word problems. They do so much better on them in the morning. I better check my plan book. I just don't remember what I planned. Five or six different preparations everyday is just too much.* "Okay class let's switch for math. Hi, Chrissy, go on in. Where's Tommy?" *He's still absent? How will he ever get caught up? I love working with this group. It's funny how a certain mixture of kids can sometimes really click!*

Prep period: *Clean up. pack up. Walk the class to the art room. When my prep is at the end of the day, I'm too exhausted to be productive. Don't the flowers smell nice...and look! Who left a note...*

"Dear Mrs. Miller,

   I'm sorry, I didn't have my homework again. I promise I'm going to try harder. If I do my homework can I still stay in with you at recess?

   Love,
   Aaron"

Oh gosh, look at the clock. I've got to get the kids to the bus. Thirty minutes isn't even enough time to get a full set of papers graded. "Thanks for the note Aaron. I'm glad to hear that you're going to try hard. Kelly, please take this note home to your mom. No, it's not bad, it's about our class trip. Jerry where are you going? Oh, that's right you gave me a note this morning. Goodnight Susie, goodbye Joe, yes, I'll be there Jenny..."

After school: *I hope the teacher's meeting doesn't last long. I promised Jenny I'd watch the field hockey game. Why don't her parents ever come? I better take the reading papers home tonight and I'll have to run into town to get the salt and flour for the salt dough maps tomorrow. I still haven't called Mrs. Shay about Bryan's work... I'd like to get my hands on some of those people who call this a nine to five job!*

Adapted from the experiences of Marion Miller, 5th grade teacher in New Jersey

Copyright © 1998 by Allyn and Bacon

Handout Master 2.4

A Day in the Life of a Secondary School Teacher

Random Thoughts on the Way to Work: "My life happens in segments just like my eight-period day. . . lots of homework last night. . . hate grading essay papers, but really enjoyed working out today's lessons. I think they're going to work. . . Hope I can keep Ralph quiet during fourth period. . . ."

Homeroom: "At least the flag salute quiets them down. Do I have all the attendance cards in order? Almost forgot to collect insurance forms. I figured those two would forget theirs again. 'Lost,' they say. I'll have to send a student to the office for extra forms."

Period 1: U.S. History (Standard) : "I really feel sharp today, but I think my students are half-asleep. Is it just that the lesson's not going as well as it could or that they're tired? Maybe the material isn't as good as I thought."

Period 2: Preparation Period: "I have a million things to do! I'd better beef up that U.S. history lesson before sixth period. I don't want to put another class to sleep. My turn to use the phone in the lounge-my only link with the outside world. Coffee! A few minutes to talk with friends and check the mail."

Period 3: Economics: "I love this course, partly because it's elective. All the kids want to be here. We can really tackle some difficult subjects. Great lesson today! The students are really getting excited. Madeline told me before class that she wants to major in economics in college. This kind of class makes it all worthwhile."

Period 4: U.S. History (Basics) : "Basics. They're rowdy but I love them. They've got character even though they don't give a damn about history. We have great lessons. . . . 'Get away from the window!'. . . 'Wait until the bell rings!'"

Period 5: Lunch Duty: "How demeaning to have to sit and watch kids eat!"

Period 6: U.S. History (Standard): "Much better lesson than in first period. Maybe you really can learn from your mistakes. Or maybe these kids are just more awake."

Period 7: Library Duty: "It's remarkable how many students don't know the first thing about using a library. In the beginning I thought I would get some reading done during this period, but the interruptions make it impossible-a frustrating 40 minutes."

Period 8: Economics: "This lesson went so well this morning. What's different? I guess last period is a terrible time to have to talk about supply and demand. We all want to go home."

End of the Day: "I'm glad I got to speak to Jane after school. Intramurals are a great way to get to know the kids. It's easier to work with them in class now that I am learning more about them after school. . . but I'm exhausted . . .just don't want to face three new lessons tonight. Sometimes I wish I could leave my work at the office."

Adapted from the experiences of Howard Schober, high school social studies teacher in New Jersey

Copyright © 1998 by Allyn and Bacon

Handout Master 2.5
Children's Conceptions of Death

Imagine a 4-year old who has just been told that a beloved and recently active, caring grandmother, has died. Given what we know about young children's thinking, what reactions can be expected? What aspects of the situation are particularly difficult to understand? Are there specific fears and anxieties the child might experience? Finally, how should caregivers reassure the child?

A number of researchers have studied the difference between young children's understanding of death and how older children and adults view death (Speece & Brent, 1984). They have focused on three major aspects of the death concept: (1) Death is always irreversible, final, permanent; (2) The absence of life functions is characteristic of death; and (3) Death is universal—everyone must die. The researchers found that young children under the age of 5 lack all three of these components in their concept of death. They interviewed children of different ages and asked them a variety of questions. What is death? But more often they asked specific questions. Such questions might include: Can a dead person come back to life? Can a dead person talk? Or feel? Or see? Or dream? Or think? Does everyone die? Can you think of someone who might not die?

Young children often see death as a temporary state, something like sleeping or "going away." They will sometimes suggest that dead people wake up or come back to life after a while. Is this reversibility? Some authors suggest that it does not mean that children see death as reversible in all cases, but that they have not established distinct categories of dead and alive. After all, when one is asleep one is also alive, so why not when one is dead?

Young children also do not seem to understand that all functions cease when one is dead. However, they may think that there is reduced functioning. One child suggested "you can't hear very well when you are dead." Often children think that the deceased can't do visible things like eating and speaking, but they can do less visible things like dreaming and knowing. Finally young children do yet realize that death is universal. They often believe death can be avoided by being clever or lucky, and that certain people are exempt from death, such as teachers, or members of their immediate family, or themselves. Some believe that you can do fairly magical things to keep from dying—for example, a child may think that if he or she prays a lot, he or she won't die. Is it any wonder that it is very difficult to explain the death of a friend or relative to a young child under age 5?

Researchers generally agree that the concept of death develops between ages 5 and 7. Most 7-year-olds have at least a rudimentary knowledge of the three basic components of death. This seems to parallel the transition in the child from Piaget's stage of preoperational thought to concrete operational thinking (Speece & Brent, 1984).

But explaining the death of a grandmother to a young child does not involve coping with the child's limited cognitive understanding. The reality of someone's death is difficult for adults as well as children. Adults may intellectually understand the reality of death, its finality and permanence, its absence of life functions, and its universality. But emotionally they must struggle to cope with their loss. Young children, too, face emotional upheaval while trying to understand the realities of death. However, there are a number of factors that further complicate the adjustment for children. First, they are to some extent egocentric—they will be primarily concerned with how situations and events affect them. Second, they have trouble understanding cause and effect. Hence, when a young child asks, "Why did Grandma die?" she may not be asking what we think she is asking. She may not want to know about disease and old age; she may be wondering, instead, why her grandmother left her. Children wonder if they control such situations: "Did she leave because I was bad?" "If I'm good, will she come back?" "Will Mommy or Daddy die and leave me?" They may feel anger or guilt, or they may wonder if they own angry thoughts caused the death. Children told that "death is like sleep" may be afraid to close their eyes at night in fear that they, too, will die. Sometimes young children will try to get a deceased loved one to return with a variety of magical strategies.

All of these factors influence children's understanding of death. The preschool child needs simple, correct information combined with lots of reassurance and emotional support to cope with the reality of death.

From Craig, G. (1986). <u>Human Development</u>, 4th edition. Englewood Cliffs, NJ: Prentice Hall, 245

Handout Master 2.6

Four Tasks That Assess Children's Thinking

<u>Interpretation of Stories:</u> Read one of Aesop's fables. Ask the children, What do you think this story means?

Preoperational response: Response is often to on emotional, person-level, and is based on the children's affective reaction to the story. They are apt to mention something that happened in their own life. They may not be interested in explaining or justifying the answer.

Concrete operational response: Response is based on the literal content of the story.

Formal operational response: Response goes beyond the literal content of the story and indicates same understanding of the moral.

<u>Classification</u>
Give the children the following group or objects and ask them to make a group of things that go together. Objects: picture, from a magazine or newspaper, pencil, Magic Marker, piece of chalk, notebook paper, drawing papa, thumb tack, straight pin, masking or scotch tape, paper sack.

Early preoperational: Grouping is based on a functional relationship. Example: Pencil and paper because you write on the paper with a pencil; thumb tack and picture because you use the tack to put the picture on the wall.

Late operational: Grouping is based on perceptual feature. Example: Pencil, pin, and tack because they all have a sharp point; paper and picture because they are the same shape (have four corners); paper and chalk because they are both white.

Concrete operational: Grouping based on a common element 80 that each object is an example of the classification basis. Example: Things made of paper, things you can write with, things you can we to put things on a bulletin board

<u>Conservation</u>
Line up two sets of wooden beads side by side. Ask the children if you both have the same amount. If they answer "yes," then spread out one set and ask who has more beads. Return them to their original position and bunch up one set. Then ask who has more.
Get two equal balls of clay. Ask the children if you both have the same amount. Make adjustments until they answer "yes." Make a "snake" or a "pancake" out of one ball and ask who has the most clay now.

Preoperational: Response will indicate that one person has more than the other when changes are made.

Concrete operations: Responds that you both still have the same amount and explains his answer by wing identity, reversibility, or compensation as a rationale.

<u>Combinatorial Logic:</u>   Give the children five different one-digit numbers on separate small pieces of paper. Ask them to make as many different 3-digit numbers as they can.

Concrete operational: Goes about the task in a random, haphazard manner.

Formal operational: Will approach the task in an orderly and systematic way.

Copyright © 1998 by Allyn and Bacon

Handout Master 2.7

Observation Checklist

<u>Classroom as a Whole</u>

Use Y for "yes" and N for "no."

   _____   Are children working independently?
   _____   Are they working in groups or clusters?
   _____   Does the teacher scan the classroom?
   _____   Are there manipulatives available to the children?
   _____   Do the children appear to be happy?

Would you conclude that the classroom is developmentally appropriate?

Your Comments:

<u>Select One Child for Observation</u>

Describe the child's behavior (what is he/she doing? What evidence do you see of the child's status with respect to Piaget's stages of cognitive development?

Copyright © 1998 by Allyn and Bacon

Handout Master 2.8

Water Levels

Jesse was shown the jar labelled 'A" which contained water. The water line is marked with the "f." The jar was then tipped so that it leaned to one side. From the jars marked "B," "C," and "D," choose the one that shows where the water line will be when the jar is tipped. Which Piagetian stage would Jesse be in if she chose "A?" If she chose "B?" If she chose "C?"

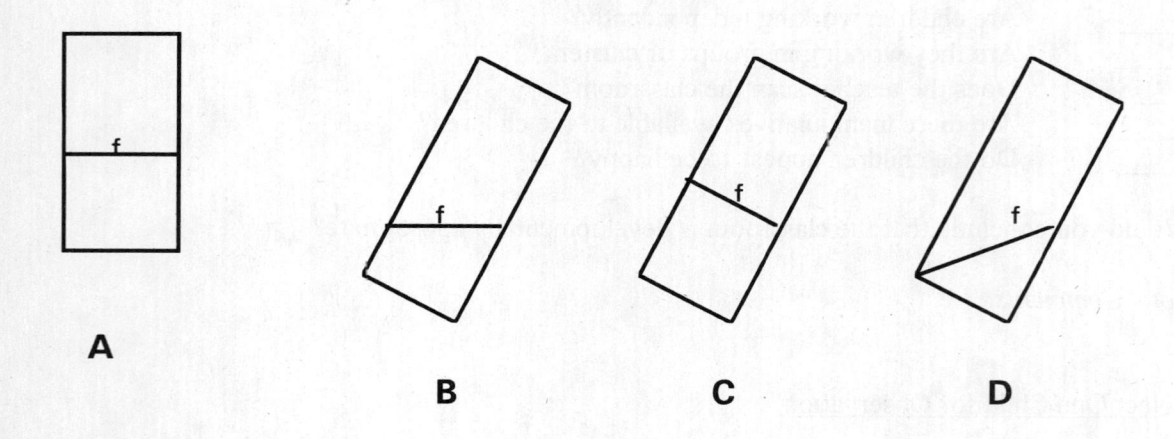

A   B   C   D

Copyright © 1998 by Allyn and Bacon

Handout Master 2.9

Cognitive Disequilibrium

Select an incident in which you (or someone you know) experienced a "disequilibrating event." Describe that event.

How did you respond to this event? Characterize your response in terms of Piaget's ideas about accommodation and assimilation.

Describe alternative ways in which you could have responded. Characterize these alternatives in terms of Piaget's theory.

How would working with peers assist a student to experience disequilibrium and re-equilibration?

Copyright © 1998 by Allyn and Bacon

Handout Master 2.10

Teacher Roles in the Classroom

List the roles you expect to play in your classroom (you might refer back to Chapter 1 to help you identify roles). How would Piaget and Vygotsky have wanted you to play those roles?

Teacher Role	Piaget	Vygotsky

Copyright © 1998 by Allyn and Bacon

Handout Master 2.11: Links to Other Chapters

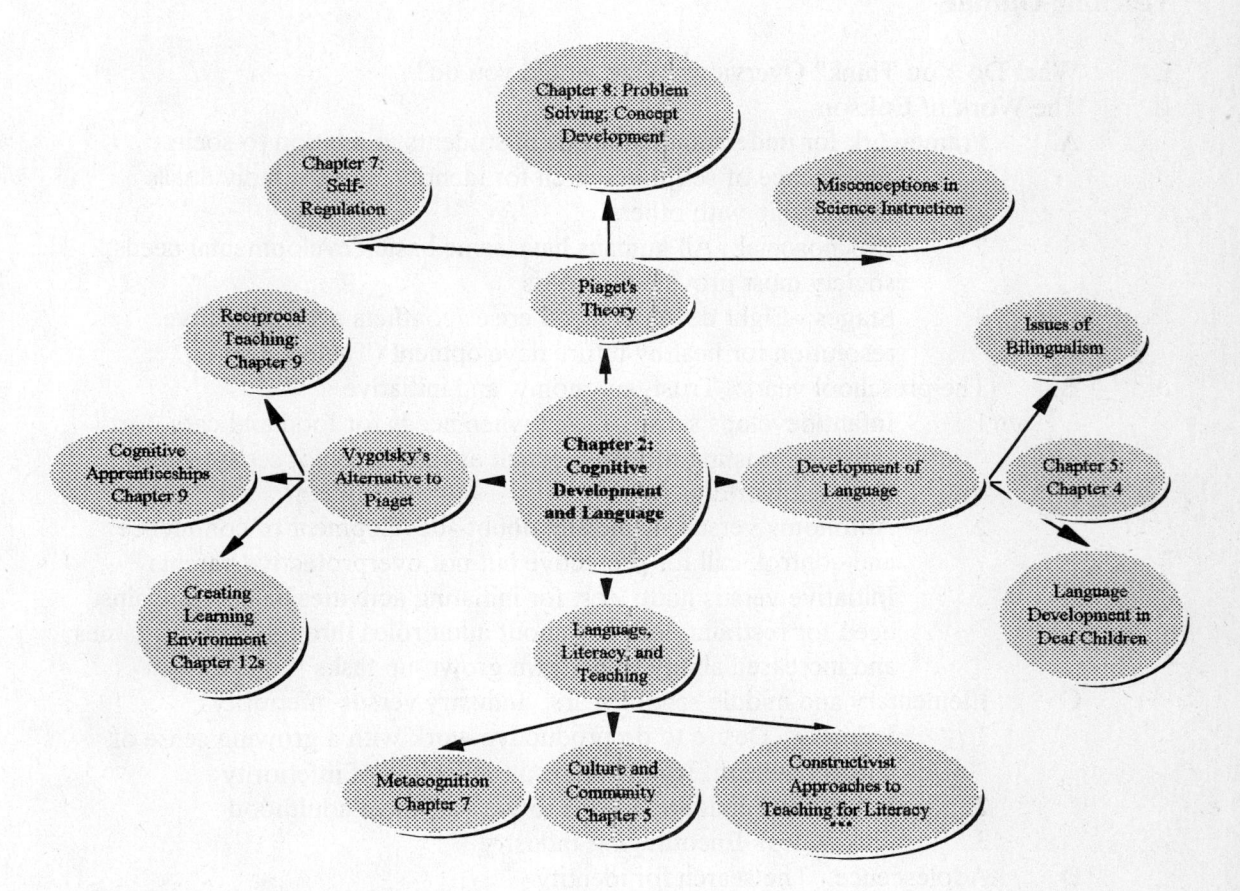

- Chapter 2: Cognitive Development and Language
  - Piaget's Theory
    - Chapter 7: Self-Regulation
    - Chapter 8: Problem Solving; Concept Development
    - Misconceptions in Science Instruction
  - Vygotsky's Alternative to Piaget
    - Reciprocal Teaching: Chapter 9
    - Cognitive Apprenticeships Chapter 9
    - Creating Learning Environment Chapter 12s
  - Development of Language
    - Issues of Bilingualism
    - Chapter 5; Chapter 4
    - Language Development in Deaf Children
  - Language, Literacy, and Teaching
    - Metacognition Chapter 7
    - Culture and Community Chapter 5
    - Constructivist Approaches to Teaching for Literacy

Copyright © 1998 by Allyn and Bacon

3

Personal, Social, and Emotional Development

Teaching Outline

I. What Do You Think? Overview/ What would you do?
II. The Work of Erikson
    A. Framework for understanding needs of students in relation to society
        1. Emergence of self, the search for identity, and the individual's relationship with others.
        2. Pyschosocial: All humans have same basic developmental needs; society must provide for needs
        3. Stages: Eight developmental crises/conflicts need a positive resolution for healthy future development (Table 3.1)
    B. The preschool years: Trust, autonomy, and initiative
        1. Infant develops sense of trust when needs for food and care satisfied; trusting more important as realization of separateness from the world grows
        2. Autonomy versus shame and doubt--development of confidence and control; call for protective but not overprotective parents
        3. Initiative versus guilt: Zest for initiating activities balanced against need for restraint; learning about adult roles through pretend games and increased ability to perform grown-up tasks
    C. Elementary and middle school years: Industry versus inferiority
        1. Industry: Desire to do productive work with a growing sense of competence; difficulty can result in feeling of inferiority
        2. Industrious childhood leads to well-adjusted adulthood
        3. Guidelines: Encouraging Industry
    D. Adolescence: The search for identity
        1. Identity: The organization of person's drives, abilities, beliefs, and history into a structure of self
        2. Identity versus role confusion: Answer to the question Who Am I? is based on earlier resolutions
        3. Identity statuses
            a) identity achievement
            b) identity foreclosure
            c) identity diffusion
            d) moratorium
        4. Guidelines: Supporting Identity Formation
    E. Beyond the school years: Human relations in adulthood
        1. Intimacy versus isolation: Ability to have a close personal relationship

Personal, Social, and Emotional Development

        2.   Generativity versus self-absorption: Caring for the needs for future generations in a broad sense. Productivity and creativity are essential features

        3.   Integrity versus despair: Integrity means consolidating one's sense of self

III.   Understanding Ourselves And Others
- A. Self-concept; a cognitive structure representing a composite of ideas, feelings, attitudes a person has about themselves
- B. Self-esteem: an affective reaction involving an evaluation of the self-concept
- C. Structure of self-concept (Figure 3.1) is hierarchical
  1. General concept is made up of more specific concepts and is a general view of self
  2. Secondary concepts are made up in turn of more specific concepts such as nonacademic self-concept as well as self-concept in English and mathematics
  3. A third level of differentiation includes perceptions of physical ability, appearance, relations with peers and family
  4. Hierarchical structure is strongest in early adolescence.
  5. Self-concept is more situation specific in adults
- D. How self-concept develops
  1. Evolves through constant self-evaluation in different situations
  2. Children's understandings of themselves moves from concrete to abstract
  3. Early views of self based on immediate behaviors and appearances; thinking rule-bound, segmented, not flexible
  4. In later years, children think abstractly about internal processes—beliefs
  5. Self-concept continues to evolve, influenced by parents/family in early years, friends/peers in later years
- E. Self-esteem and school life
  1. Higher self-esteem related to more positive attitudes and success in school
  2. Student self-esteem influenced by teachers' caring, feedback, and evaluation
  3. Lack of competence in an area that is not valued does not threaten self-esteem
  4. Greatest increases in self-esteem come when students become more competent in areas they value
  5. Suggestions for Encouraging Self-esteem (Table 3.2)
- F. Gender, ethnicity, and self-esteem
  1. Younger children tend to have positive and optimistic views of themselves
  2. As they mature, children tend to develop more realistic views but may nevertheless underestimate their competence

53

Personal, Social, and Emotional Development

        3. Girls gradually lower their perceptions of their own ability relative to boys
        4. Boys in most ethnic groups are more confident than girls
        5. Personal and collective self-esteem
        6. Guidelines for working with families to strengthen student self-esteem
    G. The self and others
        1. Intention: Differentiates accidental and proposed actions
        2. Taking the perspective of others develops over time
        3. Selman's five stages of perspective-taking (Table 3.3)
            a) undifferentiated perspective-taking
            b) social-informational perspective-taking
            c) self-reflective perspective-taking
            d) third-party perspective-taking
            e) societal perspective-taking

IV. Moral Development
V. Point/Counterpoint: Should Schools Teach Values?
VI. Kohlberg's Stages of moral development
    A. Pre-conventional (Stages 1,2): Judgment based on person's own needs and perceptions
    B. Conventional (Stages 3,4): Taking into account expectations of society and law
    C. Post-conventional (Stages 5,6): Judgments based on principles that go beyond specific laws
    D. Moral Dilemmas: hypothetical situations in which no choice is absolutely right--used to evaluate moral reasoning
    E. Level of moral reasoning related to both cognitive and emotional development
VII. Alternatives to Kohlberg's Theory
    A. The problem with stages:
        1. In real life, stages not separate, sequenced and consistent
        2. Ordering of stages indicates a sex and cultural bias
    B. Criticisms
        1. Social conventions versus moral issues are not distinguished
        2. Cultural differences in moral reasoning are ignored
    C. Morality as caring
        1. Empathy
        2. Friendships
        3. A curriculum of caring (Table 3.5)
    D. Moral behavior
        1. Influences on moral behavior
            a) internalization
            b) modeling
        2. Typical moral issues in classrooms

Personal, Social, and Emotional Development

                a)   Cheating: Involves specific situations; not just beliefs about right and wrong
                b)   Aggression: Role models often seem to condone violent behavior
            3. Guidelines: Dealing with Aggression and Encouraging Cooperation
VIII. Socialization: The Home And The School As Influences On Development
    A. American families today
    B. Growing up too fast
        1. developmentally appropriate preschools
    C. Children of divorce
        1. Single-parent family may be stressed economically and socially
        2. Guidelines: Helping Children of Divorce
IX. New Roles For Teachers
    A. Guidelines: Supporting personal and social development
X. Challenges for Children
    A. Physical development
        1. The preschool years/Elementary school
            a) Physical growth steady and predictable for boys and girls
            b) Control increases in gross-motor skills
            c) Fine motor skills develop greatly
        2. Adolescence
            a) Significant impact on identity
            b) Early maturation can have positive or negative effects
XI. Children and Youth at Risk
    A. Child abuse
        1. Factors influencing child abuse (Table 3.7)
        2. Indicators of child abuse (Table 3.8)
        3. Responsibilities to report child abuse
    B. Teenage sexuality and pregnancy
        1. Majority of American teenagers aged 15+ have had intercourse
        2. Rate of teenage pregnancy is higher in the US than in other developed countries
        3. Many teenagers are uninformed about birth control
    C. Eating disorders
        1. Bulimia: Binge eating
        2. Anorexia nervosa: Self-starvation
    D. Drug Abuse
        1. Nearly all high school seniors report experience with alcohol, 20% are smokers; and 30% have used an illegal drugs
    E. Aids
    F. Suicide
        1. Common myths and facts about suicide
XII. Summary
XIII. Key Terms And Concepts
XIV. Teachers' Casebook/What Would They Do?

Personal, Social, and Emotional Development

Learning Activities and Related Research

ACTIVITIES	HANDOUTS
Chapter 3	3.0 Lecture Outline
Cooperative Activities	
3.1 Differences in Judgment of Offense	3.1 Twelve Offenses
3.2 Moral Dilemmas	3.2 Eisensberg
	3.3 Concept map: Kohlberg & Eisenberg
3.3 Unpopular Children	3.4 Helping unpopular children
Research Activities	
3.4 Learning about Social Relations	3.5 Sociogram
	3.6 Example of nominations
Using Technology	
3.5 Challenges for Children	3.7 Locating sources on the world wide web
Field Experience	
3.6 Interviewing children about friendship	
Other Teaching Activities	
3.7 Resolving Developmental Crises:	3.8 Conditions that Encourage Positive Resolutions of Erikson's Developmental Crises
	3.9 Resolving Developmental Crises
3.8 Cheating and Plagiarism	3.10 Reducing the incidence of cheating & plagiarism
	3.11 Concept Map: Links to other chapters

Cooperative Activities

3.1   Differences in Judgment of Offense

Adapted from Shweder, R., Mahapatra, M., & Miller, J. (1987). Cultural and moral development. In J. Kagan, & S. Lamb (Eds.). The emergence of morality in young children. Chicago: University of Chicago Press, pp. 4041. Reprinted with permission.

    Begin this activity by distributing **Handout Master 3.1**, "Twelve Offenses," and having the students rank-order the offenses from "worst" (1) to "least bad" (12).   Different students will have different rank orders of the items. Use these differences among students to begin a discussion of different values. Note that different people excuse certain behaviors, pay more attention to specific information, or ignore certain information.

Personal, Social, and Emotional Development

3. 2 Moral Dilemma

The following scenario is a Kohlbergian moral dilemma. Have your students classify the responses that follow the dilemma according to Kohlberg's stages of moral development. Then do the same using Eisenberg's classification of stages of moral reasoning (see **Handout Masters 3.2 and 3.3**).

Sharon is a student in a math class. Her parents often become abusive when she gets bad grades. She has not been doing very well and is considering cheating on an upcoming math test. Should she cheat on the exam?

1. Yes, because if she cheats and does well on the test, her parents will think she is a good daughter and will be proud of her.

2. No, because if she gets caught she will be punished severely.

3. No, because cheating is against all the rules of the school.

4. No, because cheating is unfair to all the other individuals in the class. A person should complete his or her own work.

5. Yes, because if she cheats and gets a good grade on her test, her parents will probably reward her by letting her go to a movie.

Are the responses categorized differently depending on whose system for describing the development of moral reasoning one uses?

3.3 Unpopular Children

The following descriptions of three unpopular children are taken from *Harvard Education Letter* (January/February 1989), 5, 1-3.

Jeannie is 9. She talks loudly over the voices of the other fourth-grade girls. Sometimes, out on the playground, she hits hard to get what she wants. Although her classmates may give way, later they complain about Jeannie, how bossy she is and how much they hate her.

Michael, 12, is a little older than many of his classmates, and not doing well in school. Maybe by keeping his sixth-grade class in an uproar he is trying to ensure that others won't do well either. In class a few boys sometimes get caught up in his disruptive games; mostly, though, other kids shun Michael. Out on the playground, he plays "Star Wars" alone.

Although David makes no trouble in his fifth grade class, he isn't any better liked than Michael or Jeannie. He has always seemed hesitant and maladroit; now that he is 11, he is always alone. No one chooses him as a partner for class projects, and his

Personal, Social, and Emotional Development

classmates groan if he's assigned to their side for team games. His teachers find him cooperative, but peers have no use for him.

Here are a few suggestions for coping with the problems of unpopular children:

1. Without overreacting, intervene early, before a pattern of rejection is established.

2. Set firm limits and stick with difficult children, but give them extra help in improving their behavior. Do not give up on them. Try to establish a personal relationship.

3. Help all students learn social skills such as anticipating the consequences of behaviors, recognizing feelings, effective communication, etc.

4. Experiment with cooperative learning and peer tutoring to improve performance.

5. Establish clear expectations for all students behavior.

Research Activities

3.4   Learning about Social Relations

Schmuck, R., and Schmuck, P. (1992). Group processes in the classroom (6th ed.). Dubuque, IA: Wm. C. Brown Company Publishers.

In classrooms with diffusely-structured friendship patterns, most students have at least one or two close friends. In classrooms with centrally-structured friendship patterns in which only a few students are highly liked, a few are strongly disliked, and most are not chosen as friends. Classroom groups with diffuse friendship patterns in which leadership roles are dispersed tend to have a more positive classroom climate, more complete use of intellectual abilities, and a more positive attitude toward self and others.

A sociogram reveals friendship patterns in a classroom. Since diffuse friendship patterns are more supportive of individual students, a teacher should try to change a centrally structured class to a more diffusely structured class. Here are some suggestions for encouraging change adapted from Schmuck and Schmuck (1992). Group processes in the classroom. The following activity can be done in class for practice. If students have access to a classroom of students (kindergarten through high school), they could assess student friendship patterns with the two activities. An example of the sociogram appears in **Handout Master 3.5** and an example of a peer nomination form can be found in **Handout Master 3.6.**

Sociometric test: Explain to the class that everybody likes some people and dislikes other people. There are also some people who like one person a lot and some people who don't like that person at all. It is helpful to the teacher in making plans for the class to know how people in the class really feel about one another. Then ask the students in a class to list in confidence the three people in the class with whom they would most like to work (You may want to provide a list of class members that is numbered so the students can just write down the number. This is especially useful with younger children who might not know how to spell somebody's name.) Some sociometric tools ask students for names of people that they dislike. Before asking questions about disliked individuals, you should consider whether the information you would learn would be helpful. You will probably find that some children are not nominated by anyone as a "liked" individual. This information may allow you to draw the conclusions necessary. There is some possibility that asking students about disliking individuals can raise anxiety for some students or even provide rehearsal of negative thoughts. Before asking such questions, therefore, you should very carefully consider what information you think you will get and whether or not you could find that information without risking hurting anyone. You might want to discuss this issue with your class.

Sociogram: Have the students construct a sociograms for positive choices. They should answer the following questions: Does the classroom have a diffusely structured or centrally structured friendship pattern? What other conclusions can you make? If changes seem desirable, how would you go about implementing change? What are the limitations of this kind of information?

Using Technology

3.5   Challenges for Children

Chapter 3 provides a brief description of many of the challenges faced by children and youth today. Because of the availability of the World Wide Web, it is easier than ever before to locate important information about necessary resources for assistance or information. **Handout Master 3.7** provides a list of some links to important agencies. Have students locate additional links to complete the handout and provide themselves with a compendium of information related to the challenges facing children.

Personal, Social, and Emotional Development

Field Experience

3.6   Interviewing Children About Friendship

Adapted from Berk, L. (1991). Instructor's manual child development (2nd ed.) Boston: Allyn & Bacon, p. 132. Copyright 1991. Reprinted with permission of Allyn and Bacon.

The activity explores children's social-cognitive understanding of friendship using Piaget's flexible, open-ended clinical interviewing technique. Have students locate three children to interview about their understanding of friendship: (1) a 5- to 7-year old, (2) an 8- to 10-year-old, and (3) an 11- to l5-year-old. Prepare a list of questions to ask including: What is a friend? Why is it nice to have a friend? Students should interview each child separately, assuring the youngsters that their answers will be confidential and using a tape recorder or taking careful notes.

Make sure that your students have received the necessary and appropriate permission to interview children and record their responses. How do the three children differ in their responses? Why do they differ?

Other Teaching Activities

3.7   Resolving Developmental Crises

This activity will assist students learn about Erickson's theory of the developmental crises faced by individuals (see **Handout Master 3.8**). Have students apply their knowledge as they complete **Handout Master 3.9** by deciding on what kind of crisis is being resolved.

3.8   Cheating And Plagiarism

From the *Harvard Education Letter* (1987, September), some suggestions for handling cheating and plagiarism:

1. Try to keep the work interesting and convince students that it is important to learn. Make it challenging but never beyond the capacity of the class.

2. Admit frankly before the first test of the year that cheating often occurs in schools and say that it is only sensible to move desks apart and cover answers that are easy to see. Without making students feel any distrust on your part, you will convey the idea that you know what's what.

3. Find an early opportunity for class discussion of reasons for cheating and its effects. This is also the time to talk about plagiarism - what it is, what it is not,

and why it is a serious offense. (Before holding this discussion, be sure you know the school's policy on cheating and plagiarism.) It is surprising how many students have never thought much about these things.

4. Keep alert during tests and, when marking papers, watch for verbatim duplications. Do not be blindly trusting. That may reward dishonesty.

5. Take away any paper from a student who is clearly cheating, give no credit for the test, and after class arrange a time to talk alone to the student. "Setting an example" by drastic, overt action is not only unnecessary but creates such bitterness and alarm that no lessons in honesty can be taught - or learned.

6. When you talk with the student, find out why he or she cheated and try to help the student overcome the need for it. Get the student to explain, if possible, how cheating is self-defeating. But you must also explain that cheating is quite frequent and that this particular episode, while serious, does not put a permanent blot on the student's record, especially if it does not happen again.

7. Ask the student whether he/she would like to have you tell his/her parents or whether the student would rather do it herself. Explain that parents need to know when their child is in trouble so that they may help. If the child is obviously afraid of the parents and a surprising number of those who cheat are, you might let the student off this one time without telling the parents. If she says she will talk to them, then check in a day or two and ask how they reacted.

Using **Handout Master 3.10,** have your students list the reasons why college students cheat and what could be done to reduce the incidence of cheating and plagiarism.

Discussion Questions

1. What is moral education? How is morality learned? Should public schools be concerned with moral education or is it an area that should be left to the family and church? Are teachers moral educators whether they intend to be or not?

2. What does "identity formation" mean? What is one's sense of identify based on? Is identity fixed or variable? Explain your answers.

3. In what ways might a failure to resolve earlier crises positively be manifest in an adolescent who is attempting to establish his or her identify? In other words, how would failure to develop trust (or autonomy, initiative, or industry) hinder an adolescent in the identity versus role confusion stage of development?

Personal, Social, and Emotional Development

4. Moral action does not necessarily follow directly from moral judgment. But is it necessary for moral judgment to precede moral action? That is, can one behave in a moral way if one cannot make a cognitive statement about how a person "should" behave?

5. William Glasser talks about self-concept in terms of failure and success identities. The "failure identity" is characterized by loneliness, apathy, and withdrawal for delinquency; the "success identity" is characterized by the ability to give and receive love and the feeling of doing something that is important to self or others. Given these characteristics, what kind of experience can a teacher provide to help a student change a failure identity to a success identify, that is to develop a more positive self concept?

6. In a classroom discussion about stealing, the teacher finds that many students express the opinion that it is all right to steal if you don't get caught. How should a teacher respond? Would the socioeconomic level of the students influence the teachers' response?

Additional Resources for Teaching This Chapter

REFERENCES

Bandura, A. (1997). Self-efficacy in changing societies. New York, NY: Cambridge University Press.

Beane, J. A. (1991, September). Sorting out the self-esteem controversy. Educational Leadership, 49 (1), 25-30.

Damon, W. (1988). The moral child : nurturing children's natural moral growth. New York, NY : Free Press.

Damon, W. (1995). Greater expectations : overcoming the culture of indulgence in America's homes and schools. New York, NY : Free Press.

Gilligan,C. (1982). In a different voice. Cambridge: Harvard University Press.

Kohn, A. (1991, February). Don't spoil the promise of cooperative learning. Educational Leadership, 48 (5), 93-94.

Lockwood, A. (1979). The effects of value clarification and moral development curricula on school-age subjects: A critical review of recent research. Review of Educational Research ,48, 325-364.

Sears, J. T. (1991, September). Helping students understand and accept sexual diversity. Educational Leadership, 49 (1), 54-57.

Solomon, D., & Battistich, V. (1993, August). Students in caring school and classroom communities. Paper presented at the Annual Convention of the American Psychological Association (101st, Toronto, Canada.

Steinberg, L.(1986). Latchkey children and susceptibility to peer pressure: An ecological analysis. Developmental Psychology, 57, 433-440.

Personal, Social, and Emotional Development

Vogel, P. R. (1991, October). Crisis in youth fitness and wellness. Phi Delta Kappan, 73 (2), 154-156.

Walker, H. & Sylvester, R. (1991, September). Where is school along the path to prison? Educational Leadership, 49 (1), 14-16.

Websites of Interest

Alcoholics Anonymous	http://www.aa.org
Al-Anon/Alateen	http://www.al-anon.org
American Foundation for Suicide Prevention	http://www.asfnet.org/
Government Health Links	http://www.uhs.wisc.edu/government.html
American Psychological Association	http://www.apa.org

FILMS, VIDEOTAPES, AND AUDIOCASSETTES

An American stepfamily, video, 26 minutes. This program examines the problems conflicting loyalties and rivalries, dealing with former spouses, and the three categories of kids--his, hers, and theirs. (From Films for the Humanities & Sciences, Inc.)

Anorexia, video. Females are 10 times as likely as males to become anorexic, usually, bright, verbal, aggressive, teenagers and young women in their early twenties. The video explores how it starts and how it can be detected and cured.#CC-1164.

Anorexia and bulimia, video, 19 minutes, color. This program explains the addictive nature of anorexia and bulimia, and their possible effects on cardiovascular and central nervous system. A nutritionist demonstrates the extremes to which people with these disorders commonly go in their addiction. #EC-1380. VHS or Beta: $149.

Behind closed doors: Crisis at home, video 30 minutes, color). Produced by NBC News, this program presents three real stories told by teenagers who experienced them. In the first, a teenage girl tries to break up her new family after her mother remarries. The second concerns a family devastated by sexual abuse. The third examines the lives of runaways in Los Angeles. (Insight Media, 1988)

Bulimia, video, 28 minutes, color. Bulimics alternate between gross overeating and vomiting. Low self-esteem, anger, and depression are both the cause and result of their illness. In this Phil Donahue program, the issues are discussed. #EC-1165. VHS or Beta S149.

Child abuse, video, 19 minutes. This program deals with the delicate subject of sexually and physically abused children. A therapist who deals with sex offenders

Personal, Social, and Emotional Development

describes the common characteristics of offenders; a clinical social worker trained to talk with sexually abused children discusses the effects of child abuse on the child. The program also offers tips on selecting a day care center. (From Films for the Humanities & Sciences, Inc.)

Childhood physical abuse, video, 26 minutes. This program covers the range of problems in the area of physical abuse of children: The kinds of adults likely to abuse their children physically; The tell-tale signs of such abuse; The effects on the children, both in the short term and the long term; The ways in which abuse should be dealt with; How the abusive parents can break the cycle of their own behavior and whether and how they should be punished; And whether the physical abuse of children can be prevented. (From Films for the Humanities & Sciences, Inc.)

Childhood sexual abuse, video, 26 minutes. This program looks at the ways in which adult women learn to work out problems caused by their sexually abusive fathers and how they seek to protect their own children from a recurrence of the pattern. (From Films for the Humanities & Sciences, Inc.)

Internet Links to Inforrmation on Childhood Sexual Abuse
http://www.commnet.edu/QVCTC/student/LindaCain/sexabuse.html

Children of divorce, video, 28 minutes. Studies are now making clear that children of divorce almost never recover totally from the pain, confusion, guilt, and displacement that the divorcing parents have inflicted on them; instead, they continue into adulthood with academic, behavioral, and psychological problems. This specially adapted Phil Donahue program examines the legacy of divorce for children. (From Films for The Humanities & Sciences, Inc.)

Dying to be heard...is anybody listening? video 25 minutes. This program offers specific advice on how to recognize teens in danger of committing suicide and successfully intervene. It talks to teens who have attempted suicide about their reasons for trying and about their lives after treatment, and profiles a Texas community that banded together to stop a rash of teen suicides, showing how they turned tragedy into triumph. (From Films for the Humanities & Sciences, Inc.)

Eating disorders, video 26 minutes. This program covers the personality profiles of the likeliest anorexia patients; explains their inability to acknowledge that they are thin enough, shows how anorexia develops and demonstrates its symptoms; and explores with some anorexics how they were cured. (From Films for the Humanities & Sciences, Inc.)

Everything to live for, video, 52 minutes. Suicide occurs in every racial, ethnic, religious, and economic group. Suicides leave survivors guilt-ridden for not recognizing the warning signs. This documentary features the stories of four

Personal, Social, and Emotional Development

youngsters and their families who talk about the presumed causes; the cries for help; and the warning signals. (From Films for the Humanities & Sciences, Inc.)

Family in crisis, video, 28 minutes. This specially adapted Phil Donahue program centers on the plight of poor children growing up in single parent households. Experts examine the problems facing children who are growing up without fathers and the seemingly irreversible cycle of poverty that especially affects minority families. (From Films for the Humanities & Sciences, Inc.)

Family and survival, video, 52 minutes. Less than 5% of American households fit the profile of the traditional nuclear family. Broken homes, battered wives, estranged children, corporate nomads--these are today's commonplaces. From "The Human Animal" Series. (From Films for the Humanities & Sciences, Inc.)

Family and survival, part of the series, The Human Animal, film, 28 minutes, color. Focuses on modern threats to survival of the family, including divorce, unemployment, and inattentive, preoccupied parents and shows how children are affected. (Humanities and Sciences, 1986)

Keeping kids off drugs, video, 25 minutes. Why are some children susceptible to drugs? A school principal, police officers, drug counselors and parents in a high-incidence neighborhood confront the question. (From Films for the Humanities Sciences, Inc.)

Kids talk to kids about drugs, video 28 minutes. This program presents a group of inner-city youngsters who describe the experience living in the center of a drug-infested culture. The scene is New York City, but they could come from any of America's urban areas. Each youngster tells how he learned to say "no" to drugs in the face of pressures which could overwhelm any impressionable child. (From Films for the Humanities & Sciences, Inc.)

Kids under the influence, video, 58 minutes. This For Kid's Sake documentary examines school problems and run-ins with the law as well as the long-term physical and psychological disorders caused by alcohol consumption. It also demonstrates the enormous influence of peer pressure and the seductive advertisements in the mass media Visiting alcoholism treatment centers, it shows the damage done by alcohol and the process of rehabilitation, explains why alcohol presents increased health and safety risks for children and adolescents; and clarifies why alcohol is so easily abused by youngsters and what can be done about it. (From Films for the Humanities & Sciences, Inc.)

Latchkey families, video, 23 minutes. This program offers specific guidance to working parents with children who are left on their own after school. Educational and law enforcement specialists explain how parents can provide for the physical safety and emotional needs of their children and how rules for conduct can best be

Personal, Social, and Emotional Development

set and chores assigned, so that experience can help teach children maturity and independence. (From Films for the Humanities & Sciences, Inc.)

Morality: The process of moral development, 16 mm film, 28 minutes, color. Traces moral development, starting with preschool children and continuing into young adulthood. Kolhberg's stages are illustrated in interviews with adolescents. (Insight Media, 1990)

Moral development, 16 mm film, 28 minutes, color. Reviews the classic experiments on morality performed by Stanley Milgram and provides an overview of Kohlberg's theory and social learning approach to moral development. (CRM, 1975)

Moral judgment and reasoning, 16 mm film, 17 minutes. Describes moral development from three theoretical perspectives: psychoanalytic, social learning, and cognitive developmental. A variety of vignettes illustrate moral development, with special attention given to Kohlberg's stages. (MP 402, Campcut Film Distributors, 1971)

No more secrets, video, 24 minutes. This program discusses the long-term damage that results from sexual abuse, offers the personal stories of children and of adults who were abused as children, follows the trial of an adult accused of abusing eight girls; and shows how children can be encouraged to share their secret with those who can help put an end to the abuse. (From Films for the Humanities & Sciences, Inc.)

Preventing teen pregnancy, video, 28 minutes, color. This program recommends sex education beginning in the preteens, sexual abstinence by teenagers, and education about contraceptives. #CC-1438. VHS or Beta   U-Matic:

Self-esteem in school age children, video, 30 minutes, color. Presents a comprehensive research-based overview of self development during middle childhood. Practical suggestions for fostering self-esteem are offered. (Virginia Tech Intellectual Properties, 1988)

Suicide: The teenager's perspective, video, 26 minutes. This program deals with one promising solution to the problem of teen suicide: Peer groups. Teenagers are accustomed to going to their friends with their problems; in this case, the friends have been trained to recognize the signs of impending suicide. (From Films for the Humanities & Sciences)

Teenage suicide, video, 28 minutes, color. This Phil Donahue show brings together parents of teenage suicide victims, teenagers who have attempted suicide, and a psychotherapist to discuss ways to stem adolescent suicide.(Films for Humanities and sciences, 1987)

Teenage pregnancy, video, 26 minutes. Teenage pregnancy is not a new problem, but the social costs are higher than ever. Teen parents who drop out of school cannot earn enough to raise a family; young mothers and their babies are at high risk to suffer abuse. This program follows several teenagers through the births of their children and subsequent changes in their lives. (From Films for the Humanities & Sciences, Inc.)

Teenage suicide, video, 19 minutes. This documentary explores some of the reasons why teens commit suicide, the recent increase in suicide, and describes some of the behavior patterns to which family and friends should be alert. (From Films for the Humanities & Sciences, Inc.)

Telling teens about AIDS, video, 52 minutes. Helping teachers and parents to confront the issue of AIDS with respect to their own children and speaking directly to teenagers, this programs shows, without moralizing, how one seemingly innocent liaison can lead to death. Former NBA star Julius Irving is the host. #CC-1688: Films for the Humanities and Sciences, Inc., P. O. Box 2053, Princeton, NJ 08543. Or call 1-800-257-5126 (in NJ, 609-452-1128).

Telling teens about sex, video, 28 minutes, color. Do today's teenagers know all about sex? Phil Donahue's audience of teenagers tells a panel of sex educators what they really know and what they would like to know. #CC-1234. VHS or Beta.

The bizarre trial of the pressured peer, video, 28 minutes, color. This is a fast-paced, entertaining film designed for high school students that illustrates the potentially negative consequences of peer pressure. Classroom teachers will find that this film contains excellent discussion topics for health education, social development, and drug prevention programs.

The discovery year, video, 52 minutes, color. Christopher Reeve hosts this look into the first year of human life. Personality develops during the first year. The program watches how three sets of parents respond to the different personalities of their infant daughters, how they learn to adapt and communicate with the individuals who are their children. #EC-1626.

The impact of the classroom environment on children's development, film is 18 minutes, color. Describes the classroom environment of three teachers and their implications for children's development. (Davidson Films, 1980)

The skillstreaming video. How to teach students prosocial skills, video, 26 minutes, color. Illustrates an innovative for teaching students the skills they need for coping with typical social and personal problems. Order from: Research Press, Box 3177, Dept. K, Champaign, IL 61821 or call (217) 352-3273.

Personal, Social, and Emotional Development

What's the difference being different, film or video, 19 minutes, color. Demonstrates how a multicultural program can be implemented in a school system. It shows students and teachers participating in activities that increase feelings of self-worth and understanding of others. Order from: Research Press, Box 3177, Dept. K, Champaign, IL 61821 or call (217) 352-3273.

When society's problems walk through the door. This 30 minute film (1993) profiles three schools that have instituted programs to address the non-academic concerns of their students. (Insight Media, 2162 Broadway, New York, NY). (212-721-6316).

Handout Master 3.0

Lecture Outline ----- Personal, Social, and Emotional Development

- The Work of Erikson

- Understanding Ourselves and Others

- Moral Development

- Socialization: The Home and the School

- Challenges for Children

Copyright © 1998 by Allyn and Bacon

Handout Master 3.1

Twelve Offenses

Adapted from R. Shweder, Mahapatra, M., and Miller, J. (1987). Culture and moral development. In J. Kagan and S. Lamb (Eds.) *The Emergence of Morality in Young Children*. Chicago: University of Chicago Press.

Please rank order the twelve offenses from worst (1) to least bad (12) in your opinion.

___1.   The day after his father's death, the eldest son had a haircut and ate chicken.

___2.   A woman cooked rice and wanted to eat with her husband and his elder brother. Then she ate with them.

___3.   Once a doctor's daughter met a garbage man, fell in love with him, and decided to marry him. The father of the girl opposed the marriage and tried to stop it because the boy was a garbage man. In spite of the opposition of the father, the girl married the garbage man.

___4.   A beggar was begging from house to house with his wife and sick child. A homeowner drove him away without giving him anything.

___5.   In a family, a 25-year-old addresses his father my his first name.

___6.   A poor man went to the hospital after being seriously hurt in an accident. At the hospital they refused to treat him because he could not afford to pay.

___7.   A woman is playing cards at home with her friends. Her husband is cooking for them.

___8.   A father told his son to steal flowers from the neighbor's garden. The boy did it.

___9.   Two people applied for a job. One of them was a relative of the interviewer. Because they were relatives, he was given the job although the other man did better on the exam.

___10. A letter arrived addressed to a 14-year-old son. Before the boy returned home, his father opened the letter and read it.

___11. A young married woman went alone to see a movie without informing her husband. When she returned home, her husband said, "If you do it again, I will beat you black and blue." She did it again; he beat her black and blue.

___12. A boy played hooky from school. The teacher told the boy's father and the father warned the boy not to do it again. But the boy did it again and the father beat him with a cane.

Copyright © 1998 by Allyn and Bacon

Handout Master 3.2

Eisenberg's Levels of Prosocial Moral Reasoning

	LEVEL	APPROXIMATE	DESCRIPTION
1.	Hedonistic, pragmatic orientation	Preschool, early elementary school	Right behavior satisfies one's own needs. Reasons for helping or not helping another refer to gains for the self, e.g., "I wouldn't help because I might be hungry."
2.	"Needs of others" orientation	Preschool, elementary school	Concern for the physical, material, and psychological needs of others is expressed in simple terms, without clear evidence of perspective-taking or empathic feeling, e.g., "He needs it."
3.	Stereotyped, approval-focused orientation	Elementary school and high school	Stereotyped images of good and bad persons and concern for approval justify behavior, e.g., "He'd like him more if he helped."
4.	Empathic orientation	Older elementary and high school	Reasoning reflects an emphasis on perspective-taking and empathic feelings for the other person, e.g., "I'd feel bad if I didn't help because he'd be in pain."
5.	Internalized values orientation	Small minority of high school	Justifications for moral choice are based on internalized values, norms, desire to maintain contractual obligations, and belief in the dignity, rights, and equality of all individuals, e.g., "I would feel bad if I didn't help because I'd know that I didn't live up to my values."

From: Eisenberg, N. (1982). The development of reasoning regarding prosocial behavior. In N. Eisenberg (Ed.), <u>The development of prosocial behavior</u>, (pp. 219-249). NY: Academic Press.

Copyright © 1998 by Allyn and Bacon

Handout Master 3.3

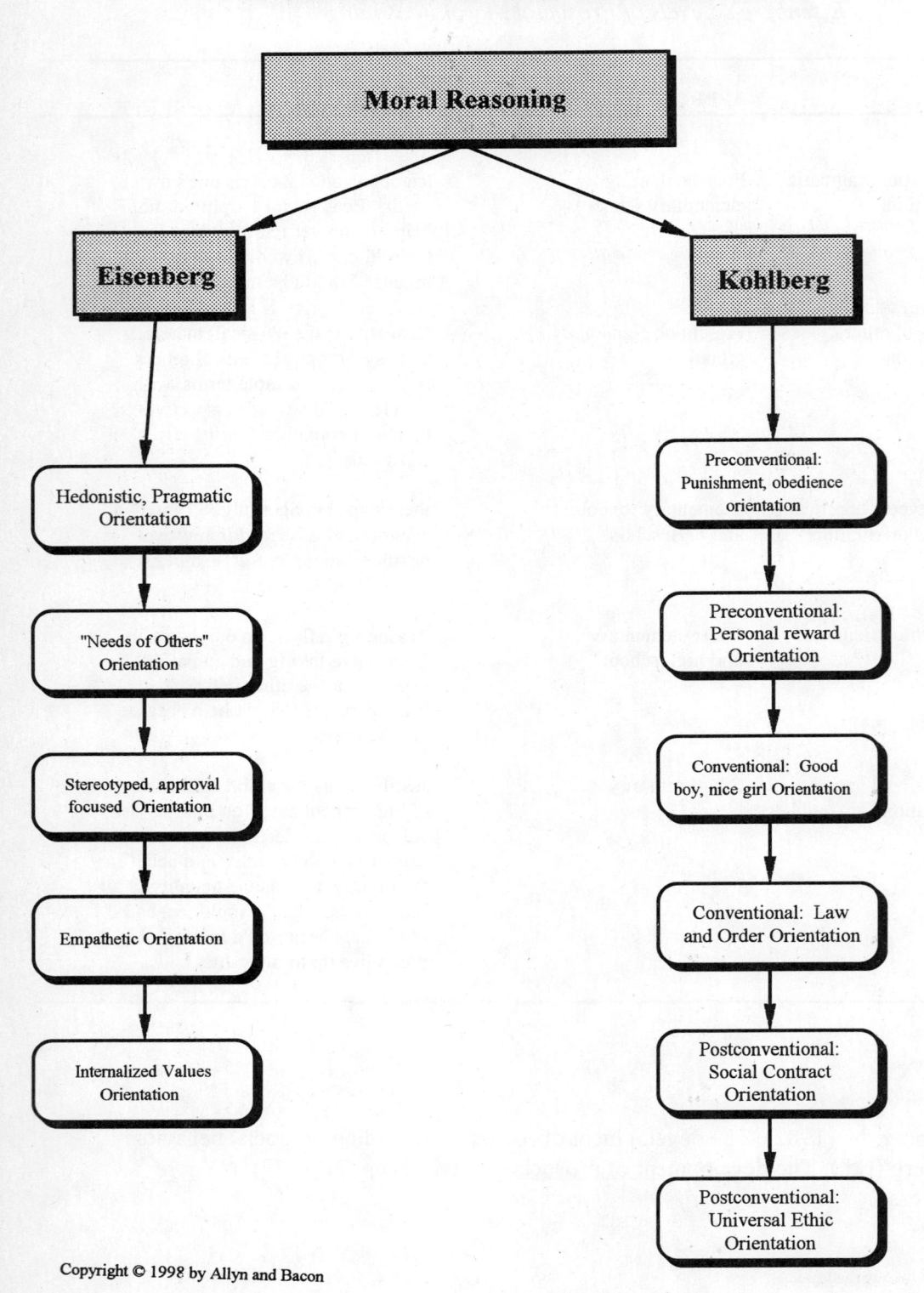

Moral Reasoning

Eisenberg

- Hedonistic, Pragmatic Orientation
- "Needs of Others" Orientation
- Stereotyped, approval focused Orientation
- Empathetic Orientation
- Internalized Values Orientation

Kohlberg

- Preconventional: Punishment, obedience orientation
- Preconventional: Personal reward Orientation
- Conventional: Good boy, nice girl Orientation
- Conventional: Law and Order Orientation
- Postconventional: Social Contract Orientation
- Postconventional: Universal Ethic Orientation

Copyright © 1998 by Allyn and Bacon

Handout Master 3.4

Helping Unpopular Children

Read the descriptions of the following children from the point of view of their classroom teacher and describe how you would help them become more accepted in your class.

Jeannie is 9. She talks loudly over the voices of the other fourth-grade girls. Sometimes, out on the playground, she hits hard to get what she wants. Although her classmates may give way, later they complain about Jeannie, how bossy she is and how much they hate her.

Michael, 12, is a little older than many of his classmates, and not doing well in school. Maybe by keeping his sixth-grade class in an uproar he is trying to ensure that others won't do well either. In class a few boys sometimes get caught up in his disruptive games; mostly, though, other kids shun Michael. Out on the playground, he plays "Star Wars" alone.

Although David makes no trouble in his fifth grade class, he isn't any better liked than Michael or Jeannie. He has always seemed hesitant and maladroit; now that he is 11, he is always alone. No one chooses him as a partner for class projects, and his classmates groan if he's assigned to their side for team games. His teachers find him cooperative, but peers have no use for him.

Suggestions for Helping

Jeannie?

Michael?

David?

Copyright © 1998 by Allyn and Bacon

Handout Master 3.5: Sociogram

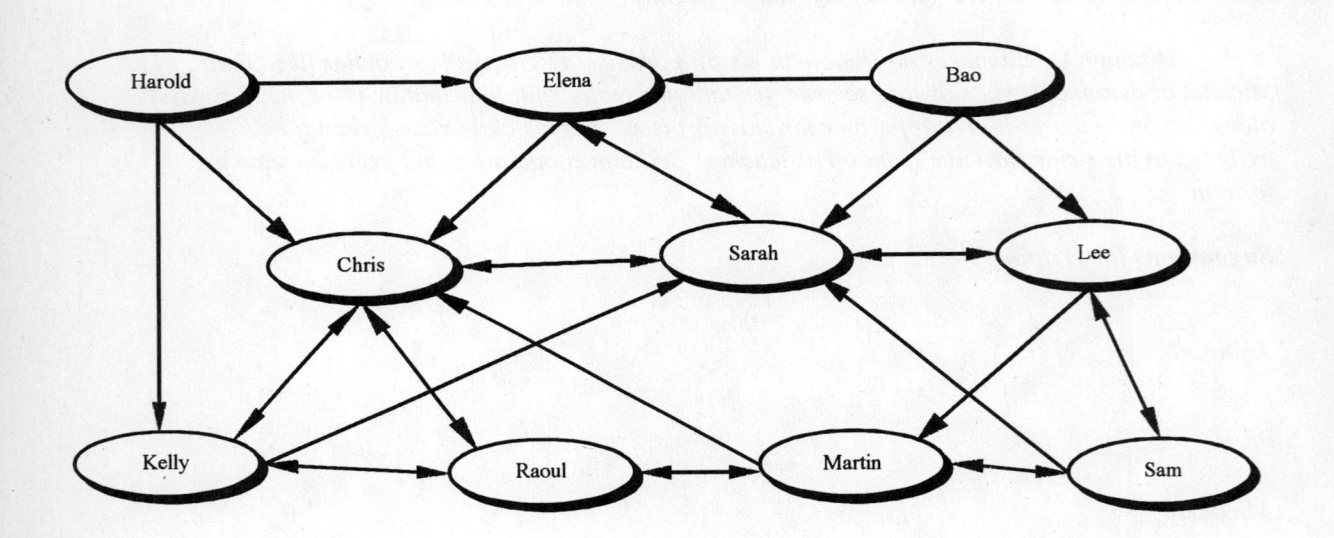

Handout Master 3.6

Peer Nomination

Explain to the child that you are trying to make up groups in the class and you want to make sure that the people in the group get along. If the child cannot remember everyone in the class, you might use a class photo to help the child pick out other children and you can supply the name.

Examples of kinds of questions you might ask are listed below.

1. Whom do you like best in the class?

2. Who is your best friend here?

3. Who do you think does the best job at (mathematics, reading, etc.)?

Copyright © 1998 by Allyn and Bacon

Handout Master 3.7

Locating Sources on the World Wide Web

As part of the activities in Chapter 1, you practiced using the World Wide Web Search Engines. Use this knowledge to add to the list of websites that can provide helpful information about some of the challenges that face children today.

Agency	Website
Alcoholics Anonymous	http://www.aa.org
Al-Anon/Alateen	http://www.al-anon.org
American Foundation for Suicide Prevention	http://www.asfnet.org/
Government Health Links	http://www.uhs.wisc.edu/government.html
American Psychological Association	http://www.apa.org

Copyright © 1998 by Allyn and Bacon

Handout Master 3.8

Conditions that Encourage Positive Resolutions of Erikson's Developmental Crises

1. **Trust vs. mistrust**: Development of a sense of trust in the world based on basic needs being met.

2. **Autonomy vs. doubt**: Development of self-control and self-confidence based on encouragement and limit setting without rejection and blame for failure to meet demands.

3. **Initiative vs. guilt**: Testing of personal power through exploration and manipulation of the environment based on encouragement and tolerance rather that overprotection from or punishment for exploration.

4. **Industry vs. inferiority**: Desire to complete productive work and master developmental tasks of childhood based on success experiences and recognition of progress.

5. **Identity vs. role diffusion**: Attempt to answer "Who am I?" and achieve a satisfying sense of identity based on personal success and satisfaction combined with peer acceptance.

6. **Intimacy vs. isolation**: Ability to relate intimately with another person based on self-disclosure and satisfying experiences with intimate others.

7. **Generativity vs. stagnation**: Act of caring extended beyond a single person to future generations based on a satisfying personal life and freedom from self-preoccupying pressures.

8. **Integrity vs. despair**: Adjustment to aging and death with a sense of satisfaction about the past.

Copyright © 1993 Allyn and Bacon

Copyright © 1998 by Allyn and Bacon

Handout Master 3.9

Resolving Developmental Crises

The positive resolution of a developmental crisis is based on consistent experiences that encourage and support such a resolution. Match the following types of experiences with the crisis in which they would have the most impact. Then indicate whether the experience would support a positive or a negative resolution of the crisis.

Crisis

A. Trust vs. mistrust
B. Autonomy vs. shame and doubt
C. Initiative vs. guilt
D. Industry vs. inferiority
E. Identity vs. role confusion

Resolution

\+ Positive Resolution
\- Negative Resolution

_____ a. When a student finally completes a complex and involved science project, the teacher criticizes him for taking so much time.

_____ b. The baby sitter loudly bangs pots together and the baby cries with fear. She continues to do this so that the baby will not be afraid of loud noises.

_____ c. When the baby is hungry and cries, his mother feeds him.

_____ d. When a student wants to pour water in a clay bowl, which he has made, the teacher lets him because she tries to let students carry out their own ideas.

_____ e. Little Susan wants to feed herself, but her mother, annoyed by the mess her daughter creates, insists on feeding the child herself.

_____ f. Students in Mrs. Jones' class decide to sell candy to make money for the local muscular dystrophy association. Mrs. Jones praises the children for this project, even though it means considerable work for her.

_____ g. Mrs. Ross purchases tennis shoes with Velcro closings rather than shoe laces so that her children can take their own shoes off and put them on themselves.

_____ h. Mr. Shumard allows his seniors in government class the opportunity to discuss not only the current events of the day, but also the views and opinions regarding those current events.

_____ i. Claire built a boat of cardboard and wood. When Claire decided to sail her boat, the Big Dipper, in the lake, her parents gave the launching of her boat the same fanfare and attention that they gave to the launching of the model boat her father built.

_____ j. Mrs. Clark, the 11th grade English teacher is all business. She believes that classroom time should be spent on lessons and not discussion of students' feelings about the meaningful of the poem to their lives. Therefore, her class time is spent telling the students the appropriate interpretations of the plays and poems.

Correct Answers: (D -, A -, A +, C +, B -, D +, B +, E +, D +, E -)

Copyright © 1998 by Allyn and Bacon

Handout Master 3.10

Reducing the Incidence of Cheating and Plagiarism

Why do People Cheat or Plagiarize in College? List 5 reasons in order of importance.

1.

2.

3.

4.

5.

What could teachers do to minimize the incidence of these kinds of behaviors?

Handout Master 3.11: Links to Other Chapters

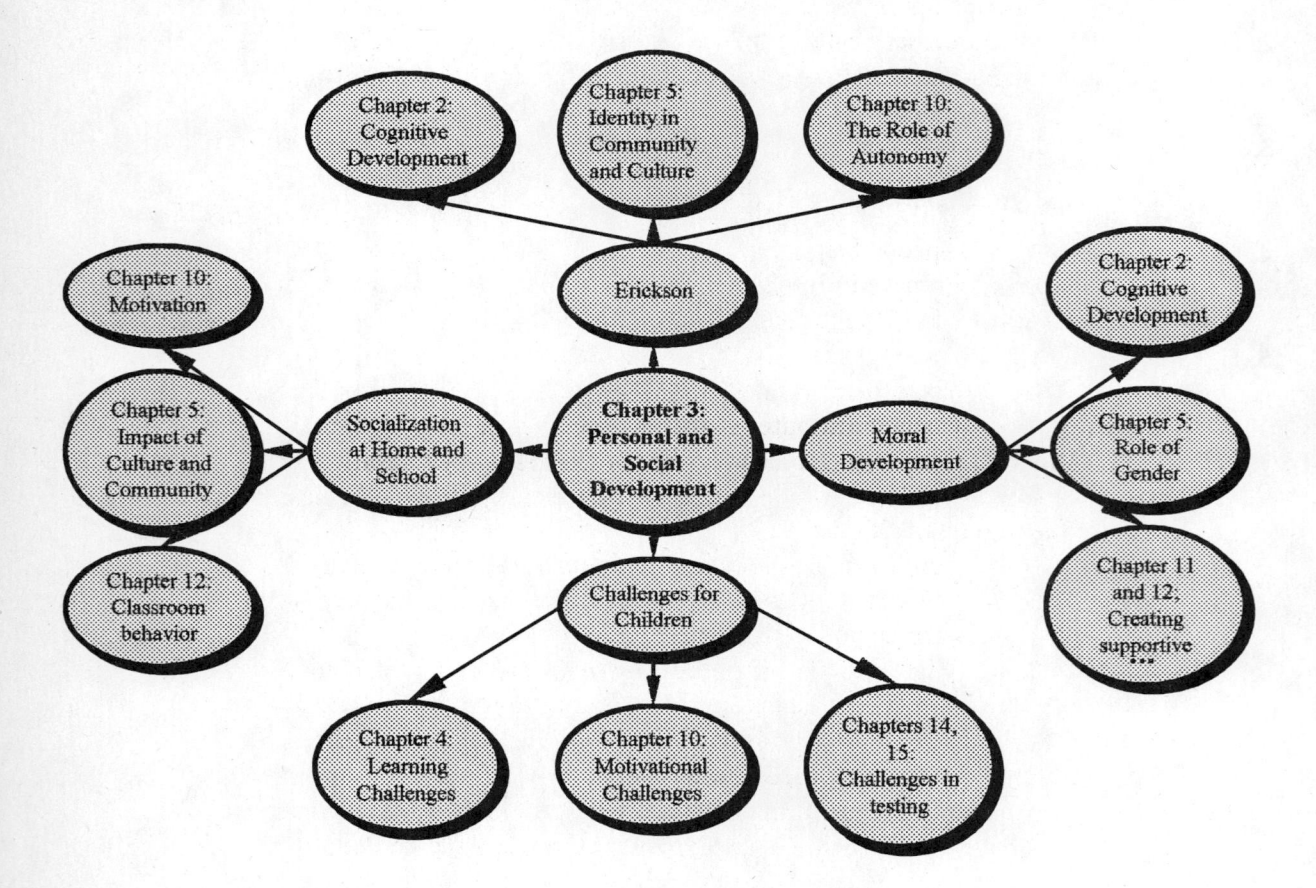

- Chapter 3: Personal and Social Development
  - Erickson
    - Chapter 2: Cognitive Development
    - Chapter 5: Identity in Community and Culture
    - Chapter 10: The Role of Autonomy
  - Socialization at Home and School
    - Chapter 10: Motivation
    - Chapter 5: Impact of Culture and Community
    - Chapter 12: Classroom behavior
  - Moral Development
    - Chapter 2: Cognitive Development
    - Chapter 5: Role of Gender
    - Chapter 11 and 12: Creating supportive...
  - Challenges for Children
    - Chapter 4: Learning Challenges
    - Chapter 10: Motivational Challenges
    - Chapters 14, 15: Challenges in testing

Copyright © 1998 by Allyn and Bacon

4

Learning Abilities and Learning Problems

Teaching Outline

I. What Do You Think? Overview/ What Would You Do?
II. Language And Labeling: What Does It Mean To Be Exceptional?
   A. Some children are exceptional because they need special education/services
   B. Labeling or "diagnosis" of exceptionalities can both stigmatize and help students
      1. Expectations and assumptions may be self-fulfilling prophecies
      2. Labels may, however, protect students and/or open doors to special help
III. Individual Differences In Intelligence
   A. What does intelligence mean?
      1. Intelligence: One ability or many?
      2. Spearman: There is one general intelligence factor or mental attribute 'g' that is used to perform any mental test but each test also requires some specific abilities
      3. Thurstone: There are several "primary mental abilities"
   B. Multiple intelligences
      1. Guilford: Three faces of intellect (mental operations, contents, and products) with each divided into multiple subcategories
      2. Gardner: There are at least seven separate intelligences (linguistic, musical, spatial, logical-mathematical, bodily-kinesthetic, understanding others, understanding self)
   C. Intelligence as a process: Sternberg's Triarchic Theory
      1. Three parts: analytic, creative, and practical intelligence
      2. Analytic intelligence involves the component mental processes that lead to more or less intelligent behavior: metacomponents, performance components, and knowledge acquisition components
      3. Creative intelligence involves coping with new experiences and is characterized by insight and automaticity
      4. Practical intelligence involves selecting an environment in which one can succeed, adapting to that environment, and reshaping it if necessary

Learning Abilities and Learning Problems

    D.   How is intelligence measured?
        1.   Binet's dilemma: how to identify children at risk for school failure
        2.   Binet's mission: To identify students needing special teaching by measuring intellectual skills necessary for success in school
        3.   Mental age: A score based on average abilities for an age group
        4.   IQ: Comparison of mental age and chronological age
        5.   Deviation IQ: Score identifying where a person's score lies in the distribution of scores for that person's age group
        6.   Group versus individual IQ tests
            a)   Group test is much less accurate than individual test
            b)   Group tests require reading and writing skills more than individual tests
    E.   Point/Counterpoint: Are Intelligence Tests Biased against Minority-Group Students?
    F.   What does an IQ score mean?
        1.   Intelligence and achievement: IQ scores strongly predict school achievement, but not good predictors of success in life
        2.   Heredity and environment both affect intelligence
        3.   Guidelines: Interpreting IQ scores

IV.   Ability Differences And Teaching
    A.   Ability grouping: Grouping students based on ability
        1.   Between-class ability grouping: Formation of separate ability-based classes
            a)   For low-ability students, does not improve learning and may cause problems
            b)   High-ability or cross-grade groupings are effective
        2.   Within-class grouping based on ability
            a)   Common with reading and math in elementary schools
            b)   Offers positive results when based on current performance and sensitively tailored to student needs
    B.   Mental retardation
        1.   Student should never be classified as mentally retarded only on the basis of IQ scores alone
        2.   Definition
            a)   Low IQ score: Below 70 on the WISC-R
            b)   Deficient adaptive behavior, social inadequacy (Table 4.3)
            c)   Deficiencies apparent before age 18

Learning Abilities and Learning Problems

3. Causes of retardation
   a) organic causes account for 10-25% of those identified as retarded
   b) up to 50% of cases of retardation could be prevented by better prenatal care, improved nutrition and disease prevention, and high quality parent training and preschool services for children at risk
4. Goals for teaching retarded students
   a) Basic reading, writing, and arithmetic, the environment, social behavior, and personal interests
   b) Transition programming: Preparing the retarded student to live and work in the community
5. Guidelines: Teaching students with below average intelligence

C. Gifted and talented
D. Who are the gifted?
1. Lack of agreement about identification of giftedness
2. Renzulli's identified 3 criteria:
   a) above average ability
   b) high level of creativity
   c) high level of task commitment
3. The Terman study of gifted students
   a) Gifted tend to be larger, stronger, and healthier than the norm
   b) Some gifted students are more emotionally stable and become better adjusted adults
4. Problems of gifted students in school
   a) Boredom, isolation from peers, difficulty in facing emotions, impatience with friends & peers
5. Terman follow-up: Popular gifted children less likely to pursue intellectual pursuits; more-accomplished adults may have preferred adult company as children
6. Recognizing students' special abilities
   a) Teacher observation successful in identifying 10 to 50 percent of the time
   b) Individual IQ tests imperfect best single predictor of academic giftedness
7. Teaching gifted students
   a) Enrichment and acceleration both may be appropriate
   b) Teachers need to encourage abstract thinking, creativity, independence; must be imaginative, flexible, and non threatening

Learning Abilities and Learning Problems

V. Creativity And Cognition
    A. Requirements
        1. a rich store of knowledge
        2. ability to break set, cognitive flexibility
        3. continual reorganization of ideas
    B. Assessing creativity
        1. Torrance's paper and pencil tests of graphic and verbal creativity
            a) responses are scored for fluency, originality, and flexibility
        2. teacher judgments are very unreliable
    C. Promoting creativity in the classroom
        1. Brainstorming: separating the generation of ideas from their evaluation
        2. Play
        3. Guidelines: Encouraging creativity

VI. Cognitive And Learning Styles
    A. Cognitive styles: Patterns of behavior and performance by which an individual approaches learning; composite of cognition, affect, and physiology
    B. Field dependence and field independence
        1. Field-dependent style: Tendency to see pattern as a whole; orientation
        2. toward people and relationships
        3. Field-independent style: Tendency to perceive separate parts of a pattern; ability to analyze its components; greater task orientation
    C. Impulsive and reflective cognitive styles
        1. Impulsive student works very quickly but makes many mistakes
        2. Reflective student works slowly with few errors
        3. Students tend to becomes more reflective with age and can be taught to become more reflective through self-instruction
    D. Learning style preferences: Individual preferences for particular approaches and environments
        1. Deep-processing approaches underscore the meaning of concepts
        2. Surface-processing approaches underscore memorization
        3. Several instruments available to assess students' learning preferences
            a) Instruments have been criticized for lack of reliability and validity

Learning Abilities and Learning Problems

    4. Tailoring instruction to learning styles
      a) Learning may be enhanced if students study in preferred settings
      b) Students may not expand repertoire of strategies if their instruction is too closely tailored to their learning style preferences

VII. Students With Learning Challenges
  A. Disability (specific inability) distinct from handicap (disadvantage in specific situation)
  B. Physically challenged students
    1. Epilepsy: Seizures that result from uncontrolled firing of neurons in the brain
    2. Cerebral palsy: Characterized by spasticity
    3. Hearing impairment: Results from multiple factors
    4. Vision impairment: Mild problem requires only glasses; severe impairment may require specialized materials and strategies
  C. Communication disorders
    1. Speech impairments: Articulation disorder, stuttering or voicing problems
    2. Oral language disorders: Absence, difference, delay, or interruption of language development
  D. Emotional/behavioral disorders: Behavior that deviates enough to interfere with growth and development or the lives of others
    1. Six dimensions
      a) Conduct disorders: Aggressiveness, destructiveness, disobedience
      b) Anxiety-withdrawal disorder: Anxiety, shyness, and depression
      c) Attentional-problems-immaturity: Short attention span, frequent daydreaming, little initiative, messiness, poor coordination
      d) Motor excess: Restlessness, tension, inability to sit still or stop talking
      e) Socialized aggression: Members of gangs; may steal or vandalize
      f) Psychotic behavior: Extremely bizarre behavior
  E. Hyperactivity and attention disorders
    1. Hyperactivity is a set of behaviors, not a single condition
    2. Characteristically children are physically overactive, inattentive
    3. have difficulty in responding appropriately and little control of behavior

Learning Abilities and Learning Problems

           4.   Main difficulty for children is in directing and maintaining attention
           5.   Children with this problem may be identified as having attention-deficit-hyperactive disorder (ADHD)
           6.   Certain stimulants bring manageable behavior but can cause negative side effects
                a)   rapid increase in the number of children who receive drug therapy for attention disorders
                b)   long term effects of drug therapy are unknown
           7.   Most successful ways to improve academic learning and social skills are based on behavioral principles
      F.   Specific learning disabilities: What's wrong when nothing is wrong?
           1.   Little agreement on definition
           2.   Most definitions agree that students with learning disabilities have at least average intelligence and significant academic problem
           3.   Problems experienced by students learning disabilities can include
                a)   difficulties with reading
                b)   difficulties with mathematics
                c)   poor learning strategies
           4.   Early diagnosis is important to prevent students becoming frustrated or discouraged
           5.   Promising approaches to teaching learning disabled students includes training in information processing and emphasis of study skills

VIII.   Integration, Mainstreaming, and Inclusion
      A.   Legislation relevant to educating children with special needs
           1.   PL 94-142: Education for All Handicapped Children Act (1975)
           2.   PL 99-457: Extended the requirement for a free and appropriate education to all handicapped children between the ages of 3 and 5
           3.   1990: Amendment of PL 94-142 by the Individuals with Disabilities Education Act (IDEA)
           4.   1990 Americans with Disabilities ACT (ADA) extended civil rights protection in employment, transportation, public accommodations, telecommunications to people with disabilities
      B.   Point/Counterpoint: Is full inclusion a reasonable approach to teaching exceptional students?
      C.   Educational Implications
           1.   Least restrictive placement: Educating the child in the mainstream as much as possible

    2. Individualized Education Plan (IEP): Written plan and objectives, updated each year
    3. Rights of students and parents, including confidentiality, right to see all records and right to challenge program developed for their child
  D. Effective teaching in inclusive classrooms
    1. Practices of effective teachers
    2. Support from resource rooms, collaborative consultation, and cooperative teaching
    3. Guidelines: Families as partners: Productive conferences
  E. Computers and exceptional students
    1. Computer programs help record keeping and program planning
    2. Can support learning of students with learning
IX. Summary
X. Key Terms And Concepts
XI. Teachers' Casebook/ What Would They Do?

Learning Abilities and Learning Problems

Learning Activities and Related Research

ACTIVITIES	HANDOUTS
Chapter 4	4.0 Lecture Outline
	4.1 Myths about special education
Cooperative Activities	
4.1 Defining Intelligence	4.2 Definitions of Intelligence
4.2 Teaching Students with Mental Retardation	4.3 Characteristics of Mental Retardation
4.3 Adapting instruction for different learners	4.4 Concept map: Adapting instruction for learner differences
	4.5 The needs of special needs children
Research Activities	
4.4 What is intelligence?	
4.5 Special Needs Students as Tutors	4.6 Guide to literature search
4.6 Should we group according to ability?	
Using Technology	
4.7 Technology for Special Needs	4.7 Technology for Special Needs: Resources
Field Experience	
4.8 Interview on the IQ testing	
Other Teaching Activities	
4.9 Teaching the Gifted	4.8 Indicators of giftedness
4.10 Examination of Special Education Services	
4.11 Communication disorders	
4.12 Assisting the ADHD child	4.9 Checklist for monitoring behavior
	4.10 Guidelines for teaching the hearing-impaired student
	4.11 Myths and facts about vision impairment
	4.12 Indicators of learning problems
	4.13a An Educational Plan
	4.13b An Educational Plan (cont.)
	4.13c An Educational Plan (cont.)
	4.14a Individualized Educational Program
	4.14b Individualized Educational Program (cont.)
	4.15 Concept Map: Links to other chapters

Cooperative Activities

4.1   Defining Intelligence

   These definitions of intelligence taken from Sattler, J. (1988). Assessing children's abilities. (3rd ed.) San Diego: Jerome Sattler Publisher, (p. 45), show the historical development of the concept of intelligence.

   Have students in groups discuss the quotations on **Handout Master 4.2** and determine what has changed in the definition of intelligence in the last century.

Binet (in Terman, 1916) "The tendency to take and maintain definite direction; the capacity to make adaptations for the purpose of attaining a desired end; and the power of autocriticism" (p.45).

Binet and Simon (1916) '...judgment, otherwise called good sense, practical sense, initiative, the faculty of adapting one's self to circumstances. To judge well, to comprehend well, to reason well, these are the essential activities of intelligence" (pp. 42-43).

Spearman (1923) "...everything intellectual can be reduced to some special case...of educating either relations or correlates" (p. 300). Education of relations-"The mentally presenting of any two or more characters...tends to evoke immediately a knowing of relation between them" (p. 63). Education of correlates-"The presenting of any character together with any relation tends to evoke immediately a knowing of the correlative character" (p.91).

Stoddard (1943) "...the ability to undertake activities that are characterized by (1) difficulty, (2) complexity, (3) abstractness, (4) economy, (5) adaptiveness to a goal, (6) social value, and (7) the emergence of originals, and to maintain activities under conditions that a demand a concentration of energy and a resistance to emotional forces" (p.4).

Wechsler (1958) "the aggregate or global capacity of the individual to act purposefully, to think rationally and to deal effectively with his environment" (p. 7).

Gardner (1983) "...a human intellectual competence must entail a set of skills of problem solving- enabling the individual to resolve genuine problems or difficulties that he or she encounters, and when appropriate, to create an effective product-and must also entail the potential for finding or creating problems-thereby laying the groundwork for the acquisition of new knowledge" (pp. 60-61).

Sternberg (1986) "...mental activity involved in purposive adaptation to, shaping of, and selection of real-world environments relevant to one's life" (p. 33).

References

Binet, A. (1916). <u>The measurement of intelligence</u>. Boston: Houghton Mifflin.
Binet, A. and Simon, T. (1916). <u>The development of intelligence in children</u>. Translated by Elizabeth S. Kite. Baltimore: Williams and Wilkins.
Gardner, H. (1983). <u>Anticipation of gains in general information: A comparison of verbal aptitudes, reading comprehension, and listening</u>. Harvard University, Cambridge, Mass: Harvard Project Zero.
Spearman, C. (1923). <u>The nature of intelligence and the principles of cognition</u>. London: Macmillan.

Learning Abilities and Learning Problems

Sternberg, R. (1986). Geniuses: A framework for intellectual abilities and theories of them. Intelligence, 10, 239-250.

Stoddard, D. G. (1943). The meaning of intelligence. New York: Macmillan.

Wechsler, D. (1958). Bellevue intelligence scale--Data on the youth of intelligence between sixteen and twenty-one years as measured by the Education Index #11. Journal of Genetic Psychology, 90, 3-15.

Sternberg, R. (1986). Geniuses: A framework for intellectual abilities and theories of them. Intelligence, 10, 239-250.

4.2   Teaching Students with Mental Retardation

Have the students review the material in **Handout Master 4.3** and decide how teaching students who are mentally retarded would be different from teaching children of normal intelligence. Students should then work together to suggest a set of guidelines for teaching retarded students in mainstreamed classes. Use the following list to help students achieve clear, complete consensus on the guidelines. You might wish to copy and distribute the final composite list the students develop.

1. Determine readiness: However little a child may know, he or she is ready to learn a next step.
2. Objectives should be simply stated and presented.
3. Specific learning objectives should be based on an analysis of the child's learning strengths and weaknesses.
4. Present material in small, logical steps. Practice extensively before going on to the next step.
5. Skills and concepts should be practical, based on the demands of adult life.
6. Do not skip steps. Students with average intelligence can form conceptual bridges from one step to the next. Retarded children need every step and bridge made explicit. Make connections for the students. Do not expect them to "see" the connections.
7. You may have to present the same idea in many different ways.
8. Go back to a simpler level if you see the student not follow.
9. Be especially careful to motivate the student and maintain attention.
10. Find materials that do not insult the student. A junior high boy may need low vocabulary of "See Spot run" but will be insulted by the ages of the characters and the content of the story.
11. Focus on a few target behaviors or skills so you and the student have a chance experience success. Everyone needs positive reinforcement.
12. Retarded students must overlearn, repeat, and practice more than children of average intelligence. They must be taught how to study and they must frequently review and practice their newly acquired skills in different settings.

Learning Abilities and Learning Problems

4.3 <u>Adapting Instruction for Different Learners</u>

Have students locate a lesson plan on the Internet (see two sources below) or use a lesson plan they have already developed. Have them redesign the lesson to accommodate specified types of learners. **Handout Master 4.5** should be used with this task.

http://www.cea.berkeley.edu./~edsci/lessons/lessons_teacherdeveloped.html
http://teachers.net/lessons/

Research Activities

4.4 <u>What is Intelligence?</u>

Have your students (with appropriate permissions in place) ask 10 people to describe three characteristics of intelligent people. Once they have collected this information, place each characteristics (e.g., able to solve problems) on a separate card and have a subgroup of the class group those characteristics that appear to go together. Have an additional group perform the same task. Compare the results of the two groupings. Use this categorization to lead a discussion of what things are usually considered to be evidence of "intelligence" and the consistency with which people make judgments of what characteristics go together. Once groupings of characteristics have been agreed upon, have students provide a single label to define the category. Use this labeling technique to introduce information about latent traits.

4.5 <u>Effects Of Handicapped Students Tutoring Regular Students</u>

From Top, B. L., & Osguthorpe, R. T. (1987). Reverse-role tutoring: The effects of handicapped students tutoring regular class students. <u>The Elementary Journal, 87</u>, 413-24.

Read the following to your students. Then assign them the task of finding additional research articles that address the issue of special needs students as tutors. Have them summarize the current knowledge on this topic. Use **Handout Master 4.6** with this activity.

The purpose of this study was to examine the effects of having handicapped students tutor younger, non handicapped children in reading. Included in the study were 78 fourth-through sixth-grade learning disabled or behaviorally disordered students attending either a resource or self-contained special education class and 82 non-handicapped first graders. Students enrolled in a resource program were randomly assigned to an experimental (tutor) or control (non tutor) group, whereas students in self-contained, special education classes were assigned randomly by class to either group. Tutors and tutees scored significantly higher on both criterion and standardized reading

Learning Abilities and Learning Problems

tests than students assigned to control groups. Although overall self-esteem scores were similar for both groups, analyses showed that tutors increased more than control students in their perceptions of their "general academic ability" and their "reading/spelling" ability.

4.6   Should We Group According to Ability?

Ask students to give an opinion on whether students should be grouped according to ability. Ask them to explain their reasoning. Have students then find 5 research articles that support their views. Compare and contrast the research findings that students locate and in a group discussion, summarize the findings and draw a conclusion about the question. Ask students to consider which information they would attach greater importance to: 1) information from a friend, peer; or 2) information based on the process they just finished.

Using Technology

4.7   Technology for Special Needs

Technology can help your students to work with children with special needs by providing accessibility to students, by supporting the skills they have, and by providing easy access to a variety of resources available on the Internet (see **Handout Master 4.5**) for some starting places.
1. Have your students examine their own computers and their help systems for accommodations made for special users. They are most likely to find this kind of information by consulting the help systems on the computer.
2. Have your students develop a comprehensive list of devices/supports that are available that can help students with special needs. They might begin by using the listing of types of special problems students might have (see text by Woolfolk) and using that list to organize their search.
3. Have your students complete the listing of Internet resources that is begun in **Handout Master 4.5.**

Field Experience

4.8   Interview on IQ Testing

Arrange to have a school psychologist, member of a child study team, or counseling psychologist visit your class. Have students brainstorm the kinds of questions that they will be asking the psychologist. Some questions might be: What is the value of IQ testing? What useful information does it provide? How valid is IQ testing? Are children likely to be misclassified? After the visit, students should analyze the information they gained from the experience. How will they use the information it in the future? Students should select the best 10 questions from among those generated and be able to explain why the questions are good questions to ask.

Learning Abilities and Learning Problems

Other Teaching Activities

4.9   Teaching the Gifted

From On Being Gifted (New York: American Association for Gifted Children, 1978), pp. 19-21. Used by permission of Walker & Co.

Distribute **Handout Master 4.8 a & b** on characteristics of gifted students. Then relate the following information about unhappy feelings associated with being gifted.

To many students with exceptional talents, a problem arises concerning their peers, their role in classroom instruction, and their relationships with teachers. *On being Gifted*, written by twenty gifted and talented high school students, contains the following comments by fourth-, fifth-, and sixth graders from Norwich, Connecticut that illustrate the negative self-perceptions and social stigma that gifted and talented students sometimes experience. The following are excerpts:

Peer Pressure
People with special gifts get a great deal of attention from the society around them. For me it is not as great as for others because I am in my own age group. However, prodding, teasing, and resentment do present themselves as foolish obstacles. Students in my peer group are jealous about my ability. I do my best to share with them my knowledge and I try to help them whenever possible but all this is to no avail.

Caught in the Middle
As I sit in a classroom of a small town high school, I am listening to the teacher begin a lecture for the day. He asks a question regarding the homework, chapter 25 in our book. I raise my hand and respond correctly to his query. He continues to ask questions and I continue to answer them. After a couple of rounds I begin to look around sheepishly to see if anyone else has his hand raised. No one does so I answer again. I hear annoyed mutterings from my classmates. I just know they're thinking, "She thinks she knows everything." So in a futile effort to conform and satisfy them, I sink in my seat just a little and let the rest of the questions slide by. The teacher becomes angry that no one has read the assignment and feels he must repeat the chapter. And another day is wasted.
So goes it, and unfortunately, too often. As a result, I do not feel challenged nor do I attempt to be when I find myself in such a class. One alternative, which in my school is extremely limited, is to sign up for courses which are designed for people planning to major in that specific area. But alas, not enough teachers, nor enough money in the budget for books or supplies. So suffer, kid!

Pressures from Teachers
Often our peers get their cues when our teachers begin to reject us. This often happens when an instructor feels threatened by the exceptional student. In my school this

takes the form of neglect. The teacher does not fill my needs because he will not devote extra time to me and often totally ignores my suggestions.

Often, instructors, though not actually threatened, feel that the gifted student has had enough recognition and therefore bypass him. Many times one of my teachers has preferred to work extremely hard with his favorite remedial workshop student than to talk to me. This sort of behavior has caused me to doubt my priorities concerning education.

Who's on Our Side

Occasionally teachers seem to be foes rather than allies. Many times teachers are on an ego trip, preferring to help slower students so that they can appear to be all-powerful and all-knowing.

If a student happens to learn rapidly or already has a knowledge of the subject from prior exposure, the teacher begins to resent the student. In my case, I had a teacher of algebra who developed this type of resentment. I understood the material because of previous contact with the subject. I seldom missed problems on tests, homework on the board; when I did, I caught his wrath.

Ask students to develop a set of guidelines for teaching gifted students and to give examples of each. You may wish to suggest they include the following points:

Guidelines for Teaching Gifted Students

Allow time, quiet, and privacy for independent work.

Examples
1. Allow students to pursue independent projects in the library, community, or art room.
2. Some class time can be devoted to independent work.
3. Help students find the resources they need. If you can't help, try to find a community expert or mentor who can.

Use advanced learning materials and computers to allow students to master material independently.

Examples
1. Have a variety of advanced texts available to take home.
2. Keep an advanced reading list to which students can add titles and comments.
3. If computers are available, encourage students to design teaching programs for computer-based instruction.

Use delayed, intrinsic, and social reinforcement rather than immediate and concrete rewards.

Examples
1. Avoid emphasizing grades.
2. Have students share their creations with the class.
3. Have students analyze and criticize their own work.

Learning Abilities and Learning Problems

4. Use gifted students as peer tutors.

Involve students in planning their own curriculum.
Examples
1. Help students set their own learning goals.
2. Have problem-solving sessions to identify assignments.

Focus on problem solving, divergent thinking, and long-term projects rather than on frequent tests of factual information.

Examples
1. Avoid frequent testing and grading.
2. Focus on a few large projects instead of many small assignments.

4.10   Examination Of Special Education Services

Invite a number of teachers to your class to engage in a panel discussion about the evaluation, placement, and educational programming for students with special needs in their classrooms. Some of the following questions may be helpful but groups of students should generate questions about teaching special needs children who are in the age groups they hope to teach.

1. How frequently are handicapped students placed in their classes?
2. What types of handicapping conditions have been represented?
3. What types of special teaching methods or adaptations have they tried?
4. Have any types of handicaps been more difficult to accommodate than others?
5. Is there any type of teacher training, not provided by their college programs, that they feel would be helpful to them in working with handicapped students?

4.11   Communication Disorders

Read the language sample accompanying the explanation to your class. Have your students respond to the questions.

Delayed Verbal Development

Teacher: "Sam, what is your favorite thing to do on a weekend?"
Sam: "Ride my minibike."
T: "What color is it?"
S: "Red."
T: "Where do you ride it?"
S: "In the field."
T: "Tell me more."
S: [ ]
T: "It must break down sometimes; how do you fix it?"

95

Learning Abilities and Learning Problems

S: "Take the engine out."
T: "Then what do you do?"
S: "Fix it."

      This language sample was taken when Sam was conversing alone with his teacher. It is apparent that Sam is uncomfortable when urged to speak; he does not contribute spontaneously and does not elaborate. When you take into consideration that Sam is 12 years old and talking to a familiar person about a subject he is interested in and knowledgeable about, then you realize the extent of the problem.
      Sam is an extremely reserved, cooperative sixth-grader who is struggling with reading. Perhaps because he has never posed a behavioral problem, his previous teachers have not taken note of Sam's sparse verbalizations. Although he is seeing the remedial reading teacher, he has never been referred to supplementary help in language. He scored at the 2.0 level on the California Achievement Test, Lower Primary, Form W, in September. When he reads Sam makes numerous substitutions particularly on basic words. He tends to substitute words such as "house" for "home." In both reading and speaking, Sam omits words or distorts the order of words, uses incorrect tenses, and makes errors of syntax.
      Sam has an <u>expressive language problem</u>. He is unable to plan and organize words for the expression of ideas in complete sentences. This in turn contributes to the reading problem. Your objective in working with Sam is that he generate sentences that include more descriptive language in the form of adjectives and adverbs.

Questions

1. What are some learning activities you could plan in order for Sam to achieve the performance objective?

2. How would you encourage Sam to talk more so that his confidence in speaking will increase?

Ask students to develop guidelines for helping students who stutter to succeed in regular classrooms. You may wish to suggest the following guidelines with samples to stimulate students' thinking in this activity.

- **Concentrate on what is said, not on the trouble the student has in saying it**.

Examples
1. Don't correct or finish the sentence for the student. Allow the student the time to speak.
2. Monitor your nonverbal communication. Does your expression show impatience?

Learning Abilities and Learning Problems

- **Give the student some classroom responsibility.**

Examples
1. Appoint the student to a position that will gain him or her respect from classmates.
2. Let the student demonstrate skills that require speaking.

- **Try to establish a regular routine.**

Examples
1. The student should follow the same rules as any other student, but pressure should not be put on speaking.
2. Develop a schedule so the student knows what's coming next most of the time.
3. Do not call on the student suddenly, with no warning.
4. Signal the student a little before his or her turn is coming. You might use patterned turns, such as going around the circle.

- **Do not allow the student to use stuttering to avoid a class assignment.**

Examples
1. If a task is oral and the student feels unable to do it, assign the work in written form.
2. Some days will be easier than others. Encourage interaction and recitation on good days.

- **Do not allow peers to make fun of the stutterer.**

Examples
1. Model patience and interest when the child talks.
2. Read a story written from an exceptional student's viewpoint and discuss it with the class.
3. Talk privately with any students who ridicule and explain the effects of their behavior on the stutterer.

4.12   Assisting the ADHD Child

Handout Master 4.9 provides a checklist that a child might use to help monitor their own performance. It requires the child to note assignments and rate their own behavior in various aspects of the school day.

Have your students discuss with a teacher what kinds of strategies he or she might use to assist the child with attention deficit/hyperactivity disorder to manage in school.

Learning Abilities and Learning Problems

Discussion Questions

1. How should a teacher interpret an IQ score that is recorded in a students' cumulative folder?
2. Can children with hyperactivity disorders learn effectively in school without medication?
3. If there were a large discrepancy (in either direction) between a child's performance level in school and his or her measured IQ score, which score would you be more concerned about? Consider more valid? What hypotheses might you entertain about the student?
4. Do labels have the negative influences people think they do?
5. Gifted children have not received the same attention as other categories of exceptionality. Do you think they should have special classes and teachers? What has caused them to receive more attention in recent years?
6. Often when students fail a grade or course they are "recycled" through the same material on the assumption that repetition will produce learning. Use the concept of cognitive style to argue against this.
7. What are the main difficulties you would anticipate in having a special needs students "included" in your class? What kinds of support or assistance would you need and where might you find it?
8. What are limitations of IEPs?
9. Do you think parents should have the right to prevent their child from being placed in a special education class?

Additional Resources for Teaching This Chapter

REFERENCES

Adams, P. (1989). Who cares about disabled people? Child's Play Ltd., Singapore.

Althea, (1987). I have epilepsy. Dinosaur Publications, 8 Grafton Street, London WIX3LA.

Barkley, R. A. (1995). Taking charge of ADHD. New York, NY: Guilford Press.

Beisser, A. (1989). Flying without wings. Doubleday, Inc. 666 Fifth Ave. New York, NY 10103

Bergman, T. (1989). In our own terms: Children living with physical disabilities. Gareth Stevens, Inc. 7317 West Green Tree Road, Milwaukee, Wisconsin, 53223.

Caine, R. N. & Caine, G. (1991). Making connections: Teaching and the human brain. Association for Curriculum Development.

Dykman, R. A., & Ackerman, P. T. (1993). Behavioral subtypes of attention deficit disorder. Exceptional Children, 60, 1332-141.

Eysenck, H. J. (Ed.). (1982a). A model for intelligence. Heidelberg: Springer-Verlag.

Eysenck, H. J. (1982b). The psychophysiology of intelligence. In C. D. Spielberger and J. N. Butcher (Eds.) Advances in personality assessment. (Vol 1, pp. 1-33). Hillsdale, NJ: Erlbaum.

Fiore, T. A., Becker, E. A., & Nero, R. C. (1993). Educational interventions for students with attention deficit disorder. Exceptional Children, 60, 163-173.

Hocutte, A. M., McKinney, J. D., & Montague, M. (1993). Issues in the education of students with attention deficit disorders: Introduction to the special issue. Exceptional Children, 60, 103-106.

Jensen, A. R. (1981). Straight talk about mental testing. New York: The Free Press.

Jordan, N. C., & Goldsmith-Phillips, J. (Eds.). (1994). Learning disabilities: New directions for assessment and intervention. Needham Heights, MA: Allyn and Bacon.

Letch, R. (1989). Special people. Child's Play, Ltd., Singapore.

Manning, B., & Payne, B. D. (1996). Self-talk for teachers and students. Needham Heights, MA: Allyn and Bacon.

McKinney, J. D., Montague, M, & Hocutte, A. M. (1993). Educational assessment of children with attention deficit disorders. Exceptional Children, 60, 125-131.

Reed Martin, J. D. (1991). Extraordinary children, ordinary lives (Stories behind special education for case law). IL: Research Press.

Swift, M. S. & Spivach, G. (1991). Alternative teaching strategies: Helping behaviorally troubled children behave. IL: Research Press.

Zentall, S. S. (1993). Research on the educational implications of attention deficit hyperactivity disorder. Exceptional Children, 60, 143-153.

Ziefert, H. (1991). Sometimes I share. Harper Collins Publishers.

WEBSITES

http://www.state.sd.us/state/executive/deca/special/taguide.htm

Provides a listing of technical assistance documents available from the Office of Special Education.

http://www.access.digex.net/~edlawinc/

Guides to legislation in special education.

http://teach.virginia.edu/curry/dept/cise/ose/new.html

New site for the Office of Special Education

http://tecfa.unige.ch/info-edu-comp.html#disabled

Technology for the disabled

Learning Abilities and Learning Problems

FILMS, VIDEOTAPES, AND AUDIOCASSETTES

Many of the following materials are available through the Association for Supervision and Curriculum Development, 125 N. West St., Alexandria, VA 22314-2798. Telephone orders: (7030 549-9110).

A language for Ben, video, 52 minutes. This is the story of Ben's first year in an English nursery school. The only deaf child in the class, he is helped by a "signing" teacher. There are more questions than answers-should he be taught to speak? Will he prefer to continue school among deaf or hearing children?--but it is clear his parents, teachers, schoolmates, and community have given him the self-confidence to be his best. (From Films for the Humanities & Sciences, Inc.)

Breaking free, video, 50 minutes. Documents the moving story of 40 mentally retarded people who broke free from their handicaps to achieve world-wide acclaim on the stage of the Sydney Opera House. Viewers are given a new image of handicapped people as they demonstrate their potentials and their rightful place in the mainstream. This is a vital addition to the mainstreaming movement. (From MTI/Coronet)

Children no more, video, 51 minutes. The second in a series of three programs begun with *So many children*, the programs shows the children, now adolescents, their development, and the change in public feelings toward the mentally handicapped. (From Films for the Humanities & Sciences, Inc.)

Hi, I'm Dan, video, 9 minutes. A delightful story of a young child with impaired hearing who becomes discouraged in his efforts to join in a football game at a local playground. Upon returning home, he reads the fable "The Tortoise and the Hare" which comes to life on screen through a captivating dance interpretation. Encouraged by the moral of the story, the boy runs outside to try again. (From MTI/ Coronet, Inc.)

How difficult can this be?, video, 70 minutes. Children with learning disabilities face an inordinate amount of frustration, anxiety, and tension in their daily lives. This unique and highly acclaimed program allows viewers to experience learning abilities firsthand. (From PBS Video)

Learning disabilities, video, 19 minutes. This program examines the frequently misdiagnosed and misunderstood problem and the importance of early diagnosis and treatment. A nine year old boy is profiled, as his parents and teacher detail the problem he faces in school and home. (From Films for the Humanities & Sciences, Inc.)

Learning-- Matter of style, video, 30 minutes, color. Learning styles expert, Rita Dunn, explains her research and observations. Classroom examples show teachers how to accommodate different learning styles. A videotaped case study helps apply what is presented in video. Stock #614-106, v2.

Learning Abilities and Learning Problems

Learning/teaching styles and brain behavior, audio. A panel of experts on learning styles answers questions from an audience of ASCD members and presents conclusions of learning styles research. Stock #612-87551c2.

Nature and nurture, video, 52 minutes. This program from the critically acclaimed "Human Animal" series looks at identical twins separated at birth and finds that biology is not everything: A supportive environment helps to produce well-adjusted adults while a hostile home can produce the contrary. (From Films for the Humanities & Sciences, Inc.)

One percent of us, video, 53 minutes. The third segment in the series about five mentally handicapped children. Now ages between 25 and 31, they are leading full and active lives and appear to have fulfilled much of their potential. (From Films for the Humanities & Sciences, Inc.)

Recent research on learning styles and practical implications for supervisors and teachers, audio. Learn how schools have boosted test scores and created more positive classroom environments by adapting teaching strategies to individual learning styles. Stock #612-20232c2.

Regular lives, video, 30 minutes. This video provides a model for parents, teachers, and communities interested in obstacles, strategies, and goals of mainstreaming as a way to integrate people with disabilities into the ordinary routines of living. (From PBS Video)
Social expectations of the learner and students' ability/inability to respond, audio. How strongly do physical, sociological, and emotional elements influence the learning that takes place in your class? Stock #612-87574c2.

So many children, video, 39 minutes. This is the first in a series of three programs that document 20 years in the lives of five mentally handicapped people. This segment looks at parents' efforts to come to terms with their children's disabilities. (From Films for the Humanities & Sciences, Inc.)

Training intellectual skills--A triarchic model, audio, approximately 45 minutes. Psychologist Robert Sternberg discusses his theory of intelligence and how it can be applied to the teaching of thinking skills. Stock #612-20372c2

What do we really know about learning styles and reading and math achievement, audio. Hear the research on learning styles and learn how the findings can be applied easily and economically in your classroom. Stock #612-20447c2.

Many videos are available on exceptionality from Films for the Humanities & Sciences, Inc., P. O. Box 2053, Princeton, NJ 08543, (800) 257-5126.

Autism: Breaking through, video, 26 minutes. Causes, symptoms, and treatment are discussed, latest research is reviewed.

Learning Abilities and Learning Problems

Autism: Childhood & beyond, video, 19 minutes. Discussion of current therapies; 26-year-old man is profiled.

Down's syndrome, video, 28 minutes. Medical and psychological research is discussed on this Phil Donahue program.

Dyslexia: Disabled or different, video, 26 minutes. Difficulties in learning to read and write and how this is diagnosed and treated in the public school system.

Dyslexia: One corrective procedure, video, 14 minutes. Demonstrates the use of specially-adapted colored lenses which offer an effective cure for a substantial number of dyslexics.

Education for all children, video, 28 minutes. This film or video examines traditional attitudes toward handicapped individuals, reviews legislative history, and reviews the future of the Right of Education Movement.

Effective behavioral programming, video. Eight video tapes demonstrating the use of behavioral procedures for training mentally handicapped persons. Nearly five hours of instruction.

Epilepsy: Taming the brain storm, video. Explores misconceptions related to epilepsy and looks at recent advances in research.

Gifted adolescents & suicide, video, 26 minutes. Phil Donahue program about intelligent and accomplished, but emotionally immature, isolated, and vulnerable adolescents. Points out how to recognize pressures on gifted teens.

Hearing, video, 19 minutes. This program explores some of the difficulties encountered by the hearing impaired and examines principal methods of communication: Signing and reading.

Stuttering & other speech disorders, video, 19 minutes. Profiles a 41-year-old stutterer and how his life was affected; describes treatment.

Special Needs Individuals on Film

See http://teach.virginia.edu/curry/dept/cise/ose/new.html for a listing of films depicting a special needs individual.

Handout Master 4.0

Lecture Outline ----- Learning Abilities and Learning Problems

- Individual Differences in Intelligence

- Ability Differences and Teaching

- Creativity

- Cognitive and Learning Styles

- Students with Learning Challenges

- Integration, Mainstreaming, & Inclusion

Copyright © 1998 by Allyn and Bacon

Handout Master 4.1

Myths and Facts about Special Education

From Exceptional Children, Sixth Edition, Daniel Hallahan and James Kaufmann (Needham Heights, MA: Allyn & Bacon, 1994), p 5.

MISCONCEPTIONS ABOUT EXCEPTIONAL CHILDREN

MYTH	FACT
Public Schools may choose not to provide education for some children.	Federal legislation specifies that to receive federal funds, every school system must provide a free, appropriate education for every child regardless of any disabling condition.
By law, the handicapped child must be placed in the least restrictive environment (LRE). The LRE is always the regular classroom.	The law does require the handicapped child to be placed in the LRE. However, the LRE is not always the regular classroom. What the LRE does mean is that the handicapped child shall be segregated as little as possible from home, family, community, and the regular class setting while appropriate education is provided. In many, but not all instances this will mean placement in the regular classroom
The causes of most disabilities are known, but little is known about how to help children overcome or compensate for their disabilities.	In most cases, the causes of children's disabilities are not known, although progress is being made in pinpointing why many disabilities occur. More is known about the treatment of most disabilities than about their causes.
People with disabilities are just like everyone else.	First, no two people are exactly alike. People with disabilities, just like everyone else, are unique individuals. Most of their abilities are much like those of the "average" person who is not considered to have a disability. Nevertheless, a disability is a characteristic not shared by most people. It is important that disabilities be recognized for what they are, but individuals with disabilities must be seen as having many abilities—other characteristics that they share with the majority of people.
A disability is a handicap.	A disability is an inability to do something, the lack of a specific capacity. A handicap, on the other hand, is a disadvantage that is imposed on an individual. A disability may or may not be a handicap, depending on the circumstances. For example, inability to walk is not a handicap in learning to read, but is can be a handicap in getting into the stands at a ball game. Sometimes handicaps are needlessly imposed on people with disabilities. For example, a student who cannot write with a pen but can use a typewriter or word processor would be needlessly handicapped without such equipment.

Copyright © 1998 by Allyn and Bacon

Handout Master 4.2

Definitions of Intelligence

These definitions of intelligence taken from Sattler, J. (1988). Assessing children's abilities. (3rd ed.) San Diego: Jerome Sattler Publisher, (p. 45), show the historical development of the concept of intelligence.

Binet (in Terman, 1916) "The tendency to take and maintain definite direction; the capacity to make adaptations for the purpose of attaining a desired end; and the power of autocriticism" (p.45).

Binet and Simon (1916) '...judgment, otherwise called good sense, practical sense, initiative, the faculty of adapting one's self to circumstances. To judge well, to comprehend well, to reason well, these are the essential activities of intelligence" (pp. 42-43).

Spearman (1923) "...everything intellectual can be reduced to some special case...of educating either relations or correlates" (p. 300). Education of relations-"The mentally presenting of any two or more characters...tends to evoke immediately a knowing of relation between them" (p. 63). Education of correlates-"The presenting of any character together with any relation tends to evoke immediately a knowing of the correlative character" (p.91).

Stoddard (1943) "...the ability to undertake activities that are characterized by (1) difficulty, (2) complexity, (3) abstractness, (4) economy, (5) adaptiveness to a goal, (6) social value, and (7) the emergence of originals, and to maintain activities under conditions that a demand a concentration of energy and a resistance to emotional forces" (p.4).

Wechsler (1958) "the aggregate or global capacity of the individual to act purposefully, to think rationally and to deal effectively with his environment" (p. 7).

Gardner (1983) "...a human intellectual competence must entail a set of skills of problem solving- enabling the individual to resolve genuine problems or difficulties that he or she encounters, and when appropriate, to create an effective product-and must also entail the potential for finding or creating problems-thereby laying the groundwork for the acquisition of new knowledge" (pp. 60-61).

Sternberg (1986) "...mental activity involved in purposive adaptation to, shaping of, and selection of real-world environments relevant to one's life" (p. 33).

References

Binet, A. (1916). The measurement of intelligence. Boston: Houghton Mifflin.

Binet, A. and Simon, T. (1916). The development of intelligence in children. Translated by Elizabeth S. Kite. Baltimore: Williams and Wilkins.

Gardner, H. (1983). Anticipation of gains in general information: A comparison of verbal aptitudes, reading comprehension, and listening. Harvard University, Cambridge, Mass: Harvard Project Zero.

Spearman, C. (1923). The nature of intelligence and the principles of cognition. London: MacMillan.

Sternberg, R. (1986). Geniuses: A framework for intellectual abilities and theories of them. Intelligence, 10, 239-250.

Stoddard, D. G. (1943). The meaning of intelligence. New York: MacMillan.

Wechsler, D. (1958). Bellevue intelligence scale--Data on the youth of intelligence between sixteen and twenty-one years as measured by the Education Index #11. Journal of Genetic Psychology, 90, 3-15.

Sternberg, R. (1986). Geniuses: A framework for intellectual abilities and theories of them. Intelligence, 10, 239-250.

Copyright © 1998 by Allyn and Bacon

Handout Master 4.3

Myths and Facts about Mental Retardation: Misconceptions About Persons With Mental Retardation

MYTH	FACT
Once diagnosed as mentally retarded, a person remains within this classification for the rest of his or her life	The level of mental functioning does not necessarily remain stable, particularly for those in the mild classification.
In most cases, we can identify the cause of retardation	In most cases (especially within the mild classification), we cannot identify the cause. For many of the children in the mild classification, it is thought that the poor environment may be a causal factor. However, it is usually extremely difficult to document.
Most mentally retarded children look different from nondisabled children	The majority of mentally retarded children are mildly retarded, and most mildly retarded children look like nondisabled children.
Most mental retardation can be diagnosed in infancy	Because the majority of retarded children are mildly retarded, because infant intelligence tests are not as reliable and valid as those used in later childhood, and because intellectual demands on the child greatly increase upon entrance to school, most children eventually diagnosed as retarded are not so identified until they go to school.
Retarded individuals go through different learning stages compared to nondisabled individuals	Many studies indicate that the learning characteristics of retarded individuals, particularly those classified as mildly retarded, do not differ from those of nondisabled people. That is, retarded people go though the same stages, but at a slower rate.
Children classified as moderately retarded (once called "trainable") require a radically different curriculum from that appropriate for children classified as mildly retarded (once called "educable")	Although academic subjects re generally stressed more with mildly retarded students, and vocational skills are stressed more with moderately and severely and profoundly retarded students, there is actually a great deal of overlap in curricular goals for all retarded students.
When a worker with mental retardation fails on the job, it is usually because he or she does not have adequate job skills	There is substantial research indicating that when mentally retarded workers fail on the job, it is more often because of poor job responsibility (e.g., poor attendance and lack of initiative) and social competence (e.g., not interacting appropriately with co-workers) than because of any competence in task production.
Transition programming for students with mental retardation begins in secondary school	Although the degree of emphasis should be greater for older students, most authorities agree that transition programming for students with mental retardation should begin in elementary school.
Severely retarded people are helpless	With appropriate educational programming,. Many severely retarded people can lead relatively independent lives. In fact, with appropriate professional support, some can live in the community and even enter competitive employment.

From Exceptional Children, Sixth Edition, Daniel Hallahan and James Kaufmann (Needham Heights, MA: Allyn & Bacon, 1994), p.117.

Copyright © 1998 by Allyn and Bacon

Handout Master 4.4: Adapting Instruction for Learner Differences

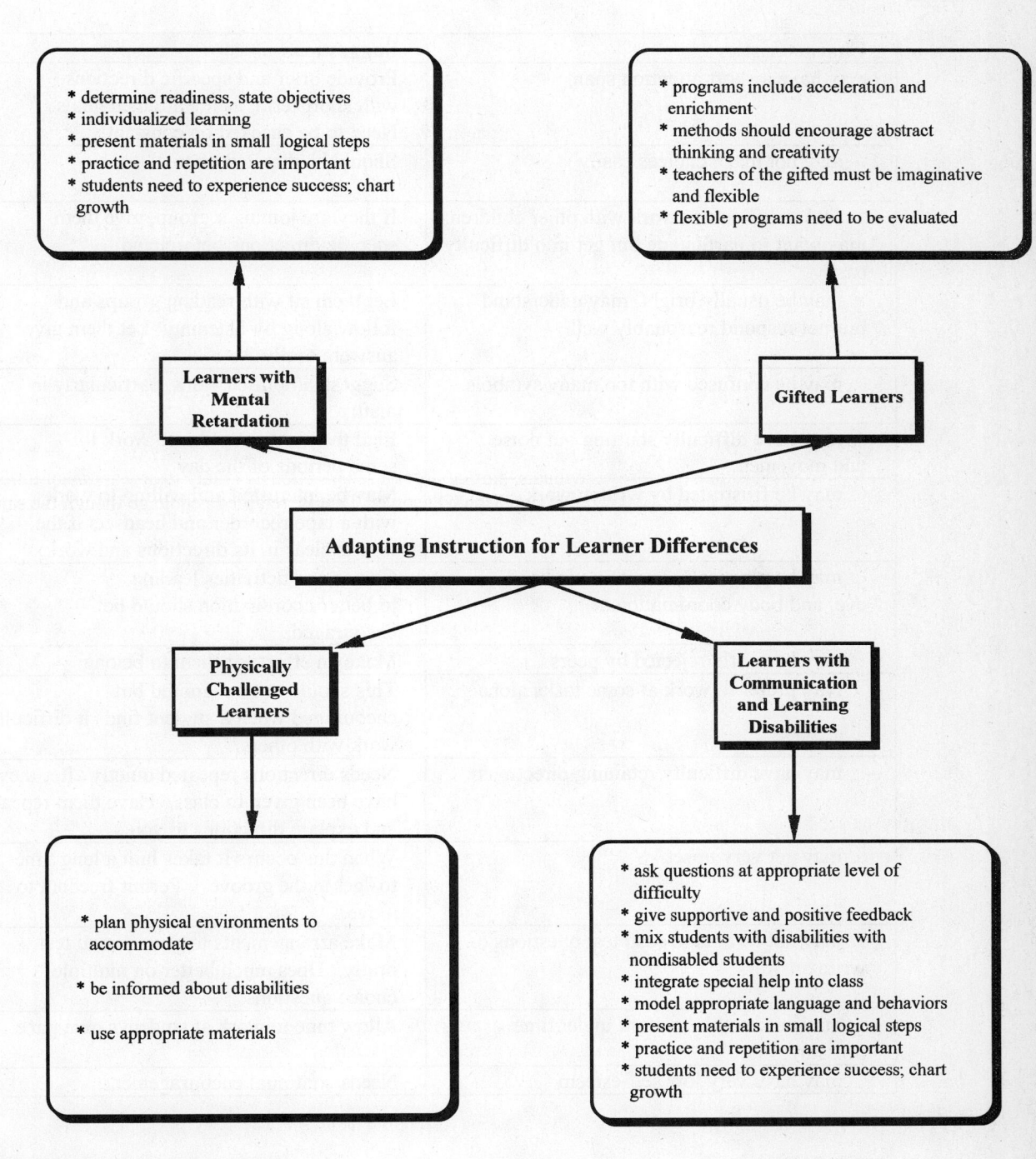

Learners with Mental Retardation
* determine readiness, state objectives
* individualized learning
* present materials in small logical steps
* practice and repetition are important
* students need to experience success; chart growth

Gifted Learners
* programs include acceleration and enrichment
* methods should encourage abstract thinking and creativity
* teachers of the gifted must be imaginative and flexible
* flexible programs need to be evaluated

Adapting Instruction for Learner Differences

Physically Challenged Learners
* plan physical environments to accommodate
* be informed about disabilities
* use appropriate materials

Learners with Communication and Learning Disabilities
* ask questions at appropriate level of difficulty
* give supportive and positive feedback
* mix students with disabilities with nondisabled students
* integrate special help into class
* model appropriate language and behaviors
* present materials in small logical steps
* practice and repetition are important
* students need to experience success; chart growth

Copyright © 1998 by Allyn and Bacon

Handout Master 4.5

The Needs of Special Needs Children

From Karge Dunnick, B., Associate Professor, San Diego State. <u>Children with special needs</u>

Characteristics	Suggestions
may have a short attention span	Provide brief and specific directions with short-term, easily attained goals. Need to be checked on constantly.
...may not make choices easily	Should be directed often.
...find it difficult to work with other children; may want to participate but get into difficulty easily.	If they are joining a group, give them specific directions beforehand
...may be usually bright, may understand but not respond reasonably well.	Let them sit with reading groups and follow along by listening. Let them give answers orally.
...may be confused with too many symbols	Suggest simplified work, particularly in math.
...may have difficulty shutting out noise and movement.	Find them a quiet place to work for some periods of the day.
...may be frustrated by written work	May be interested and willing to work with a tape recorder and headsets if the tape is clear in its directions and work
...may be physically immature in hand, eye, and body coordination.	Games and activities leading to better coordination should be encouraged.
...may be subtly rejected by peers.	Make an effort for them to belong.
...may prefer to work at some tasks alone	This should not be ignored but encouraged when a student finds it difficult to work with others.
...may have difficulty retaining directions	Needs directions repeated quietly after they have been given to class. Have them repeat and explain directions to you.
...may get very upset.	When this occurs it takes him a long time to "get in the groove." Permit freedom to move.
...may not be able to read test questions or write answers.	Make arrangements to give crucial test orally. Does much better on multiple choice questions.
...may not be able to work under time pressure.	Allow time to work at student's own pace.
...may have very low self-esteem	Needs continual encouragement.

Copyright © 1998 by Allyn and Bacon

Handout Master 4.6

Guide to Literature Search

You have a number of possible strategies for searching for information. Your main sources of information are:
1. reference librarians
2. computer searches
3. manual browsing among the library stacks.

In order to use any of these resources appropriately, you will need to understand your topic. Fill in the concept map below as a way of beginning to identify search terms or subtopics you might use.

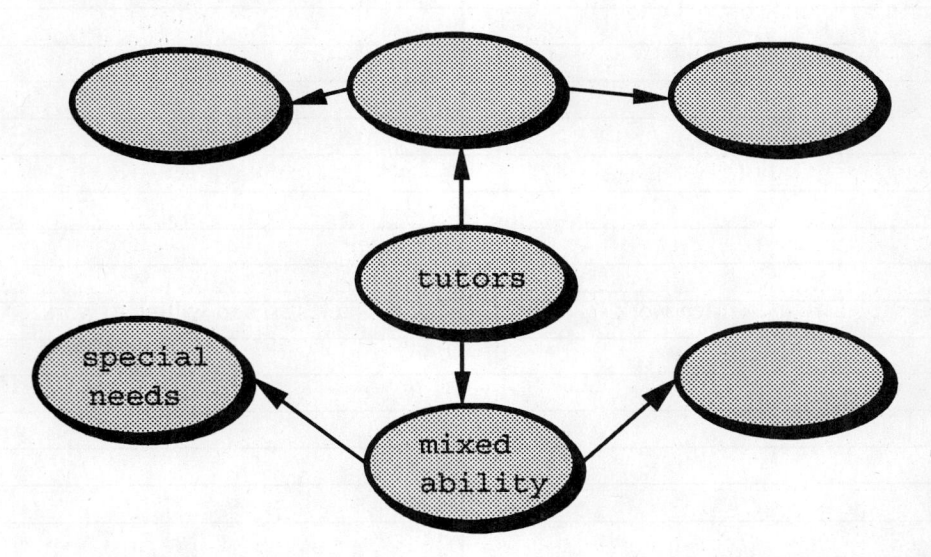

```
   ( )  <—  ( )  —>  ( )
             ↑
          tutors
             ↕
  special        ( )
  needs  ←  mixed  →
           ability
```

Use the search terms identified to seek help. If you are using a computerized search, you will be able to seek combinations of terms easily.

Copyright © 1998 by Allyn and Bacon

Handout Master 4.7

Technology for Special Needs: Resources

Complete the following table for a list of Internet Resources on Special Education. The first item in the table below will provide an excellent startpoint. It is a search engine from Yahoo that is linked to special education resources.

http://www.yahoo.com/Education/Special_Education	Search for special education resources
http://www.access.digex.net/~edlawinc/	Law related to special education
http://teach.virginia.edu/curry/dept/cise/ose/new.html	New site for the Office of Special Education

Copyright © 1998 by Allyn and Bacon

Handout Master 4.8 a

Indicators of Giftedness

Giftedness Observable in the Classroom			
Intellectual (General)	**Intellectual (Critical Thinking)**	**Academic**	**Creative**
Demonstrates understanding of cause-and-effective relationships	Shows ability to judge the following:	Possesses a large store of information	Generates many ideas, solutions to problems, and answers to questions
Has rapid mastery and easy recall of information	whether a statement follows from the premises	Has advanced vocabulary and uses terms in a meaningful way within the subject area	Shows curiosity about many things and asks many questions
Has rapid insight into underlying principles and ability to make valid generalizations quickly in many areas	whether something is an assumption	Understands abstract concepts or key ideas important to the structure of the subject area	Demonstrates concern with changing, improving, and modifying objects, systems, and institutions
	whether an observation is reliable		
Reasons in more sophisticated ways than age-mates, including the use of logic and common sense	whether a simple generalization is warranted	Makes valid generalizations about information and ideas in the subject area	Prefers complexity to simplicity
	whether a theory is warranted		Possesses cognitive flexibility, the ability to use perceptions and processes typical of several developmental levels in the development of products or ideas
	whether an argument depends on an ambiguity	Understands and effectively uses the problem-solving methods or inquiry techniques characteristic of the field of study	
	whether a statement is overvague or overspecific		
	whether an alleged authority is reliable	Recognizes and uses major sources of information in the subject area	Possesses a great degree of perceptual openness or an awareness of openness to both the outer world and the inner self
		Possesses advanced skills in the use of reference tools related to the subject area	Is uninhibited in expression of opinion and nonconforming; does not fear being different
			Shows ambivalence toward traditional sex roles, interests, and characteristics

Source: Renzulli et al., 1976; Ennis, 1964, pp. 600-610; Dellas & Gaier, 1970; Maker, 1982a.

Courtesy of Maker, C. J. (1987). Gifted and talented. In V. Richardson-Koehler (Ed.), Educator's notebook: A research perspective. White Plains, NY: Longman.

Copyright © 1998 by Allyn and Bacon

Handout Master 4.8 b

Indicators of Giftedness (Continued)

Giftedness in Student Products	
Intellectual and Academic	**Creative**
Demonstrates an application of basic information and methodology appropriate to the problem or question being investigated Extends or transforms raw data, the student's existing knowledge, and/or the general principles in the applicable area of study. Demonstrates the use of critical and higher-level thinking skills Designs for effective communication to an appropriate audience Acknowledges information sources in a suitable way Demonstrates consideration of varying points of view, conflicting data, and primary sources and reflects a reasonably thorough search of relevant sources Demonstrates the use of details or explanations that enhance their meaning or appeal to the audience	Product shows evidence of the following: viewing from a different perspective (visual, philosophical, historical, theoretical, logical, emotional) reinterpreting (adapting objects to new ideas, shifts in meaning, redefining a problem, illustrating ideas, "highlighting") elaborating (addition of details, adding to richness and color of a visual image, enhancing the product's appeal and uniqueness) extending (going beyond) the known information (predicting, extrapolating, generalizing)

Observation of Effects Following Classroom Modifications	
Intellectual and Academic	**Creative**
Include more teacher questions or activities that require critical thinking or higher levels of thinking. Observe the child's ability to answer, excitement, and interest. Teach more abstract and sophisticated ideas or concepts. Observe the child's ability to comprehend the ideas, excitement, and interest.	Include more open-ended teacher questions or activities that require the production of unusual ideas or products. Observe the student's originality, flexibility, and elaboration in these ideas or products. Include more open-ended teacher questions or activities that require the production of many different ideas or products. Observe the student's fluency (number of different ideas or different products) and flexibility (number of different categories of ideas and products)

Source: Renzulli et al., 1976; Ennis, 1964, pp. 600-610; Dellas & Gaier, 1970; Maker, 1982a.

Courtesy of Maker, C. J. (1987). Gifted and talented. In V. Richardson-Koehler (Ed.), <u>Educator's notebook: A research perspective.</u> White Plains, NY: Longman.

Copyright © 1998 by Allyn and Bacon

Handout Master 4.9

Checklist for Monitoring Behavior

Name: _____   Day/Date: _____

Subject	Work Completion	Class Behavior
Language Arts	NA 2 1 0	NA 2 1 0
Math	NA 2 1 0	NA 2 1 0
Science	NA 2 1 0	NA 2 1 0
Reading	NA 2 1 0	NA 2 1 0
Social Studies	NA 2 1 0	NA 2 1 0
Lunchroom Behavior	NA 2 1 0	

Total =

Ratings - Please circle

NA = not applicable
2 = satisfactory
1 = needs improvement
0 = poor

Language Assignment   **Math Assignment**
_____   _____

Teacher initials _____   Teacher initials _____

Test/Quiz Grades _____   Test/Quiz Grades _____

Reading Assignment   **Science Assignment**
_____   _____

Teacher initials _____   Teacher initials _____

Test/Quiz Grades _____   Test/Quiz Grades _____

Social Studies Assignment   **Previous Assignments Overdue**

_____   _____

Teacher initials _____

Test/Quiz Grades _____

(used with Permission, Richard S. Zakreski, Ph.D.)

Copyright © 1998 by Allyn and Bacon

Handout Master 4.10

Guidelines For Teaching The Hearing-Impaired Student

Make sure the student is seated where he or she can see your lip and facial movements clearly.
Examples
1. Lighting should be sufficient for clear vision, but students should not be facing windows or bright light.
2. Do not stand with your back to the windows or a bright light; this casts your face in shadow and makes lip reading difficult.
3. Don't seat the child too close to you, either. A distance of about six feet is best.

Speak naturally, in complete grammatical sentences.
Examples
1. Do not overemphasize lip movements or speak more slowly than usual.
2. Do not speak too loudly, especially if the student is wearing a hearing aid.

Make it easy for the student to see your face.
Examples
1. Use an overhead projector so you can speak and write while maintaining eye contact with students. Don't talk to the chalkboard.
2. Try not to move around the room while speaking.
3. Avoid visual distractions that would draw attention away from lips.
4. Do not overuse hand gestures.

Encourage the student to face the speaker during class discussions.
Examples
1. Allow the student to move around the room to get the best possible view of the speaker.
2. Use small-group discussions.

Make sure directions, assignments, and class materials are understood
Examples
1. Write assignments or directions on the board, or use handouts. Use visual aids as much as possible.
2. If necessary, ask a hearing student to take notes for the hearing-impaired student.
3. Ask hearing-impaired students to repeat or explain class material. Do not simply ask, "Do you understand?" these children often become good imitators, following the lead of other students and appearing to understand.

Learn how a hearing aid operates
Examples
1. Ask the child or special teacher to demonstrate it to the class.
2. Encourage the child to assume responsibility for the care of the hearing aid.

If applicable, give the whole class some exposure to sign language.
Examples.
1. Ask a hearing-impaired student if she or he is willing to give a mini-lesson in signing. Offer your assistance.
2. Arrange to see a play performance that is simultaneously interpreted in sign language.

Keep in close contact with other professionals involved in the child's education.
Examples
1. Exchange visits with the special-class teacher.
2. Check with the child's therapist regularly, noting changes and different needs.

Copyright © 1998 by Allyn and Bacon

Handout Master 4.11

Myths and Facts about Vision Impairment

MISCONCEPTIONS ABOUT PERSONS WITH VISION IMPAIRMENT

MYTH	FACT
Legally blind people have no sight at all	Only a small percentage of those who are legally blind have absolutely no vision
Most legally blind people use Braille as their primary method of reading	The majority of legally blind individuals use print (even if it in large type) as their primary method of reading,. In addition, a recent trend shows that more blind people who cannot benefit from the use of print are now using more aural methods (listening to tapes or records) rather than Braille.
Blind people have an extra sense that enables them to detect obstacles	Blind people do not have an extra sense. They can develop an "obstacle sense" provided they have the ability to hear.
Blind people automatically develop better acuity in their own senses	Through concentration and attention, blind individuals learn to make very fine discriminations in the sensations they obtain. This is not automatic but rather represents a better use of received sensations.
Blind people have superior musical ability	The musical ability of blind people isn't necessarily any better than that of sighted people. Apparently many blind individuals pursue musical careers because this is one way in which they can achieve success.
Blind people are helpless and dependent	With a good attitude and favorable learning experiences, a blind person can be as independent and possess as strong a personality as a sighted person.
If people with low vision use their eyes too much, their sight will deteriorate	Only in rare conditions is this true; visual efficiency can actually be improved through training and use. Wearing strong lenses, holding books close to the eyes, and using the eyes as much as possible cannot harm vision.
Blind children automatically develop superior powers of concentration that make them good listeners	Good listening is primarily a learned skill. Although many visually impaired individuals do develop good listening skills, this is the result of work on their part because they depend on these skills for so much of the information they gain from the environment.
Guide dogs take blind people where they want to go	The guide dog does not "take" the blind person anywhere; the person must first know where he or she is going. The dog is primarily a safeguard against unsafe obstacles.
The long cane is a simply constructed device that is easy to use	The National Academy of Sciences has drawn up specifications for the manufacture of the long cane, and to use it properly, most visually impaired individuals require extensive instruction from mobility specialists.

Copyright © 1998 by Allyn and Bacon

Handout Master 12

Indicators of Learning Problems

Indicators of Learning Problems

Match the category of exceptionality with the behavior that could indicate its presence:

A	gifted and talented	B	physical/health problems
C	visual impairment	D	hearing impairment
E	communication disorder	F	behavior disorder
G	specific learning disability	H	mental retardation

1. _____ A student behaves in one of two extremes: he is either loud, hostile, and disruptive or he is subdued, withdrawn, and uncommunicative.
2. _____ A student often turns one ear toward the speaker and seems intent on looking at the speaker's face.
3. _____ A student is at the top of the class academically and is a leader in the class because of his advanced social development.
4. _____ A student seldom speaks in class, and when he does, he speaks jerkily in very short phrases or sentences.
5. _____ A child seems to daydream frequently, and at times he "blanks out" or "spacers out" of what is happening in the classroom.
6. _____ A student seems quite bright when answering questions orally, but writing is a very tedious task for him and he writes slowly and poorly.
7. _____ A student starts reading his assignment, but after a few minutes he begins clowning around or says how dumb the story is or exhibits some other behavior which allows him to avoid reading.
8. _____ This student is a very low achiever in all areas and frequently acts like a much younger child in social situations.

Copyright © 1998 by Allyn and Bacon

Handout Master 4.13 a

An Educational Plan

This educational plan was written for an eight-year-old second-grade boy. Did the person who wrote this plan follow the steps in the diagnostic-prescriptive cycle? Does the plan seem feasible to you? What aspects of the plan are the most helpful? What additional information would you like to be included?

NAME: BOB	Address: 1900 Forest Park
Age: 8.3 years	School: Bell Elementary
Grade: 2	

Presenting Problem

The resource teacher describes Bob as being obstinate and not willing to mind anybody except her. He refuses to do his work most of the time and then will work only for short periods if the teacher stays with him. He has difficulty being in a group. His classroom teacher considers him to be mildly disruptive. He enters and leaves the classroom noisily. talks out in class often. wants a lot of attention. likes to be the boss. and is anxious about the time to go home. His mother says she has no problems with him. Bob has been diagnosed by physicians as "brain damaged" and near-sighted. He was in a class for learning disabled last year. He had a hearing loss which was corrected by surgery last spring. Previous testing shows him to be in the dull normal range (WISC IQ=75). The validity of this regarded as questionable by the psychometrician because of his visual-motor problems as well as lack of motivation and attention during testing. He is deficient in all areas of visual perception (Frostig) and his visual-motor skills are at the kindergarten level (Bender).

Educational Planning

<u>Behavior</u>: Bob continually tests limits. This behavior intensifies when he is in a new situation. If there is a change in a familiar situation. and if he doesn't know what the reaction to his behavior will be. Bob is very skillful in manipulating people with words and getting them involved in long verbal discussions. He may agree to something because it is expedient for him to do so. However, we found he cannot be expected to follow through on the agreement. He also uses words to get out of doing his work by distracting the teacher to another subject. Bob has the idea that he is different from other children and he doesn't like it. He over-reacts to teasing and derogatory remarks from his classmates.

General Suggestions

1. Since Bob uses words to procrastinate and manipulate, the teacher should not allow herself to be drawn into verbal arguments with Bob. He uses such tactics as: promising to do something later, asking the teacher to wait until he does something else first, asking her to substitute some other task, and generally using conversation to divert attention from the work he is supposed to be doing. All actions intended to be nonrewarding should be carried out with as little verbalization as possible. Action, not conversation .is affective with Bob.
2. Many times Bob is surprisingly cooperative with requests stated in a friendly manner. When it was suggested that he raise his hand like the other children when he was through with his work instead of yelling out. he did. This carried over into later class periods. He was also cooperative when told to talk more softly because he was disturbing the other children who were working. He enjoyed doing helpful jobs in the room-erasing the board, cleaning his desk, shining the window, etc.

Copyright © 1998 by Allyn and Bacon

Handout Master 4.13 b

An Educational Plan (Continued)

Suggestions for the Resource Room

Since Bob especially tests limits when he doesn't know what the consequences will be, there should be a set routine with which all the resource teachers are familiar. Then if, one teacher is absent ,Bob will still know what to expect. An effective routine was to explain to Bob that if he doesn't behave like a student, he will be given a warning. If he continues his behavior, he will be taken out of the room. Then, if Bob doesn't behave like a student:

1. Teacher states what is expected of him and gives him a warning. For example, "Bob, it is time for you to do your work at your desk. This is a warning."
2. If his behavior persists, teacher calls another person to remove him from the room. He is removed quickly and quietly. If he starts running away, all teachers can corner him, but show no concern or involvement with him. This probably won't have to be done more than once or twice, just enough to let Bob know what will happen if he behaves in that way.
3. "Time-out"-While outside the classroom he sits in a chair for five minutes. If he acts up, time starts over again. During this time, there should be no conversation. Physical arrangements should be such that he cannot attack the teacher.
4. At the end of five minutes he is welcomed back by his regular teacher and work continues as usual. In this format. Bob has worked for as long as an hour and forty minutes.

Suggestions for the Classroom

1. If Bob continues to be disruptive in lines and in entering the classroom. A program of rewards for proper behavior can be initiated. Some suggestions for rewards are: Let him help in the room. If he still chooses to misbehave. Then the teacher needs to try to find more rewarding activities.
2. A wall clock in the room should eliminate Bob's badgering the teacher about the time to go home.

Academic Area

<u>Achievement Skills</u>: In reading. Bob knows most of the letter sounds. He can hear and identify initial and final consonants, but has trouble with vowels. It is difficult for him to blend three sounds into a word. Bob sometimes does not identify even simple pictures correctly. Because of his visual-motor deficiencies, Bob has very poor handwriting, and it is hard work for him to try to write. In math, he can count easily to twelve with understanding. He understands the concept of addition and can find any sum up to twelve if he has concrete materials to work with. He has very few combinations memorized.

<u>Behavior in Learning Situation</u>: Bob's negative verbalization is profuse ("I'm not going to do this, this is too hard," etc.) and should be ignored. He is in a hurry to be done with his work. In group situations, he wants to be through whenever others are. If the work is difficult, Bob either quits or, if he is doing a worksheet, he'll just start marking anything for an answer.

Copyright © 1998 by Allyn and Bacon

Handout Master 4.13 c

An Educational Plan (Continued)

General Suggestions for Academic Work

1. Since Bob hurries to be "finished" with his work when others are about to finish, it is better to keep him out of a group and in a non-competitive situation. Although doing something with a group will get Bob started, he also stops with the group. Since he does not work quickly with accuracy, he produces sloppy work in this kind of situation.
2. In order to reduce Bob's concern with finishing his work, it is helpful to have a card which lists all the work he is to do that day as well as a folder which contains all the materials he will need. Then he can check them off as he finishes with each one. We found that this format worked well.
3. Because Bob's involving the teacher in conversation interferes with his doing a specific lesson, Bob's lesson should be structured in such a way that he works independently, so that he has less opportunity to involve the teacher in nonproductive conversation. The following format is effective:
4. Teacher shows him what to do, checks to see if he understands, and leaves him;
5. he does the work independently (mistakes can be corrected later);
6. he lets the teacher know in some prearranged manner that he is finished;
7. then the teacher gives attention.
8. This format can be followed in a regular classroom. It is more effective than a routine of constant teacher involvement to get him to work (e.g., Bob doesn't do work; teacher comes over, he works; teacher leaves, he doesn't work).
9. Since Bob has a tendency to mark just any answer on a worksheet, it is helpful to separate the problems and have only one or two on a page. This is especially necessary if the work is difficult for him.
10. Handwriting is very difficult for Bob and should be attacked separately rather than combining it with language. Materials which can be used to improve his visual-motor skills are listed in the appendix. Also contained in the appendix is a list of ways to teach spelling and reading which do not involve writing.
11. If Bob is to do his math independently with a minimum of teacher involvement, he will need simple concrete aids. Manipulation of these aids will also help his fine muscle coordination. The SRA Math Discovery Board is an excellent material.
12. The following approaches were ineffective with Bob: I told him I would wait at his desk until he was ready to work, but he didn't come and I could no longer ignore his bad behavior; I tried to offer a reward by showing him some of the things he could do after he had finished his work; I asked if he'd like for one of the other boys to help him since he seemed so anxious to make friends with them; I joked with him about funny places where he could do his work. These approaches were unsuccessful because they either ignored his misbehavior or rewarded it with teacher attention.

Copyright © 1998 by Allyn and Bacon

Handout Master 14 a

Individualized Education Program

Student <u>Tom Example</u>　　　　　　　　　　IEP Period F<u>rom: 1-2-97 to 1-2-98</u>
School: <u>Any Elementary School</u>　　　　　Grade: <u>K</u>
Primary Language of Parent: 　<u>English</u>　　Birthdate: <u>4/23/92</u>
SS #: 　<u>99-142-0000</u>　　　　　　　　　　　Classification: 　<u>Developmental Delay</u>

Tom speaks in 4-6 word sentences. He interacts with both peers and teachers. Speech intelligibility is good with 5 developmental errors. Tom answers "where, what, and how" questions with 45% accuracy. Groups objects with 60% accuracy. He also has difficulty understanding basic concepts such as same/different, location, top (combined less than 1/10 trials). He is able to construct sentences but he is having a hard time developing morphological rules (more than 5 errors). His current mean length of utterance is 4.2. Tom copies 1-0 but needs assistance to copy +, -, /. He traces his name. Tom cuts across the page and attempts to cut on a line. He is independent in self-help skills (dressing, eating, toileting). He walks to circle time in the morning and participates 95% of the time. He needs verbal prompts to wait his turn (> 4 times daily) and keeps his hands to his own body (> 7 times daily). He makes transitions to small group activities but starts before directions are complete 75% of the time. He names 11 basic colors, 5 shapes, 3 numbers (1,2,4). He is unable to object count.

Annual Goal: Tom will increase receptive language skills.

A. Tom will classify objects according to environment, placement, function, or size 80% of the time during a 10 minute activity across three therapy session. Evaluation will occur using pre/post tests and classroom reported observations.

Persons responsible:　　_____ Special Ed　　_____ Student　　_____ SLP
　　　　　　　　　　　　_____ Guidance　　　_____ Other　　　　_____ Parent

B. Tom will answer "where" questions 90% of the time, "what" questions 60% of the time, and "how" questions 50% of the time during three consecutive therapy sessions. Evaluation procedures will include pre/post tests and classroom reported observations.
C. Tom will demonstrate knowledge of concepts hard/soft, dry/wet, same/different, and bottom/top with 80% accuracy during three consecutive therapy sessions. Evaluation procedures will include pre/post tests and classroom reported observations.

Annual Goal: Tom will increase expressive language skills.

A. Tom will use "he, she, we, they" when semantically appropriate 70% of the time across three consecutive therapy sessions. Evaluation procedures will include pre/post tests and classroom reported observations.

Persons responsible:　　_____ Special Ed　　_____ Student　　_____ SLP
　　　　　　　　　　　　_____ Guidance　　　_____ Other　　　　_____ Parent

Copyright © 1998 Allyn and Bacon

Handout Master 14 a (continued)

Individualized Education Program

B. Tom will increase mean length of utterances to 5.0 during a 10 minute language sample across three therapy sessions. Evaluation procedures will include pre/post tests and classroom reported observations.

Placement Review (to be reviewed by the IEP team within one year after IEP date. Sign and date below).

- Maintain current placement of:

    ___ Regular class/resource   ___ Special class   ___ Special school
    ___ Home instruction   ___ Other _____

- Change Current placement to : (this requires prior notice form):

    ___ Regular class/resource   ___ Special class   ___ Special school
    ___ Home instruction   ___ Other _____

- Discontinue special education:

    ___ Remediated/declassified ___ Parent request
    ___ Other _____

My signature signifies that I have participated in the development of the goals outlined in this IEP and I have received a copy of Parent Rights

IEP	**Participants**	**Date**	**IEP**	**Participants**	**Date**
LEA	_____		LEA	_____	
Parent	_____		Parent	_____	
Parent	_____		Parent	_____	
Student	_____		Student	_____	
Reg. Ed.	_____		Reg. Ed.	_____	
Special Ed.	_____		Special Ed.	_____	
Guidance	_____		Guidance	_____	
Speech/Lang	_____		Speech/Lang	_____	
Other	_____		Other	_____	

Copyright © 1998 Allyn and Bacon

Handout Master 4.15: Links to Other Chapters

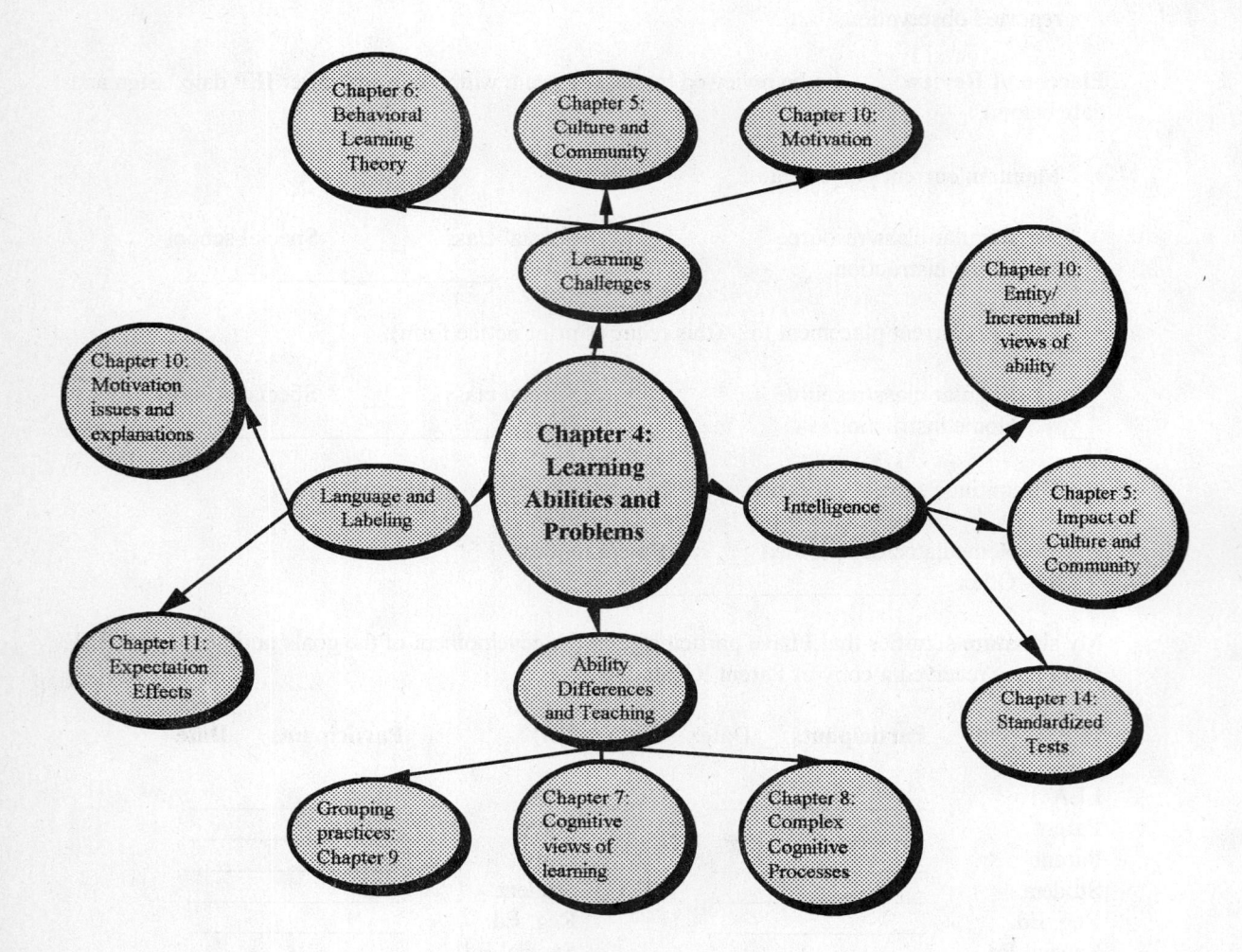

Chapter 4: Learning Abilities and Problems

- Learning Challenges
  - Chapter 6: Behavioral Learning Theory
  - Chapter 5: Culture and Community
  - Chapter 10: Motivation
- Language and Labeling
  - Chapter 10: Motivation issues and explanations
  - Chapter 11: Expectation Effects
- Intelligence
  - Chapter 10: Entity/Incremental views of ability
  - Chapter 5: Impact of Culture and Community
  - Chapter 14: Standardized Tests
- Ability Differences and Teaching
  - Grouping practices: Chapter 9
  - Chapter 7: Cognitive views of learning
  - Chapter 8: Complex Cognitive Processes

Copyright © 1998 by Allyn and Bacon

5

The Impact of Culture and Community

Teaching Outline

I. What Do You Think/What Would You Do?
II. Today's Multicultural Classrooms
    A. Individuals, groups, and society
        1. Banks' 5 dimensions of multicultural education
            a) content integration
            b) understanding relationship of knowledge and belief
            c) reducing prejudice
            d) creating social structures to support learning
            e) using teaching methods to reach all students
        2. Goal of a multicultural education is to educate ALL students irrespective of the groups to which they belong
III. Point/Counterpoint: Should Multicultural Education Emphasize Similarities or Differences?
IV. American Cultural Diversity
    A. Culture and group membership: Defined by the knowledge, rules, traditions, attitudes, and values that guide behavior in a group
V. Cautions In Interpreting Cultural Differences
    A. Differences should not be considered in isolation; children are complex beings who are members of many groups simultaneously
    B. Membership in particular group does not determine behavior
VI. Social Class Differences: Usually Defined By Socioeconomic Status.
    A. Who are the poor?
        1. One in five Americans under age 18 live in poverty
        2. Defined as income less than $13,359 for a family of four
        3. The US has the highest rate of poverty for children among industrialized nations
    B. SES and achievement
        1. High-SES students of all ethnic groups score higher on achievement tests, get higher grades, and stay in school longer
        2. Family attitudes to education are important in considering a relationship between SES and achievement
        3. Low SES may cause low expectations and low self-esteem
        4. Repeated failure may result in learned helplessness
        5. Resistance cultures: Doing well in school may mean selling out.

Impact of Culture and Community

        6.   Low SES students may be tracked into "general ability" classes that emphasize memorization and passive behavior
        7.   Childrearing styles may differ between low SES and middle class families with low SES children having more trouble adjusting to the school norms

VII.   Ethnic And Racial Differences:
     A.   Based on geography, religion, race, or language
     B.   By 2020, almost half of the population will be from African-American, Asian, Hispanic, or other ethnic groups
     C.   Cultural differences: Some differences between cultural groups are very visible whereas others are subtle
     D.   Cultural conflicts
        1.   Differences in conducting interpersonal relationships
        2.   Misunderstanding arising from mannerisms, gestures
     E.   Cultural compatibility
     F.   Ethnic and racial differences in school achievement
        1.   Major concern: Some ethnic groups score lower than the average on standardized tests
        2.   Differences may be due to discrimination, or socioeconomic status
     G.   The legacy of discrimination
        1.   Continuing prejudice and racism
        2.   Education is one of the strongest influences counteracting prejudice
     H.   The development of prejudice
        1.   Prejudice may be learned from family and friends
        2.   Extreme prejudice may develop as part of authoritarian personality
        3.   Prejudice about groups can be represented as stereotypes, a schema of organized knowledge about a group
     I.   Continuing discrimination

VIII. Women And Men: Differences In The Classroom
     A.   Gender-role identity: Children learn very early from parents male and female roles
        1.   Gender-role stereotyping in the preschool years
        2.   Boys are encouraged to be physically active and independent
        3.   Girls encouraged to be affectionate and tender
     B.   Developing gender schemas
     C.   Gender bias in the curriculum: Stereotyped views of gender roles
        1.   Books in the 1970s often portrayed males and females in sexually stereotyped roles
        2.   Books in the 1990s may still portray females as more helpless
        3.   Teacher attitude about sex differences are influential

Impact of Culture and Community

- D. Sex discrimination in classrooms
    1. Teachers give boys more comments, praise, criticism, and correction than girls
    2. Teachers can perpetuate stereotypes by asking boys to do physical tasks, to be leaders; asking girls to arrange flowers, be secretaries
- E. Sex differences and mental abilities
    1. In early years, little difference in mental and motor development
    2. In school years, little difference in intelligence tests but tests have been balanced so that neither sex is favored
- F. Sex and mathematics
    1. Prior to 1974, males outperformed females but recently differences seem to be disappearing
    2. In the beginning of high school, boys and girls take an equal number of math classes but by end of senior year boys have taken more math courses
    3. Teachers treat male and females differently in mathematics classes
    4. Differences in achievement between boys and girls are more pronounced for academically talented students
- G. Eliminating gender bias
    1. In schools in which there are no significant gender-based differences in mathematics achievement, teachers are enthusiastic about and have strong backgrounds in mathematics, engineering, or science
    2. Girls tend to do better in math when they work in cooperative groups
- H. Guidelines: Avoiding Sexism in Teaching

IX. Language Differences In The Classroom
- A. Dialect: A variation of a language spoken by a particular ethnic, social, or regional group
- B. Dialects have rules and order
- C. Dialects and teaching
    1. Focus on understanding the child
    2. Accept the dialect as valid but teach the Standard form of English or dominant language
    3. Teachers may need to repeat instructions using different words
- D. Guidelines: Teaching Dialect-Dominant Students

X. Bilingualism
- A. Increase in numbers of children for whom English is not their native language
- B. Definitions of bilingualism include the idea that an individual speaks two languages

Impact of Culture and Community

        C. Difficulties of being bilingual and bicultural
        D. Higher degrees of bilingualism are associated with increased cognitive abilities
        E. Language acquisition is slower when two languages develop simultaneously, but this problem diminishes by age four
        F. Two aspects to proficiency in a second language: face-to-face communication and academic uses of language
            1. face-to-face communication skills takes about 2 years to develop
            2. academic skills take between 5-7 years to develop
        G. Bilingual education: Two approaches
            1. Teach all subjects in English as early as possible
            2. Teach students in their primary language and increase English-language instruction over time

XI. Creating Culturally Compatible Classrooms
        A. Goal is to eliminate racism, sexism, and prejudice
        B. Social organization: Classrooms need to be organized to promote productive participation by ALL children
        C. Learning styles of cultural groups
            1. validity of learning styles research has been strongly questioned
            2. dangers of promoting stereotypes by describing cultural groups by global characteristics
            3. Identifying ethnic-group differences may be misleading
        D. Sociolinguistics: Study of the courtesies and conventions of conversations across cultures
            1. Participation structure: students need to know the communication rules, when, where, and how to communicate cues about effective participation structures
            2. Different groups of children bring different participation structures to the classroom
            3. Teachers need to teach clear and explicit rules for communication and activities
            4. Teaching every student
            5. Guidelines: Creating Culturally Compatible Classrooms

XII. Summary
XIII. Key Terms And Concepts
XIV. Teachers' Casebook: What Would They Do?

Impact of Culture and Community

Learning Activities and Related Research

ACTIVITIES	HANDOUTS
Chapter 5	5.0 Lecture Outline
Cooperative Activities	
5.1 Clarifying the goals of a multicultural curriculum	5.1 Goals of education in a multicultural society
5.2 Similar, Different, or Neither	
5.3 Identity: One or many?	5.2 Identity or Identities
5.4 Cultural Differences: Sources of Conflict	5.3 Cultural Differences: Sources of Conflict
5.5 Historical Perspectives	5.4 Multicultural societies: A definition guide
Research Activities	
Using Technology	
5.6 Sources on multicultural education;	5.5 Internet resources on multicultural education;
Field Experience	
5.7 Experiencing social class differences	
5.8 Patterns of Differentiation	5.6 Who is in?
Other Teaching Activities	
5.9 Cultural Differences	
5.10 Immigrant Student Project	
5.11 Lesson planning	5.7 Lesson Planning
5.12 Status in the Classroom	5.8 Status in the Classroom
5.13 Teaching Different Students	5.9 Concept Map: Creating culturally compatible classrooms
	5.10 Adapting instruction

Cooperative Activities

5.1   <u>Clarifying the Goals of a Multicultural Curriculum</u>

Adapted from Bennett, C. (1986). *Comprehensive multicultural education*. Boston: Allyn & Bacon, p. 130. Copyright 1986. Reprinted with permission by Allyn & Bacon.

Listed below are five goal statements concerning purposes of education necessary in a society comprising diverse racial and cultural groups. Using **Handout Master 5.1**, have your students first individually rank order the goals from one to five, with the first indicating the goal they value most, and the fifth, the goal they value least.

After they complete the rank ordering of goals individually, have them try to reach a consensus in groups. After about thirty minutes, have one member of each group share their decisions with the class. The five goals are the following:

- To preserve ethnic heritage, promote ethnic identification, and raise ethnic consciousness.

Impact of Culture and Community

- To increase intercultural competence, including empathy, acceptance, and trust of those from other culture groups, and the ability to interpret customs and nonverbal behavior in differing cultural styles.
- To build the skills, knowledge, and values that predominate in the mainstreamed culture.
- To eradicate ethnic and racial prejudice.
- To strengthen the social action skills that will enable students to become effective change agents.

Discuss any difficulties in coming to consensus and any differences there are among groups. You might also raise the issue of the relationship between values/attitudes that are verbally expressed and any subsequent behavior.

5.2   Same, Different, or Neither

Divide your students into 3 sets of groups to consider whether a multicultural education should focus on similarities among groups (e.g, Italians, Russians), focus on differences among groups (Asians or African-Americans), or should not be concerned with either similarities or differences. Give students 20 minutes to come up with a set of arguments that they will then share with the class. Once all groups have presented their arguments to the larger group, have a general discussion on the issue. Ask students to note which arguments were persuasive and why.

5.3   Cultural Identity

An important part of self-knowledge is being aware of one's cultural identity. Have your students individually describe themselves in regard to the attitudes, values, beliefs, and ethnic group membership that make up their cultural identity. Have students in groups make an exhaustive list of the items included in individual descriptions. Sort the items into categories to highlight the various ways in which "culture" is defined. **Use Handout Master 5.2** for this activity.

5.4   Cultural Differences: Possible Sources Of Conflict

Using **Handout Master 5.3,** have the students work in groups to discuss possible sources of clash between the culture of the school and that of the home. See if students can generate additional categories or examples. Ask your students to consider what they might do as teachers to minimize these difficulties.

5.5   Historical Perspectives

Draw a continuum on the chalkboard showing the range of consequences in a society when there is one predominant macroculture and any number of microcultures. Point A, cultural assimilation, represents an extreme where the predominant culture (sometimes called the host society) completely absorbs the microculture(s). Point C, suppression,

Impact of Culture and Community

represents the other extreme where the predominant culture keeps the microculture(s) totally separate and suppressed. Point B, cultural pluralism. represents a compromise. Everyone is governed according to laws established by the macroculture, and everyone must follow certain customs as is necessary for harmonious living in one society. At the same time, members of the various ethnic groups or microcultures are encouraged to retain their traditions (such as language, religion, and artistic expressions) if they wish to do so.

For example, the people from Jewish decent have retained their customs, traditions, but have also become absorbed into the macroculture, so they fall along the middle of the continuum labeled cultural pluralism. Have your students try to place the following ethnic groups along the continuum: Irish, Afro-American, Japanese, Italian, Mexican, Navajo, German, Chinese, Vietnamese, and Sioux.

Use **Handout Master 5.4**, *Multicultural Societies: A Definition Guide*, to help students grasp these concepts. Ask students to give examples of microcultures in American society that fit each type of consequence.

Using Technology

5.6   Sources on Multicultural Education

Handout Master 5.5 provides the Internet addresses for a number of sites that have relevance to multicultural education. Have your students visit these sites and evaluate the quality of information provided. They will need to articulate a set of criteria against which "quality" can be defined. For example, a site that is mostly propaganda related to a particular point of view may not be helpful as an instructional aid.

Field Experience

5.7   Experiencing Social Class Differences

The following excerpt is adapted from the Instructor's Manual of Popenoe, D. (1989). Sociology (7th ed.). Englewood Cliffs, NJ: Prentice Hall, p. 1-44.

Students tend to shop in stores and eat in restaurants that they consider class-appropriate and with which they are generally familiar. For this exercise, have each student identify four different stores or restaurants: One the student identifies as upper-class, one middle class, one working class, and one lower class. Ask the students to visit each. They should perhaps do this activity in groups. Students should write a brief report in which they describe the following:

Impact of Culture and Community

1. the establishment and how they classify it
2. the quality of the product sold or food prepared
3. the general atmosphere
4. the quality and style of service
5. where they were the most comfortable, least comfortable, and explain why.
6. what they could have done to be more comfortable in the setting.

The exercise will expose students to social-class lifestyles with which they are not generally involved, and help them become aware of the social distance that exists between social classes.

To explore these lifestyle differences further, have students describe and compare the interpersonal interactions that they witnessed in each establishment. Who were the clientele of each establishment? How were they dressed? What was the nature of the verbal interactions between staff and customer?

5.8   Patterns of Differentiation

Have your students visit 2 different classrooms for a one hour period. Before the observation period, students should draw a diagram of the class and the location of each child. During the observation period, students should use **Handout 5.6** to record the number of times specific children are called upon in favorable and unfavorable ways. At the end of the period, students should characterize the children in terms of identifiable characteristics (e.g., gender) to answer such questions as "Were boys called upon more than girls?"

Other Teaching Activities

5.9   Cultural Differences

Read the following letter to your students that appeared in the June, 1988 issue of the Harvard Education Letter.

Dear Editors:

I applaud your article "Cultural Differences in the Classroom" (March 1988). My own research on Alaska Native education, however, suggests a number of abuses perpetrated in the name of "being sensitive to the children's cultural backgrounds." Our teacher education program--Teachers for Rural Alaska--sensitizes teachers to these abuses and at the same time emphasizes the importance of taking cultural background into account in teaching. When teachers overreact to cultural background, we see problems like these:

1. "I'll make it special for you." Teachers often exempt Native students from academic expectations and standards applicable to other students. A touching essay on coming

to the city from the village substitutes for a research paper. Non-Native students resent the double standard and accuse Native students of getting good grades because they are Native.

2. "What do they need this for?" Worried that schooling really is an agent of Western imperialism, some teachers lack a sense of legitimacy. When students get bored or frustrated, teachers are quick to say, "Well, they're going to stay home in the village. What do they really need (algebra, English, chemistry . . .) for anyway?

3. Give me a C(ulture)."Teachers often assume that the behavior of Native students will invariably have a cultural explanation. Even researchers fall into this error. Once I was watching a young Eskimo boy complain to his school counselor about the emotional, erratic behavior of the middle-aged woman he was living with. Knowing that the woman had just left a small, traditional village, I was thinking about the sociocultural consequences of migration. The school counselor, who knew the particular woman, put a hand on the boy's knee and said, "Oscar, have you ever heard of menopause?"

4. "Genuflect, genuflect, genuflect." Teachers create lessons ad nauseam featuring kayaks and caribou. Many of these lessons have no point other than to display the teachers' reverence for the traditional culture and teachers often get the culture wrong. The dangers arising from ignoring the cultural context are as serious as the dangers arising from exaggerated reverence toward it. But this does not mean that teachers should "mirror" the traditional culture in the classroom or that teachers should base their instruction on stereotypes about "cultural learning styles."

It does mean that teachers should attempt to understand the particular cultural context in which their students are growing up. We say to our teacher education students. "Think about students' background knowledge. Think about how you are interpreting or misinterpreting their abilities. Think about what this community and the parents want for their children. Think about these issues not in terms of cultural stereotypes and abstractions but in terms of this particular community and these particular students. Use this knowledge to design a classroom that fits the context. Fine teaching anywhere involves a similar process of design.

       Judith Kleinfeld, Director
       Teachers for Rural Alaska Program
       University of Alaska, Fairbanks

5.10   <u>Immigrant Student Project</u>

The National Coalition of Advocates for Students identified in 1988 some recommendations for local school districts in dealing with immigrant students.

- School districts should provide comprehensible information about the schools to immigrant parents. Information should be disseminated through print and electronic

Impact of Culture and Community

media including native-language publications and radio and television programs that regularly reach immigrant communities; through bilingual, bicultural outreach workers; and through community-based self-help and resettlement organizations.

- School districts should help "front-line" personnel, such as school secretaries, to gain cultural sensitivity and to understand the legal rights of immigrant children and their families.

- School districts should adopt policies that prevent harassment of children within school buildings by immigration officials or by officials of any another agency seeking contact with immigrant children.

- Where significant numbers of immigrant children are present, districts should create a centralized intake and assessment center with a trained staff that includes individuals skilled in the languages and cultures of the new immigrants. Districts should conduct evaluations of immigrant children that include speaking, reading, writing, and comprehension in English and in the native language for those arriving after grade 2; math and basic skills in both languages; and educational background.

- School districts should act on the research evidence demonstrating that nearly all students learn equally well in heterogeneous classes, that children who experience academic difficulties achieve better when promoted than when retained, and that strong connections exist between repeating grades and dropping out.

- School districts should organize elementary schools so that children progress through road cross-age groupings, rather than through rigid grade levels; they should organize middle schools so that they resemble elementary schools more closely than high schools.

- School districts should evaluate student progress using broadly based assessment techniques rather than standardized tests. Important decisions about the educational future of an immigrant child should not be made on the basis of a single test score or on professional judgment alone.

- Districts should restructure the curriculum to move away from a scope-and-sequence approach and toward an emphasis on central ideas and themes as the focal points for student learning.

- School districts should provide supplementary services to students with limited proficiency in English, through the "English Plus" approach. Depending on individual need and the resources available, the added services of "English Plus" may range from respectful support of the student's primary culture and language to extensive instruction in the student's first language.

Impact of Culture and Community

- Districts should provide multicultural education for all students, even if no immigrant children are enrolled.

- Districts should encourage immigrant children to tell their own stories, orally and in writing.

- Districts should make it clear that teachers should supplement, not replace, an immigrant child's first language and culture by teaching English language and American culture.

- At both the district and building levels, mission statements should be developed that express strong commitment to the success of immigrant students.

- Districts should hire bilingual/bicultural staff members (both professional and paraprofessional), so that immigrant students have appropriate role models.

- Districts should require administrators and teachers to model respect for all children and adults, regardless of their race or the language they speak.

- Districts should forge links with community-based agencies, advocacy groups, and self-help organizations to insure the availability of physical and mental health services for immigrant families.

- School psychologists must be encouraged to become active advocates for the provision of appropriate educational services for immigrant children within regular classrooms, rather than assuming that all academically troubled immigrant children are best served in special education.

5.11 <u>Lesson Planning</u>

In this activity, using **Handout Master 5.7**, your students should develop a lesson plan on any topic that they might expect to teach during student teaching experiences. They should include the following in their lesson plans:

1. A clear statement of the topic.
2. Purposes of the lesson (what do they hope to accomplish).
3. Materials and equipment needed.
4. Procedures for implementing the lesson.
5. Methods for evaluating the success of the lesson.

Have your students explain <u>in detail</u> how they will accommodate individual differences in gender, race, ethnicity, language, socioeconomic status in the lessons. What elements of the designed lesson were specifically included with such accommodations in mind. What would students do procedurally to guarantee the inclusion of <u>all</u> children.

Impact of Culture and Community

5.12   Status in the Classroom

Ask students to consider all the classes they are currently taking in college (without mentioning who is teaching them). Ask them to group the classes according to whether they are in the natural sciences, social sciences, or humanities using **Handout Master 5.9.**. For each class, ask them to consider what kinds of students appear to have high status in the class. Ask them to clarify what this means and why it would matter educationally, Are there classes in which all the students have low status? Do the same kinds of students have high status in each kind of class? What behaviors signify students as having high status?

5.13   Teaching Different Students

James Vasquez of the University of Washington, Seattle, advocates adapting instruction to cultural traits. **Handout Master 5.10** features his three-step model for adapting instruction. Use this model as the basis for a discussion about the advantages and pitfalls of adapting instruction.

Additional considerations may be found below, adapted from Bennett, C. I. (1986). Comprehensive multicultural education. Boston: Allyn and Bacon, p. 130.

Below is a list of teaching strategies that have proven effective.

Instructional Qualities

- Provide each student with an opportunity to make an important contribution to class activities.
- Provide each student with an opportunity to experience success.
- Provide students with effective feedback or helpful information about their progress; be prompt; be clear about the criteria for success.
- Shift patterns of instruction; use a variety of strategies and sensor channels.
- Alter the physical learning environment when necessary to make it compatible with the purpose of the lesson. (For example, desks in a circle facilitate equal communication, rows may be more effective for a film, and opposing blocks of chairs can enhance a classroom debate).

Suggestions About Content

- Begin with clear objectives that are challenging but attainable.
- Make clear why the objectives are important and worth attaining.
- Cultivate curiosity and creativity.
- Invite students to participate in planning and evaluating their curriculum.
- Build on students' existing interests while trying to create new ones.
- Organize at least part of the curriculum around real life problems.

Suggestions About Personal Qualities

- Search for ways to express care for each student.
- Never belittle or ridicule a student.
- Project enthusiasm.
- Avoid distracting behaviors and overuse of terms such as "uh" and "you know."
- Use movement don't stay behind the desk.
- Be genuine.

Suggestions About Climate

- Get to know students. Learn their names right away.
- Find ways to help students know each other.
- Insist that students show respect for each other; create a classroom climate of trust and acceptance.

Discussion Questions

1. What is the relationship between special education and multicultural education? Why do some school systems assign disproportionate numbers of students from particula groups to special education classes?

2. What evidence is there for pervasive individual differences in learning styles?

3. At a local PTA meeting, some non-African-American parents complained about the emphasis on Black History Month in the school curriculum. How would you respond to these parents?

4. There are often criticisms regarding school programs that emphasize Christian beliefs, such as the traditional Christmas program of Christmas carols and religious plays. How do you think schools should respond to this issue?

5. Discuss the roles of social class and culture in shaping similarities and differences among individuals.

6. Analyze the effects of poverty on a child's ability to profit from schooling.

7. Select one of the social problems mentioned in the text and discuss the steps that should be taken to solve that problem. Which of these steps should be undertaken by the schools?

8. Do you believe that schools reproduce the existing class and social structure—that students from lower socioeconomic classes are not really being prepared for upward social mobility? Explain.

Impact of Culture and Community

Additional Resources for Teaching This Chapter

REFERENCES

Baker, G. (1983). Planning and organizing for multicultural instruction. Reading, MA: Addison-Wesley.

Brabeck, M. and Weisberger, K. (1989). College students' perceptions of men and women choosing teaching and management. The effects of gender and sex role egalitarianism. Sex Roles: A Journal of Research, 2, 841-857.

Brutsaert, H. (1990). Changing sources of self-esteem among girls and boys in secondary schools. Urban Education, 24, 432-439.

Chunn, E. W. (1988). Sorting black students for success and failure: The inequality of ability grouping and tracking. Urban League Review, 11, 93-108.

Cohen, E. (1982). Expectation states and interracial interaction in school settings. Annual Review of Sociology, 8, 209-235.

Cohen, E. (1991). Teaching in multiculturally heterogeneous classrooms: Findings from a model program. McGill Journal of Education, 26, 7-23.

Cohen, E. (1994). Designing groupwork: Strategies for the heterogeneous classroom. New York, NY: Teacher' College Press.

Cuban, L. (1970). To make a difference: Teaching in the inner city. New York: The Free Press.

Cummins, J. (1979). Linguistic interdependence and the educational development of bilingual children. Review of Educational Research, 49, 222-251.

Gonzalez, J. M. (1981). Special report: Short answers to common questions about bilingual education. Agenda, 11, 29-35.

Gould, S. J. (1981). The mismeasure of man. New York, NY: Norton.

Hyde, S. H. and Linn, M. C. (1986) (Eds.). *The psychology of gender: Advances through meta-analysis*. Baltimore: Johns Hopkins University Press.

Lomotey, K. and Swanson, A. (1989). Urban and rural schools research: Implications for school governance. *Education and Urban Society, 21* (4), 436-454.

Maruyama, G. M., Knechel, S., & Petersen, R. (1992). The impacts of role reversal and minority empowerment strategies on numerically unbalanced cooperative groups. In R. Hertz-Lazarowitz & N. Miller (Eds.), Interaction in cooperative groups: The theoretical anatomy of group learning (pp. 228-249). New York: Cambridge University Press.

McCarthey, C., & Crichlow, W. (1993). Race identity and representation in education. New York: Routledge.

Mickelson, R. A., & Smith, S. S. (1992). Education and the struggle against race, class, and gender inequality. In M. L. Andersen & P. H. Collins (Eds.), Race, class, and gender (pp. 82-87). Belmont, CA: Wadsworth Publishing Co.

Miller, N., & Harrington, H. (1992). Social categorization and intergroup acceptance: Principles for the design and development of cooperative teams. In R. Hertz-Lazarowitz & N. Miller (Eds.), Interaction in cooperative groups: The theoretical anatomy of group learning (pp. 203-229). New York: Cambridge University Press.

Rendon, L. I., & Hope, R. O. (1996). <u>Educating a new majority: Transforming America's educational system for diversity.</u> San Francisco: Jossey-Bass Publishers.

Selkow, P. (1984). <u>Assessing sex bias in testing</u>. Westport, CT; Greenwood Press.

Slavin, R. (1989). <u>Effective programs for students at risk</u>. Boston: Allyn and Bacon.

FILMS, VIDEOTAPES, AND AUDIOCASSETTES

Accomplished women, 3/4 or 1/2 inch videotape, 16 mm, 25 minutes. Profiles several women who have attained high levels of prominence and accomplishment despite innumerable explicit and implicit barriers. Katherine Graham of the Washington Post; Dr. Virginia Apgar, specialist in problems of newborn infants; LaDonna Harris, Comanche Indian and founder of Americans for Indian Opportunity; Shirley Chisholm, U.S. congresswoman; Nicki Giovanni, American poet; and Helen Reddy, singer, discuss a wide range of topics from politics to personal feelings, all pointing to a new attitude and image women have about themselves. (From Films, Inc., 1974)

Bilingual education: An inside view, 1/2 inch VHS, 3/4 inch, 25 minutes. (From University of California, 1985).

Black on Black violence, video, 26 minutes. An American Black male has a 1 in 29 chance of being murdered; for white men, the odds are one in 186. Some inner-city residents and experts, including Harvard psychiatrist Dr. Alvin Poussaint, discuss Black on Black violence. (From Films for the Humanities & Sciences, Inc.)

Children of poverty, video, 26 minutes. This program profiles some of America's children of poverty, -and shows the toll taken on the children and their mothers by the problem of finding shelter and enough food to survive, trying to prevent kids from becoming either the victims or the perpetrators of crimes, trying to nurture self-esteem in poor children. (From Films for the Humanities & Sciences, Inc.)

CNN special reports: Black men, mean streets, video, 30 minutes. Young black men in American society are at risk. The social fabric that binds black families and provides role models has disintegrated. CNN's award-winning Special Reports unit has put together a moving and highly sensitive view of the black man's position in today's world. These poignant vignettes present the problems, myths realities, and the young men who have broken the cycle to achieve success. (From Turner Multimedia)

Hablas Ingles?, video, 26 minutes. This program looks at the movement to make English the official language of the United States and presents the arguments on the issue. (From Films for the Humanities & Sciences, Inc.)

I Only Want You to be Happy, video, 16 minutes. Two sisters with very different views of the feminine role in American society discuss their ideas. Could be used to structure a discussion of role confusion. (From CRM, 1976)

Impact of Culture and Community

Multicultural education: A teaching style, 16 mm, 3/4 or 1/2 inch videotape, 29 minutes. (From Films Inc.)

Racism in America, video, 26 minutes. This program examines the resurgence of racially motivated violence and vandalism; the reasons why people vent anger against minorities; the social and economic implications of racist acts; how a community successfully responded to its racial problems. (From Films for the Humanities & Sciences, Inc.)

Sexism, stereotyping and hidden values, 16 mm., 29 minutes.(From Films Inc., 1978).

Status treatments for the classroom. A 1994 videotape (30 min) that accompanies Elizabeth Cohen's book on designing groupwork. Available from Teacher's College Press, NY.

The Asianization of America, video, 26 minutes. Asians are the nation's fastest growing racial group--a fact with enormous significance for our culture and the economy. This program examines Asian's successes in academia and to what extent they can or want to blend into the America melting pot. (From Films for Humanities & Sciences, Inc.)

The next minority: White Americans, video. All indications point to whites becoming the new American minority. Samuel Bentances and Ben Wattenberg consider the possible sociological and political consequences of such a scenario in the specially adapted Phil Donahue program.

Woman and man, video, 52 minutes. As part of the "Human Animal" series, Phil Donahue speaks with men and women in many walks of life and finds the role differences between woman and man beginning to fade.

The following titles on the topic of equity in schools are available from Insight Media, 2162 Broadway, New York, NY

- *Valuing diversity: Multicultural communication*
- *Prejudice: Eye of the storm*
- *Shortchanging girls, Shortchanging America*
- *Increasing motivation through gender equity*
- *The psychological residuals of slavery*
- *Voices*
- *Dealing with diversity in the classroom*

Handout Master 5.0

Lecture Outline ----- The Impact of Culture and Community

- Today's Multicultural Classrooms

- Social Class Differences

- Ethnic and Racial Differences

- Gender Differences in the Classroom

- Language Differences in the Classroom

- Creating Culturally Compatible Classrooms

Copyright © 1998 by Allyn and Bacon

Handout 5.1

Goals of Education in a Multicultural Society

Listed below are five goal statements concerning purposes of education necessary in a society comprised of diverse racial and cultural groups. Rank order the goals from 1 to 5 either 1 indicating the goal you value most and 5 the goal you value least. After completing your rank order, work with a small group of classmates to try to reach a consensus. After about 30 minutes, share your group's decisions with the class. The five goals are:

1. To preserve ethnic heritage, promote ethnic identification, and raise ethnic consciousness.
2. To increase intercultural competence, including empathy, acceptance, and trust of those from other culture groups, and the ability to interpret customs and nonverbal behavior in differing cultural styles.
3. To build skills, knowledge, and values that predominates in the mainstreamed culture.
4. To eradicate ethnic and racial prejudice.
5. To strengthen the social action skills that will enable to become effective change agents.

Ranking by Self   **Ranking by Group**

_____   _____

_____   _____

_____   _____

_____   _____

_____   _____

Reasons for choices in self-ranking:

1.

2.

3.

4.

5.

Reasons for choices in group ranking:

1.

2.

3.

4.

5.

Based on ideas in Bennett, C.1. (1995). Comprehensive Multicultural Education. 3rd ed. Needham Heights, MA: Allyn & Bacon.

Copyright © 1998 by Allyn and Bacon

Handout 5.2

Identity or Identities

Make a list of those groups to which you belong and identify the characteristics of that group that might make it possible to consider them separate cultural groups.

GROUPS	CULTURAL CHARACTERISTICS

Handout 5.3

Cultural Differences: Sources of Conflict

Here are a few examples of possible clashes between the culture of the school and that of the home. These are only examples. They do not hold for all individuals within a group.

Some Potential Areas of Cultural Conflict

Areas in which the culture *"Teaches Lessons"*	School's Expectation *(Majority* **Culture Belief)**	Student's Expectation **(Minority Culture Belief)**
Interpersonal Relationship	Students will compete and value individual achievement	Students will help each other; the group, not the individual is the source of accomplishment (many Native American and Mexican American Groups
Orientation Toward Time	Plan for the future, work and save now for a better future for yourself	Focus on the present, trust the central group to provide for the future (certain Native American groups) or Value the past, tradition, and ancestors (certain Asian cultures)
Valued Personal Qualities	Busy	Methodical, relaxed, meditative (some Asian and Hispanic cultures)
Relationship of People to Nature	Control nature, use technology to "improve" nature	Be at one with nature; respect and live with nature
Most Cherished Values	Individual freedom	Group loyalty, tradition

From Bennett, C.1. (1995*).* <u>Comprehensive Multicultural Education</u>, 3rd ed. Needham Heights, MA: Allyn & Bacon.

Copyright © 1998 by Allyn and Bacon

Handout Master 5.4

Multicultural Societies: A Definition Guide

ASSIMILATION	PLURALISM	SUPPRESSION
The ethnic minority group: • Gives up its original culture • Identifies with and is predominant Anglo Western European culture • Is no longer identifiable as distinct from the predominant Anglo-Western European culture	The ethnic minority group: • Retains many of its traditions, such as language, religion, artistic expression, and social customs • Adopts many aspects of the predominant Anglo Western European culture such as language; monogamy; military service; local, state, and federal laws; and full civil rights of citizenship • Develops an ethnic perspective and also identifies with the nation as a whole. • Respects and appreciates different ethnic traditions that they may or may not choose to experience.	The ethnic minority: • Is segregated from the rest of society, including schools, churches, jobs, housing, restaurants, etc. • Develops a unique culture, or retains its original culture, or a combination of both • May develop a "dual" consciousness" in order to survive
The macoculture: • Accepts members of other ethnic groups once they give up their original ethnic identity • View other cultures as unacceptable, inferior or a threat to social harmony and national unity • Suppresses the culture and their original ethnic identity contributions of other groups	**The macoculture:** • Respects and appreciates ethnic diversity • Encourages ethnic minorities to keep many of their traditions alive • May or may not adopt some of society's different ethnic traditions and current way of live	**The macoculture:** • Regards the ethnic minority as inferior beings • Controls society's economy, government, schools, churches, news and other media • Accepts the doctrine of White supremacy and sets up policies to preserve it • Suppresses the culture and contributions of other groups

From Bennett, C.1. (1995). Comprehensive Multicultural Education, 3rd ed. Needham Heights, MA: Allyn & Bacon.

Copyright © 1998 by Allyn and Bacon

Handout Master 5.5

Internet Resources on Multicultural Education

Visit these sites (or others that you find by typing in "Multicultural education" to any search engine. Evaluate the quality of the site in terms of the relevance of the material presented. Are there any problems with the information presented?

WWW address	Site Name	Your Comments on the Utility of the Site
http://www.ncrel.org/sdrs/areas/issues/educatrs/leadrshp/le4pppme.htm	Promising programs and practices in multicultural education	
http://www.weber.edu/MBE/htmls/MBE-Resource.html	Weber State: Multicultural/Bilingual Education Resource Guide	
http://edweb.camcnty.gov.uk/services/multi/multi/multi03.htm	Cambridgeshire County Multicultural Services	
http:/igc.apc.org.nmci/	National Multicultural Institute	
http://eric-web.tc.columbia.edu/	Urban Education Web	

Copyright © 1998 by Allyn and Bacon

Handout Master 5.6

You should draw a diagram of the classroom, indicating the placement of each child. Using the key below, place a mark beside the location of a child on your diagram to indicate the gender and racial/ethnic status of the child. Also indicate on the diagram when he or she was called upon in favorable or unfavorable ways.

KEY:

*	Boy
**	Girl
@	White
#	Non-White
□	Teacher asks a question
+	Teacher praises
®	Teacher reminds to pay attention
&	Teacher reprimands
$	Teacher does not wait for child to answer question

At the end of the observation period, calculate the amount of teacher attention given to each student and answer the following questions.

Do all children participate equally?
Is the nature of children's participation the same?
What might explain differences in students' participation?
Were boys called upon more than girls?

What other questions can you answer based on this observation?

Copyright © 1998 by Allyn and Bacon

Handout Master 5.7

Lesson Planning

Design a lesson plan on a topic of your choosing. You will need to specify the age group for whom it is intended. In designing your lesson plan, you need to consider how you will accommodate individual differences in gender, race, ethnicity, language, socioeconomic status in the lessons.

Lesson Topic:

Target Age Group:

Purposes of the Lesson:

Materials And Equipment Needed.

Procedures

Evaluation of the Lesson

What Accommodations to Individual Differences Did You Make?

Copyright © 1998 by Allyn and Bacon

Handout Master 5.8

Status in the Classroom

In the table below, describe the kind of student who *appears* to have high status in the class (be mindful that perceiving some pattern of events does not necessarily mean that the perception is accurate). List the behaviors that are associated with these students.

General Domain	Class	High Status Students	High Status Behaviors
Natural Science			
Social Science			
Humanities			

Copyright © 1998 by Allyn and Bacon

Handout Master 5.9: Culturally Compatible Classrooms

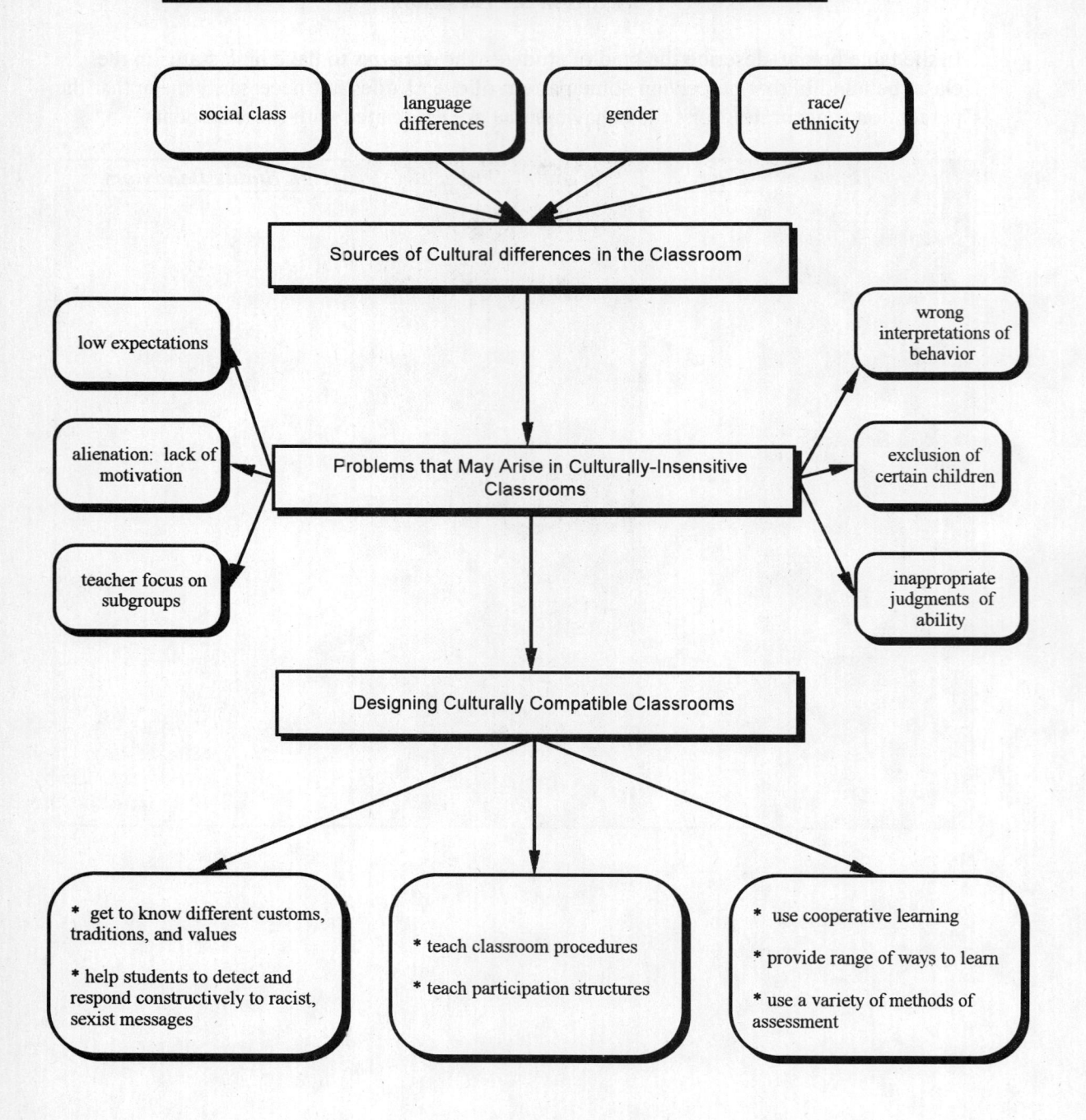

Sources of Cultural differences in the Classroom
- social class
- language differences
- gender
- race/ethnicity

Problems that May Arise in Culturally-Insensitive Classrooms
- low expectations
- alienation: lack of motivation
- teacher focus on subgroups
- wrong interpretations of behavior
- exclusion of certain children
- inappropriate judgments of ability

Designing Culturally Compatible Classrooms

- * get to know different customs, traditions, and values
- * help students to detect and respond constructively to racist, sexist messages

- * teach classroom procedures
- * teach participation structures

- * use cooperative learning
- * provide range of ways to learn
- * use a variety of methods of assessment

Copyright © 1998 by Allyn and Bacon

Handout 5.10

Adapting Instruction

Three step Procedure for Adapting Instruction to Cultural Traits

STEP 1	STEP 2	STEP 3
Teacher observes/ identifies student trait	Trait is passed through "filter" of three questions to identify which aspect of teaching (content, context, mode) should be affected. Content a. Does any aspect of the trait suggest the kind of material I should be teaching? Context b. Does any aspect of the trait suggest the physical or psychological setting I should create in the classroom? Mode c. Does any aspect of the trait suggest the manner in which I should be teaching?	Teacher verbalizes/writes out the new instructional strategy.
1. Carlos is very concerned about pleasing his family.		1. I'll tell Carlos that I'll inform his parents when he really does good work. (Carlos should work with greater effort and expectation and thus for him, the context is changed).
2. Sammy and Joanna seem disinterested when given individual work and more "turned on" when interacting with others.		2. I'll provide more activities that allow Sammy and Johanna to work on projects with others in small groups.
3. Ben seems intimidated and shy when I ask him questions to which he might not know the answer.		3. I'll focus on asking Ben questions in class that I'm fairly sure he can answer correctly, and work with him individually in areas in which he is less knowledgeable. (This strategy affects both the mode of instruction and the psychological context for Ben).
4. Charlotte does better when the material I teach involves other people interacting with one another; she is not strongly "object oriented."		4. I will teach more math concepts in the context of people dealing with one another, as in buying, trading, and borrowing. (The mode is basically changed to suit Charlotte's preferred method of learning).

From: Vasquez, J. A. (1990). Clearinghouse, 63(7), 299-304.

Copyright © 1998 by Allyn and Bacon

Handout 5.11: Links to Other Chapters

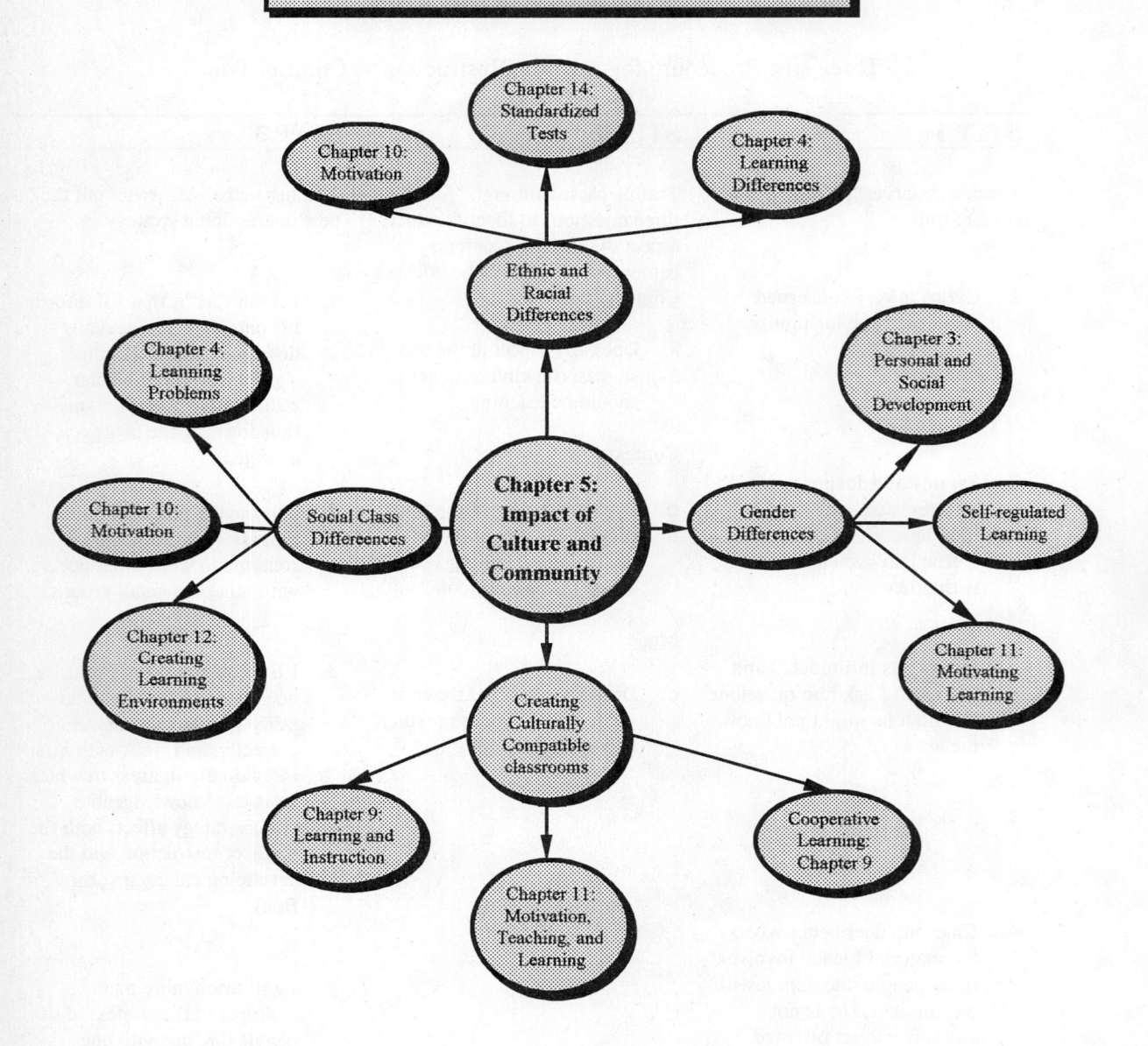

Chapter 5: Impact of Culture and Community

- Ethnic and Racial Differences
  - Chapter 10: Motivation
  - Chapter 14: Standardized Tests
  - Chapter 4: Learning Differences

- Social Class Differences
  - Chapter 4: Learning Problems
  - Chapter 10: Motivation
  - Chapter 12: Creating Learning Environments

- Gender Differences
  - Chapter 3: Personal and Social Development
  - Self-regulated Learning
  - Chapter 11: Motivating Learning

- Creating Culturally Compatible classrooms
  - Chapter 9: Learning and Instruction
  - Chapter 11: Motivation, Teaching, and Learning
  - Cooperative Learning: Chapter 9

Copyright © 1998 by Allyn and Bacon

6

Behavioral Learning Theory

Teaching Outline

I. Overview/What Would You Do?
II. Understanding Learning
    A. Learning: A definition
        1. Permanent changes in knowledge or behavior brought about by experience, not merely through maturation or temporary conditions
        2. Cognitive view: Learning as internal process that cannot be observed directly; changes in behavior reflection of internal change
        3. Behavioral view: Learning as change in observable behavior
    B. Learning is not always what it seems: Learning processes vary
III. Early Explanations Of Learning: Contiguity And Classical Conditioning
    A. Repeated pairings of two events (stimulus and response) cause them to be associated
    B. Pavlov's dilemma and discovery: Classical conditioning
        1. Pairing neutral stimulus with an unconditioned stimulus
        2. Classical Conditioning: Unconditioned responses become conditioned the formerly neutral stimulus (Figure 6.1)
    C. Generalization, discrimination, and extinction
        1. Generalization: Responding to new stimuli as though it were the original stimulus
        2. Discrimination: Responding differently to two similar but not identical stimuli
        3. Extinction: Gradual disappearance of conditioned response when conditioned stimulus is presented repeatedly but not followed by the conditioned stimulus
        4. Guidelines: Using Principles of Classical Conditioning
IV. Operant Conditioning: Trying New Responses
    A. The work of Thorndike: The Law of Effect
    B. The ABCs of operant conditioning: Antecedents--behavior--consequences
        1. Operants: Deliberate actions influenced by the consequences that follow them
        2. Operant conditioning: Effort to influence learning control of the consequences of behavior

Behavioral Learning Theory

      C.   The Work of Skinner: Behavior can be changed by changes in its antecedents (stimuli that precede it) and/or its consequences

V.   Types Of Consequences
- A. Reinforcement: Use reinforcers to strengthen behavior
  1. Positive reinforcement: Presentation of a pleasant stimulus
  2. Negative reinforcement: Disappearance or avoidance of as aversive stimulus
- B. Punishment: Use of punishers to decrease or suppress behavior
  1. Presentation punishment: Presentation of a punisher
  2. Removal punishment: Disappearance of a removal of a reinforcer
- C. Reinforcement schedules
  1. Continuous reinforcement: Reinforcing behavior every time it occurs to teach a new behavior faster
  2. Intermittent reinforcement: Reinforcing behavior periodically (not every time) to maintain an established behavior (Table 6.1)
     a) Interval schedules (based on time interval): Fixed or variable
     b) Ratio schedules: fixed or variable (based on number of responses)
- D. Summarizing the effects of reinforcement schedules
  1. Speed of performance: Ratio schedules produce faster response time than interval schedules
  2. Persistence: Variable schedules produce behaviors more resistant to extinction then those on fixed schedules
  3. Extinction: Removal of reinforcement leads to ceasing of behavior
- E. Antecedents and behavior change
  1. Antecedents (events preceding a behavior): Provide information about which behaviors will lead to positive and negative behavior
  2. Cueing: Providing an antecedent stimulus just before a certain behavior is to occur; nonjudgmental cues help prevent negative confrontations
  3. Prompting: Providing students help in responding to cues (See Figure 6.2)

VI.   Applied Behavior Analysis:
- A. Application of behavioral learning principles to change behavior
- B. Methods for encouraging behavior
  1. Reinforcing with teacher attention
     a) Behavior improves when teachers give attention to constructive behavior while making rules explicit and ignoring problem behavior

                b)   Praise must be contingent on the desired behavior, the behavior must be specified, and praise must be believable
        2.   Selecting the best reinforcers
                a)   Premack principle using preferred activity as reinforcer for a less-preferred activity
                b)   Important: The less-preferred activity must precede the preferred activity.
        3.   Shaping: Reinforcing progress in successive approximations
                a)   Reinforce each subskill
                b)   Reinforce improvements in accuracy
                c)   Reinforce longer and longer periods of performance
                d)   Reinforce longer and longer periods of participation
        4.   Positive practice: When students make academic errors, having them practice correct responses
        5.   Guidelines: Using Reinforcement
    C.   Coping with undesirable behavior
        1.   Negative reinforcement
        2.   Satiation: Requiring students to continue inappropriate behavior until they are tired of it
        3.   Reprimands: Private, quiet reprimands most effective
        4.   Response cost: Loss of reinforcer
        5.   Social isolation or time out: Often impractical or impossible to use
        6.   Some cautions: Teachers should pair punishment with reinforcement
        7.   Guidelines: Using Punishment Appropriately
VII.   Social Learning Theory
    A.   Elements of social cognitive theory
    B.   Bandura distinguished between acquisition of knowledge and observable performance based on that knowledge
    C.   Internal and external factors (reciprocal determinism) are important in shaping behavior
    D.   Bandura distinguished between enactive and vicarious learning
        1.   Enactive learning is learning by doing
        2.   Vicarious learning is learning by observing others
    E.   Learning by observing others (modeling)
        1.   Vicarious conditioning: Learning based on seeing others rewarded or punished for their actions
        2.   Imitation: Copying behavior of model
        3.   Example from Bandura's research: Learning aggressive behavior through modeling
    F.   Elements of observational learning

Behavioral Learning Theory

        1. Attention: Teachers must attract student's attention to critical features of lessons
        2. Retention: To imitate behavior you have to remember it
        3. Production: Practice makes behavior smoother and more expert
        4. Motivation and reinforcement: Incentives may be necessary to encourage performance and maintenance of newly acquired skills
    G. Forms of reinforcement that encourage observational learning
        1. direct reinforcement
        2. vicarious reinforcement
        3. self-reinforcement
    H. Factors that influence observational learning (Table 6.3)
        1. Developmental status
        2. Model prestige and competence
        3. Vicarious consequences
        4. Outcome expectations
        5. Goal setting
        6. Self-efficacy
    I. Observational learning in teaching
        1. Teaching new behaviors: Teacher's own behavior may be most prevalent influence on learning
        2. Encouraging already learned behaviors: Children receive cues by observing others
        3. Strengthening or weakening inhibitions: "Ripple effect" means tendency to imitate or not imitate behavior depending upon the observed consequences of that behavior
        4. Directing attention: Observation can direct attention to new aspects of situation
        5. Arousing emotion: Observations can cause fears and anxieties to develop or be reduced
        6. Guidelines: Using Observational Learning

VIII. Self-Regulation And Cognitive Behavior Modification
    A. Focusing on helping students take control of their own learning
    B. Self-management
        1. Goal setting: Setting specific goals and making them public
            a) Higher standards lead to higher performance
            b) Student-set goals have a tendency to decline; need monitoring and reinforcement of high standards by teacher
        2. Recording and evaluating performance
            a) self-recording/monitoring
            b) self-evaluation
        3. Self-reinforcement
        4. Guidelines: Instituting Self-Management Programs

Behavioral Learning Theory

       C.   Cognitive behavior modification and self-instruction
            1.   Adds emphasis on thinking and self-talk to behavior change program
            2.   Self-instruction on skills associated with achievement
            3.   Direct teaching of how to use self-instruction through "private speech"

IX.   Problems And Issues
       A.   Ethical issues
            1.   Goals
            2.   Strategies
       B.   Criticisms of behavioral methods

X.   Point/Counterpoint: Should students be rewarded for learning?
XI.   Summary
XII.   Key terms
XIII.   Teacher's Casebook/What Would They Do?

ACTIVITIES	HANDOUTS
Chapter 6	6.0 Lecture Outline
Cooperative Activities	
6.1 Reinforcement and Punishment	6.1 Differentiating punishment and reinforcement
6.2 Behavior problem scenarios	6.2a Intervention techniques
	6.2b Behavior problem scenarios
Research Activities	
6.3 Do we repeat the past?	
6.4 What is rewarding?	
6.5 Reinforcer preferences	6.3 Survey of reinforcement preferences
6.6 Analyzing an intervention	6.4 Concept map: Applied behavior analysis
	6.5 Behavior Checklist
Using Technology	
6.7 Video game analysis	6.6 Handout to guide analysis
Field Experience	
6.8 Behavioral principles in action	6.7 Behavior analysis chart
6.9 Self-talk	
Other Teaching Activities	
6.10 Schedules of reinforcement	
6.11 Positive practice	
6.12 Self-management	6.8 Success log
6.13 Behavioral principles in the world	6.9 Behavioral analysis chart
6.14 Peer modeling	
	6.10 Concept Map: Links to Other Chapters

Behavioral Learning Theory

Learning Activities and Related Research

Cooperative Activity

6.1   Reinforcement and Punishment

Have your students describe at least three kinds of positive reinforcement as well as negative reinforcement that they plan to use in their classrooms. How will they go about emphasizing the positive more than the negative? Will there be a way they can monitor themselves so that they are not giving out more negative consequences than positive consequences? Each group should provide a summary of their responses using **Handout Master 6.1**.

6.2   Behavior Problem Scenarios

Have students read **Handout Master 6.2a**, "Intervention Techniques." They should identify in the situation the following techniques: Positive reinforcement, satiation, punishment, negative reinforcement, and modeling. Then divide your class into cooperative learning groups and give each group a scenario from **Handout Master 6.2b** Have each group determine an appropriate behavioral procedure or procedures to use to help solve the problem. In addition, have each group indicate what they would anticipate happening when they use the strategy. Go around the class and students share their behavioral procedures.

Research Activities

6.3   Do We Repeat The Past?

Have your students explore the issue of whether teachers' experiences of reward and punishment in their own childhood influences the methods by which they discipline children. Students should write a brief paper summarizing their findings. They should also note any difficulties they had in locating appropriate sources.

6.4   What is Rewarding?

Have your students develop a survey to be administered to college students about what they regard as rewarding and what they regard as punitive. A preliminary survey might solicit information from students in terms of what a teacher would need to offer them in exchange for attending an additional week of classes. Based on these responses, a tentative list of possibly rewarding activities/items may be developed. A similar strategy might be adopted for identifying punishments.

Behavioral Learning Theory

6.5   Reinforcer Preferences

Handout Master 6.3 is a questionnaire taken from Martin, G., & Pear, J. (1988). Behavior modification: What is it and how to do it. (p. 35). Englewood Cliffs, NJ: Prentice Hall.

Ask the students to administer **Handout Master 6.3** to public school pupils of different ages. Be careful to remind them to select age groups that can read the questionnaire. Are there differences among children based on age?

6.6   Analyzing an Intervention

Have your students attempt an ABAB intervention (with the appropriate permissions) with a child. Use **Handouts 6.4 and 6.5** to help guide this activity and record the information from the intervention. The students should first select a target, undesirable behavior, record the frequency of this behavior during a 10 minute interval, introduce an intervention to reduce the incidence of this behavior (e.g., praising an alternative behavior), record the frequency of the undesirable behavior during a period in which the intervention is in place, and again record the frequency of the undesirable behavior after the intervention has been withdrawn.

6.7   Videogame Analysis

Using **Handout Master 6.6**, have your students observe a child playing a videogame. Their goal in doing so is to identify what they consider/observe to be reinforcing properties of the videogame and the child's affective responses to them.

6.8   Behavioral Principles in Action

Have your students select a class in which they are students and attempt to identify behavioral principles in action using **Handout Master 6.7**.

6.9   Self-Talk

One of the strategies that teachers can use is to engage in positive self-talk in which they direct themselves through a task, comment on a task, etc. Have your students write 10 negative statements that they could make about a class (e.g., the children never listen). Ask them to write 10 positive statements that counter these negative self-statements. Have them repeat negative statements twice and ask them to note how they feel. Now have them repeat the positive statements and ask them to note how they feel. Discuss the benefits of positive self-talk and attempt to identify when it might be most important to do this in a classroom.

Behavioral Learning Theory

6.10   Schedules of Reinforcement

Ask your students to imagine that they are assisting a teacher who wants to use a token economy system in his or her class. The system involves reinforcing good behavior tokens that students can trade in at the end of the week for rewards or privileges. Have students give a specific example of how the teacher might use each of the following schedules in dispensing the tokens. Students should also indicate their impressions about the relative effectiveness (possible advantages and disadvantages) of using that schedule.

1. Fixed-interval.
2. Fixed-ratio.
3. Variable-interval.
4. Variable-ratio.

6.11   Positive Practice

From Jensen, W.R., Sloan, H. N., & Young, K. R. (1988). <u>Applied behavioral analysis in education: A structured approach</u> (p. 118). Englewood Cliffs, NJ: Prentice Hall.

An excellent example of the use of positive-practice is a study conducted by Azrin and Powers (1975). This study was conducted with six boys ranging in age from seven to eleven. The target behaviors were speaking out and/or getting out of one's seat without permission. The positive practice centered around the rationale that speaking out and getting out of one's seat are not disruptive behaviors per se, but that permission should be asked and granted before the behavior is emitted. Four procedures were compared in treatment of these disruptive behaviors: (1) Warnings, reminders, and reinforcement; (2) Loss of recess (a type of response-cost); (3) Delayed positive practice; and (4) Immediate positive practice. Both delayed and immediate positive practice consisted of the following steps:

1. The teacher asked the pupil to repeat the correct procedure (getting permission) for talking in class or leaving one's seat.

2. The student repeated the procedure.

3. The student then role-played the correct procedure by raising his hand and waiting for the teacher to call on him by name.

4. The student asked for permission.

5. The student was given feedback as to the correctness of his practice and was then required to practice again.

If the practice was "delayed," it was conducted during recess. An average of five to ten practices were performed in a five-minute period. During the "immediate" practice procedure, the teacher asked the student to repeat the correct procedure for the disruptive behavior, practice the correct procedure once, and then finish the practice session during the next recess.

The results of this study showed the positive-practice procedures to be more effective than either the warnings or the loss of recess. Delayed positive practice was almost as effective as immediate positive practice.

Azrin and Powers contend that in many classrooms, delayed positive practice may be more easily implemented than other response-weakening procedures.

6.12   Self-Management

From Manning, B. H. (1988). Application of cognitive behavior modification: First and third graders' self management of classroom behaviors. American Educational Research Journal, 25 (2), 193-212.

Problem: Manning wanted to apply Meichenbaum's (1977) theory of cognitive behavior modification to elementary students who were exhibiting inappropriate classroom behaviors. The specific question Manning posed was: Would a cognitive behavior modification program significantly decrease the amount of inappropriate behavior in elementary school children?

Sample and Setting: Manning's subjects were thirty first-grade students and twenty- five third-grade students. All the students were in the average range on tests of intelligence and none was involved in special education. They had been identified by their teachers as exhibiting inappropriate behavior in class. In addition, all these students were rated by two outside observers as generally inattentive to class activities. Before the instruction began, all students were given the Nowicki-Strickland locus of control test. Both the first and third grade students were divided randomly into a control group and an experimental group.

Procedures: Both the control groups and the experimental groups met twice per week in fifty minute sessions for a total of eight hours over a four week period. The students and their regular teachers were unaware of assignments to control and experimental groups. Both groups covered similar material in the treatment classes designed to eliminate inappropriate classroom behavior; however, the experimental group received self-instructional cognitive training whereas the control group used more traditional instructional techniques.

Behavioral Learning Theory

The self-instructional cognitive training consisted of three major components: modeling, practicing, and cueing. Modeling involves viewing adults and videotaped peer models who use self-instruction to affect work habits (e.g. concentration on studies) and social responsibility (e.g. not disturbing others). The models verbally state the reasons for their actions and the outcome. For example, the students might watch a videotape of a boy debating whether to raise his hand in class or say the answer out loud. The model in the videotape will say to himself out loud "If I scream out the answer, others will be disturbed. I will raise my hand and wait my turn. Good for me - see, I can wait. "

Next the students practiced the self-instructional strategies taught by the instructor. For example, the subjects role-played classroom scenes so they could practice using self-statements and questions. The cueing component involved training the experimental group to respond to reminders to engage in the self-instruction taught during the treatment sessions. This cueing training occurred in the later phases of the experiment. Cue cards were commonly used to create associations. For example a cue card might say "Raise my hand " or "I will concentrate on my classwork". The words "I" and "my" are important key words for self-instructed cognitive training. The control group was exposed to identical cards except that the words "I" and "my" were replaced by "you" and "your".

When the training ended, and again one month and three months later, the teachers were asked to rate the appropriateness of the students' behavior. In addition to the teacher's ratings, students on-task behavior (attentiveness to class activity), and locus of control (sense of responsibility in controlling events) were also assessed. An independent t-test was used to analyze the differences between the treatment and control groups.

Results: Results of the t-tests indicated that, compared to the control group, students in the experimental group had significantly lower levels of inappropriate behavior, were more attentive, and more internal in their locus of control. These differences persisted for at least three months.

Discussions and implications: According to Manning's experiment, cognitive behavior modification is an effective way to teach students to control their outbursts and pay more attention in class. Students receiving the cognitive behavior modification instructions also developed a more internal locus of control than their control group counterparts. Cognitive behavior modification may prove to be a valuable tool in dealing with undesirable behavior in the classroom. The small amount of time it takes to administer the cognitive behavior modification lessons make it less costly and perhaps more effective than traditional treatments. Regular teachers could easily learn how to administer the lessons.

Behavioral Learning Theory

Have your students identify a goal (proximal) that they would like to accomplish. Using **Handout Master 6.8**, have them record their progress to the goal.

6.13   Behavioral Principles in the World

Have your students keep track of behavioral principles they see in the real world during a day.

6.14   Peer Modeling

From Schunk, D. H. (1987). Peer models and children's behavioral change. Review of Educational Research, 57, 149-74.   The abstract of the article follows:

This article critically reviews the research literature on peer modeling among children as a function of model attributes. Peer modeling is hypothesized to depend in part on perceived similarity between model and observer. Similarity serves as an important source of information for gauging behavioral appropriateness, formulating outcome expectations, and assessing one's self-efficacy for learning or performing tasks. Research is reviewed on the effects of model age, model sex, model competence, number of models, and model background. Peer models can foster diverse types of behavioral change in children, but attribute similarity does not automatically enhance modeling. The conditions under which similarity promotes behavioral change are discussed. Future research needs to assess children's self- perceptions, as well as maintenance and generalization of behavioral changes. It is suggested that classroom peers can help train social skills, enhance self-efficacy, and remedy skill deficiencies.

Discussion Questions

1. Differentiate between classical and operant conditioning. Discuss what practical applications each can provide for teachers.

2. A student seems very anxious about reading aloud in class. How would you use each of the following classical conditioning techniques to reduce and hopefully eliminate this fear?

3. Describe the different patterns of responding that are engendered by the four intermittent schedules of reinforcement.

4. Television programming is frequently criticized for the high incidence of violence featured.   Discuss the possible dangers of TV violence in reference to social learning theory and Bandura's work on modeling.

Behavioral Learning Theory

5. Describe what is meant by the "praise and ignore" approach to classroom management. What are the strengths and limitations of this approach? Give several examples of the types of incidents to which it might be applied.

6. Discuss how new behaviors might be developed through (a) cueing and prompting, (b) modeling, and (c) shaping.

7. Identify the ethical issues involving behavioral management. Evaluate these concerns based on your own perceptions of their importance.

Additional Resources for Teaching This Chapter

REFERENCES

Bandura, A. (1986). Social foundations of thought and action: A social cognitive theory. Englewood Cliffs, NJ: Prentice-Hall.

Ferster, C. B. and Skinner, B. F. (1957). Schedules of reinforcement. New York: Appleton-Century-Crofts.

Jacobs, P., Meier, N. and Stolurow, S. (1966). A guide to evaluating self-instructional programs. New York: Holt, Rinehart and Winston.

McDaniels, T. R. (1987, May). *Practicing positive reinforcement*. Clearinghouse, 389-392.

Meichenbaum, D. (1977). Cognitive behavior modification. New York: Plenum.

Rogers, C. and Skinner, B. F. (November, 1956). Some issues concerning human behavior. Science. 1057-1066.

Skinner, B. F. (1984). The shame of American education. American Psychologist, 39, 947-954

Schaps, E., & Lewis, C. (1991). Extrinsic rewards are education's past, not future. Educational Leadership, 48(7), p. 81

Spalzo, F. J. (1985). Behavior analysis. Teacher Educator, 21(2), 15-25.

FILMS, VIDEOTAPES, AND AUDIOCASSETTES

Behavior modification in the classroom, 16 mm, 24 minutes). Shows teachers using behavior modification techniques to help students reduce distractibility and overcoming daydreaming. (From UCB, 1969)

B. F. Skinner and behavior change: Research, practice, and promise, 16 mm, 48 minutes. Using a panel of social scientists the film addresses the history, theory, ethics, and applications of behaviorism. (From REPR, MG, 1975)

B. F. Skinner on education, Parts I and II, 16 mm, 25 minutes. A discussion of Skinner's views regarding freedom and control in the classroom as these relate to the purpose of schooling. (From ASCD, 1972)

Contracting, 3/4 or 1/2 inch video, 30 minutes. Explains the use of contracting in educational settings. (From DMCPB)

Conversations on learning, No. 1, 16 mm, 28 minutes. Dr. Robert Mager discusses the use of task analysis as a technique of teaching and determining how measurable objectives may be determined. (From EDUC)

Learning, 16 mm, 3/4 inch Umatic, 1/2 inch VHS, 1/2 inch Beta, 30 minutes. Shows a variety of experiments (e.g., imprinting, behavior shaping, teaching language to a mentally retarded child) using principles of operant conditioning. B. F. Skinner and David C. McClelland narrate the closing sequence and touch on human dignity, motivation training, and the power of rewards. Can be used as an introduction to the section on operant conditioning. (From CRM, 1971)

Operant learning, 16 mm, 10 minutes. Shows the use of operant techniques in a 3rd grade classroom in dealing with both inappropriate as well as appropriate problem-solving behaviors. (From MSU, 19 75)

Pavlov: The conditioned reflex, video, 25 minutes, B & W. This documentary shows Pavlov's pioneering work in behavioral psychology, including the famous dog experiment. It provides rare documentary footage of Pavlov at work, focusing on his revolutionary studies of the conditioned reflex and covering his concerns with the extension of conditioned research methodology to the problems of neurology and psychiatry. (From Films for the Humanities & Sciences, Inc.)

Positive reinforcement, 16 mm, 10 minutes. Illustrates a variety of possible reward circumstances that may be used following desired behavior.(From MSU, 1975)

Reinforcement, 16 mm, 8 minutes. Increasing Student Participation Skills. The film focuses on how teachers may use positive incentives (reinforcement) to increase student participation in class discussion. Focuses on the secondary level. (From GLC, 1968)

Behavioral Learning Theory

Reward and punishment, 16 mm, 3/4 inch Umatic, 1/2 inch VHS, 1/2inch Beta, 14 minutes. Appropriate uses of reward and punishment to shape child behavior are illustrated. Viewers are asked at the end of the film to consider how to use behavior modification techniques without violating humanistic values. (From CRM, 1972) The ABC's of behavioral education, 16 mm, 20 minutes. Describes the use of behavior modification programming at a school for adolescent delinquent students. Emphasizes the relationship between antecedents, behaviors, and consequences in program development and implementation. (From INFORM, NBUC, WAU, 1971)

The Skinner revolution, 16 mm, 1/2 inch VHS, 22 minutes. A biographical sketch of B. F. Skinner that attempts to clarify his main ideas. (From REPR, IU, PST, WAU, 1978)

Handout Master 6.0

Lecture Outline ----- Behavioral Views of Learning

- **Understanding Learning**

- **Contiguity Learning**

- **Operant Learning**

- **Applied Behavior Analysis**

- **Social Learning Theory**

- **Self-Regulation and Cognitive Behavior Modification**

Copyright © 1998 by Allyn and Bacon

Handout Master 6.1

Differentiating Punishment and Reinforcement

List examples of reinforcements and punishments you might use in your class.

Reinforcement	Punishment

Copyright © 1998 by Allyn and Bacon

Handout Master 6.2a

Intervention Techniques

This is an example of a situation where several intervention techniques were utilized.

Situation

Several times a week, attendants dragged Charlie down the hall to one of his classes s the boy screamed and buckled his knees. On several occasions, the boy threw himself on the floor in front of a classroom door. A crowd of staff members inevitable gathered around him. The group usually watched and commented as the boy sat or lay on the floor, kicking, and screaming. Some members of the group hypothesized that such behavior seemed to appear after the boy was teased or frustrated.

Observing one such situation that occurred before her class, the teacher asked the attendant to put the boy in the classroom at the desk and leave the room. Then she closed the door. The boy sat at his desk, kicking and screaming; the teacher proceeded to her desk and worked there, ignoring Charles. After 2 or 3 minutes, the boy, crying softly, looked up at his teacher. Then she announced that she would be ready to work with him as soon as he indicated that he was ready to work. He continued to cry and scream with diminishing loudness for the next 4 or 5 minutes. Finally, he lifted his head and stated that he was ready. Immediately the teacher looked up at him, smiled, went to his desk, and said, "Good. Now let's get to work." The boy worked quietly and cooperatively with the teacher for the remainder of the period.

From Zimmerman, E., & Zimmerman, J. (1972). The alteration of behavior in a special classroom situation. In K. D. O'Leary and S. G. O'Leary, Classroom management. Elesford, NY: Pergammon Press, Inc. Reprinted from Journal of Experimental Analysis of Behavior, 5(1), 59-60.

Copyright © 1998 by Allyn and Bacon

Handout Master 6.2b

Behavior Problem Scenarios

Listed below are five scenarios. For each, determine appropriate behavioral procedures to use to help solve the problem. Additionally, indicate what you anticipate happening when you use the strategy.

Scenario 1: Jim, a fourth grader, would much rather carve desks than do his assignments. His carvings are not random but involve a definite design—a complete circle with tiny circles around it. His carving tools consist of pens, pencils, rulers, and compass. Year and year, Jim produces a new masterpiece. The school can no longer afford to allow Jim to carve desks.
Design a strategy to eliminate the carving behavior. Explain what you anticipate happening with this strategy.

Scenario 2: Mr. Horatio Stevens is a second-grade teacher at Green Elementary School. He has only been teaching for a few weeks and is having problems. He has a class of 25 overeager children who consistently blurt and yell out their answers instead of waiting and raising their hands. He finds the blurting out disruptive and it is difficult to respond to each student. He is pleased with their eagerness but need a calmer setting.

Design a strategy to help Mr. Stevens. Explain what you anticipate happening with the strategy.

Scenario 3: Polly is very adept at mimicking her teacher's idiosyncrasies, for example, hand gestures, and facial expression, and this behavior is being reinforced by Ms. Garcia's tirades and the applause reaction of classmates. The more Ms. Garcia has lectured Polly about her behavior, the greater the frequency and exaggeration of the mimicking behavior.

Design a strategy too remedy this situation. Explain what you anticipate happening with this strategy.

Scenario 4: Jim, a 13-year-old boy, was transferred from Berry School to Tampa County School. His passivity and lack of assertiveness have pervaded all aspects of his classroom adjustment and are especially noticeable in gym class. He seems interested in but afraid of athletic activities, as evidenced by his hovering on the fringe of the action. The teacher's attempts to involve him directly have been met with stubborn resistance by Jim.

Design a strategy to help Jim. Explain what you think will happen.

Scenario 5: Toni flusters and irritates her teacher by playing the role of the "dumb, slow student." Toni constantly asks questions to which the answers are evident. For example, after the teacher had given the pages of an assignment out loud, and written them on the board, Toni asked what pages the assignment was on. She also manipulated her teacher to give her a negative, flustered response by pretending not to be able to do an assignment in which she has been previously successful. This behavior was exemplified by her reading assignment. Toni was called upon to read some words, she read them very well, and the teacher praised her reading. The other students did not do as nearly as well, so for the next day's assignment the class was to study the words and to be able to read them correctly. The next day, when Toni was called to read the same words, she faltered and pretended that she could not read the words. The teacher is certain that Toni knew the words, became irritated and reassigned them as homework.

Design a strategy to help this situation. Explain what you think will happen.

Copyright © 1998 by Allyn and Bacon

Handout Master 6.3

Survey of Reinforcement Preferences

This questionnaire is designed to help you find some specific activities, objects, events, or individuals that can be used as reinforcers in an improvement program. Read each question carefully and then fill in the appropriate blanks.

I. Consumable reinforcers: What does this person like to eat or drink?
   A. What things does this person like to eat most?
      1. regular meal-type foods
      2. health foods—dried fruits, nuts, cereals, etc.
      3. junk foods—popcorn, potato chips, etc.
      4. sweets—candies, ice cream, cookies, etc.
   B. What things does this person like to drink most?
      1. milk
      2. soft drinks
      3. juices
      4. other

II. Activity reinforcers: What things does this person like to do?
   A. Activities in the home residence
      1. Hobbies
      2. Crafts
      3. redecorating
      4. Preparing food or drinks
      5. Housework
   B. Free Activities In The Neighborhood (window shopping, walking, jogging, cycling, driving, swinging, teeter-tottering, etc.)
   C. Free Activities Farther Away From Home (hiking, snow shoeing, swimming, camping, going to the beach, etc.)
   D. Activities You Pay To Do (films, plays, sports, events, night clubs, pubs, etc.)
   E. Passive Activities (Watching TV, listening to the radio, records, or tapes, sitting, talking, bathing, etc.)

Copyright © 1998 by Allyn and Bacon

Handout Master 6.4: Applying Behavioral Principles

Applying Behavioral Principles

Methods for Encouraging Behavior

reinforcement
- negative and positive reinforcement
- increases behavior

- select reinforcers (Premack Principles)
- shaping
- positive practice

ABAB Steps
* baseline measure of behavior
* intervention is applied
* intervention is stopped;
* results are recorded
* intervention is reintroduced

Maintaining Behavior
* use schedules of reinforcement to influence speed of performance, persistence of behavior

Methods for Coping with Undesirable Behavior

direct student to appropriate behavior (**reinforce**)

suppress undesirable behavior (**punish**)

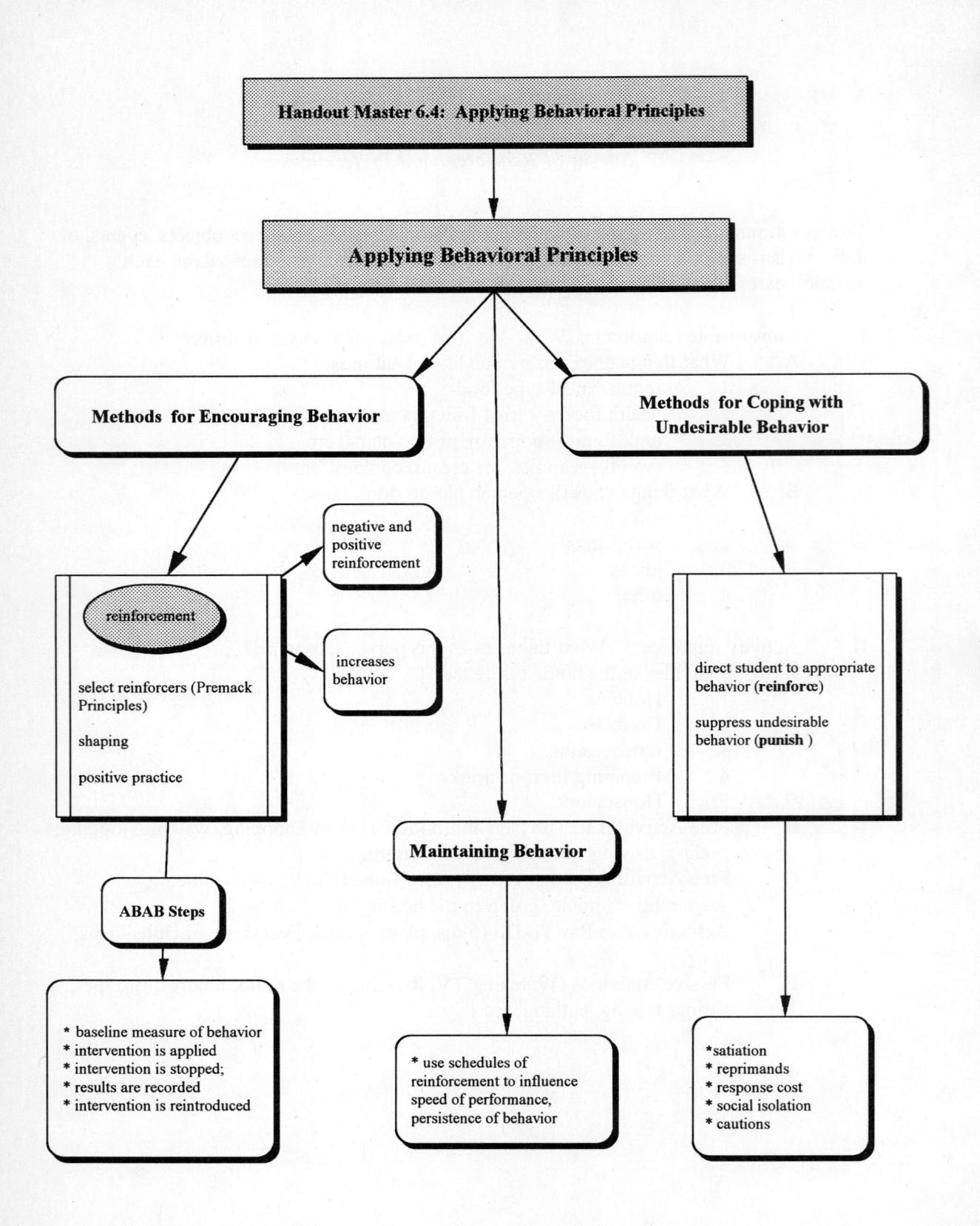

* satiation
* reprimands
* response cost
* social isolation
* cautions

Copyright © 1998 by Allyn and Bacon

Handout Master 6.5

Behavior Checklist

What is the behavior that is undesirable?

Why is it undesirable? What learning outcome is it influencing?

What is the nature of the intervention you will introduce?

Before Intervention

Record Instances of Target Behavior in 10 minute interval

Intervention

Record Instances of Target Behavior during a 10 minute interval in which the intervention is in place (to be completed some time after the intervention has been introduced)

After Intervention Has Been Withdrawn

Record Instances of Target Behavior in 10 minute interval

Copyright © 1998 by Allyn and Bacon

Handout 6.6

Videogame Analysis

How long did the child play the game?

What evidence did you note of the child's interest?

Did you observe any change in the child's behavior that would indicate that she or he had been reinforced by any elements of the game? Explain.

What affect accompanies the child's experience of reinforcement?

What elements of the game appear to be reinforcing?

Copyright © 1998 by Allyn and Bacon

Handout Master 6.7

Behavior Analysis Chart

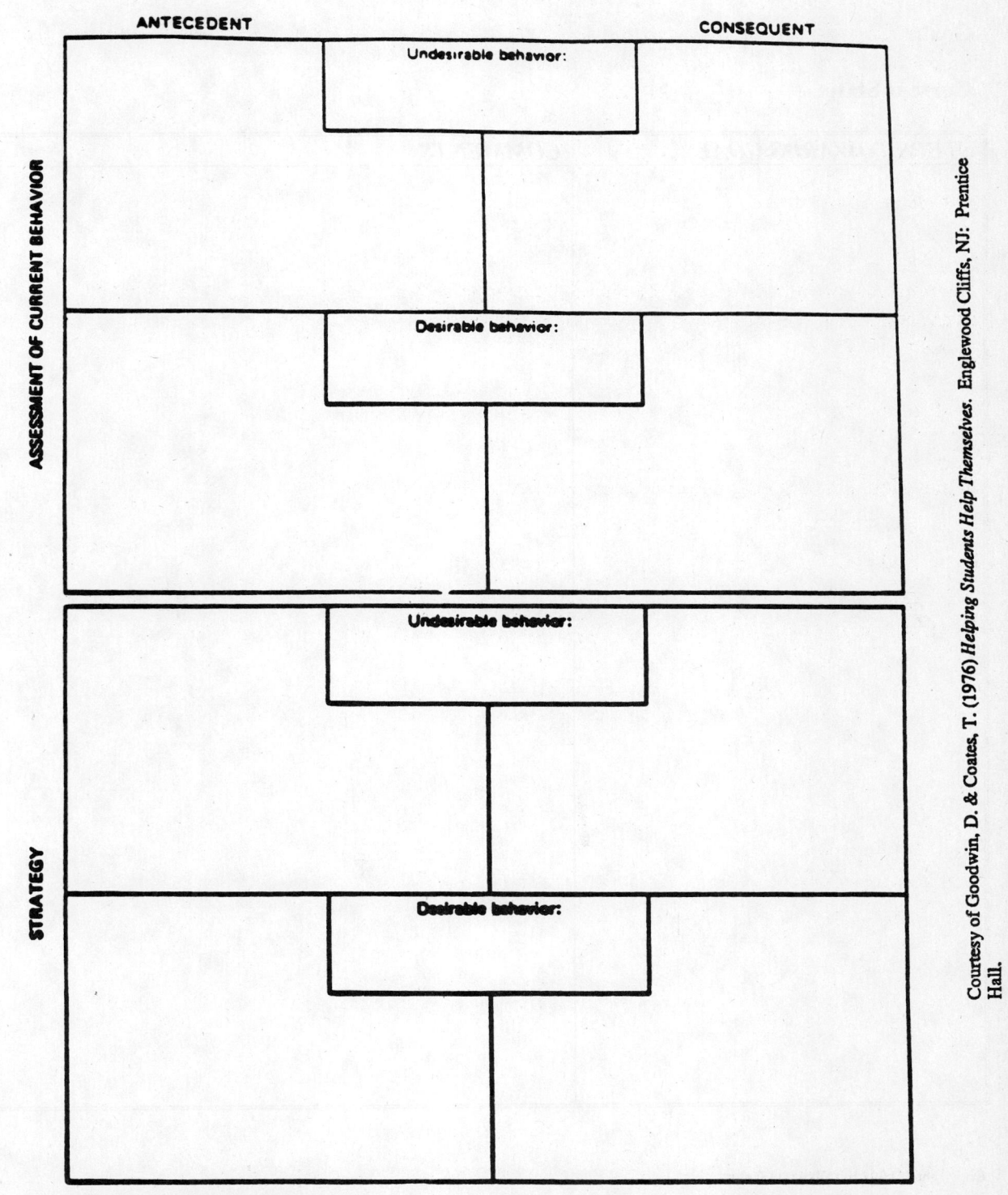

	ANTECEDENT		CONSEQUENT
ASSESSMENT OF CURRENT BEHAVIOR		Undesirable behavior:	
		Desirable behavior:	
STRATEGY		Undesirable behavior:	
		Desirable behavior:	

Courtesy of Goodwin, D. & Coates, T. (1976) *Helping Students Help Themselves*. Englewood Cliffs, NJ: Prentice Hall.

Copyright © 1998 by Allyn and Bacon

Handout 6.8

Success Log

Goal:

Current State:

STEPS TOWARDS GOAL	COMMENTS

Copyright © 1998 by Allyn and Bacon

Handout Master 6.9: Links to Other Chapters

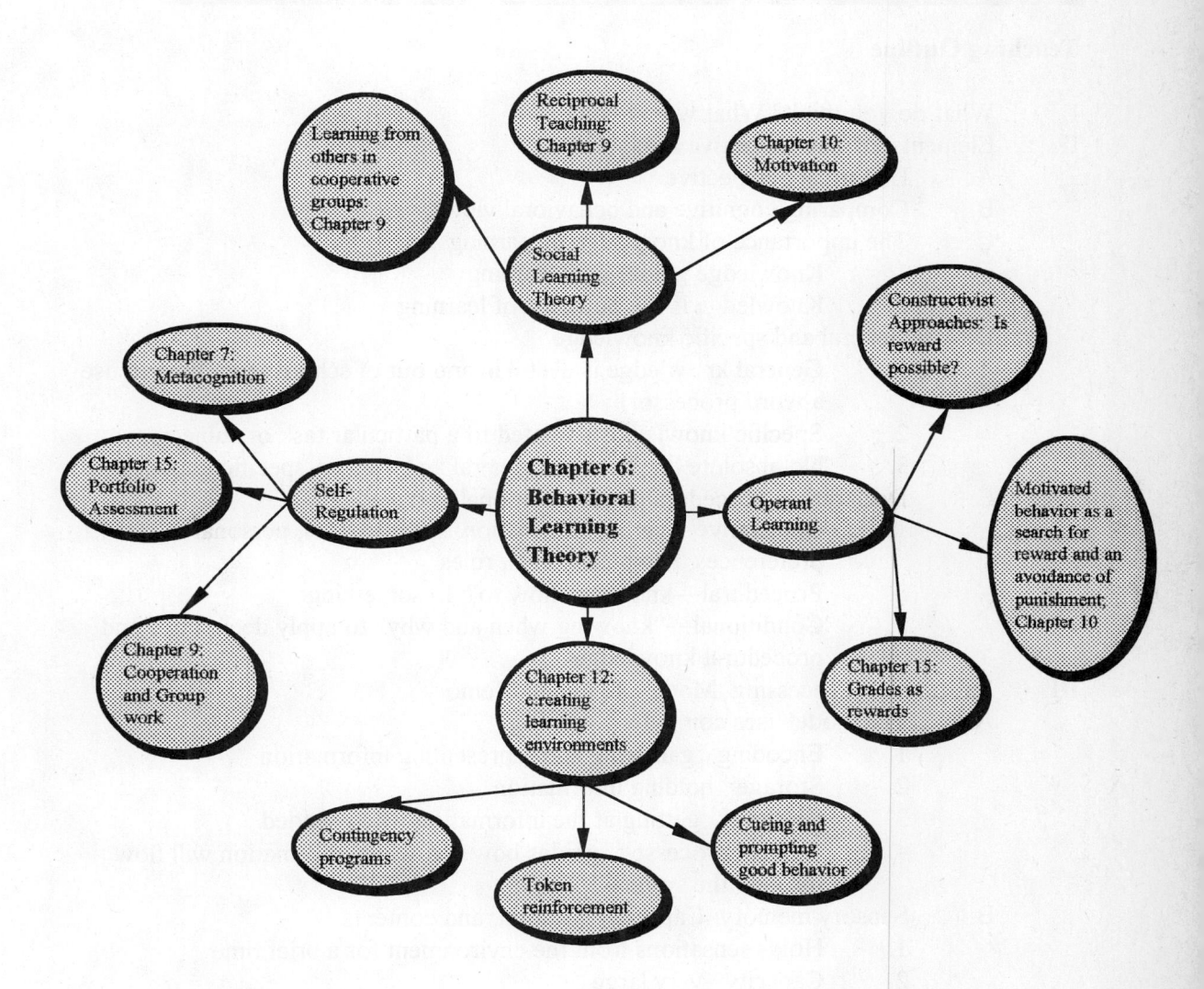

- Chapter 6: Behavioral Learning Theory
  - Social Learning Theory
    - Learning from others in cooperative groups: Chapter 9
    - Reciprocal Teaching: Chapter 9
    - Chapter 10: Motivation
  - Self-Regulation
    - Chapter 7: Metacognition
    - Chapter 15: Portfolio Assessment
    - Chapter 9: Cooperation and Group work
  - Operant Learning
    - Constructivist Approaches: Is reward possible?
    - Motivated behavior as a search for reward and an avoidance of punishment: Chapter 10
    - Chapter 15: Grades as rewards
  - Chapter 12: creating learning environments
    - Contingency programs
    - Token reinforcement
    - Cueing and prompting good behavior

Copyright © 1998 by Allyn and Bacon

7

Cognitive Views of Learning

Teaching Outline

I. What do you think? What would you do?
II. Elements Of The Cognitive Perspective
    A. Historical perspective
    B. Comparing cognitive and behavioral views
    C. The importance of knowledge in learning
        1. Knowledge guides new learning
        2. Knowledge is the outcome of learning
    D. General and specific knowledge
        1. General knowledge is useful in and out of school (e.g., how to use a word processor)
        2. Specific knowledge is related to a particular task or subject
        3. No absolute line between general and domain-specific knowledge
    E. Declarative, procedural, and conditional knowledge
        1. Declarative—verbal information, specific facts, personal preferences, personal events, rules
        2. Procedural—knowing "how to" do something
        3. Conditional—"knowing when and why" to apply declarative and procedural knowledge
III. Information Processing Model of Human Memory
    A. The model uses computer as analogy
        1. Encoding: gathering and representing information
        2. Storage: holding information
        3. Retrieval: getting at the information when needed
        4. Control processes: guides how and when information will flow through the system
    B. Sensory memory: Capacity, duration, and contents
        1. Holds sensations from the environment for a brief time
        2. Capacity: very large
        3. Duration: fragile, between 1 and 3 seconds
        4. Content: resembles the sensation from the original stimulus
    C. Perception: The meaning we attribute to sensory memory
        1. Gestalt theory: People's tendency to organize sensory information into patterns or relationships (Figure 7.2)
        2. Feature analysis: the stimulus is analyzed into features or components and assembled into a meaningful pattern (bottom-up processing)
        3. Top-down processing: based on knowledge and expectation

Cognitive Views of Learning

D. Attention
    1. Is a limited resource—can only pay attention to one demanding task at a time
    2. Attention and teaching
    3. Guidelines for gaining and maintaining attention
        a) Use signals
        b) Make sure the purpose of the lesson or assignment is clear to students
        c) Emphasize variety, curiosity, and surprise
        d) Ask questions and provide frames for answering

E. Working memory (or short-term memory): Holds the information that is currently activated
    1. Capacity, duration, and contents of working memory
        a) Capacity: limited—five to nine separate new items at once (of new information)
        b) Duration: short, about 5 to 20 seconds
        c) Contents: may be in the form of images, or structured more abstractly and based on meaning
    2. Retaining information in working memory
        a) Maintenance rehearsal (Craik & Lockhart) involves repeating the information in your mind
        b) Elaborative rehearsal involves connecting the information with something already known
        c) Chunking—grouping individual bits of information can somewhat circumvent the capacity of working memory
    3. Forgetting
        a) Interference—remembering new information interferes with the remembering of old information
        b) Decay—the activation level weakens until the information cannot be reactivated
        c) Is useful, or the working memory would be overloaded and learning would cease

F. Long-term memory: Holds the information that is well learned
    1. Capacity and duration of long-term memory
        a) Capacity: Unlimited
        b) Duration: Can remain in long-term memory indefinitely
        c) Access can be difficult
    2. Contents of long-term memory
        a) Alan Paivio: Dual coding theory—information is stored as either visual images or verbal units, or both. Information coded both ways may be easier to learn.
    3. Categories of long-term memory
        a) Semantic memory is memory for meaning
            (1) stored as propositions, images, and schemas
        b) Propositions and propositional networks

Cognitive Views of Learning

          (1) Proposition—the smallest unit of information that can be judged true or false
          (2) Propositional network—interconnected bits of information
          (3) Information may be stored and represented in propositional networks; bits of information can trigger or activate recall of another
      c) Images are representations based on perceptions
      d) Schemas are abstract knowledge structures
          (1) organize vast amounts of information.
          (2) Patterns or guides for understanding an event, a concept, or a skill
              (a) Story grammar
              (b) Event schema
    4. Episodic memory—
      a) Memory for information tied to a particular place and time, especially events in one's own life
    5. Procedural memory
      a) Memory for how to do things. Represented as condition-action rules, or productions. These tell one what to do under certain conditions

G. Storing and retrieving information in long-term memory
    1. Elaboration—the addition of meaning to new information through its connection with already existing information.
    2. Organization—material that is well organized is easier to learn and to remember that bits of information
    3. Context—aspects of physical and emotional content are learned along with other information.

H. Levels of processing theories (Craik and Lockhart)—The more completely information is processed, the better are the chances of retrieving the information later

I. Retrieving information from long-term memory
    1. Only one small area of the memory network is activated at any time
    2. Retrieval through the spread of activation
    3. Reconstruction—a problem-solving process that makes use of logic, cues, and other knowledge to construct a reasonable answer by filling in any missing parts
      a) Bartlett—stories recalled to be consistent with students' schemas
      b) Loftus—eyewitness testimony

J. Forgetting and long-term memory
    1. Once lost, information disappears
    2. Lost through time decay and interference

K. Guidelines: Using information processing ideas in the classroom

IV. Connectionism: An Alternative View Of Memory
   A. Assumes all knowledge is stored in patterns of connections among basic processing units in a vast network in the brain
   B. Information processing is distributed across this network
   C. Knowledge stored in a network of connections rather than as rules, propositions, or schemas
   D. Advantages:
      1. Can account for more than recall of information
      2. Can explain the slowly developing, incremental nature of human learning
V. Metacognition, Regulation, And Individual Differences
   A. Executive control processes—metacognitive skills
   B. Metacognitive knowledge and regulation
      1. Metacognition is thinking about thinking
      2. Involves declarative knowledge about yourself as a learner; factors that influence your learning and memory; and the skills, strategies, and resources needed to perform a task
      3. Is used to regulate thinking and learning
         a) Planning
         b) Monitoring
         c) Evaluation
   C. Individual differences in metacognition
      1. Some differences due to development (age, maturation)
      2. May be caused by biological differences or by variations in learning experiences
      3. Individual differences and working memory
         a) Developmental differences in efficiency and capacity
      4. Individual differences and long-term memory
         a) Knowledge: Memory is better when students have more domain-specific declarative and procedural knowledge
VI. Becoming Knowledgeable: Some Basic Principles
   A. Development of declarative knowledge
      1. Rote memorization
      2. Distributed practice
      3. Mnemonics (systematic procedures for improving one's memory)
         a) Loci method
         b) Acronyms
         c) Chain mnemonics
         d) keyword method
      4. Point-Counterpoint: What's wrong with memorizing?
      5. Making it meaningful
VII. Becoming An Expert: Development Of Procedural And Conditional Knowledge
   A. Experts have a wealth of domain-specific knowledge, procedural knowledge, and conditional knowledge

Cognitive Views of Learning

      B.   Much of an expert's declarative knowledge is automated
      C.   Automatic skills
           1.   Cognitive stage—rely on declarative knowledge and general problem-solving strategies
           2.   Associative stage—individual steps of a procedure are combined into larger units
           3.   Autonomous stage—whole procedure can be accomplished without much attention
           4.   Teachers can help students become experts through feedback and practice
      D.   Guidelines: Including families in students' learning
VIII.   Constructivism And Situated Learning: Challenging Symbolic Processing Models
      A.   Exogenous constructivism: focuses on the ways that individuals reconstruct outside reality by building accurate mental representations
      B.   Endogenous constructivism: assumes that new knowledge is abstracted from old knowledge and not by accurately mapping the outside world
      C.   Dialectical constructivism: suggests that knowledge grows through the interactions of internal and external factors
      D.   Knowledge: Accuracy versus usefulness
      E.   Situated learning—notion that learning is inherently social and embedded in a particular cultural setting. Learning is like an apprenticeship
IX.   Summary
X.   Key words and concepts
XI.   Teachers' casebook?: What would you do?

Cognitive Views of Learning

Learning Activities and Related Research

ACTIVITIES	HANDOUTS
Chapter 7	7.0 Lecture Outline
	7.1 Memory
Cooperative Activities	
7.1 Episodic Memory	7.2 Episodic Memory
7.2 Endangered Species Exercise	7.3 Instructional sheet for Endangered Species
7.3 Constructivism and Exogenous Constructivism	
Research Activities	
Using Technology	
7.4 Metacognition and Internet Use	7.4 Record keeping sheet
Field Experience	
7.5 Memory and Curriculum	
7.6 Metamemory	
Other Teaching Activities	
7.7 Limits of Attention	
7.8 Short term memory	
7.9 Role of Organization	
7.10 Elaborative rehearsal	
7.11 Semantic Memory	7.5 Quiz on Particularly Cats Passage
7.12 Reconstructive Memory	7.6 Sleep Schema
	7.7 Keyword Mnemonic
	7.8 Concept Map: Links to other chapters

Cooperative Activities

7.1   <u>Episodic Memory</u>

Use **Handout Master 7.2** with this activity. Ask students in their groups to recall a favorite memory drawn from the school years between kindergarten and sixth grade. Try to make the memory as vivid as possible by recalling details through such prompts as the following: the look of the room (if indoors) or the environment (if outdoors); other people involved (their identities, clothing, actions); feelings remembered; and events that made the memory a lasting one.

Ask students to recall a favorite memory drawn from the school years between seventh and twelfth grade. Using the same prompts, describe the circumstances of the memory.

Compare the experiences. How does episodic memory differ for the two events? What does this suggest about the nature of the memory coding and recall for school events at these two levels of schooling? What does this suggest about the meaning of the experiences?

Cognitive Views of Learning

7.2   Endangered Species

The following exercise was provided by Dr. Robert Lebeau. The exercise is provided in **Handout 7.3**. The article on which it is based is:

Temple, S. (1977). Plant-animal mutualism: coevolution with dodo leads to near extinction of plant." Science, 197, 887-886.

The goal of the exercise is to make students aware of the role of prior knowledge in being able to formulate hypotheses. For example, a student who is a forestry major will most likely propose a different hypothesis than a student who is a psychology major. You can also use this exercise to reinforce the important role of metacognition in knowledge management.

Students should work on this task alone initially. Group members should then share answers, coming to consensus on the hypotheses to be proposed and the evidence to be sought. Students should make an audiotape of their discussion for use in subsequent activities. Each group should present their conclusions to the class, including the reasons for the decisions they made.

Case Study of an Endangered Species: Calvaria major

The Problem

Calvaria major is a large tree, native to the island of Mauritius in the western Indian Ocean. Historical forestry records indicate that Calvaria was formerly common on the island and was frequently exploited for lumber. Today, however, only 13 old and dying trees are known to survive in what is left of the original forests of Mauritius. Experienced Mauritian foresters have estimated that these trees are all more than 300 years old. In other words, no young Calvaria major trees are currently growing to replace the older ones. The species is in danger of becoming extinct.

Your Mission

You are a member of a team of scientists that has been invited to the island to investigate the situation. Your team's mission is to explain as well as possible why the species Calvaria major is failing to produce new trees and to recommend how the species might regenerate. Today, as you travel with other team members on an airplane to Mauritius, your task is to develop a plan for approaching this problem. You may adopt any strategy you wish for developing such a plan, but for our purposes today the outcome of your discussion should be organized in the following two categories:

1. Your initial hypotheses regarding this problem.

2. Additional information you would want to know that might help you narrow these hypotheses and pursue possible solutions.

Concepts and Definitions of Potential Value in This Task

Declarative Knowledge: Knowledge of facts, definitions, generalizations, and rules; "knowing that"

Procedural Knowledge: Knowing how to perform activities; skills

Conditional Knowledge: Knowing when to apply declarative and procedural knowledge

Schemas: Associative memory structures that store general knowledge about objects, events, or situations

Metacognition: Knowledge one has of, and the regulation one exercises over, one's own cognition

Self-efficacy: Beliefs in one's capacities to organize and execute actions required to manage given situations; Perceptions about one's capacities to achieve designated levels of performance in given areas

7.3   Constructivist Lesson Plans

Ask students in groups a concept that they will prepare to teach to a sixth grade class (you might select a concept recently taught in the class).   Assign half of the students to prepare a lesson that is oriented from the position of endogenous constructivism. The other half of the group should prepare a lesson that is oriented from the position of exogenous constructivism. Once students have prepared their lesson, have each group in turn present to the class. Compare how the lessons differed. Did they actually represent the exogenous and endogenous constructivism?

Using Technology

7.4   Metacognition and Internet Use

Metacognition includes a) knowledge of oneself as a learner, b) knowledge of the effects of strategies, and c) knowledge of when to use particular strategies. Have your students access the Internet and conduct a search to locate a vacation rental with the following constraints (see **Handout 7.4**):

- need the rental for one week
- should be in a quiet, beachfront area
- average temperature in the location should be 80 degrees Fahrenheit
- can accommodate children
- can accommodate a dog

Cognitive Views of Learning

Have students monitor their metacognition about their search by noting (using **Handout 7.4**) their thoughts about themselves as a learner (in this case, searcher), their knowledge of what strategies will produce results, and when they should use those strategies.

Field Experience

7.5   Memory and Curriculum

Have students interview a classroom teacher briefly about the role of memory in the curriculum. Suggest the following questions: What type of memorization is required? What classroom activities are chosen to help students to retain the desired information? What strategies are effective at the specified grade level? How long are students required to retain information between its presentation and the required recall? What kinds of individual differences are apparent in students' ability to remember information? Compare the responses among various interviews. What attempts are evident of teachers helping students to code information meaningfully for enhanced recall?

7.6   Metamemory

Ask you students to conduct an interview with a child (approximately 7-10 years old) about their knowledge of memory. The students will need to develop an interview protocol or guide for conducting the interview. They will need to consider how to ask a young child about his or her knowledge of memory or metamemory. Have your students share what they learn from children about their memories and discuss the implications of their knowledge of memory for effective learning.

Other Teaching Activities

7.7   Limits of Attention

Select two paragraphs from a text or newspaper. Ask two students to volunteer to come to the front of the class to read the passages aloud to the rest of the class. Direct the other students in the class to pay attention to both sets of material and warn them that they will be asked to recall the material once the reading is complete. Upon your signal, both students should read aloud to the rest of the class. Once they are finished, ask the students in the class to write down all they can recall from the task. Discuss with students why this task was difficult. Did they recall much? Why not? What strategies did they use to attend to BOTH?

7.8   Short Term Memory

Ask students to listen to the following words but not to take notes.

| TULIP | PONY | TABLE |

CENTER	RUSSIA	SALAD
CAARPET	LIME	PHONE
BOOK	DISK	COFFEE
WINDOW	SIDEWALK	PILLOW

Ask them to write down as many words as they can. Then read the next list to them. This time, ask students to DO the things you say.

BLINK	SCRATCH	YAWN
COUGH	SQUINT	REACH
CLAP	TWIST	STRETCH
LEAN	SQUEEZE	GARGLE
SNEEZE	WINK	KICK

They should now write down the items they can remember. Give students the information about the words read aloud. Ask them to count how many they had correct. Compare and contrast performance on the word list with that of the actions. Use the comparison to address such concepts as the serial position effect, the possible benefits of organization (using the constraints of the possible actions of the body as an organizer), the role of elaboration, and the role of interference.

7.8   Role of Organization

For this activity, tell students that you will help them to recall as many words as they can because you will give them some hints. The words they will hear are organized into 4 categories: fruits, flowers, cities, countries. You will read a list of words aloud. Each set of four words will include a member of each category. In addition, each word in a set of 4 will begin with the same letter. Read the following words aloud (read from left to right).

TOMATO	TULIP	TORONTO	TUNISIA
RASPBERRY	ROSE	RENO	RUSSIA
LIME	LILY	LONDON	LATVIA
BANANA	BLUEBONNET	BANKOK	BRAZIL
CANTALOPE	CARNATION	CANCUN	CANADA
GRAPE	GERANIUM	GENOA	GERMANY

Performance on this list usually exceeds the typical 5-9 item recall found on the initial list. Discuss the importance of organization.

Cognitive Views of Learning

7.10 Elaborative Rehearsal: The Role of Meaning in Memory

Have the students study the following chart for one minute. They must memorize these symbols long enough to use them on a spelling test. They may remember them any way they can except by writing them.

⌋ A ⌐F
⌊ B ⌐|G
⌊ C ⌐⌐H
⌋ D ⌐|I
☐ E

Instruct the students to use the symbols above to represent the letters and administer a brief spelling test using the follow words: big, acid, cage, decide, face, headache. Tabulate the results. Compare the methods which the students used to memorize the symbols. Ask the students if they think they could remember the symbols if another test were given after one half hour of intervening discussion on another topic. Will the symbol-letter connection remain in long-term memory for a week, a month, or longer? Discuss.

Now draw the diagram below on the chalkboard or on an overhead transparency. Students will notice that each letter fits into a box, or partial box, that becomes the symbol which represents the letter. Having understood this correspondence, what do the students predict will happen to the memory task?

```
A | B | C
---------
D | E | F
---------
G | H | I
```

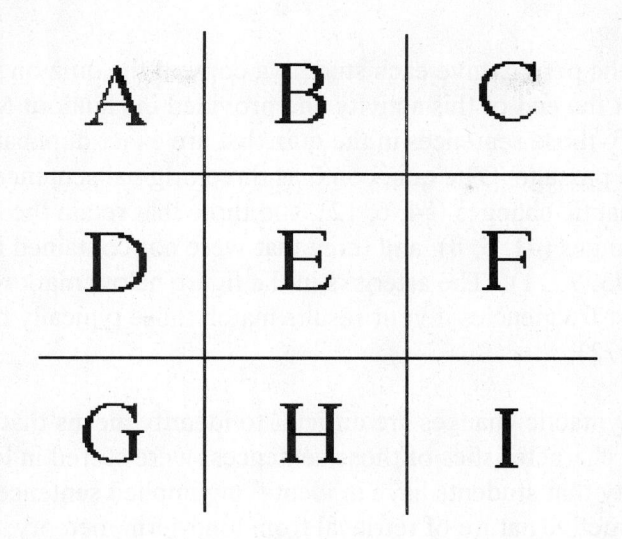

7.11 Semantic Memory

From Makosky, V.P., Whittemore, L. G., and Rogers, A.M. (Eds.) (1987). <u>Activities handbook for the teaching of psychology, Vol. 2</u>. Washington, DC.: American Psychological Association. Diekhoff, G. M. Activity 23, 75-77.

Bransford, J. D., Barclay, J. R., & Franks, J. J. (1972). Sentence memory: A constructive vs. interpretive approach. <u>Cognitive Psychology, 3</u>, 193-209; Lessing, D. (1967). Particularly cats. New York: Simon and Schuster.)

Errors in recall from long-term memory are likely to be words which are semantically similar to the correct items. Given TOAD, FROG may be recalled; given SKY, CLOUD may be remembered. This activity will demonstrate the tendency to store in long-term memory the deep structure (i.e., meaning) of a message rather than the surface structure (i.e., specific words or physical stimulus characteristics) used in transmitting that meaning.

At the beginning of the class period, read the following short passage from Doris Lessing's Particularly Cats to students:

In the big sycamore at the bottom of the garden, a thrush builds a new nest every year. Every year, the little birds hatch out and take their first flights down into the jaws of waiting cats. Mother bird, father bird, comes down after them and is caught. The frightened chittering and squealing of a caught bird disturbs the house. Gray cat has brought the bird in, but only to be admired for her skill, for she plays with it, tortures it-- and with what grace. Black cat crouches on the stairs and watches. But when three, four, five hours after gray cat has caught the thing, and it is dead, or nearly so, black cat takes it and tosses it up and about, in emulation of the games gray cat plays. Every summer I rescue birds from gray cat. When she brings a bird in she is proud. (p. 81)

Cognitive Views of Learning

At the end of the period, give each student a copy of the quiz on the Particularly Cats passage shown at the end of this activity and provided in Handout Master 7.1. Students are to identify those sentences in the quiz that are exact duplicates ("originals") of the sentences in the passage. The quiz contains three original sentences (#2, 9, 10), three that contain semantic changes (#4, 6, 12), and three that retain the original meaning but contain syntax changes (#1, 5, 8), and three that were not contained in the passage at all but were implied (#3, 7, 11). The asterisks in the figure below mark those cells that will contain the highest frequencies if your results match those typically found (Bransford, Barclay, & Franks, 1972).

The fact that syntactic changes are difficult to identify means that sentence meanings, not surface characteristics of those sentences, were stored in long-term memory. The difficulty that students have in identifying implied sentences as "new" illustrates the reconstructive nature of retrieval from long-term memory; that is, we tend to remember "what must have been" rather than what was.

The following diagram illustrates this principle:

ORIGINAL NEW

SENTENCE TYPE

*		ORIGINAL
	*	SEMANTICS CHANGE
		SYNTAX CHANGE
*		
	*	IMPLIED

You may wish to discuss some of the implications of this demonstration. What might the advantages be of retaining memory for meaning rather than for surface characteristics? What might be some disadvantages? How could we use this information to help students retain information?

7.12   <u>Reconstructive Memory</u>

You might want to introduce this task in the middle of some of the others. Read the words aloud, ask the students not to take notes. When reading this list to students, <u>OMIT</u> the words printed in **bold lettering**.

NIGHT	MOON	**PILLOW**	DARK
YAWN	CLOCK	CURTAIN	BLANKET
SHEET	LAMP	**STRETCH**	READ
QUIET	**LIGHT**	SNORE	DREAM
SLEEP	TOOTHBRUSH	ALARM	**TIRED**
PAJAMAS	STARS	BOOK	**BED**

Cognitive Views of Learning

Ask the students NOT to write anything but to move onto another task. After some time has passed, return to this task. Distribute the sheet of words represented in **Handout Master 7.6** and ask students to check whether or not you had read each of the words aloud previously.

Discuss the task. Some students will have falsely recognized some words as having been read aloud that in fact were not. Examine the various kinds of errors that were made and discuss the implications for a an understanding of memory.

Discussion Questions

1.   Is the digital computer an appropriate model for the human information processing system? Give reasons why the fit is appropriate and why it is not. Consider some of the implications of the victory of "Deep Blue" (a computer chess master) over the world champion Kasparov.

2. Much of the current emphasis in cognitive research is on problem-solving activities and thinking skills. Is there a place for rote memory in the curriculum?

3. How are factual knowledge and effective problem-solving linked?

4. How effective is levels of processing theory in explaining memory?

5. Compare and contrast constructivist and symbol processing models of learning. How would you determine which provided the better explanation for learning.

6. How do you promote the development of metacognition or can you? Explain.

Additional Resources for Teaching This Chapter

PRINT RESOURCES

For entertaining examples of mnemonics see Susan Ferrar's "You must remember this" (Education Life Supplement, New York Times, April 1989, pp. 34-35). She describes three types and gives many examples from history, music, mathematics, literature, science, medicine and others. These are the three types:
1. Acrostic-like sentences, in which the first letters of each word should cue a response.
2. Jingle mnemonics using rhythm or rhyme.
3. Acronym mnemonics in which each letter of a word stands for a piece of information.

REFERENCES

Bartlett, F. C. (1932). *Remembering.* New York, NY: Cambridge University Press (reissued 1995).

Benton, S., Glover, J., and Bruning, R. (1983). Levels of processing: Effect of number of decisions on prose recall. *Journal of Educational Psychology, 75*, 382-90.

Borkowski, J., Peck, V, Reid, M., & Kurtz, B. (1983). Impulsivity and strategy transfer: Metamemory as mediator. *Child Development, 54*, 459-74.

Carrell, P. L.., Pharis, B. G., and Liberto, J. C. (1989). Metacognitive strategy training for ESL reading. *TESOL Quarterly, 23*, 647-678.

Deshler, D. D. (1986). Learning strategies. An instructional alternative for low achieving adolescents. Exceptional Children, 52, 583-90.

Heller, M. F. (1986). How do you know what you know? Metacognitive modeling in the content areas. *Journal of Reading, 29*, 415-22.

Luria, A. (1968). *The mind of a mnemonist: A little book about a vast memory*. New York: Basic Books.

Reyes, M. L. & Molner, L. A. (1991). Instructional strategies for second-language learners in content areas. *Journal of Reading, 35(2)*, 96-103.

Steffe, L. P., & Gale, J. (1995). *Constructivism in education.* Hillsdale, NJ: Lawrence Erlbaum.

White, S. (1983). Pre-passage questions: The influence of structural importance. *Journal of Educational Psychology, 75*, 234-44.

FILMS, VIDEOTAPES, AND AUDIOCASSETTES

Memory: Fabric of the mind. What kind of brain chemistry can explain memory? Are different types of memory located at different areas of the brain? What is the process of forgetting? Is it possible to improve memory? This program seeks answers to these and other fascinating questions about the brain and memory at several internationally-renowned memory-research labs. From Films for the Humanities and Sciences, Inc. 28 min.

Teaching reading as thinking. This 30-minute video combines extensive research with practical experience to offer teachers this 3-step approach:

Before Reading: Help students bring purpose, prior knowledge, and focus to assignments.

During Reading: Keep students involved and accountable for reading.

After Reading : Ensure that students apply reading and go back to the text.

Teachers observe an exceptional teacher in action as she guides an elementary school class through all 3 steps. Plus, the manual contains learning activities that encourage teachers to contribute their own classroom practices to the training.
Order from: Association for Supervision and Curriculum Development (ASCD), 125 N. West St., Alexandria, VA, 22314-2798. Telephone: (703) 549-9110; FAX: (703) 549-3891.

Handout Master 7.0

Lecture Outline ----- Cognitive Views of Learning

- **Elements of the Cognitive Perspective**

- **Information Processing Model of Memory**

- **Metacognition, Regulation, and Individual Differences**

- **Becoming Knowledgeable**

- **Constructivism, Situated Learning, and Symbol Processing**

Handout Master 7.2

Episodic Memory

Characteristics	Memory 1: K - 6 grade	Memory 2: 7 - 12 grade
Location		
People Present • who • what they wore • what they did		
Feelings About the Event		
Sensory Memories of Event • smells • sounds • sights • tastes • touch		

Copyright © 1998 by Allyn and Bacon

Handout Master 7.3

Endangered Species

Case Study of an Endangered Species: Calvaria major

The Problem

Calvaria major is a large tree, native to the island of Mauritius in the western Indian Ocean. Historical forestry records indicate that Calvaria was formerly common on the island and was frequently exploited for lumber. Today, however, only 13 old and dying trees are known to survive in what is left of the original forests of Mauritius. Experienced Mauritian foresters have estimated that these trees are all more than 300 years old. In other words, no young Calvaria major trees are currently growing to replace the older ones. The species is in danger of becoming extinct.

Your Mission

You are a member of a team of scientists that has been invited to the island to investigate the situation. Your team's mission is to explain as well as possible why the species Calvaria major is failing to produce new trees and to recommend how the species might regenerate. Today, as you travel with other team members on an airplane to Mauritius, your task is to develop a plan for approaching this problem. You may adopt any strategy you wish for developing such a plan, but for our purposes today the outcome of your discussion should be organized in the following two categories:

1. Your initial hypotheses regarding this problem.

2. Additional information you would want to know that might help you narrow these hypotheses and pursue possible solutions.

Handout Master 7.4

Metacognition and Internet Search

YOUR TASK is to use the Internet to locate a vacation rental with the following characteristics:

- need the rental for one week
- should be in a quiet, beachfront area
- average temperature in the location should be 80 degrees Fahrenheit
- can accommodate children
- can accommodate a dog

What search strategies will help you find the information you need? List them here.

1.
2.
3.

How effective are you as a searcher?

================================

As you conduct your search, keep track of the actions you took and your comments on what you thought in response to the task and how you felt. you follow and complete the table below. (Hint: Most browsers keep track of where you have been. Look in the help menu of your browser for where to find a "history" of your search). An example is included.

Step/Search action	Comments/What I Thought/Felt
1. tried "vacation rental" in Altavista search engine	produced a set of links that really aren't very specific, I know I need to work harder

Copyright © 1998 by Allyn and Bacon

Handout 7.5

Quiz on Particulary Cats Passage

<u>Directions</u>: Place a check mark next to each of the sentences below that appeared verbatim in the passage from <u>Particularly Cats.</u>

_____ 1. Thrushes build nests in the big sycamore at the bottom of the garden every year.
_____ 2. Every year, the little birds hatch out and take their first flights down into the jaws of waiting cats.
_____ 3. And every year, grey cat waits at the bottom of the sycamore tree.
_____ 4. The frightened chittering and squealing of a caught bird no longer disturbs the house.
_____ 5. Crouching on the stairs, black waits.
_____ 6. Mother bird, father bird, comes down after them but are not caught
_____ 7. She waits patiently for her turn as she knows it will inevitably come.
_____ 8. But when three, four, five hours after grey cat has caught the thing and it is dead, or nearly so, black cat emulates grey cat's games, by tossing it up and about.
_____ 9. When this happens, grey cat is furious, puts her ears back, glares.
_____ 10. Grey cat has brought the bird in, but only to be admired for her skill, for she plays with it, tortures it—and with what grace.
_____ 11. She does not understand, no, not at all.
_____ 12. When she brings a bird in, she is not proud.

When your instructor rereads the passage, circle your errors in recall. In the space below, explain each error in terms of what you have learned about semantic memory.

Copyright © 1998 by Allyn and Bacon

Handout Master 7.6

Memory

Directions:

For each word listed below, decide if the word was read aloud by your instructor. Rate your confidence in your decision using a scale of 1 to 5. If you choose "1", you are indicating that you are not at all confident. If you choose a "5," you are indicating that you are absolutely confident in your decision.

    1   Not at all confident
    2   Unsure
    3   Somewhat confident
    4   Fairly confident
    5   Absolutely confident

WORD	READ ALOUD? INDICATE "Y" OR "N"	CONFIDENCE 1-5 RATING
night		
moon		
pillow		
dark		
yawn		
clock		
curtain		
blanket		
sheet		
lamp		
stretch		
read		
quiet		
light		
snore		
dream		

Copyright © 1998 by Allyn and Bacon

Handout Master 7.7

Keyword Mnemonic

SURPLUS (SYRUP) having some left over, having more than was needed

Levin, J.R., McCormick, C.B., Miller, G.E., Kessler, J., & Pressley, M. (1981). Mnemonic versus nonmnemonic vocabulary-learning strategies for children. Report from the Project on Studies in Language: Reading and Communication.

Copyright © 1998 by Allyn and Bacon

Handout Master 7.8: Links to Other Chapters

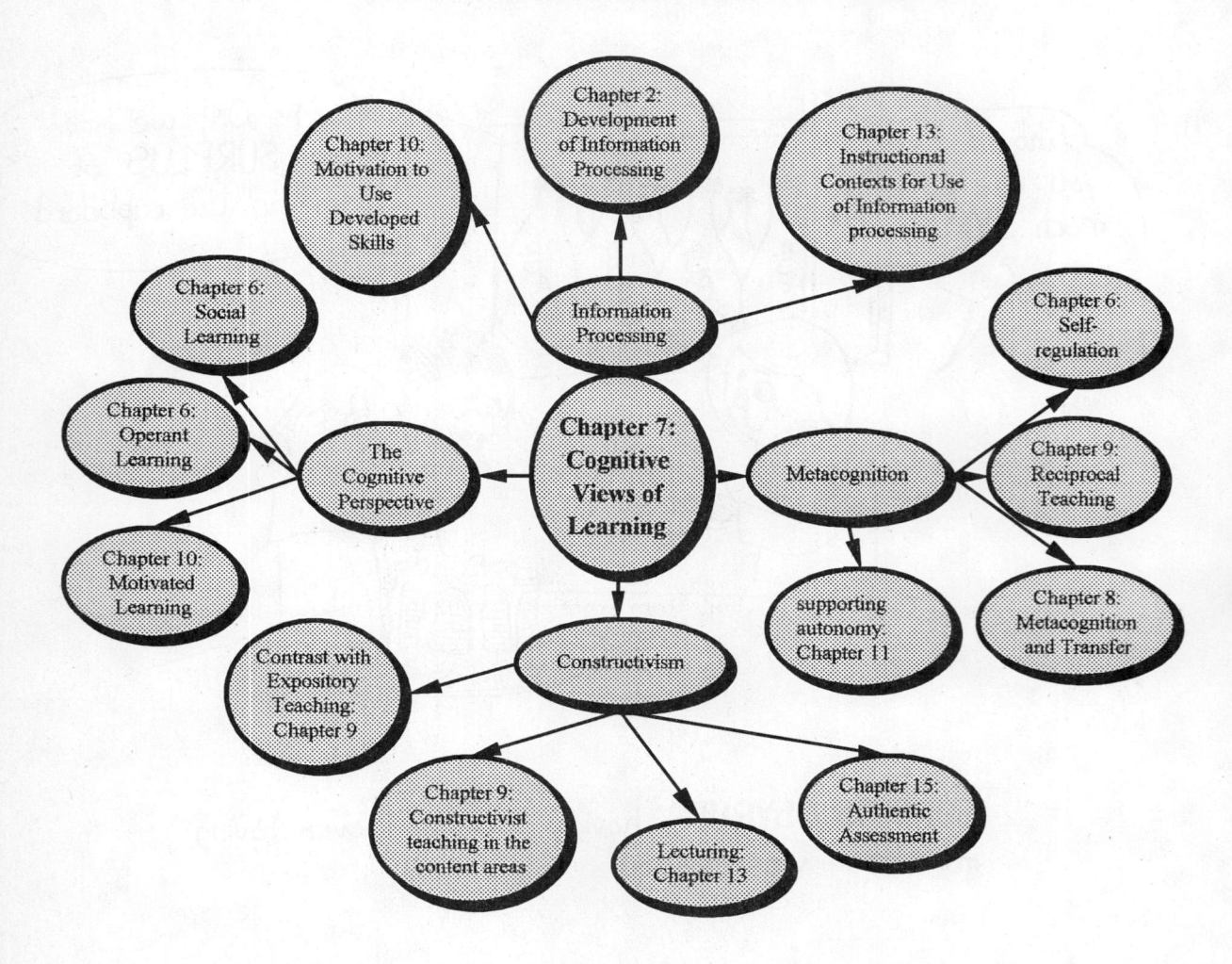

- Chapter 7: Cognitive Views of Learning
  - Information Processing
    - Chapter 10: Motivation to Use Developed Skills
    - Chapter 2: Development of Information Processing
    - Chapter 13: Instructional Contexts for Use of Information processing
  - The Cognitive Perspective
    - Chapter 6: Social Learning
    - Chapter 6: Operant Learning
    - Chapter 10: Motivated Learning
  - Metacognition
    - Chapter 6: Self-regulation
    - Chapter 9: Reciprocal Teaching
    - Chapter 8: Metacognition and Transfer
    - supporting autonomy Chapter 11
  - Constructivism
    - Contrast with Expository Teaching: Chapter 9
    - Chapter 9: Constructivist teaching in the content areas
    - Lecturing: Chapter 13
    - Chapter 15: Authentic Assessment

Copyright © 1998 by Allyn and Bacon

8

Complex Cognitive Processes

Teaching Outline

I. What Do You Think?
II. What Would You Do?
III. The Importance Of Thinking And Understanding
    A. Understanding involves appropriately transforming and using knowledge, skills, and ideas
IV. Learning And Teaching About Concepts
    A. A concept is a category used to group similar events, objects, ideas, or people
    B. A concept is an abstraction which does not exist in the real world
    C. Concepts help organize information into manageable units
    D. Views of concept learning
        1. Defining attributes or distinctive features
        2. Prototypes and exemplars
            a) prototype—the best representative of its category. Are built from experiences with many exemplars
            b) Categories have fuzzy boundaries and graded membership
            c) Exemplars—actual memories of members of a category used to compare with an item in question
        3. Concepts and schemas
    E. Strategies for teaching concepts
        1. Concept attainment
        2. Lesson components
            a) examples and nonexamples
            b) relevant and irrelevant attributes
            c) the name of the concept
            d) a definition
            e) visual aids can improve learning of many concepts
        3. Lesson structure
            a) Present examples and nonexamples before discussing attributes or definitions
            b) Show a wide variety of examples to avoid undergeneralization or overgeneralization
        4. Extending and connecting concepts
            a) Have students use concept
            b) Can use concept "map" to illustrate understanding of a concept

Complex Cognitive Processes

V. Problem Solving
   A. Problems have:
      1. an initial state
      2. a desired outcome
      3. a path for reaching that outcome.
   B. Problem solving: General or domain-specific?
   C. A general problem-solving strategy (IDEAL)
      1. Identify problems and opportunities
      2. Defining goals and representing the problem
         a) Focusing attention
         b) Understanding the words
         c) Understanding the whole problem
         d) Translation and schema training
         e) Results of problem representation
      3. Exploring possible solution strategies
         a) Algorithms—step-by-step prescription for achieving a goal. Usually domain-specific
         b) Heuristics—general strategies that might lead to the right answer
            (1) means-end analysis—dividing the problem into a number of intermediate (sub) goals and then figuring out a way to solve each subgoal
            (2) distance reduction
            (3) working-backwards strategy
            (4) analogical thinking
      4. Anticipating, acting, and looking back
   D. Factors that hinder problem solving
      1. Functional fixedness—the inability to consider unconventional uses for materials that have a specific function
      2. Response set
   E. The importance of flexibility
   F. Insight—the sudden reorganization or reconceptualization of a problem that clarifies the problem and suggests a feasible solution.
   G. Effective problem solving: What do the experts do?
      1. Expert knowledge
         a) Background knowledge that is elaborated and well practiced and can be used to organize information for easier learner and retrieval
         b) Pattern recognition
         c) Representation of the problem
         d) Large store of productions or condition-action schemas about how to solve problems
         e) Planning and monitoring
      2. Expert teachers

Complex Cognitive Processes

                a)   Have a sense of what is typical in classrooms
                b)   Many of their teaching routines have become automatic
                c)   Work from integrated sets of principles instead of individual events
                d)   Deep and well-organized knowledge of their subjects
                e)   Novice knowledge may involve misconceptions about things that are counterintuitive, for example, in physics
         3.   Guidelines: Problem Solving
    H.   Becoming an expert student: Learning strategies and study skills
         1.   Learning strategies—ideas for accomplishing learning goals (plans)
         2.   Learning tactics—specific techniques that make up the plans
         3.   Students must be exposed to a variety of different strategies
         4.   Students need to be taught conditional knowledge about when, where, and how to apply the various strategies
         5.   Students must develop the desire to use these skills
         6.   Direct instruction in schematic knowledge
         7.   Specific strategies
                a)   Underlining and highlighting
                b)   Taking notes
                c)   Visual tools, e.g., "maps"
                d)   PQ4R—Preview, Question, Read, Reflect, Recite, and Review (appropriate for older children)
         8.   Guidelines: Study Skills and Learning Strategies
VI.   Teaching And Learning About Thinking
    A.   Stand-alone programs for developing thinking
    B.   Developing thinking in every class—encourage analysis, problem solving, and reasoning through the regular lessons of the curriculum
    C.   The language of thinking
    D.   Critical thinking
    E.   Thinking as a "State of Mind"
VII.   Teaching For Transfer
    A.   Defining transfer—when something previously learned influences current learning or when solving an earlier problem affects how a subsequent problem is solved
    B.   Specific transfer—when knowledge is applied to a very similar situation
    C.   General transfer—when knowledge is applied to a dissimilar situation
    D.   A contemporary view of transfer (Salomon and Perkins)
         1.   Low-road transfer (automatic transfer of highly practices skills)
         2.   High-road transfer (consciously application of abstract knowledge learned in one situation to a different situation);
                a)   forward-reaching transfer (looking forward to applying the knowledge gained)
                b)   backward-reaching transfer (looking back to other problems to solve a current one)
         3.   Transfer of learning strategies

Complex Cognitive Processes

       E.   Teaching for positive transfer
            1.   Transfer cannot be expected, because learning is situated
            2.   What is worth learning?
            3.   How can teachers help?
                a)   have students be actively involved in the learning process; encourage them to form abstractions
                b)   overlearning—practicing a skill past the point of mastery
       F.   Stages of transfer for strategies
            1.   Acquisition phase (receive instruction about a strategy and how to use it; practice the strategy)
            2.   Retention phase (more practice with feedback)
            3.   Transfer phase (solve new problems that appear different than the original ones)

VIII.   Guidelines: Enlisting Family Support for Encouraging Transfer
       A.   Keep families informed about their child's curriculum so they can support learning
       B.   Give families ideas for how they might practice, extend, or apply learning from school
       C.   Show connections between learning in school and life outcomes
       D.   Make families partners in practicing learning strategies

---

Learning Activities and Related Research

ACTIVITIES	HANDOUTS
Chapter 8	8.0 Lecture outline
Cooperative Activities	
8.1 Teaching a concept effectively	
8.2 Expert and novice teachers' problem-solving	8.1. Concept map: Problem-solving
	8.2 Teacher's Problem Solving: A case study
Research Activities	
8.3 Can thinking be taught?	
Using Technology	
8.4 What kind of knowledge?	
Field Experience	
8.5 Critical thinking in the classroom	8.3 Strategy list: 35 dimensions of critical thought
Other Teaching Activities	
8.6 Learning a concept: Weetags Experiment	8.4 Weetags
8.7 Concept attainment lesson	
8.8 Students' ideas in the science classroom	
8.9 The need for representation	
8.10 Functional fixedness	
8.11 Critical thinking strategies and fallacies for learning	
8.12 Analyzing learning strategies	
	8.5 Concept Map: Links to Other Chapters

Complex Cognitive Processes

Cooperative Activities

8.1   Teaching A Concept Effectively

Have students work in pairs or small teams to prepare and give a brief lesson on one concept. Have the students alternate as they role-play presenters, subjects, and observers. Discuss with students how they would evaluate subjects' attainment of the concept.

8.2   Expert and Novice Teacher's Problem Solving

Have your students interview new teachers and more experienced teachers about how they would respond to the dilemma in the Teacher's Casebook. In groups, have them compare and contrast more expert and novice teacher's problem-solving. Use the information from the text on the nature of problem solving to guide this discussion. What effect does experience have? Use **Handout 8.2** to practice this discussion on.

Research Activities

8.3   Can Thinking Be Taught?

Have your students locate information in the library that speaks to this issue. They should locate research on the topic and evaluate the quality of the work they find. They should prepare a one page summary of their findings and be able to defend it to their peers.

Using Technology

8.4   What Kind of Knowledge?

Have your students locate an article related to any topic relevant to education on the World Wide Web. Ask them to analyze the type of knowledge needed to locate the information effectively and the nature of the kind of knowledge utilized in the article.

Field Experience

8.5   Dimensions Of Critical Thinking

Observe a classroom in which the students are having a literature, science, or social studies lesson. Can you find evidence of encouragement of critical or creative thinking or problem solving? Examine **Handout Master 8.3**, *Strategy List: 35 Dimensions Of Critical Thought* (taken from R. Paul, A. J. A. Binker, D. Martin, and K. Adamson. *Critical thinking handbook: High school.* Center for Critical Thinking and

Complex Cognitive Processes

Moral Critique, Sonoma State University, Rohnert Park, CA.). Using one or more of the dimensions of critical thinking given, provide a critique of the lesson you have seen.

Other Teaching Activities

8.6   <u>Learning A Concept-- Weetags Experiment</u>

Display or distribute **Handout Master 8.4**, "WEETAGS," to the class and ask them to figure out what *weetags* are. (The defining attribute is that the head and body are the same shape.) Discuss the following questions:
1. What irrelevant attributes did you consider as defining attributes?
2. What is the purpose of the non-instances?
3. Would the non-instances have been sufficient if the second one was omitted (the non-instance of 2 ears and 4 arms)? (No, because then you could reach the conclusion that WEETAGS are defined by 2 ear and 4 arms.)
4. What process did you go through to formulate a definition?
5. Would it have been easier if you had been told the defining attribute at the beginning? Would it have been as interesting?
6. Was this an eg-rule or a rule-eg presentation?

8.7   <u>Concept Attainment Lesson</u>

From Joyce, B., & Weil, M. (1988). *Models of teaching*, (3rd ed.) Englewood Cliffs, NJ: Prentice-Hall, pp. 25-26.

Mrs. Stern's eighth grade class in Houston, Texas, has been studying the characteristics of the largest cities in the United States. They have collected data on size, ethnicity of population, types of industry, location, and proximity to natural resources. Working in committees, the students have collected information and summarized it on a series of charts now pasted up around the room. One Wednesday in November, Mrs. Stern says, "Today let's try a series of exercises designed to help us understand these cities better. I have identified a number of concepts that help us compare and contrast them. I will identify the ideas that I have in mind. I'm going to start with the city that's a 'yes' and then one that's a 'no', and so forth. Think about what the 'yeses' have in common. Then write down after the second 'yes' the idea that you think connects those two places, and keep testing those ideas as we go along. Let's being with our own city," she says. "Houston is a 'yes'." The students look at the information about Houston, its size, industries, location, ethnic composition. Then she points to Baltimore, Maryland. "Baltimore is a 'no'," she says.

Then she points to San José, California. "Here is another 'yes'," she comments. The students look for a moment at the information about San José. Two or three raise their hands. "I think I know what it is," one offers. "Hold on to your idea," she replies. "See if you're right." She then selects another 'yes' -- Seattle, Washington. Detroit, Michigan is a 'no'. Miami, Florida is a 'yes'. She continues until all students think they know what the concept is, and then they begin to share concepts. "What do you think it is,

Jill?" "The 'yeses' all have mild climates," says Jill. "That is, it doesn't get very cold in any of them." "It gets pretty cold in Salt Lake City." objects another. "Yes, but not as cold as in Chicago, Detroit, or Baltimore," another student counters. "I think the 'yeses' are all rapidly growing cities. Each one of them increased more than 10 percent during the last ten years."

There is some discussion about this. "All the 'yeses' have lots of different industries," volunteers another. "That's true, but almost all these cities do," replies another student. Finally the students decide the 'yeses' are all cities that are growing very fast and have relatively mild climates. "That's right," agrees Mrs. Stern. "That's exactly what I had in mind. Now let's do this again. This time I want to begin with Baltimore, Maryland, and now it is a 'yes'." The exercise is repeated several times. Students learn that Mrs. Stern has grouped the cities on the basis of their relationship to waterways, natural resources, ethnic composition and several other dimensions.

The students are beginning to see patterns in their data. Finally she says, "Now, each of you try to group the cities in a way that you think is important. Then take turns and lead us through this exercise, helping us to see which ones you place in which category. Then we'll discuss the ways we can look at cities and how we can use different categories for different purposes.

8.8 Students' Ideas In The Science Classroom

From *Harvard Education Letter* (1988, January). Students' ideas in the science classroom, 4-6.

A second-grade teacher brought mealworms to school so her students could observe metamorphosis at first hand. As she expected, youngsters eagerly watched the transformation from larva to pupa - but when the adult form emerged they were flabbergasted and asked her who had put a beetle in the jar. Once persuaded that mealworms were really turning into beetles, the children attributed the change to the mealworms' diet of potato bits and the beetles' color to the color of the food they had eaten as larvae. Straightening out these misconceptions required a series of experiments in which they kept mealworms in several containers and fed them different diets. As we all do every day, these children constructed an intuitive explanation for a phenomenon they had observed. They were fortunate that their teacher encouraged them to talk about their theories and then arranged experiences that would help them develop a better understanding of what they had seen.

Not all students are so lucky. As many as 80 percent of beginning college students -- even those who have taken up to two years of high school physics -- predict that if a heavier object and a lighter object are dropped simultaneously from the same height, the heavier object will hit the ground first. Audrey Champagne and Leopold Klopfer of the University of Pittsburgh and Richard Gunstone of Monash University in Australia, who have questioned college students about a variety of physical situations, think instruction has had such a shallow impact on most of them because their own intuitive theories were never exposed, challenged, and transformed. They point out that even very young children come to the classroom with definite notions about how and why objects move.

Complex Cognitive Processes

Having developed these ideas through experience, students stick to them and find them more sensible than the science they are taught in school. While they may play along with new vocabulary or produce textbook-perfect answers on tests, their basic ideas often remain unchanged.

Discussion: How can teachers work with students to build upon and transform their intuitive ideas about such concepts as the nature of objects, the movement of objects, and the physical and chemical changes which take place in nature? How can the following cognitive learning theories be applied to assist in these processes: Concept attainment, transfer of learning, problem solving, and teaching critical thinking skills.

8.9   The Need for Representations

Read the following to your students.

> I am going to read a problem to you but I would like you not to take notes. Listen carefully.
>
> A bus-driver leaves the terminus at 7.00 a.m. It is the first run of the morning and save for the bus-driver, the bus is empty. At the first stop, the driver picks up 7 passengers. At the next stop, 4 people get off the bus and 7 more people get on. It is now raining and the new passengers are very wet. At the next stop, 5 passengers get on the bus and 8 get off. At the next stop, one person gets off but no-one gets on. At the next stop, 4 people get on but no-one gets off. It has stopped raining and people are complaining less. At the next stop, 6 people get off and 2 get on.
>
> **How many stops did the bus make?**

Students are usually counting the number of people on the bus as the problem structure suggests one of addition and subtraction. Because they are being prevented from making any external representation that might allow them to go back and check, they are often unable to answer the question. This activity can be used to demonstrate the important of external representations as supports for a limited working memory system. If the students could make any marks that represent the bus-stops, they can easily check for the answer to the question.

8.10   Functional Fixedness

The following activity is taken from the *Instructor's manual for Morris, C. Psychology: An introduction*, (6th ed., 1988) Englewood Cliffs, NJ: Prentice Hall, p. I-39.

The negative impact of functional fixedness is evident in several examples. Many people fail to arrive at insight into a problem because they become "fixed" on an incorrect set of responses. Fixation can be caused by any one of a number of factors, including the following:

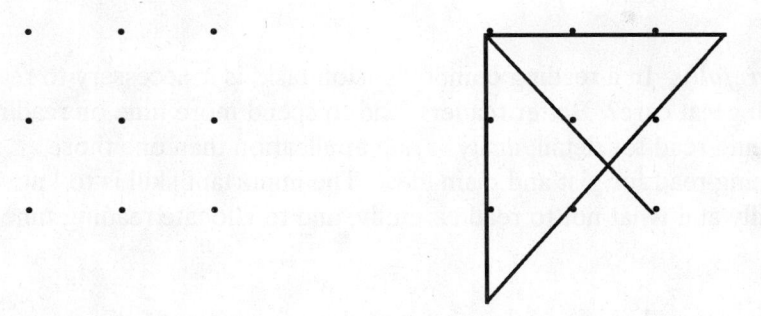

A. The person may make an implicit but incorrect premise. For example, consider the problem of connecting all nine dots in the following figure with 4 lines, without lifting your pencil from the page. So long as the subject cannot break the implicit premise that the lines should not go outside the bounds of the figure, the problem is not solvable. The person may fail to recognize the suitability of an object for solving the problem; e.g., a shoe to pound a nail, the pop top from a soft drink can as a loop to hang a picture on the wall, or a dime as an emergency screwdriver.

B. The person may fail to abandon the most obvious (but incorrect) solution to reach the actual solution.

C. The person may continue to use habitual mode of response which makes it more difficult to see a new and better approach to the solution of the problem.

Discuss the ways in which the present educational system is conducive to the development of these types of fixations. Is it possible to teach students to avoid these patterns?

8.11   Strategies And Fallacies For Problem Solving

The following is taken from R. J. Sternberg (1987), "Teaching intelligence: The application of cognitive psychology to the improvement of intellectual skills," in J. B. Baron and R. J. Sternberg, *Teaching thinking skills: Theory and practice."* New York: W. H. Freeman.

Training students with specific instructions on how to take tests will often lead to one or more of the unfortunate strategies listed below.

Complex Cognitive Processes

1. *Work as quickly as you can.* Research shows that it is not the total time spent on a task that is important, but rather how one allocates one's time. Good reasoners on a complex task spend more time structuring what they are going to do. They know when to work faster and when to work slower. One must budget one's time in an effective way.

2. *Read everything carefully.* In a reading comprehension task, is it necessary to read all of the passages with great care? Better readers tend to spend more time on reading passages that are being read for detail, analysis and application than one those passages that are being read for gist and main idea. The important skill is to know what to read carefully and what not to read carefully, and to allocate reading time accordingly.

3. *Memorize a lot of new vocabulary.* If the goal is to do well on standardized tests, should one memorize large numbers of vocabulary words? People who have a good vocabulary are not those who have memorized lists of long words. They are good at learning words in context. Teaching people to learn from context puts them in a position to be able to increase their vocabularies.

4. *Learn the best strategy for solving each type of problem.* Is learning a process of acquiring specific strategies for solving problems of a given type? Probably not. There is often no one best strategy for solving problems. One should prepare a range of strategies, along with intelligent strategy selection.

5. *Use all of the information in a problem.* Is all the information in a problem relevant? Probably not. Some information my be misleading or irrelevant. Very often the problem itself is to figure out which information is relevant. We need to encode selectively, not to attempt to fully encode everything in sight.

8.12   Analyzing Learning Strategies

Have your students complete the LASSI (Learning and Study Strategies Inventory; Weinstein, C. E., Palmer, D. R., & Schulte, A. C.; Available from H & H Publishing Co., Inc., 1231 Kapp Drive, Clearwater, FL 34625-2116; Phone Number (813) 442-7760). The inventory takes about 25 minutes to complete and score. Your students will be able to self-score the inventory and develop a profile of their strengths and weaknesses in terms of their learning strategies. Ask them to analyze their profiles as described below.
1. identify a weakness in their learning strategy profile.
2. identify a course they are currently taking in which this weakness might be a problem.
3. develop a plan for addressing the weakness within the context of the course they identified.
4. implement and evaluate the plan.

Complex Cognitive Processes

For example, a student might have decided that "Time Management" was a problem. The student would need to describe how time management problems might be a problem in a course he or she are taking (e.g., Physics). He or she would need to describe how he or she plans to improve time management in the course identified. The student should also evaluate his or her success.

Discussion Questions

1. Why do you think research has shown teachers' assessments of students' creativity to be poorly related to the creativity these students have shown later in life? How could teachers be more on target?

2. Many programs for teaching thinking skills have been developed and implemented in the classroom. Use the articles by Bransford et al., Sternberg and Kastoor, and Feldman to instigate a discussion. What is the instructional theory on which these programs are based? How effective are the programs? What are some of the concerns about valid evaluation of these programs?

3. Why is transfer so hard to do? How can transfer be improved?

4. Should learning strategies need to be taught explicitly?

5. What role does factual knowledge play in expert problem solving?

Additional Resources for Teaching This Chapter

PRINT RESOURCES

Chance, P. (1985). Thinking in the classroom. A survey of programs. Wolfeboro, NH: Teachers College Press. This book thoroughly describes eight of the most important curriculum programs and instructional strategies intended to develop thinking abilities: CoRT Thinking Lessons (Edward deBono), Productive Thinking Program (Martin V. Covington), Philosophy for Children (Matthew Lipman), Odyssey, Instrumental Enrichment (Reuben Feuerstein), Problem Solving and Comprehension, Techniques of Learning, and Thoughtful Teaching.

Little, L. W. and Greenberg, I. W. (1991). Problem solving: Critical thinking and communication skills. White Plains, NY: Longman Pub. Co. Activities for limited English proficient students which combine reading, dialogue, and discussion. Targeted for the junior and senior high school student. Characters involved in the vignettes are drawn from a wide variety of cultures.

Marzano, R. (1986). A framework for teaching thinking. Educational Leadership, 43 (8), 20-27.) Marzano, at the Mid-Continent Regional Educational Laboratory, incorporated a set of thinking skill tactics into a program of K-12 thinking skills used by

Complex Cognitive Processes

several school districts. These tactics are now featured in an ASCD Training Program called TACTICS for Thinking.

Midwest Publications has a wide variety of critical thinking print materials and computer software. For a catalog, write Midwest Publications, P. O. Box 448, Garden Grove, CA, 93950.

Perkins, D. (1986) Thinking frames. Educational Leadership, 43 (8), 4-10. Perkin's work in building mental "frameworks" or concept mapping is summarized.

Raths, L. E., Wasserman, S., Jonas, A. and Rothstein, A. J. (1986). Teaching for thinking: Theory, strategies, and activities for the classroom *(2nd Ed.)*. New York: Teachers College Press. The authors make specific recommendations and practical suggestions on how to implement critical thinking through classroom applications at both the elementary and secondary levels. Special attention is given to the teacher's role as well as to problems that may be preventing more widespread acceptance of thinking programs.

Sternberg, R. J. (1986). Intelligence applied. San Diego: Harcourt Brace Jovanovich. Robert J. Sternberg has distilled and simplified his Triarchic Theory of Human Intelligence into a training program on critical thinking and problem solving skills. His book provides a theoretical base for understanding as well as increasing intellectual skills. Many practical examples drawn from many fields, and discusses concretely why the program will benefit students.

Stice, J. E., Ed., (1987). Developing critical thinking and problem solving abilities. San Francisco: Jossey-Bass. This book offers methods for successfully teaching problem solving and critical analysis to students in all disciplines. It provides exercises that students can use to improve critical thinking skills. Order TL#28 from Jossey-Bass Inc., Publishers, 350 Sansome St., San Francisco, CA 94104.

The following titles are an excellent source of additional application activities:

Benjamin, L. T.. & Lowman, K. D. (Eds.) (1981). Activities handbook for the teaching of psychology. Washington, DC.: American Psychological Association. The following activities are applicable for this chapter:

Engle, T. L. & Snellgrove, L. Performance and negative transfer. (Activity 30). Subjects in the demonstration are timed on how fast they sort cards, in a particular pattern. After 10 trials the pattern is reversed for a second set of 10 trials, after which the two sets of scores can be compared and discussed with respect to negative transfer.

Snellgrove, L. (1981). Problems of set. (Activity 42). Eight problems are presented in which the first six require a particular type of solution, but problems #7 and #8 can be solved more directly. The class can be split into two groups with the first given all the problems in order and the second given some of the first six problems and #7 and #8, to demonstrate that the first group is more likely to experience response set.

REFERENCES

Bransford, R. J., Burns, M. S., Delclos, V. R., & Vye, N. J. (1987). Teaching thinking: Evaluating evaluations and broadening the data base. Educational Leadership, 44, 68-70.

Collins, C., & Mangieri, J. (1992). Teaching thinking: An agenda for the 21st century. Hillsdale, NJ: Lawrence Erlbaum.

Feldman, R. D. (1986). What are thinking skills? Instructor, 95, 34-38.

Schiever, S. W. (1991). A comprehensive approach to teaching thinking. Needham Heights, MA: Allyn & Bacon.

Sternberg, R. J., & Kastoor, B. (1987). Synthesis of research on the effectiveness of intellectual skills programs: Snake-oil remedies or miracle cues? Educational Leadership, 44, 60-67.

Tishman, S., Perkins, D. N., & Jay, E. (1995). The thinking classroom: Learning and teaching in a culture of thinking. Needham Heights, MA: Allyn & Bacon.

FILMS, VIDEOTAPES, AND AUDIOCASSETTES

The following resources can be ordered from Association for Supervision and Curriculum Development (ASCD), 125 N. West St., Alexandria, VA, 22314-2798:

Analyzing approaches to teaching thinking, by R. Brandt and D. Perkins, audio. An outline for choosing a successful program, and three examples of thinking skills programs that work. Stock #612-87616C2, $9.00.

ASCD Library of Teaching Episodes. The following is an example of a video from the *ASCD Library of Teaching Episodes*. Each features an actual scene from a classroom which has been selected and edited for use with pre- or in-service teachers. *Crimes*. 7th grade social studies, 20 min.

Critical thinking in elementary school, by R. Paul, audio. Understand how to revise lesson plans in reading, social studies, and science to emphasize critical thinking. Stock #612-87617C2.

Planning a thinking skills program, by B. Beyer, audio. Discover which thinking skills can be most readily taught and how to incorporate them into your current curriculum. Stock #612-87618C2.

Tactics for thinking. This video training program introduces teachers to 22 instructional techniques that help students become better thinkers through concentration, memorization, and compare/contrasting. The complete package contains a 250-page trainer's manual and 8-hr video presentations.

Complex Cognitive Processes

Teaching skillful thinking. Four videotapes in this training program summarize research on thinking skills, demonstrate how teachers can facilitate it among their students, and how several schools are using the program to improve student achievement.

Teaching thinking in elementary schools. A complete framework for how to teach thinking in elementary schools with this set of audiotapes. Stock #612-87630C2.

The creative spirit. Ideas, inventions, solutions. How do they happen? And how can we nurture the process, the creative spirit, that produces innovation? This four-part PBS series from IBM, produced by Alvin H. Perlmutter, blends celebrity sketches, animation and everyday examples in an entertaining look at creativity. The series takes us to the home, the workplace, the classroom and the community to illustrate that creativity is not the domain of the intellectual elite. The series looks at ways to increase your own creativity. Scientists, artists, doctors, musicians, actors, and students share their thoughts to create a vivid experience, a celebration of the creative spirit in us all. *Inside creativity, creative beginnings, The creative spirit at work, The creative community,* series of 4 one-hour videos:

The development of children's thinking and teaching in the River Edge, New Jersey, Schools, by E. Fusco and J. Barell, audio. The important "why-to" information you need about adapting instruction to children's cognitive development is in this tape. Stock #612-87619C2.

What human beings do when they behave intelligently, by A. Costa, audio. Know when your thinking skills program is working by using this tape's list of 12 characteristics that indicate growth in student thinking abilities.

A complete catalog of audio- and videotape resources for critical thinking can be obtained by writing The Foundation for Critical Thinking, 4655 Sonoma Mountain Road, Santa Rosa, CA 95404 (707) 546-4926 or contact the Center for Critical Thinking and Moral Critique, Sonoma State University, Rohnert Park, CA 94928.

Handout Master 8.0

Lecture Outline ----- Complex Cognitive Processes

- **Thinking and Understanding**

- **Learning and Teaching about Concepts**

- Problem Solving

- Learning Strategies and Study Skills

- Teaching and Learning about Thinking

- Teaching for Transfer

Handout Master 8.1 : Problem Solving

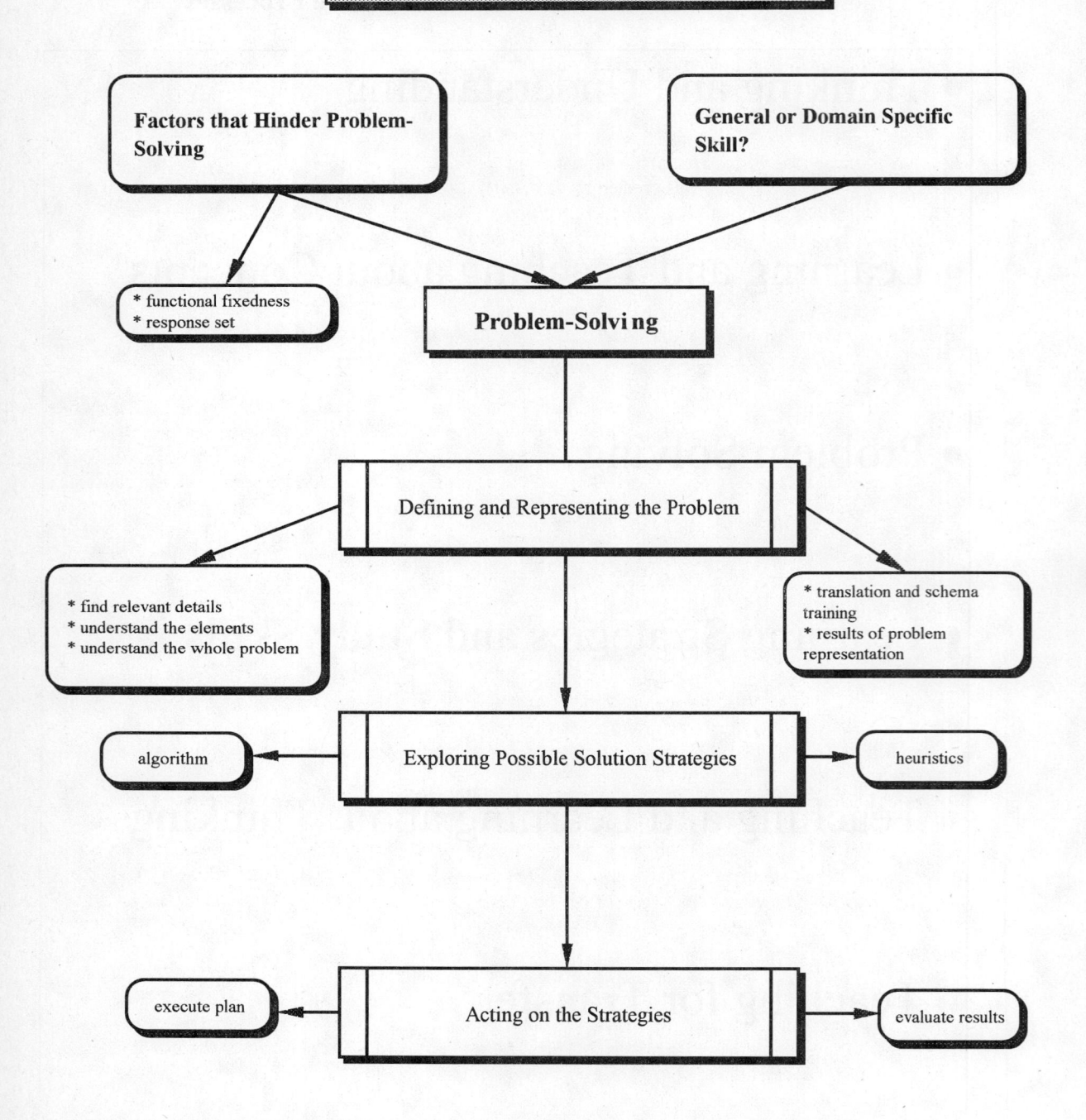

Factors that Hinder Problem-Solving

General or Domain Specific Skill?

* functional fixedness
* response set

Problem-Solving

Defining and Representing the Problem

* find relevant details
* understand the elements
* understand the whole problem

* translation and schema training
* results of problem representation

algorithm ← **Exploring Possible Solution Strategies** → heuristics

execute plan ← **Acting on the Strategies** → evaluate results

Copyright © 1998 by Allyn and Bacon

214

Handout Master 8.2

Teacher Problem Solving: A Case Study

Elizabeth Rhodes sighed as she unplugged the overhead projector and pushed it to the back of the room. Well," she thought, "at least when I do all the talking it is easier." "Only two months until the calculus exam, "she mused aloud. "Will they be ready?" This question was one she asked herself every year at this time; it was always accompanied by the same uncomfortable uncertainty. But this year, her cause for concern ran deeper. She looked toward the back of the room and the projector. "Am I really helping them by standing in front of them day after day talking to them?" As she left the room and headed toward the faculty lounge, she was greeted by her long-time friend Clare, from the English department. Clare could see something was bothering Elizabeth. "What's the matter?" "It's those kids in my AP calculus class again," responded Elizabeth. She plunked herself down next to Clare with a fresh cup of coffee. "I still don't think I'm teaching them all I could be. All I'm doing is assigning homework and giving them tests. They seem happy that everything is teacher-directed, but I don't think that's the right way to teach this class." Elizabeth leaned forward and spoke earnestly. "What I want-these kids are seniors, after all- -is to make them independent thinkers and problem solvers. Math is a tool for philosophers and explorers. These kids are smart enough to use math to create and discover, not just to pass tests."

[Elizabeth goes on to describe her efforts to have the class work in cooperative groups. Many of the superior students resent receiving a grade based on an average of the group's performance. Several students disliked having to share their problem solutions with others. Here is a typical class session:]
"Are the tests corrected yet, Ms. Rhodes?" Ralph spoke politely as he and Bill burst through the classroom door. "Yeah, how'd we do? Asked Bill as they both made a beeline for her desk. Elizabeth replied, "Yes, yes they're corrected, but first we have some work to do. Take a seat, OK?" At this, Bill and Ralph turned and noticed the configuration of desks in the room. "Oh, no, not again," moaned Bill under his breath. Karen and several others students were now entering the room. "We're not working in groups again, Ms. Rhodes, are we?" asked Karen. Elizabeth had known this would not be an easy period. "Sit anywhere you like for now, class; later we'll count off by numbers and get into groups. I have your tests from yesterday, but I'll return them at the end of class so you won't be distracted from our activity." "Could we please see the tests?" entreated Melissa. Her question prompted several others to join in. "How many A's?" "What was the top score?" "No, no, I said later! You did not do badly, any of you, so relax. But I do think you all benefit from some exercises that force you to consider opinions and discuss alternative solutions. So we're going to work together today to do just that. Count off by fives; Bill, you start."

[The class begins to work on problems which Elizabeth has given them in packets. After a brief period of letting the groups work on their own, she circulates among the tables to find one pair of girls discussing a yearbook writing assignment, another girl covertly doing a homework assignment that is due at the end of the class period, another group who has let one boy do the problems for everyone, and a fourth group listening while two members argued over a solution. As one student asked Elizabeth if they would be graded on their group work, other students started a chorus of complaints against being graded as a group.]

With only ten minutes remaining in the period, Elizabeth returned yesterday's tests and began reviewing a difficult problem. "Can anyone share an alternative idea about the best answer to this problem? She scanned the room for volunteers but saw, from the expressions on students' faces, that she might easily wait forever. "All right, then, listen. In this case, B is the better answer because it is expressed as a coordinate, not a point, and when dealing with graphs…"As Elizabeth was finishing the explanation, the students interrupted her. "One answer's the same as the other! Anybody with either answer ought to get credit!" The bell rang before Elizabeth could attempt an answer, and five or six students immediately headed for her desk as the rest gathered books and papers and rose to leave. As the line of students asking for extra points formed, Elizabeth looked past her students and gazed at the overhead projector sitting silently and invitingly in the rear.

Copyright © 1998 by Allyn and Bacon

Handout Master 8.2

Teacher Problem Solving: A Case Study (continued)

Discuss with the students the importance of incorporating creative and alternative problem solving techniques in math. How is the emphasis placed on individual grades and test points detrimental to this process? Since the students are preparing for the Advanced Placement calculus examination, which is graded individually, it is fair to them to encourage them to work in groups during their calculus class?
Source: Silverman, R., Welty, W.M. and Lyon, S. (1992). <u>Case studies for teacher problem solving</u>. New York: McGraw-Hill. Inc., pp.79-85.

Copyright © 1998 by Allyn and Bacon

Handout Master 8.3

Strategy List: 35 Dimensions of Critical Thought

A. Affective Strategies

S-1 Thinking independently
S-2 Developing insight into egocentricity or sociocentricity
S-3 Exercising fair-mindedness
S-4 Exploring thoughts underlying feelings and feeling underlying thoughts
S-5 Developing intellectual humility and suspending judgment
S-6 Developing intellectual courage
S-7 Developing intellectual good faith or integrity
S-8 Developing intellectual perseverance
S-9 Developing confidence in reason

B. Cognitive Strategies - MACRO-ABILITIES

S-10 Refining generalizations and avoiding oversimplifications
S-11 Comparing analogous situations: Transferring insights to new texts
S-12 Developing one's perspective: Creating or exploring beliefs, arguments, or theories
S-13 Clarifying issues, conclusions, or beliefs
S-14 Clarifying and analyzing the meanings of words or phrases
S-15 Developing criteria for evaluation: Clarifying values and standards
S-16 Evaluating the credibility of sources of information
S-17 Questioning deeply: raising and pursuing root or significant questions
S-18 Analyzing or evaluating arguments, interpretations, beliefs, or theories
S-19 Generating or assessing solutions
S-20 Analyzing or evaluating actions or policies
S-21 Reading critically: Clarifying or critiquing texts
S-22 Listening critically: The art of silent dialogue
S-23 Making interdisciplinary connections
S-24 Practicing Socratic discussion: Clarifying and questioning beliefs, theories, or perspectives
S-25 Reasoning dialogically: Comparing perspectives, interpretations, or theories
S-26 Reasoning dialectically: Evaluating perspectives, interpretations, or theories

C. Cognitive Strategies - MICRO-SKILLS

S-27 Comparing and contrasting ideals with actual practice
S-28 Thinking precisely about thinking: using critical vocabulary
S-29 Noting significant similarities and differences
S-30 Examining or evaluating assumptions
S-31 Distinguishing relevant from irrelevant facts
S-32 Making plausible inferences, predictions, or interpretations
S-33 Evaluating evidence and alleged facts
S-34 Recognizing contradictions
S-35 Exploring implications and consequences

Source; R. Paul, A.J.A. Binker, D. Martin, and K. Adamson. Critical Thinking Handbook; High School. Center for Critical Thinking and Moral Critique (Sonoma State University, Rohnert Park, CA), 56.

Copyright © 1998 by Allyn and Bacon

Handout 8.4

Weetags

These are all WEETAGS --

These are not WEETAGS --

Which of these are WEETAGS?

218

Handout Master 8.5: Links to Other Chapters

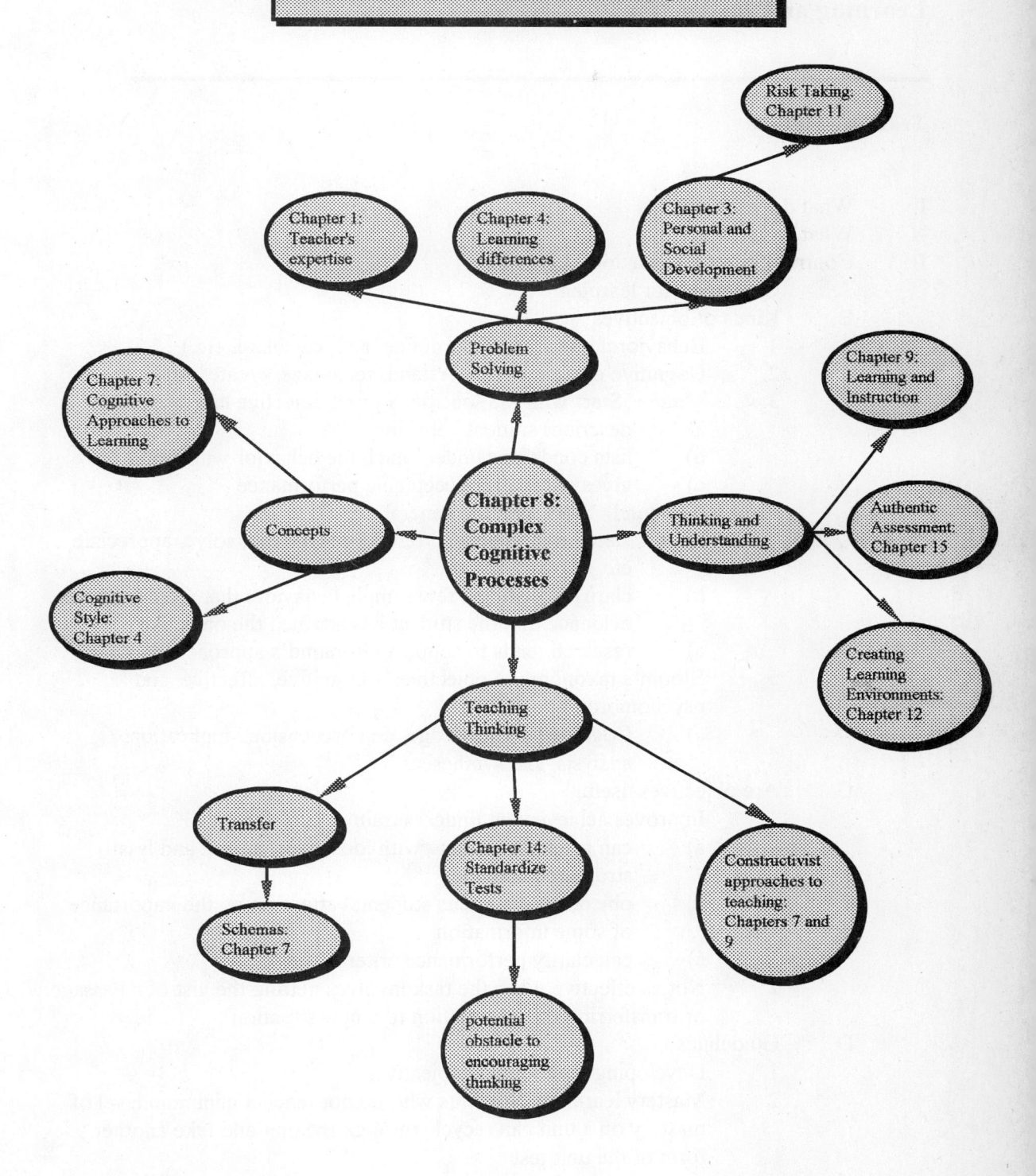

```
                                              Risk Taking:
                                              Chapter 11
                                                  ↑
      Chapter 1:      Chapter 4:        Chapter 3:
      Teacher's       Learning          Personal and
      expertise       differences       Social
                                        Development
           ↖            ↑            ↗
                  Problem
                  Solving
                      ↑                              Chapter 9:
  Chapter 7:                                         Learning and
  Cognitive                                          Instruction
  Approaches to                                          ↑
  Learning
      ↖                                              Authentic
        Concepts ← Chapter 8:    → Thinking and →    Assessment:
      ↙            Complex         Understanding     Chapter 15
  Cognitive       Cognitive                              ↓
  Style:          Processes                          Creating
  Chapter 4                                          Learning
                      ↓                              Environments:
                  Teaching                           Chapter 12
                  Thinking
              ↙       ↓        ↘
     Transfer    Chapter 14:    Constructivist
        ↓        Standardize    approaches to
     Schemas:    Tests          teaching:
     Chapter 7      ↓           Chapters 7 and 9
                 potential
                 obstacle to
                 encouraging
                 thinking
```

Copyright © 1998 by Allyn and Bacon

Learning and Instruction

9

Learning and Instruction

Teaching Outline

I. What do you think?
II. What would you do?
III. Contributions Of Behavioral Learning
    A. Objectives for learning
    B. Kinds of objectives
        1. Behavioral objectives (list, define, add, calculate, etc.)
        2. Cognitive objectives (understand, recognize, create, apply, etc.)
        3. Mager: Start with the specific; a good objective has three parts
            a) describes student behavior
            b) lists conditions under which the behavior with occur
            c) gives criteria for acceptable performance
        4. Gronlund: Start with the general
            a) stated first in general terms (understand, solve, appreciate, etc.)
            b) clarify by listing a few sample behaviors that would provide evidence that the student has attained the objective
            c) research tends to support Gronlund's approach
        5. Bloom's taxonomy of objectives—cognitive, affective, and psychomotor
            a) Cognitive—knowledge, comprehension, application, analysis, and synthesis
    C. Are objectives useful?
        1. Improves achievement under certain circumstances
            a) can promote learning with loosely organized and less-structured activities
            b) objectives can focus students' attention on the importance of some information
            c) can clarify performance criteria
        2. Not as effective when the task involves getting the gist of a passage or transferring the information to a new situation
    D. Guidelines
        1. Developing instructional objectives
        2. Mastery learning: Students who do not reach a minimum level of mastery on a unit can recycle through the unit and take another form of the unit test
            a) Advantages

Learning and Instruction

                (1)   gives students the time to learn foundational information, for example, in mathematics
                (2)   gives student extra time and support they need to learn
            b)   Disadvantages
                (1)   teachers need a variety of materials to allow students to recycle through the objectives since repeating the same material probably won't help
                (2)   has not helped to erase achievement differences among student—individual differences still persist
                (3)   some students may get frustrated rather than encouraged by being able to recycle through the information
        3.   Direct Instruction—focuses on teaching basic skills in a group setting (a.k.a. explicit teaching, active teaching)
            a)   Rate of students' interruptions is very low
            b)   Teacher maintains a strong academic focus
            c)   Teacher carefully chooses appropriate tasks, clearly presenting Subject-matter information and solution strategies
        4.   Rosenshine's six teaching functions (for teaching basic skills)
            a)   Review and check the previous day's work
            b)   Present new material
            c)   Provide guided practice
            d)   Give feedback and correctives
            e)   Provide independent practice
            f)   Review weekly and monthly
        5.   Criticisms of direct instruction
            a)   Limited to lower-level objectives
            b)   Based on traditional methods, ignoring innovative models
            c)   Discourages students' independent thinking
            d)   Student is "empty vessel" to be filled with knowledge rather than an active constructor of knowledge
        6.   Benefits of direct instruction
            a)   Can help students learn actively, not passively
            b)   Especially helpful with younger and less prepared learners who need guidance to construct knowledge
IV.   Cognitive Models Of Teaching
    A.   Discovery learning (Jerome Bruner)—method in which the teacher presents examples and the students work with the examples until the discover the interrelationships (the subject's structure)
        1.   Structure and discovery—structure is the essential information underlying what is being studied
        2.   Students must be active in identifying the principles for themselves, not just accepting the teachers' explanations

Learning and Instruction

    3. Inductive reasoning
    4. Discovery in action—gives students a chance to develop their intuitive thinking
    5. Guidelines: Applying Bruner's Ideas in the Classroom
    6. Point-Counterpoint: Is Discovery Learning Effective?
  B. Expository teaching / reception learning (David Ausubel)—assumes that people acquire knowledge through reception rather than through discovery.
    1. Meaningful verbal learning rather than rote learning
    2. Teachers present information in an organized way, delivering materials to students in the most efficient way
    3. Learning should progress deductively (from the general to the specific)
    4. Advance organizers act to better fit the students' schemas and the material to be learned—will provide scaffolding or support for the new information
     a) Comparative organizers activate already existing schemas
     b) Expository organizers provide new information that students will need to understand the upcoming information
     c) Good advanced organizers have been shown to help students learn
    5. Steps in expository lessons
     a) Present advance organizer
     b) Present basic similarities and differences, using specific examples
    6. Making the most of expository teaching
     a) Most appropriate when trying to teach about the relationships among several concepts
     b) Students need background knowledge first
     c) Developmentally appropriate for students at, or above, later elementary school
    7. Guidelines: Applying Ausubel's Ideas in the Classroom
V. The Instructional Events Model (Robert Gagne)
  A. Based on the information processing model of learning; concerned with the quality, permanence, and usefulness of students' learning
  B. Steps in learning
    1. Gain students' attention
    2. Set an expectancy
    3. Remind students of what they already know that is related to the material to be learned
    4. Present the new material
    5. Provide learning guidance
    6. Students demonstrate understanding through responding
    7. Reviews at the end of the lesson, week, and unit to encourage transfer by extending practice over time
VI. Constructivist And Situated Learning

Learning and Instruction

- A. Elements of constructivist perspectives
  1. Complex learning environments and authentic tasks
  2. Social negotiation to encourage development of higher mental processes through social interaction
  3. Multiple representations of content
  4. Understanding the knowledge construction process
  5. Student-centered instruction
- B. Inquiry and problem-based learning (John Dewey)
  1. The teacher presents a puzzling event, question, or problem
  2. The students:
     a) Formulate hypotheses to explain the event or solve the problem
     b) Collect data to test the hypotheses
     c) Draw conclusions
     d) Reflect on the original problem and on the thinking processes needed to solve it
- C. Group work and cooperation in learning
  1. Group work and cooperation not the same thing. Students can be involved in group work without having to work together, or cooperate
  2. Beyond groups to cooperation
     a) Helps students rehearse, elaborate, and expand their knowledge
     b) Through questioning and explaining, students organize their knowledge, make connections, and review
     c) Can create the disequilibrium necessary to question one's understanding and try new ideas
     d) Social interaction can help develop higher thinking abilities
- D. Elements of cooperative learning groups (Johnston & Johnston)
  1. Face-to-face interaction
  2. Positive interdependence
  3. Individual accountability
  4. Collaborative skills
  5. Group processing
- E. Setting up cooperative groups
  1. Size of group depends on task—for review, rehearse, or practice, 4, 5, or 6 students is about right; for problem solving and participation, 2 to 4 is better
  2. Balance the number of boys and girls
  3. Assign roles to encourage cooperation and full participation
- F. Formats for cooperative learning
  1. Jigsaw—emphasizes high interdependence
  2. Reciprocal questioning
  3. Scripted cooperation
- G. What can go wrong: Misuses of group learning

Learning and Instruction

        1. Interactions can be unproductive and unreflective if there is pressure in the group for conformity
        2. Misconceptions might be reinforced, or the worst, not the best, ideas may be combined to construct a superficial understanding
        3. Ideas of low status students may be ignored or ridiculed in favor of contributions of high status students, regardless of the merit of the respective ideas
        4. Speed and finishing take precedence over thoughtfulness and learning
        5. Socializing and interpersonal relationships may take precedence over learning
        6. Students may shift dependency from teacher to "expert" in the group, remaining passive in their learning
        7. Status differences may be increased rather than decreased
    H. Instructional conversations
        1. Provide necessary opportunities for students to operate within their zones of proximal development
        2. Reduces dominance of teacher talk in the classroom
    I. Cognitive apprenticeships
        1. Students observe an expert model the performance
        2. Students get external support through coaching or tutoring
        3. Conceptual scaffolding is provided and gradually removed as the student becomes more competent
        4. Students continually articulate their knowledge
        5. Students reflect on their progress through comparison with the expert and with their own earlier efforts
        6. Students are required to explore new ways to apply what they have learned

VII. Cognitive And Constructivist Approaches To Reading, Mathematics, And Science
    A. Learning to read and write
        1. Whole language
            a) Learning to read as a natural process
            b) Reading as a kind of guessing game
            c) Teaching and learning seen as reciprocal and collaborative
            d) Authentic writing
            e) Integrated curriculum
        2. Do students need skills and phonics?
            a) Skill in recognizing sounds and words supports reading
            b) Knowing words helps make sense of context
            c) Fluency in word identification is a prerequisite to successful reading comprehension, word identification becomes automatic in skilled readers
            d) The poorest, not the best, readers use context to help them understand meaning
        3. Being sensible about reading and writing

Learning and Instruction

        a) Whole language approach is most effective in preschool and kindergarten
        b) Phonemic awareness in kindergarten and first grade predicts literacy in later grades
        c) Excellent primary school teachers use a balance of explicit phonics teaching and whole language instruction
    4. Reciprocal teaching
        a) Helps students understand and think deeply about what they read through strategies used automatically by skilled readers, but not by poor readers
            (1) summarize
            (2) asking a question
            (3) clarifying
            (4) predicting
        b) Applying reciprocal teaching
            (1) shift gradually
            (2) match demands to abilities
            (3) diagnose thinking
  B. Learning and teaching mathematics
    1. Thinking processes of the students are the focus of attention
    2. One topic considered in depth rather than covering many topics
    3. Assessment is ongoing and mutually shared by teacher and students
  C. Learning science
    1. Students need to directly examine their own theories and confront their shortcomings
    2. Six stages: Initial discomfort, attempts to explain away inconsistencies, attempts to adjust measurements or observations to fit personal theories, doubt, vacillation, and finally conceptual change.
    3. Teachers are committed to teacher for understanding rather than for covering the curriculum
    4. Students are encouraged to make sense of science using their current ideas
    5. Dialogue is key
  D. Working with families
  E. Guidelines: Communicating with Families about Innovative Teaching Approaches
  F. Be confident and honest
  G. Treat parents as equal partners
  H. Communicate effectively
  I. Have examples of projects and assignments available for parents when they visit the class
  J. Develop family involvement packages
VIII. Teachers' casebook: What would they do?

Learning and Instruction

Learning Activities and Related Research

ACTIVITIES	HANDOUTS
Chapter 9	9.0 Lecture Outline
Cooperative Activities	
9.1 Effective Teaching	9.1a Principles of Effective Teaching I
	9.1b Principles of Effective Teaching II
9.2 Role-playing an expository lesson	9.2 An example of an expository lesson
9.3 Group Presentations on teaching approaches	9.3 Group Presentations on teaching approaches
9.4 Reciprocal Teaching: Analyzing dialogue	9.4a Reciprocal Teaching I
	9.4b Reciprocal Teaching II
Research Activities	
9.5 Critique Research: Discovery Learning in Action	
9.6 Effective group interaction	
Using Technology	
Field Experience	
9.7 Teaching Functions	
Other Teaching Activities	
9.8 Direct vs. indirect instruction	9.5 Concept Map: Direct Instruction
	9.6 An example of direct instruction
	9.7 Concept Map: Constructivist Approaches
9.9 Children's understanding of science	9.8 Children's thinking about science
9.10 Comparison of Teaching Models	9.9 BICEPS: Models of Teaching
9.11 Cooperative learning strategies for elementary reading	9.10 Structures of the Cooperative Classroom
9.11b Cooperative Structures	
9.12 Teaching methods and classroom management	
	9.11 Concept Maps: Links to other chapters

Cooperative Activities

9.1   <u>Effective Teaching</u>

Handout Masters 9.1A and **9.1B** list principles and behaviors that were compiled from the results of four prominent studies. Before presenting the list of principles to the students, have them write their own teaching principles based on their studies so far. As volunteers read their principles aloud to the class, have other students respond with examples of teacher behavior which illustrate those principles. Ask the students to save their principles for discussion later in the class. Then divide the class into groups and assign each group one of the thirteen principles listed (have each written separately on a piece of paper). In a group, the students should write exemplary teacher behaviors for their principle and share their results with the class. Then distribute **Handout Master 9.6** and ask the whole class to discuss the example.

Learning and Instruction

9.2   <u>Role-playing an Expository Lesson</u>

From Eggen, P. D., & Kauchak, D. P. (1988). <u>Strategies for teachers: Teaching content and thinking skills,</u> (2nd ed.) Boston, MA, Allyn & Bacon, 253-55.

   Have the students perform and discuss the dialogue presented in **Handout Master 9.2** as a role play. Analyze with students the elements of expository teaching and compare examples of discovery learning and expository teaching. End by asking students to generate a list of the strong and weak points of each teaching method.

9.3   <u>Group Presentations on Teaching Approaches</u>

   Use **Handout 9.3** to structure a teaching experience for students. They will be using one of the teaching models below to experience instruction in the classroom. They can use the subsequent activity to observe actual instruction using the same models.

Directions to the students:

1. You must develop your presentation in your assigned groups of 4 to 5 members each.
2. Each group will be responsible for preparing a lesson (maximum-10 minutes) using one of the following approaches: See the appropriate pages in the text for reference.
   - Guided Discovery:
   - Expository:
   - Direct Instruction (low ability):
   - Recitation (high ability class):
   - Class Discussion:
   - Teaching Study/Learning Strategies:
   - Whole Language:
   - Inquiry:
   - Constructivist:
3. One or two people assume the role of the teacher and the remaining people play the "students." Specify the age of your students and the topic of your lesson. The purpose of the presentations is to demonstrate an actual "slice of classroom life." Your group should provide a good example of the type of lesson assigned and be ready to describe what you included in your lesson and why. Your lesson should reflect appropriate applications of learning principles as well.
4. Your group will be evaluated on the following:
   - Clarity of objectives.
   - Accuracy in presenting an example of the assigned approach.
   - Reflection of the guidelines or suggestions from text pages indicated above.
   - Success in capturing and maintaining the interest of the class.
   - Involvement of all group members.

Learning and Instruction

- Ability to justify the elements of the lesson as good examples of the approach presented.
- Reflection of principles of motivation in the teaching.

Each group is given approximately 60 minutes to prepare the lesson and 10 minutes to simulate the teaching. Each group will evaluate itself and receive feedback from other groups.

9.4   Reciprocal Teaching: Analyzing Dialogue

Use **Handouts 9.4a and 9.4b** which provide an example of the dialogue from a reciprocal teaching episode. Have students identify the key steps of reciprocal teaching in the dialogue. Ask students to describe the cognitive processes being used throughout the course of this dialogue. Are there statements that should not have been made or could have been better stated?

Research Activities

9.5   Critique Research: Discovery Learning in Action

From Joyce, B., and Weil, M. (1986). *Models of teaching.* Boston, MA, Allyn & Bacon, 40-41.

The following lesson compares an inductive approach to teaching a botany lesson with the more traditional teacher presentation method. Have your students read the lesson, and then use the questions that follows as the basis for discussion. Encourage them to critically evaluate the quality and appropriateness of the research methods and measurements used in the study.

Contrasting lessons: At the Motilal Nehru School of Sports in the state of Haryana, India, two groups of tenth grade students are engaged in the study of a botany unit that focuses on the structure of plant life. One group is studying the textbook with the tutorial help of their instructor, who illustrates the structures with plants found on the grounds of the school. We will call this group the presentation *cum* illustration group. The other group, which we will call the inductive group, is taught by Bharati Baveja, an instructor at Delhi University. This group is presented with a large number of plants that are labeled with their names. Working in pairs, the students build classifications of the plants based on the structural characteristics of their roots, stems, and leaves. Periodically, the pairs share their classifications and generate labels for them.

Occasionally, Mrs. Baveja employs concept attainment to introduce a concept designed to expand the students' frame of reference and induce more complex classification. She also supplies the scientific names for the categories the students invent. Eventually Mrs. Baveja presents the students with some new specimens and asks them to see if they can predict the structure of one part of the plant from the observation of another part (as predicting the root structure from the observation of the leaves). Finally, she asks them to collect some more specimens and fit them to the categories they have developed so they can determine how comprehensive their categories have become. They discover that most of the new plants will fit into existing categories but that new categories have to be invented to hold some of them.

Posttest: After two weeks of study, the two groups take a test over the content of the unit and are asked to analyze some more specimens and name their structural characteristics. The inductive group has gained twice as much on the test of knowledge and can correctly identify the structures of eight times more specimens than the presentation cum illustration group.

Discussion: What characterizes the discovery learning lessons that the inductive group experienced? How does the instructor use the following components of concept learning: concept labeling, concept attainment, categorization, relevant and irrelevant attributes, and examples/non-examples?

9.6 Group Interaction

Each group should use the tape made in exercise 7.2 *"Endangered Species."* If they have not made a tape of that exercise, group members will need to record another problem-solving session.

The first task of the group will be to transcribe their tape. Once they have an agreed-upon transcript, they should analyze the transcript for evidence that their group was productive, the interaction was supportive of effective cognitive processing. They should also note what kinds of interaction seemed to take time from the assigned tasks and other evidence of non-productivity.

Field Experience

9.7 Teaching Functions

Have your students observe a classroom and note the degree to which Rosenshine's 6 teaching functions are being deployed? Do teachers give reasons for why things are being done in the class? Is previous material reviewed?

Other Teaching Activities

9.8 Direct vs. Indirect Instruction

Present the following list of topics in earth science which are a part of the scope and sequence for a fifth-grade class. Discuss which topics would be better suited for direct instruction and which would be more suitably taught through a discovery approach or through student discussion. Have the students give reasons for their selection.

How volcanoes are formed
Why fossils are found on land
Where earthquakes happen
How earthquakes are measured

Learning and Instruction

> What happens to people when earthquakes occur
> The inner make-up of the earth
> Comparing metamorphic, sedimentary and igneous rocks
> Minimizing earthquake damage

9.9   Children's Understanding of Science

The Harvard Education Letter (1988), 4-6, described a second grade science class in which students, observing the transformation of mealworms into adult beetles, constructed the intuitive explanation that it was the food they were eating that had caused the change. Their teacher arranged a series of demonstrations that helped them to understand that food was not a factor in this metamorphosis.

Evidence shows that encouraging students to examine and question their own intuitive theories in such ways leads to better, more durable understanding of a variety of physical science situations. Unfortunately, many college age students, estimates range up to 80%, who may have not had the benefit of such instructional strategies, enter college with very shallow, and often inaccurate, knowledge of science.

Discussion: How can teachers present subject material and work with students to build upon and transform their intuitive ideas about such concepts as the nature of objects, the movement of objects, and the physical and chemical changes which take place in nature?

Have your students examine **Handout 9.8** which illustrates changes in children's thinking about science. What changes? How would this influence the design of a lesson?

9.10   Comparison of Teaching Models

Using **Handout Master 9.9**, have your students compare two different models of teaching using the categories of information presented in the handout.

9.11   Cooperative Learning Strategies For Elementary Reading

Whisler, N. and Williams, J. (1990). Literature and cooperative learning. Sacramento, CA: Literature Co-Op. (page numbers reference pages from source)

Expose the students to the following strategies by modeling in a class activity. They may also be adapted to middle and high school.

Strategy: "Two/Four -- Question Some More" (pp. 61-63)

Structuring Cooperative Learning

- **Grouping**: Partners and groups of four
- **Interdependence**: Roles are assigned - questioner, paraphraser

Learning and Instruction

- **Accountability**: Partner groups are randomly called on to share questions and possible answers
- **Social skills**: Paraphrasing, sharing ideas, listening

"*Two/Four -- Question Some More*" begins with partners and then moves to pairs of partners to make a group of four students. This strategy can be used during read-aloud time. It incorporates several worthwhile procedures. Most educators acknowledge the importance of reading aloud to children. Readers and listeners can use their personal schemata to anticipate/make predictions and ask themselves questions about the text before and during reading. They are then active listeners (or readers) seeking to confirm/prove their predictions and find answers to their questions. This strategy teaches students to become active questioners when they read.

Before beginning: Mark the turning point in the story. Prior to reading aloud, read through the story or chapter and mark several usually exciting parts or turning points where you will stop and have the students discuss what they will want to know. Now you are ready to begin.

We will describe "Two/Four -- Question Some More" as we have used it with O. Henry's "After Twenty Years." This is a suspenseful story about two friends who have promised to met each other after twenty years. (As a schemata-enhancing activity before reading, we have students write what it would be like to meet a friend they have not seen for twenty years and where they would meet that person. Students share these in their group of four. Some youngsters take the opportunity to share with the whole class.) The steps follow:

1. **Teacher reads aloud several paragraphs.** We usually read a paragraph or two from the story up to a point where students will have some questions. In this story we read the first page, which sets the scene with a police officer on his night beat in a rather run-down part of the city. He encounters a man standing in the doorway of a hardware store.
2. **Students share questions with a partner.** We stop and ask the students, "What questions do you have about the story so far? What do you want to know? Discuss this with a partner." Students enthusiastically turn to their partner and begin to discuss the questions they want answered in the story.
3. **Students share questions and suggest answers** in their group of four. After several minutes of discussion with a partner, the teacher signals the students to now talk with their group of four. Explain that they are to share their questions and speculate some answers to their questions, providing rationales for their responses. The discussions become more and more lively as two students now bring their ideas together with two more students. Having two students work together before joining another pair of students provides the opportunity for students to formulate more questions, predictions, and speculations.
4. **Questions and speculated answers are shared** in a whole class discussion. Time should be provided for sharing with the whole class. To structure positive

Learning and Instruction

interdependence and individual accountability the student partners are assigned to be either a paraphraser or a question asker. When one set of partners is called on to share, the question asker shares one of the questions their group had. The paraphraser then explains what possible answers their group discussed. You will find that when one group shares a question and some possible answers, other groups will want to share their answers. Our responses are nonjudgmental. "That's interesting. What makes you say that? How could that happen? I haven't thought about that. That's a possibility. Could that happen? That makes sense. Any more ideas?" All of this discussion builds curiosity. There is no more powerful motivator that the curiosity and desire to find out, which of course can only be accomplished by reading. The bottom line for many youngsters is, of course, did they predict the same thing the author writes in the story.

5. **Steps 1-4 are repeated** several more times.

Application: (intermediate level) In The House of Dies Drear by Virginia Hamilton, Thomas explores the hidden passages and rooms under his new home in a huge mansion that was once a stop on the underground railroad. It was scary alone, even with a flashlight. Thomas drops the light. We stop reading. Questions are at the tips of students' tongues as are possible answers in the groups of four.

Strategy: "Panel of Experts" (pp. 102-103)

Structuring Cooperative Learning

- **Grouping**: Groups of four
- **Interdependence**: Roles are assigned: Facilitator, quizzer, judge, and Master of Ceremonies. One group set of questions is collected.
- **Accountability**: Each student writes one question/answer. Any student in the panel of experts may be called on to answer.
- **Social skills**: Paraphrasing, sharing information

"Panel of Experts" is an exciting game in which cooperative groups develop and ask each other questions after having read a selection. New information is often made more meaningful by elaborating on and embellishing what was read, and asking questions is one form of elaboration. Teachers, however, need not be the ones to ask the questions. The goal is to have students become strategic readers who ask their own questions to guide their reading. "Panel of Experts," in addition to being an activity for reprocessing information, is also helpful in providing models for students to become self-questioners as they read. The steps for using "Panel of Experts" follow:

1. **Students read selected pages** in a chapter of portion of a nonfiction book. ("Panel of Experts" works better with informational text where the focus may be more on high consensus information, although we have used it with fiction)

2. **Students take notes for possible quotations.** Students may jot down notes/ideas/questions/page numbers during the reading in preparation for the group formulation of questions after reading.
3. **Teacher assigns roles.** You will need a quizzer, judge, facilitator, and an MC (Master of Ceremonies/Announcer) in each group.
4. **Students write questions.** After reading, students in each group discuss and agree on four questions and their answers. Each student writes one of the four questions along with the answer and page number where the answer may be located. (No true/false or yes/no questions are permitted).
5. **One panel of experts is selected.** One group is selected to be the first panel of experts. They may bring their individual notes, the text, and their group questions and answers to the front of the room. They sit in the panel of experts chairs (four chairs in the front of the room facing the class). One chair is designated as the MC's chair. You may even want to label the chairs.
6. **Students ask the panel of experts questions.** The MC on the panel of experts calls on one group in the audience (the rest of the class). The quizzer in that group challenges the panel of experts by asking one of the questions from their group's list. The panel of experts huddles together and discusses possible answers. They may refer to their notes, text, and questions if needed to formulate an answer. The facilitator on the panel of experts clarifies, summarizes, and makes any final decision regarding what answer they will give. The facilitator also makes sure everyone on the panel of experts can explain the answer. The MC in the group who asked the question may then call on any panel member to present the answer orally to the class. Many times the less proficient students are called on to respond. The lesson is structured so that those students are able to succeed and will be able to give the correct answer. The judge in the group who asked the question determines if the response is correct. (Having students write the answers when they write the questions makes this process work more smoothly. The judge merely needs to refer to the answer written in their group).
7. **Play continues** until the panel of experts is either stumped or answers two questions in a row correctly. If one of the group stumps the panel of experts by asking a question they cannot answer, that group becomes the new panel of experts. When the panel of experts does answer correctly, they remain up front and the MC then calls on another group for a different question. After two correct answers the panel of experts retires and the MC selects a new panel to come up. In this way all groups get a chance to become the panel of experts.
8. **Groups turn in their questions and answers.** After the game, each student in the group signs the group questions and answers and they turn them in. Students tend to write excellent questions and frequently these are the very questions that a teacher or text would ask. These may be used later for assessment.

Learning and Instruction

Strategy: "One Minute Book Discussions" (pp. 124-125)

<u>Structuring Cooperative Learning</u>

- **Grouping**: Groups of four
- **Interdependence**: Group pencil is shared. Group turns in a single book discussion list.
- **Accountability**: Students all share.
- **Social skills**: Listening, sharing ideas

"One Minute Book Discussions" are an excellent avenue for students to participate in developing a community of readers in their classroom. The informal sharing among children is a way of promoting reading and literacy development. Children, after all, are the best sales people for introducing good books to their fellow students. Reading habits are caught, not taught; and this is more likely to happen when students share with each another what they are reading. The steps for organizing "One Minute Book Discussions" follow:

1. **Students get organized for "One Minute Book Discussions."** To put some structure into the activity of book sharing, we have divided classes into groups of four students. We ask the students in each group to number off one through four. Students have, at their desks, the books they are currently reading or have just finished.
2. **We discuss some of the ideas students may want** to address during the sharing. These are listed on a chart and students may refer to the suggestions if they need them. See below:

    Book Sharing Suggestions
    - Name of the book and author
    - What the book is about
    - Why you like or dislike the book
    - What you will remember about the book
    - What experiences does the book make you think of?
    - A funny, interesting, or unusual part you would like to share
    - Other books you want to compare with this book
3. **Student #1 shares**. A timer is used. Student #1 shows/tells something about the book he/she is reading. We allow only a short amount of time for each student to share, usually one or two minute is ample. We then call time.
4. **Student #2 shares**. Student #2 takes a turn sharing his/her book. Time is called after several minutes.
5. **Student #3 shares**. Student #3 takes a turn sharing his/her book. Time is called after several minutes.
6. **Student #4 shares**. Student #4 takes a turn sharing his/her book. Time is called after several minutes.

Learning and Instruction

7. **Students finalize discussion** and fill out the group book discussion list. Many times students have questions, want to know more about, or want to discuss in depth several of the books. Time is provided for free discussion of any of the books that were introduced. During this time, students fill out the group discussion list. Students pass the group pencil to each student to record the title and author of the book he/she is reading. All the students sign the list and turn it in. (These book lists may be displayed on the bulletin board under the title "This Week's Books on Parade.")

The whole process takes five to ten minutes and the whole class has the opportunity to share what they are reading in an informal setting. A real advantage to these book sharing sessions is that all students have an opportunity to contribute. The avid readers are rich sources of information about children's literature and other children learn from their peers about interesting books.

9.11 (b) Cooperative Learning Structures

From Kagan, S. (1989/1990). The structural approach to cooperative learning. Educational Leadership, December/January, 12-15.

Cooperative structures are content-free ways of organizing social interaction in the classroom. Among the well-known structures are **Jigsaw**, **Student-Teams-Achievement Divisions (STAD)**, and **Think-Pair-Share**. These might be contrasted with **Whole-Class-Question-Answer**, a competitive structure used repeatedly by teachers. In this arrangement, students vie for the teacher's attention and praise, creating negative interdependence among them. This is, when the teacher calls on someone, the others lose their chance to respond, while a failure by one student to give a correct response increases the chances for other students to receive praise and attention.

Numbered Heads Together is a simple, useful four-step cooperative structure. The teacher has students number off within groups, so that each student has the number 1, 2, 3, or 4. The teacher asks a question, then asks the students in each group to "put their heads together" to arrive at an answer. The teacher then calls one of the numbers, and students with that number can raise their hands to respond. This builds in individual accountability (once the number is called, the students who answer are on their own); but students also support and help one another so their team can gain points.

Many cooperative structures actually increase individual accountability simultaneously with group cooperation. In the **Three-Step Interview**, students form two pairs within their teams of four and conduct one-way interviews in pairs. Then students reverse roles. Students then round-robin, taking turns to share the information they learned during the interview. This assures equal participation; half of the class is talking at one time, in contrast to the usual procedures for group discussions, in which some individuals do all the talking while others remain silent.

Handout Master 9.10 provides an overview of group structures and their social and academic functions. A brief description is included of each structure. Ask students if

Learning and Instruction

they have seen these cooperative learning structures in operation during their field experiences in local schools. What are some of the advantages and disadvantages of each?

9.12   Teaching Methods and Classroom Management

This demonstration can be very effective in illustrating the interaction between teaching strategies and classroom behavior. You play the role of the teacher and ask six students to play the following roles: a good and attentive student; a daydreamer; two students who talk to one another; a student who wiggles, taps his pencil and is generally restless; and a student who is interested in some kind of gadget he has. Arrange the seating in a typical classroom style. Be sure that you have room to stand by each child. Choose a topic to teach, e.g., the body of an insect. Give the instructional objective of the lesson: The student will be able to identify all the parts of an insect on a diagram.

First demonstration: Give a lecture on the information. Ask everyone to look at the board while you draw the body of an insect, label its parts (head, abdomen, thorax, antennae, wings, legs) and discuss their number and location. While lecturing, ignore the good student. Interrupt your lecture frequently to reprimand individual students ("Be quiet." "Pay attention." "Put that away." "Move to another place."). In general, pay attention to the misbehaviors. Hand out the diagram and tell them to copy the names of the parts from the board. After a minute, stop and say that you are going to give the same lesson in a different way.

Second demonstration: Begin by asking questions: Do any of you know what an insect is? What kinds of insects have you seen? Do they crawl? Can they fly? Do they have feelers sticking out of their heads? Give each student a picture of an insect and say, "Can you find the parts of an insect's body? It has three big parts: a head -- Can you find the head?, a thorax -- The wings are joined onto the thorax, and an abdomen or stomach -- It's the end part of the body." Continue asking questions: "How many feelers or antennae are on the head?"; "How many legs?" "Wings?" "Now I'm going to give you a diagram of an insect. Let's see if you can label the parts. Can you find the head?" (Write HEAD on the board and continue with the other parts of the body.)

After a minute of labeling the diagram, stop the activity. Ask the class to comment on the differences of the two demonstrations. The following points should be discussed:

- Lecture does not require active student involvement. When a teacher is lecturing, student behavior that is off-task (not listening) is much more noticeable, and it is tempting to interrupt the lecture to attend to negative behavior. In effect, this calls attention to such behavior and exacerbates it.

- In the second example, student were able to volunteer what they knew about the subject as the lesson began; this related the subject to prior student knowledge and engaged student attention.

- If students are involved through questions and concrete materials, misbehavior is less likely to occur.

- Both lessons were keyed to the same objective, but the effects of the lessons were different.

Discussion Questions

1. Compare and contrast Gronlund and Mager's approaches to designing objectives?
2. Compare and contrast discovery learning and expository teaching? Pay particular attention to when these models of instruction are optimally used.
3. A focus on authentic tasks seems to propel teachers to attend less to the skills necessary to accomplish a larger task. Can authentic tasks be fruitfully accomplished if students do not have the requisite skills?
4. How can groups of children best help one another learn?
5. What does it mean to have a cognitive apprenticeship?
6. Compare constructivist and symbol processing strategies for teaching science?
7. How can families be included in the teaching and learning process?

Additional Resources for Teaching This Chapter

PRINT RESOURCES

Orlich, D. C., Harder, R. J., Callahan, R. C., Kravas, C. H., Kauchak, D. P., Pendergrass, R. A., and Keogh, A. J. (1985). Teaching strategies: A guide to better instruction. Lexington, MA: D. C. Heath and Co. In this text, the authors offer a broad spectrum of instructional methodologies, including such topics as preparing lesson plans, conducting microteaching, deciding on objectives, utilizing formative and summative evaluation, sequencing instruction, incorporating microcomputers into instruction, comparing inquiry models of teaching, teacher questioning techniques, and classroom management. This is an excellent overall resource for the classroom teacher.

Rosenshine, B. (1986). Synthesis of research on explicit teaching. Educational Leadership, 43 (7), 60-69. Rosenshine summarizes in a very readable article ten years of research on teaching which establishes the effectiveness of systematic, step-by-step instruction. This issue has several other good articles on direct instruction and teaching basic skills.

REFERENCES

Fosnot, C. T. (1989). Enquiring teachers, enquiring learners. New York and London: Teachers College Press.

Mallory, B. L. and New, R. S. (1994). Diversity and developmentally appropriate practices. New York and London: Teachers College, Columbia University.

Learning and Instruction

Tobin, K., Kahle, J. B., and Fraser, B. J. (1990). <u>Windows into science classrooms</u>. Hampshire, ENG: Falmer Press.

Well, G. (1986). <u>The meaning makers: Children learning language and using language to learn</u>. New Hampshire: Heinemann.

Wyne, M., & Stuck, G. (1982). Time and learning: Implications for the classroom teacher. <u>Elementary School Journal, 83(1)</u>, 67-75.

FILMS, VIDEOTAPES, AND AUDIOCASSETTES

S is for science. This program looks at methods being used to reverse the decline in science education: High-tech museums; new technologies like interactive videodisks and laser scanners; and the Network for Excellence in Teaching Science program, which shows teachers how to teach science. From Films for the Humanities. 26 min.

To the nth dimension. This program explores modern mathematics and the emerging crisis in American mathematics education, which may leave Americans unable to compete in the marketplace of ideas. From Films for the Humanities. 26 min.

Handout Master 9.0

Lecture Outline ----- Learning and Instruction

- **Contributions of Behavioral Learning**

- **Cognitive Models of Teaching**

- **Constructivist and Situated Learning**

- **Cognitive and Constructivist Approaches to Content Area Teaching**

Copyright © 1998 by Allyn and Bacon

Handout Master 9.1 a

Principles of Effective Teaching

I. Instruction
   A. Organization of instruction
       1. **General principle:** Effective teachers organize instructional activities so as to maximize student opportunity to learn.
       2. **Exemplary teacher behaviors:**
          a) Ensures high degree of student success
          b) Relates content to pupil interests
          c) Has reasonable work standards
          d) Stresses student understanding of meaning
          e) Uses large group or whole group instruction
          f) Maintains a brisk pace during lessons
   B. Introduction to the lesson
       1. **General principle:** Effective teachers begin lessons with an introduction which prepares students for the lesson.
       2. **Exemplary teacher behaviors:**
          a) Uses overviews to introduce lesson.
          b) States lesson objectives.
          c) Gives or seeks rationale for the lesson.
          d) Reviews content of previous lesson(s).
          e) Reviews/discusses homework or seatwork.
   C. Preparation of the lesson.
       1. **General principle:** Effective teachers assume an active role in presenting new material.
       2. **Exemplary teacher behaviors:**
          a) Actively presents new material.
          b) Provides clear presentation of content.
          c) Uses a variety of material.
       3. **General principle:** Effective teachers ensure active student participation in the lesson by providing opportunities for discussion or recitation.
       4. **Exemplary teacher behaviors:**
          a) Asks questions students can answer with high level of success
          b) Varies cognitive level of questions.
          c) Minimizes choral responses.
          d) Uses ordered turns to select respondents.
          e) Accepts volunteers.
          f) Minimizes interactions with volunteers.
          g) Minimizes call-outs.
          h) Accepts call-outs (in middle ability classes)
          i) Stresses content rather than form in student responses.
          j) Probes, rephrases, or prompts when students give incorrect responses.
          k) Provides opportunity for practice to individual students.
       5. **General principle:** Effective teachers conduct "controlled practice" of new material with the group, during which they monitor student responses and provide feedback.
       6. **Exemplary teacher behaviors**:
          a) Monitors students responses for correctness.
          b) Checks for understanding of assignment.

Copyright © 1998 by Allyn and Bacon

Handout Master 9.1 a (continued)

Principles of Effective Teaching

        c)   Provides feedback
            (1)   uses process feedback
            (2)   omits feedback after correct response
            (3)   uses praise moderately
            (4)   uses specific academic praise
            (5)   uses specific criticism
            (6)   uses behavior corrections
            (7)   uses non-evaluative feedback
            (8)   uses supportive correction

D.   Student practice after presentation

    2.   **General principle:** Effective teachers provide independent practice (e.g., seatwork, homework) which they monitor and for which students are held accountable.

    3.   **Exemplary teacher behaviors:**
        a)   Gives common seatwork assignments.
        b)   Monitors seatwork.
        c)   Works with individuals.
        d)   Holds students accountable for assignments.
        e)   Assigns homework.

Copyright © 1998 by Allyn and Bacon

Handout Master 9.1 b

Principles of Effective Teaching

II. Management
- A. Introduction to the class
    1. **General principle:** Effective teachers establish themselves as classroom leaders at the beginning of the school year.
    2. **Exemplary teacher behaviors:**
        - a) organizes first day for maximum contact with the students.
        - b) provides examples and practices when introducing rules and procedures.
- B. Learning environment
    1. **General principle:** Effective teachers create a classroom environment hat is work-, task-, and academically-oriented.
    2. **Exemplary teacher behaviors:**
        - a) Has high expectations for students.
        - b) Assumes responsibility for student learning.
        - c) Communicates expectations for behavior and academic performance.
        - d) Maintains high levels of student engagement in academic work.
        - e) Maintains an orderly classroom.
    3. **General principle:** Effective teachers create a classroom climate that is warm and supportive.
    4. **Exemplary teacher behaviors:**
        - a) Ensures a high degree of student success.
        - b) Demonstrates listening skills.
        - c) Expresses feelings.
        - d) Uses supportive correction.
        - e) Focuses on student concerns and uncertainties at the beginning of the school year.
- C. Classroom administration
    1. **General principle:** Effective teachers are well-organized in their administration of the classroom.
    2. **Exemplary teacher behaviors:**
        - a) Is well-organized.
        - b) Establishes clear rules and procedures.
        - c) Posts written rules.
        - d) Teaches rules and procedures to students.
        - e) Has classroom arranged for ease of movement.
    3. **General principle:** Effective teachers organize the classroom so as to ensure the efficient use of time.
    4. **Exemplary teacher behaviors:**
        - a) Begins class promptly.
        - b) Has smooth, quick transitions between activities.
        - c) Has materials ready to begin activities.
        - d) Has classroom arranged for ease of movement.

Copyright © 1998 by Allyn and Bacon

Handout Master 9.1 b *(continued)*

Principles of Effective Teaching

    D.   Behavior management
           1.   **General principle:** Effective teachers minimize student misbehavior by being activley involved with students and closely monitoring their behavior.
           2.   **Exemplary teacher behaviors:**
                 a)   Is actively involved with students.
                 b)   Monitors classrooms.
                 c)   Holds students accountable for behavior.
                 d)   Signals appropriate behavior.
                 e)   Establishes eye contact.
                 f)   Uses a variety of rewards.
    B.   Reactions to misbehavior
           1.   **General principle:** Effective teachers respond promptly to student misbehaviors.
           2.   **Exemplary teacher behaviors**:
                 a)   Responds quickly to disruptive behaviors.
                 b)   Ignores disruptive behavior.
                 c)   Corrects specific students for misbehavior.
                 d)   Cites specific rules when correcting misbehavior.
                 e)   Uses mild, informative types of punishment.
                 f)   Is consistent in enforcement of rules.

Borko, H., Widman, T., & Lakik, R. (1984, April). <u>Designing a classroom observation system: Accountability for principles rather than behaviors.</u> Paper presented at the Annual Meeting of the American Educational Research Association, New Orleans, LA.

Copyright © 1998 by Allyn and Bacon

Handout Master 9.2

Example of an Expository Lesson

Miss Lake began her language arts class with, *Today, class, we're going to talk about a different kind of word pair. Who remembers what other word pairs we've been studying? John?*
"Yesterday we were talking about synonyms," answered John.
"Good, and who knows what a synonym is? Mary?"
"Synonyms are word pairs that mean the same thing, like big and large."
"Very good, Mary. How about another example? Toni?" "...Fast and speedy."
"Yes, very good example, Toni. Well, today we're going to study a different kind of word pair called antonyms. When we are all done with the lesson today, you will be able to give me some examples of antonyms. Also, when I give you a word you will be able to give me an antonym for it." She then wrote the following on the board.

Word Pairs: Synonyms (Same Meaning) Antonyms (Opposite Meaning)

"Antonyms are word pairs that have opposite meaning. What do we mean by word pairs?" Miss Lake asked.
Susan hesitated and then said, "I think 'pair' means two."
"Good, Susan," Miss Lake said with a smile. *"So 'word pair' means two words. Now, what does opposite mean?"*
"It sort of means different or not the same, I think, "Joe volunteered.
*"That's very close, Joe, "*Miss lake said. She continued, *"Let me give you an example. Big and small have opposite meanings and they're two words, so they're antonyms. Opposite means having a different or almost a reversed meaning like big and small."* With that, she wrote big and small under the term, antonym. *"Another example of antonyms is 'up' and 'down'. They are antonyms because they're pairs of words whose meanings are opposite. So let's put them up here under the antonym column. Let me try another one. Are 'happy' and 'glad' antonyms? Andy?*
"No," replied Andy. *"Why not?"* asked Miss Lake.
"Because the words don't have opposite meanings. They mean the same thing."
"So what are they, Andy?"
"Synonyms." *"Fine, Andy. Let's put them under the synonyms column. Now let's try another one. Are 'cold' and 'hot' antonyms? Ted?*
"Yes, because they're a word pair, and the words have opposite meanings."
"So, let's put them over here on the board. And what about 'alive' and 'dead'? Pat?
"Those are antonyms, too, because they mean the opposite."
"Fine. Now I want to see if you can give me some examples of antonyms. Think real hard. Anyone? Lynne?"
"How about 'high' and 'low'?" *"Why are these antonyms?"*
"Because they are word pairs that have opposite meanings."
"Real fine. Now remember we had the word pair 'happy' and glad' said that they weren't antonyms? Can anyone make antonyms from these words? Jim?"
"How about 'happy and 'sad'?" *"Those are excellent antonyms. I think you've all done a good job today in learning about this new kind of word pair. Now someone tell me what we learned today. Susan?*
"...Well, we learned about antonyms." *"Good. Go on,"* Miss Lake smiled.
"Antonyms mean the opposite." *"Yes, excellent! And one more thing. Brad?*
"They're word pairs." *"Exactly. Very good, Brad."* She then closed the lesson by saying, *"Remember word pairs that mean the same are... class?"*
"Synonyms! they all shouted in unison. *"Fine, and word pairs that are opposite are...?"*
'Antonyms!" they again shouted. *"Excellent. Now I have some exercises that I would like you to do individually."* She then distributed a worksheet among the students and the lesson was completed.

From Eggen, P.D., & Kauchak, D.P. (1996). <u>Strategies for teachers: Teaching content and thinking skills,</u> (3rd ed.) Needham Heights, MA: Allyn & Bacon.

Copyright © 1998 by Allyn and Bacon

Handout Master 9.3

Group Presentations Assignment on Teaching Approaches

1. You must develop your presentation in your assigned groups of 4 to 5 members each.

2. Each group will be responsible for preparing a lesson (maximum-10 minutes) using one of the following approaches: See the appropriate pages in the text for reference.
   - Guided Discovery:
   - Expository:
   - Direct Instruction (low ability):
   - Recitation (high ability class):
   - Class Discussion:
   - Teaching Study/Learning Strategies:
   - Whole Language:
   - Inquiry:
   - Constructivist:

3. One or two people assume the role of the teacher and the remaining people play the "students." Specify the age of your students and the topic of your lesson. The purpose of the presentations is to demonstrate an actual "slice of classroom life." Your group should provide a good example of the type of lesson assigned and be ready to describe what you included in your lesson and why. Your lesson should reflect appropriate applications of learning principles as well.

4. Your group will be evaluated on the following:
   - Clarity of objectives.
   - Accuracy in presenting an example of the assigned approach.
   - Reflection of the guidelines or suggestions from text pages indicated above.
   - Success in capturing and maintaining the interest of the class.
   - Involvement of all group members.
   - Ability to justify the elements of the lesson as good examples of the approach presented.
   - Reflection of principles of motivation in the teaching.

Copyright © 1998 by Allyn and Bacon

Handout Master 9.4 a

Reciprocal Teaching

(Teacher D, Day 4: Segment 1)

T: Today, we're going to have a new story about a new animal. We will still be doing the same things. We will try to summarize, we'll ask questions, we'll try to predict, and we'll also try to clarify any words that you may not understand. Remember that we are going to try very hard to listen, and to keep the noise down. The title of today's story is "Cats do talk." Any predictions about what you think this story is going to ell us.

S3: That cats can talk.

T: Exactly. I think that is going to talk about that. How do you think that they talk, R__?

S3: The move their tails.

T: Any other predictions? Let's see if R ____'s predictions are right.

S6: When they want to go out, they scratch on the door. Or when they want to come in, they scratch on the door.

Reading: Cats have many ways of "talking." They may not speak words as people do, but cats do use sounds and movements to show their feelings. Here are some ways cats communicate.

T: How do cats show their feelings?

S: They talk. They make a sound.

T: Did the paragraph tell about any other way they talk to us.

S: They come up to you.

T: So, through their movements, they can show whether they need something.

S2: They come up to your arm.

T: What do you think they are trying to tell you when they come up to your arm?

S2: That they are your friend.

T: Very good. IF I were going to summarize, I would say that this is telling us that cats do talk through using movements and sounds. There was a word here that I'm not sure if I quite understand. There was a long word "communicate." [repeats sentence] What does that sentence mean?

S1: Um, talk.

T: There are some ways that they talk. All right. So, the talking and the movements let us know something, don't they? So communication is not just talking; it's a way to let us know something. A ____, do you want to try and be the teacher for this next one? I want you to listen and think of a question that you can ask the group.

Reading: A cat purrs. When a cat purrs, it is usually showing that it feels happy. Many cats purr after they eat, or while they are being petted. Cats purr to "talk" to each other too. A kitten communicates with its mother by purring. Even before its eyes are open, it finds its mother by sounds she makes.

T: Do you remember what this paragraph is telling you, A __? What did you learn? [pause] Did it move, or talk in some way? Who was the cat talking to?

S5: To the mother.

T: When the cat was talking to its mother, do you remember what it did? [pause] How does a cat talk to its moth? Does it make sounds? Do you remember what kind of sounds it makes? Shall we let some of the others help us out?

S1: It sometimes rubs against you on your arms.

T: So, it is trying to get your attention. It is wanting to communicate, right?

S1: Baby kittens find their mother from the sounds.

T: S o you might want to ask a question from that information. You might ask how...does the kitten know where its mother is if I cannot see, if its eyes are closed.

Copyright © 1998 by Allyn and Bacon

LESSON CONTINUES

Handout Master 9.4 b

Reciprocal Teaching (continued)

(Teacher D, Day 19, Segment 2)

Reading: Behind the front legs, there are two odor glands. They look like two extra eyes. To protect itself, a daddy longlegs can give off a smelly liquid from these glands. Birds, toads, and large insects don't like it at all. It makes them feel too sick or too weak to try and catch the daddy longlegs.

S: [question] What does the daddy longlegs do when something comes around it? J___?
S1: Use that odor and ..[not audible]
S6: Yeah. C___.
S2: When an animal comes along, he puts out his odor and they get too sick to catch him.
S6: Yeah, M__.
S4: Or too weak.
S3: They feel too weak and too sick.
S6: Everybody gave me good answers.
T: Very good.
S6: [summary] I will summarize. When an animal comes around, it gives out its bad smell, and they get weak and too old to catch it.
S1: [clarification] Who does?
S6: That's the daddy longlegs?.
S1: [clarification] Who does?
S3: The animals.
S1: [clarification] Which animals?
S3: All kinds of animals.
S6: Yeah, different kinds.
S1: Different kinds of animals put out a spray?
S3: [clarification] Um, it might be the same kind of animal as tries to catch the daddy longlegs.
T: Okay, I think you are talking about two different things. He's talking about the animals that come around to the spider and he's trying to get you to say who puts out the odor. Is it all animals?
S1: No the daddy longlegs.

[LESSON CONTINUES]

Source: Palinscar, A. S. (1986). The role of dialogue in providing scaffolded instruction. <u>Educational Psychologist, 21,</u> 73-99.

Handout Master 9.5: Direct Instruction

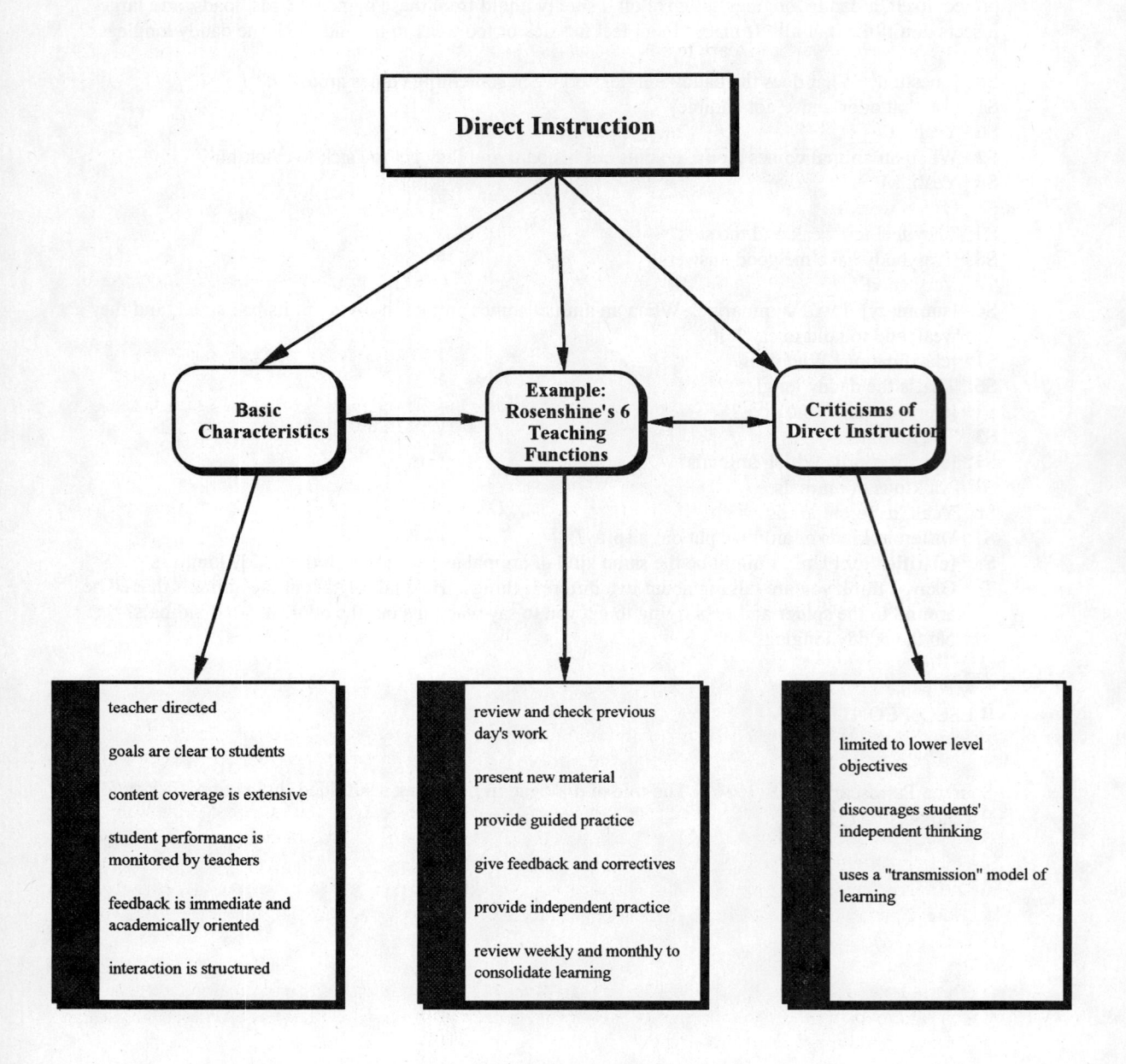

```
                    Direct Instruction
                   /       |        \
                  /        |         \
            Basic    Example:       Criticisms of
         Characteristics  Rosenshine's 6  Direct Instruction
                    Teaching
                    Functions
```

Basic Characteristics	Rosenshine's 6 Teaching Functions	Criticisms of Direct Instruction
teacher directed	review and check previous day's work	limited to lower level objectives
goals are clear to students	present new material	discourages students' independent thinking
content coverage is extensive	provide guided practice	uses a "transmission" model of learning
student performance is monitored by teachers	give feedback and correctives	
feedback is immediate and academically oriented	provide independent practice	
interaction is structured	review weekly and monthly to consolidate learning	

Copyright © 1998 by Allyn and Bacon

Handout Master 9.6

An Example of Direct Instruction

Project Follow Through direct instruction treatment. In this treatment a derivation rule was used. Through the rule, children were taught about fractions for part-whole situation. The children identified the denominator as telling how many parts are in each group and the numerator as telling how many parts are "used." For example, m 5/4, the children were to respond that there were four parts in each group and that five parts were used. An example of the presentation follows:

Teacher: We're going to learn to write fractions. Fractions tell us how many parts are in each whole unit and how many parts are used. The bottom number of a fraction tells how many parts are in each whole. What does the bottom number tell?
Students: How many parts are in each whole.
Teacher: Look at this picture and think how many parts are in each whole. (Pause) How many parts are in each whole?
Students: Four.
Teacher: So what is the bottom number of the fraction?
Students: Four.
Teacher: I'll write four as the bottom number that tells us four parts in each, whole. What does the four tell us?
Students: Four parts in each whole.
Teacher: The top number tells w how many parts are used. What does the top number tell us?
Students: How many parts are used.
Teacher: We find how many parts are used by counting the shaded parts. (Points to each shaded part.)
Students: One, two, three, four, five.
Teacher: How many parts are shaded?
Students: Five.
Teacher: So I write five as the top number of the fraction. (writes five on top). That tells us five parts are used. What does the five tell us?:
Students: Five parts are used.
Teacher: I'll say what the fraction tells w. (Points to the four.) Four parts in each whole. (Points to the five.) Five parts are used. You say what the fraction tells w. (Points to the four. Signals.)
Students: Four parts in each whole.
Teacher: (Points to the five.)
Students: Five parts are used.

Similar strategies for working from pictures and then from written problems were presented. It must be emphasized that regardless of the activity, the strategy that students used to complete the activity was the same. Initially, the teacher guided the students through each step in the Project Follow Through direct instruction group. As the students became more facile in using the strategy, the teacher offered less guidance. Finally, students were able to work problems independently. Mistakes during this phase of instruction were not corrected by just giving the correct answer. Rather, the teacher asked questions based on the derivation rule in order to help the students produce the correct response. Below is an example of a correction procedure that the teacher used when students erred on the question about the number of parts in each whole:

"Let's see how many parts are in each whole" (point to first circle); "Count the parts as I touch them" (touch each part in the first circle; repeat same procedures with next two circles); "There are four parts in this whole, and four parts in this whole."

From Kameenui, E.L., Carnine, D.W., Darch, C.B., tic Stein, M. (1986). Two approaches to the development phase of mathematics instruction. The Elementary School Journal, 86, 641-642.

Copyright © 1998 by Allyn and Bacon

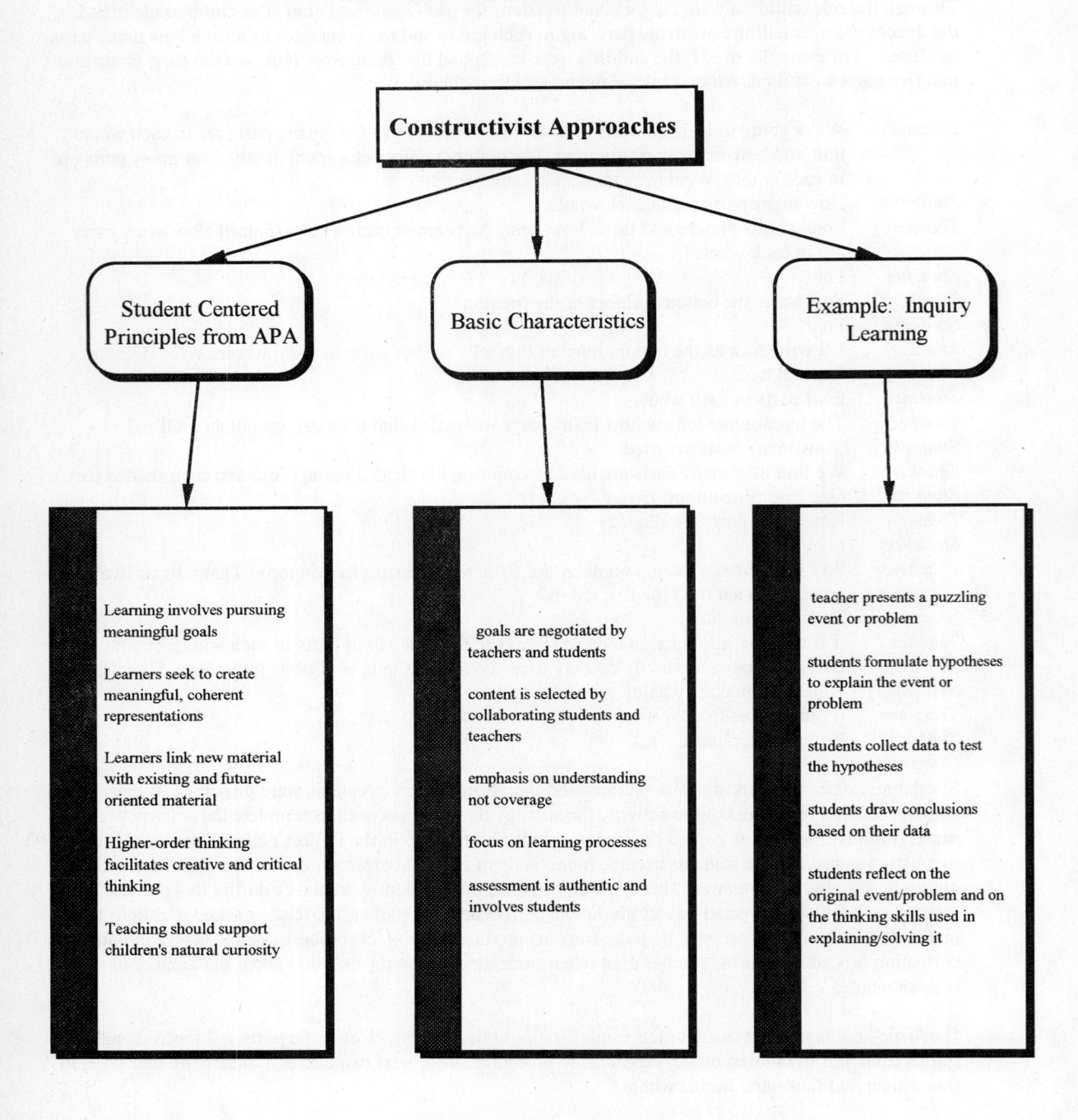

Handout Master 9.7: Constructivist Approaches

Constructivist Approaches

Student Centered Principles from APA

- Learning involves pursuing meaningful goals
- Learners seek to create meaningful, coherent representations
- Learners link new material with existing and future-oriented material
- Higher-order thinking facilitates creative and critical thinking
- Teaching should support children's natural curiosity

Basic Characteristics

- goals are negotiated by teachers and students
- content is selected by collaborating students and teachers
- emphasis on understanding not coverage
- focus on learning processes
- assessment is authentic and involves students

Example: Inquiry Learning

- teacher presents a puzzling event or problem
- students formulate hypotheses to explain the event or problem
- students collect data to test the hypotheses
- students draw conclusions based on their data
- students reflect on the original event/problem and on the thinking skills used in explaining/solving it

Copyright © 1998 by Allyn and Bacon

Handout Master 9.8a

Children's Thinking About Science

The interviews below illustrate the thinking of children at three stages of development.

Jim, Age 6

Questioner:	When you go for a walk at night, what does the moon do?
Jim:	It goes with us.
Questioner:	Why?
Jim:	Because the wind makes it go.
Questioner:	Does the wind know where you are going?
Jim:	Yes.
Questioner:	And the moon too?
Jim:	Yes.
Questioner:	Does it move on purpose to go where you are going or because it has to?
Jim:	It comes so as to give light.
Questioner:	Where did you go for a walk?
Jim:	In the park. The moon went too.
Questioner:	Did it see you?
Jim:	Yes.
Questioner:	Does it know when you go for a walk in the park?
Jim:	Yes.
Questioner:	Does it care?
Jim:	Yes, it does.
Questioner:	Does it know your name?
Jim:	No.
Questioner:	Does it know there are houses?
Jim:	Yes.

Sue, Age 9

Questioner:	When you go for a walk at night, what does the moon do?
Sue:	It follows us.
Questioner:	Why?
Sue:	Because it's high up and everyone sees it.
Questioner:	If you and I were walking in opposite directions, which of us would the moon follow?
Sue:	It stays still because it can't follow two at the same time.
Questioner:	When there are a lot of people in the town what does it do?
Sue:	It follows someone.
Questioner:	Which person?
Sue:	Several people.
Questioner:	How does it do that?
Sue:	With its rays.
Questioner:	Does it moves?
Sue:	Yes, it moves.
Questioner:	How does it do that?
Sue:	It stays still and its rays follow us.

Copyright © 1998 by Allyn and Bacon

Handout Master 9.8b

Children's Thinking About Science

Pam, Age 10

Questioner: When you go for a walk at night, what does the moon do?
Pam: When you're walking you'd say that the moon was following you, because its so big.
Questioner: Does it really follow you?
Pam: No. I used to believe it follows us and that it ran after us but I don't believe that any more.

From: Ann C. Howe and Linda Jones (1993). Engaging children in science (pp. 30-31). New York: Macmillan Publishing Company. (used with permission).

Copyright © 1998 by Allyn and Bacon

Handout Master 9.9

BICEPS: *Models of Instruction*

Complete the following table:

	Direct Instruction	Constuctivist
B Basis		
I Inventors		
C Characteristics		
E Effectiveness		
P Props needed in teaching		
S Steps in teaching		

Copyright © 1998 by Allyn and Bacon

Handout 9.10 a

Structures of the Cooperative Classroom

Structure	Brief Description	Functions: Academic and Social
Team Building		
Roundrobin	Each student in turn shares something with his or her teammates	Expressing ideas and opinions, creation of stones. *Equal participation, getting aquainted with teammates.*
Classbuilding		
Corners	Each student moves to a corner of the room representing a teacher-determined alternative. Students discuss within corners, then listen to and paraphrase ideas from other corners.	Seeing alternative hypotheses, values, problem-solving approaches. *Knowing and respecting different points of view, meeting classmates.*
Communication Building		
Match Mine	Students attempt to *match* the arrangement of objects on a grid of another student using oral communication only	Vocabulary development. *Communication skills, role-taking ability.*
Mastery		
Numbered Heads Together	The teacher asks a question, students consult to make sure everyone knows the answer, then one student is called upon to answer.	Review, checking for knowledge, comprehension. *Tutoring.*
Color.Coded Co-op Cards	Students memorize facts using a flash card game. The game is structured so that there is a maximum probability of success at each step, moving from short-term to long-term memory. Scoring is based on improvement.	Memorizing facts. *Helping, praising.*
Pairs Check	Students work in pairs within groups of four. Within pairs students alternate-one solves a problem while the other coaches. After every two problems the pair checks to see if they have the same answers as the other pair.	Practicing skills. *Helping, Praising.*
Concept Development		
Three Step Interview	Students interview each other in pairs, first one way, then the other. Students each share with the group information they learned in the interview.	Sharing personal information such as hypotheses, reactions to a poem, conclusions from a unit. *Participation, Involvement.*

Copyright © 1998 Allyn and Bacon

Handout 9.10 b

Structures of the Cooperative Classroom

Structure	Brief Description	Functions: Academic and Social
Concept Development		
Think-Pair-Share	Students think to themselves on a topic provided by the teacher; they pair up with another student to discuss it; they then share their thoughts with the class.	Generating and revising hypotheses, inductive reasoning, deductive reasoning, application. *Participation, Involvement.*
Team Word-Webbing	Students write simultaneously on a piece of chart paper, drawing main concepts, supporting elements, and bridges representing the relation of ideas in a concept.	Analysis of concepts into components, understanding multiple relations among ideas, differentiating concepts. *Role taking.*
Multifunctional		
Roundtable	Each student in turn write one answr as a paper and pencil are passed around the group. With simultaneous Roundtable more than one pencil and paper are used.	Assessing prior knowledge, practicing skills, recalling information, creating cooperative art. *Team-building, participation of all.*
Inside-Outside Circle	Students stand in pairs in two concentric circles. The inside circle faces out, the outside circle faces in. Students use flash cards or respond to teacher questions as they rotate to each new partner.	Checking for understanding, review, processing, helping. *Tutoring, sharing, meeting classmates.*
Partners	Students work in pairs to create or master content. They consult with partners from other teams. They then share their products or understanding with the other partner pair in their team.	Mastery and presentation of new material, concept development,. *Presentation and communication skills.*
Jigsaw	Each student on the team becomes an expert on one topic by working with members from other teams assigned the corresponding expert topic. Upon returning to their teams, each one in turn teachers the group and students are all assessed on all aspects of the topic.	Acquisition and presentation of new material, concept development. *Presentation and communication skills.*
Co-op, Co-op	Students work in groups to produce a particular group product to share with the whole class; each student makes a particular contribution to the group.	Learning and sharing complex information often with multiple sources; evaluation, application, analysis, synthesis. *Conflict Resolution, presentation skills.*

Source: From Kagean, S. (19989//1990). The structural approach to cooperative learning; Educational Leadership. Dec/Jan.

Copyright © 1998 by Allyn and Bacon

Handout Master 9.11: Links to Other Chapters

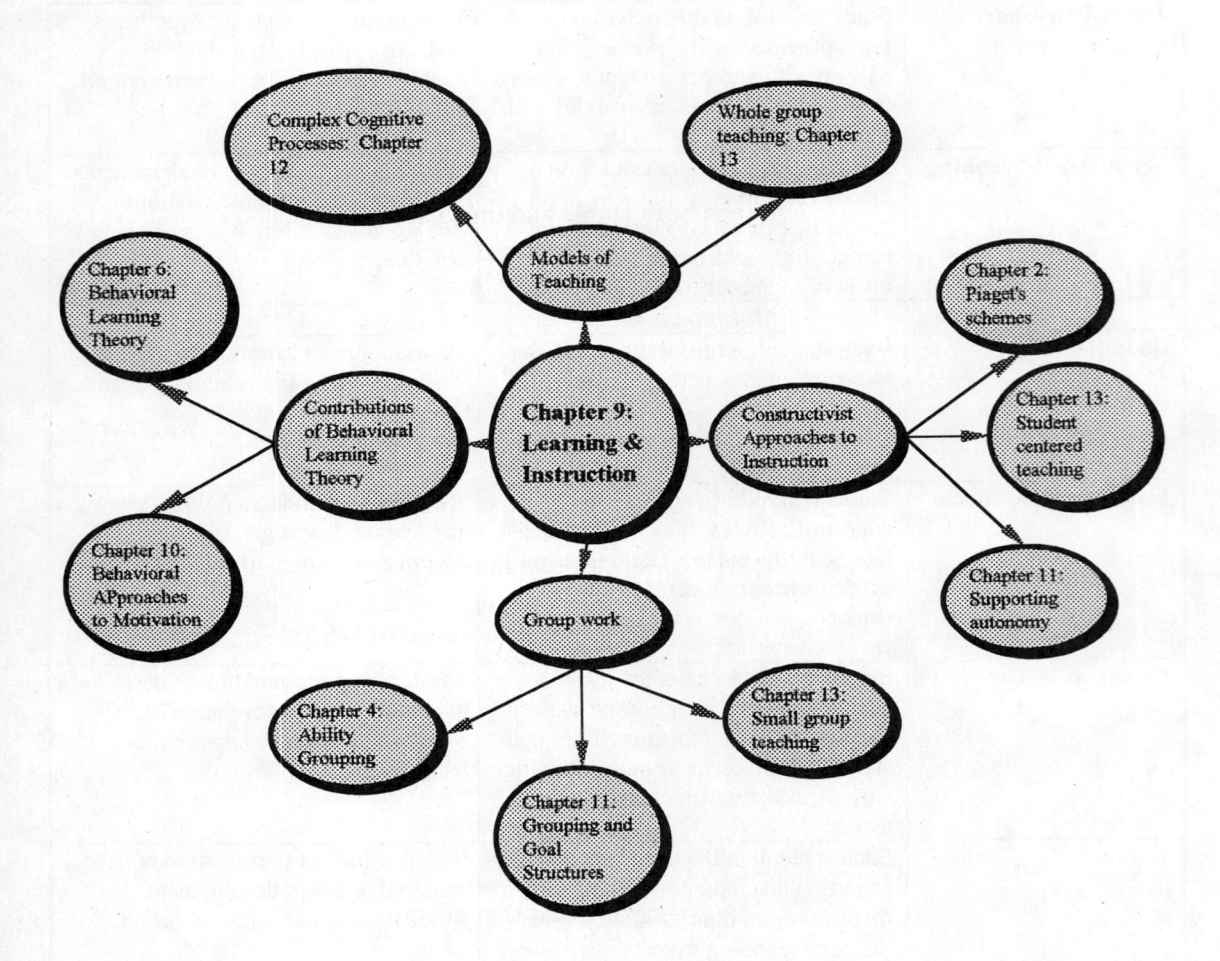

- Chapter 9: Learning & Instruction
  - Models of Teaching
    - Complex Cognitive Processes: Chapter 12
    - Whole group teaching: Chapter 13
  - Contributions of Behavioral Learning Theory
    - Chapter 6: Behavioral Learning Theory
    - Chapter 10: Behavioral Approaches to Motivation
  - Constructivist Approaches to Instruction
    - Chapter 2: Piaget's schemes
    - Chapter 13: Student centered teaching
    - Chapter 11: Supporting autonomy
  - Group work
    - Chapter 4: Ability Grouping
    - Chapter 11: Grouping and Goal Structures
    - Chapter 13: Small group teaching

Copyright © 1998 by Allyn and Bacon

10

Motivation: Issues and Explanations

Teaching Outline

I. What Do You Think?
II. What Is Motivation?
    A. Definition: an internal state that arouses, directs, and maintains behavior
    B. Often involves choice, duration, intensity, persistence, and emotional response
    C. Motivation can be seen both stable and unstable.
        1. Motivation can be seen as traits, or stable characteristics of individuals
        2. Motivation can also be seen as a temporary state that fluctuates in response to environmental or internal states.
III. Intrinsic And Extrinsic Motivation
    A. Intrinsic
        1. Intrinsic motivation is associated with activities that are their own reward
        2. Enjoyment of task or sense of accomplishment that it brings
    B. Extrinsic
        1. Motivation created by external factors like rewards and punishments
        2. Not interested in activity for its own sake, but instead for possible gains
    C. Locus of causality explains the students' reason for performing tasks
        1. Internal/intrinsic locus: Students freely choose to perform an activity
        2. External/extrinsic locus: Students are influenced by someone or something outside them
IV. Four General Approaches To Motivation
    A. Behavioral approaches to motivation
        1. Reward is an attractive object or event supplied as a consequence of a particular behavior
        2. Incentive is an object or event that encourages or discourages behavior
    B. Humanistic approaches to motivation
        1. Reaction against behaviorism and Freudian psychoanalysis
        2. Emphasis on personal freedom, choice, self-determination, and personal growth (example, Maslow's hierarchy of needs)
        3. Role of needs is central; people are motivated to fulfill their potential
    C. Cognitive approaches to motivation
        1. Behavior is determined by thinking, not simply by reward or punishment for past behavior
        2. People is initiated and regulated by plans, goals, schemas, expectations, and attributions
        3. A central assumption is that people respond not to external or physical conditions or events, but to interpretations

Motivation: Issues and Explanations

                  4.   People are seen as active and curious, searching for information to solve personally relevant problems
        D.   Social learning approaches to motivation
                1.   Integration of behavioral and cognitive approaches
                2.   Expectancy X value theories: motivation is the product of two forces,
                3.   expectation of success combined with the value of the goal (example, Bandura's Social Cognitive Theory).

V.   Elements Of Motivation To Learn In School
        A.   Planning
        B.   Concentration on a goal
        C.   Metacognitive awareness of progress
        D.   Clear perception of feedback
        E.   Pride and satisfaction in achievement
        F.   Little anxiety or fear of failure

VI.   Goals (what an individual is striving to accomplish) and Motivation
        A.   Types of goals
                1.   Most effective: Specific, moderately difficult, within reach
                2.   Learning goals
                      a)   seek challenge and mastery
                      b)   task-involved
                      c)   persist
                3.   Performance goals
                      a)   seek to perform well
                      b)   ego-involved
                      c)   give up easily
        B.   Feedback and goal acceptance
                1.   Feedback: An accurate sense of where one is and how far one has to go
                2.   Goal acceptance: Students accept goals set by teachers or establish own goals
        C.   Goals: Lessons for teachers
                1.   Students are more likely to work towards goals that are clear, specific, moderately challenging, attainable in short time
                2.   Emphasis should be on learning and improving, not just performing well

VII.   Needs And Motivation
        A.   Needs: What a deficiency person requires or thinks he/she requires for overall well-being; needs activate motivation
        B.   Maslow's believed that needs function as hierarchy
                1.   Deficiency needs (four)
                      a)   Survival, safety, belonging, self-esteem
                      b)   Must be satisfied first
                2.   Being needs (three)
                      a)   Intellectual achievement, aesthetic appreciation, and self-actualization

Motivation: Issues and Explanations

      b) Never completely fulfilled, endlessly renewed
    3. Criticisms of the theory
    4. Educational implications
      a) Enables look at full person: physical, emotional, and intellectual needs interrelated
      b) Students with deficiency needs will not seek knowledge and understanding
      c) Student needs and teacher's goals may conflict
  C. Need For Achievement: Desire To Excel For The Sake Of Achieving
    1. Origins in the family and cultural group of the child
    2. Resultant motivation: When the achievement motivation is greater than the need to avoid failure,
    3. Fear of failure: When the achievement motivation is less than the need to avoid failure,
      a) The student will usually be discouraged by failure and encouraged by success
  D. The Need For Self-Determination
    1. The desire to have our own wishes rather than external rewards
    2. People strive to become the causal agent for their own behavior
    3. DeCharms model: Origins versus pawns
  E. Need For Relatedness:
    1. The need to develop bonds with others in order to be connected to important people in our lives
    2. Two components: involvement and autonomy support
    3. Involvement: The degree to which teachers are interested in and involved with children's interests and experiences
    4. Autonomy support: The degree to which teachers and parents encourage children to make their own choices
  F. Needs And Motivation: Lessons For Teachers
    1. Meet lower level needs first, providing a secure learning environment
    2. Make sure that tasks offer a sense of achievement
    3. Students need to form positive relationships with others
    4. Teachers need to make students feel secure, competent, and cared-for
    5. Students need to feel like origins rather than pawns
VIII. Attributions, Beliefs, And Motivation
  A. Attribution theory describes how an individual's justifications and excuses influence motivation (B. Weiner)
  B. 3 dimensions: locus, stability, responsbility
  C. Locus: internal/external dimension
    1. Internal locus related to confidence and self-esteem, or loss of self-esteem
    2. Students with internal locus feel responsible for success through skill and effort
    3. Students with external locus prefer to work in situations governed by luck

Motivation: Issues and Explanations

- D. Stability: stable or unstable dimension; related to expectations about future
    1. If success attributed to stable factors, similar expectation of past to future
    2. If success attributed to unstable factors, expectation is future will differ from past
- E. Responsibility: Whether a student can control the causes of success; it is related to emotional reactions
    1. If attribution is that success or failure is due to controllable factors, the outcome is feeling of pride or shame
    2. If attribution is to uncontrollable factors, outcome will be gratitude for good luck
- F. Attributions are linked to emotional responses that may support continued activity or diminish motivated behavior
- G. Distinguishing between self-determination and control by others
    1. Deci and Ryan's concept of intrinsic motivation
    2. DeCharms's concept of origins and pawns
    3. Rotter's concept of locus of control
- H. Learned Helplessness: A belief that events and outcomes are uncontrollable
    1. Results in cognitive, motivational, and affective deficits
- I. Attributions And Student Motivation
    1. Positive, adaptive mastery-oriented response: failure attributed to lack of effort (internal and controllable); focus on strategies for succeeding next time
    2. Negative, unmotivated: failure attributed to internal, stable, and uncontrollable causes (resigned to failure and apathetic)
- J. Cues about causes
    1. teacher behavior with respect to praise, providing help, questions
    2. social comparison by self or others
- K. Beliefs about ability
    1. Entity view: Intelligence fixed, stable, uncontrollable
        a) students tend to set performance goals
    2. Incremental view: Intelligence is a set of skills that can be changed; it is unstable, yet controllable
        a) young children hold this view almost exclusively
        b) value effort
        c) Between 10 and 12 years of age, children learn to differentiate among effort, ability and performance
        d) Students tend to set learning goals
        e) Failure is not as threatening
        f) Tend to set moderately difficult goals which are the most motivating

IX. Beliefs About Efficacy
- A. Self-efficacy refers to our beliefs about competency in a certain area
    1. Sense of self-efficacy affects motivation through goal-setting
    2. Self-efficacy related to self-attributions

3. High levels of self-efficacy supports motivation
- B. Teacher efficacy
  1. Efficacy grows from genuine success
X. Attributions, Achievement Motivation, And Self-Worth
- A. Mastery-oriented students
  1. Set learning goals,
  2. Assume responsibility for success and failure
  3. Competitive
- B. Failure-avoiding students
  1. Set performance goals
  2. Seek to protect image
  3. Take few risks or may decide they are incompetent
- C. Failure-accepting students
  1. Failure avoidance leads to failure acceptance
  2. Believe that their problems are due to low ability
- D. Lessons for teachers
  1. Help failure-avoiding students to set realistic goals,
  2. Avoid encouraging self-defeating attitudes
- E. Guidelines: Encouraging Students' Self-Worth

XI. Anxiety And Coping In The Classroom
- A. Definition: General uneasiness or feeling of tension
- B. Improves performance on simple tasks; interferes on complex tasks
- C. Anxiety is negatively related to almost all school achievement
- D. What causes anxiety in school?
  1. Pressures to perform, S
  2. Severe consequences for failure
  3. Competitive
  4. Comparisons among students
- E. How anxiety affects performance.
  1. Tobias suggests that anxiety can negatively affect attention, learning, and performance
     a) Anxious students divide their attention between information to be learned and their feelings of nervousness,
     b) Anxious students perform poorly on tasks involving memory
        (1) distracted by irrelevant information and details
     c) Anxious students may have poor test-taking skills

XII. Helping Anxious Students
- A. Set realistic goals
- B. Work at moderate pace; for example, on tests; eliminate time pressures
- C. Provide structure such as repetitive lessons

XIII. Summary
- A. Key terms and concepts

XIV. Teachers' casebook/ What would they do?

Motivation: Issues and Explanations

Learning Activities and Related Research

ACTIVITIES	HANDOUTS
Chapter 10	10.0 Lecture Outline
Cooperative Activities	
10.0 What's common?	
10.1 What motivates you?	
10.3 Motivating students	10.1 Encouraging Motivation
Research Activities	
Using Technology	
Field Experience	
10.4 Comparing high and low achievers	10.2 Achievement Motivation: Observation Chart
10.5 Motivating students: teacher observation	
Other Teaching Activities	
10.6 Types of Motivation	
10.7 Levels of aspiration	
10.8 Maslow's Hierarchy	10.3 Maslow's Hierarchy and Motivation
10.9 Origins and Pawns	10.4 Training students to be origins
10.10 Explaining the same event differently	10.5 Explain this.
10.11 Locus of Control	10.6 Locus of control
10.12 Attribution of Motive	
	10.7 Concept map: Links to other chapters

Cooperative Activities

10.1   <u>What is Common?</u>

Have your students read the vignettes at the beginning of Chapter 10 (page 373). These vignettes describe the motivational difficulties of Hopeless Henry, Safe Sally, Satisfied Sam, Defensive Diana, and Anxious Amy. Your students should attempt to:
1. Identify what motivates each student.
2. Determine what is common the sources of motivation identified in 1.
3. Provide a definition of motivation that could be applied to <u>all</u> of the children on page 373.

10.2   <u>What Motivates You?</u>

Have your students in small groups develop a list of things/people that motivate them. Once a complete list has been developed, have students categorize the items that appear on the list and come up with key categories of motivators.

262

Motivation: Issues and Explanations

10.3   Motivating Students

From the list of General Motivational Approaches **(Handout Master 10.1) ENCOURAGING MOTIVATION)** indicate which ones would be appropriate in the given situations. Then describe the exact behaviors or actions which could be applied. (Can be used as a handout or in class oral exercise.)

General Motivational Approaches
1. Arrange extrinsic rewards
2. Use student interests in lessons
3. Give more challenging work
4. Praise success
5. Provide a safer learning situation
6. Communicate your expectations
7. Structure a cooperative learning task
8. Set up an individualistic goal structure
9. Use individualized instruction
10. Involve student in setting reasonable goals
11. Fulfill need for affiliation and belonging
12. Provide realistic success experiences

1. Carol is a very bright, friendly girl who has been working individually on math because she is more advanced than the rest of the class. At first she was enthusiastic about working on her own, but after three weeks she is beginning to drag and complain about doing math, and the amount of work she does is decreasing. How would you help Carol to become more motivated in math?

    General motivational approach(es):_____

    Specific action(s):_____

2. Mike seems to be interested in social studies, which is generally conducted with the entire class in an oral discussion and report format. Mike listens to whoever is speaking, nods, laughs, looks puzzled, and so on at appropriate times, so you know he's paying attention. But Mike never voluntarily contributes anything, and when you call on him, he seems so embarrassed and confused that you feel sorry for putting him on the spot. How can you encourage Mike to be motivated to participate during social studies class?

    General motivational approach(es):_____

    Specific action(s):_____

Motivation: Issues and Explanations

3. Jody is going to be a student in your class this fall, and you're already thinking about your first interactions with him. His two older brothers have a reputation for being smart, but disruptive. Jody has been living up to their reputation plus the other kids like to follow his lead. He seems to thoroughly enjoy their attention and admiration. How can you influence Jody so that he will be motivated to use his intelligence and leadership qualities in a more positive way?

    General motivational approach(es):_____

    Specific action(s): _____

4. Mary is truly a pitiful sight. Hair uncombed, poorly dressed, listless, shy, thumb in mouth, she sits at her desk in your second-grade class, hardly moving without your speaking directly to her. As far as you can tell she learned very little during her two years in the first grade and unless some changes occur, she's not going to learn much this year. How would you encourage Mary's motivation to engage in learning experiences?

    General motivational approach(es):_____

    Specific action(s): _____

Field Experience

10.4 <u>Comparing High And Low Achievers</u>

Ask students to select a classroom for observation and ask the teacher to point out three students who are considered high achievers and three who are low achievers (they do not show the teacher what they will be observing). Have them observe the classroom during a discussion or recitation session and during a period of assigned seatwork. Ask them to use the following chart to accompany the observation (See **Handout Master 10.2**). As they observe, have them make a frequency tally in the chart. When they are finished, have them compare the two groups.

	Raise hand to contribute orally	Ask for help	Receive praise/correction
Low achievers			
High achievers			

Motivation: Issues and Explanations

10.5   Motivation Students: Teacher Observation

Have your students observe a classroom teacher for a half-day. They should use **Handout Master 10.2** to record their observations of strategies used by the teacher for motivating the students.

Other Teaching Activities

10.6   Types Of Motivation

Have the students match the statements below with the appropriate view of motivation:

   A. Behavioral view (extrinsic motivation)
   B. Cognitive view (intrinsic motivation)
   C. Humanistic view (deprivation and being needs)
   D. Need for achievement
   E. Need to avoid failure
   F. Attributing success/failure to internal-stable causes
   G. Attributing success/failure to external-unstable causes

1. _____ "I'm going to stay home tonight and work on my science project. It's interesting and I've got an idea I want to try out."

2. _____ "I want to finish the week's assignment by Thursday because I get to do what I want in Friday's class if I've completed my work."

3. _____ "I just can't concentrate on the lesson because I know at lunch nobody is going to want to sit with me."

4. _____ "I tried hard and earned my 'A' in physics."

5. _____ "If at first I don't succeed, I'll try again. (This student likes challenges and doesn't need excessive praise or encouragement.)

6. _____ "If at first I don't succeed, I quit." (This student likes safe situations where he will probably succeed, and needs recognition of successes.)

7. _____ "I know I'm dumb in math, and I don't even try anymore."

Answers: 1. B   2. A   3. C   4. F   5. D   6. E   7. F

Motivation: Issues and Explanations

10.7   Level of Aspiration

From Fernald, P. S. & Fernald, L. D. Jr. (1981). Activity 76. In L. T. Benjamin, Jr. and K. Lowman, Eds. Activities handbook for the teaching of psychology. Washington, DC. : American Psychological Association.

Concept: Research has shown that our "reach" often exceeds our grasp. Several factors that influence "reach" or aspiration level are highlighted in the following activity.

Procedure: Four volunteers are asked to leave the room. Inform the remaining students that you wish to test three hypotheses: (1) Group standards influence level of aspiration (2) Level of aspiration remains close to actual performance, with a tendency to be above rather than below it (3) Success leads to an increased level of aspiration, and failure leads to a decrease. Write the following chart on the board:

Volunteer	Standard	First estimate	Score	Second estimate
1	15			
2	15			
3	35			
4	35			

Bring the volunteers into the room one at a time. Do not allow them to see the chalkboard. Have them stand facing a table on which you have placed two coffee cans 3 feet apart, one can containing 60 marbles, the other empty. Explain to the volunteers that they are going to take a text of manual dexterity. The task is to transfer as many marbles as possible from the full can to the empty can in 30 seconds. They can transfer only one marble at a time, using only one hand. Tell the first volunteers, "Most people can place about 15 marbles in the empty can during a 30 second interval."

For the second two volunteers, substitute 35 for 15. Be sure to emphasize the score of "most high school students"; if the standard is mentioned only casually, it may be ignored. Next, ask the volunteers to estimate the number of marbles they expect to transfer. Then have them perform the task. When 30 seconds are up, count the number of marbles transferred, inform the volunteers, and tell them they will have a second trial. Again ask for an estimate of expected performance and have them repeat the task. (The score on the second trial is of no consequence for the demonstration, but it may give the volunteers some satisfaction in terms of improved performance).

Motivation: Issues and Explanations

Hypothesis 1 can be tested by comparing the initial estimates of the first volunteers with those of the second volunteers. Typically, the estimates offer strong support for this hypothesis. The effect is great because the volunteers did not have prior experience with the task. Hypothesis 2 can be tested by comparing second estimates with initial scores. Typically, second estimates are very close to scores; in the majority of cases, they are higher. With regard to Hypothesis 3, comparison of the first and second estimates of the first two volunteers typically confirms the hypothesized effect of success, and a similar comparison for the last two volunteers typically supports the hypothesis about failure (providing the estimates were too high to achieve).

Discussion: Discuss the results obtained in terms of support for the three hypotheses. What happens to people when their level of aspiration is too high? Too low? How do you think the results of this activity might be applied to performance in schools? What are the factors that influence level of aspiration?

10.8   Maslow's Hierarchy

From Bragstad, B. J. and Stumpf, S. M. (1987). *A guidebook for teaching study skills and motivation* (2nd ed.). Boston: Allyn and Bacon, Inc., 209.

Use **Handout Master 10.3** to help students examine their motivation to learn. Using Maslow's hierarchy, have students match each statement of a student's positive experience to a Maslow level, then decide if it represents an internal or external locus of control. Then ask students to rank the experiences in order of importance according to Maslow's theory.

10.9   Origins And Pawns

Origins and Pawns: A Special Program to Enhance Competence. In 1976, Richard de Charms published a book called Enhancing motivation: Change in the classroom, New York: Irvington, describing the results of a four-year effort to enhance motivation in several elementary and junior high classrooms. The program was based on earlier studies of classroom motivation and the characterization of students as "origins" and "pawns." We will look first at the results of his earlier studies and then at the program itself. According to de Charms, origins are people who are in control of their own achievement, due to skills they have developed at goal setting, their ability to plan strategies to reach these goals, and their willingness to take responsibility for their own actions. Pawns are people who are at the mercy of the environment and feel helpless in the face of outside forces. Some situations seem to encourage "pawnlike" behavior, while others seem to encourage people to be achievement-oriented origins. De Charms believes that schools should create environments where students will have many chances to act as origins, although not all students may be able to do so immediately.

As a result of these earlier studies, de Charms became involved in a special program to enhance motivation in the schools. The elementary and junior high teachers in

Motivation: Issues and Explanations

the program were asked to introduce their students to a number of the concepts we have been discussing in this chapter: (1) self-concept, (2) achievement motivation, (3) realistic goal setting, and (4) the origin-pawn distinction. Games, exercises, creative writing, journals, art-work, and other techniques were used to promote student understanding. **Handout Master 10.4** shows one of the methods for teaching the origin-pawn concept to sixth and seventh graders.

Reflected in this exercise and in the others used in the program is a framework for self-motivation. Students were asked to set reasonable goals, make concrete plans to reach those goals, devise ways of evaluating their progress, and assume personal responsibility. These steps are in many ways reminiscent of the social-learning theorists' ideas about motivation as well as the research on metacognitive skills discussed in the chapters on cognitive learning. In addition, by helping students to see themselves as origins, de Charms is encouraging them to view their successes and failures as the outgrowth of internal, controllable causes. All these factors contribute to a sense of personal competence. Based on the results of the special motivation program, de Charms concluded that "motivation training for personal causation enhances both motivation and academic achievement when embedded in subject-matter material" (de Charms, 1976, p. 210). He also noted that the origin concept, with its emphasis on personal responsibility, was a much better source of motivation for both teacher and student than externally imposed tests of accountability.

10.10 Explaining the Same Event Differently

Use **Handout Master 10.5** for this activity. Ask your students to write explanations for two different audiences. Then have them analyze their attributions in terms of locus (internal vs. external), controllability (controllable or uncontrollable), and stability (unstable or stable). What changes?

10.11 Locus of Control

The following activity is taken from Morris, C. (1988). Psychology: An introduction, (6th ed.) Englewood Cliffs, NJ: Prentice Hall, p. I-74.
Objective: To give students the opportunity to determine whether they have an internal or external locus of control.
Procedure: Give the LOCUS OF CONTROL TEST **(Handout Master 10.6)** to the class. When the students are finished have them score the test according to the following procedure: Odd statements reflect "internal" and even statements reflect "external" locus of control. Count the number of true statements for odd and then the number of true statements for even.
Discussion: There is a tendency in our society toward an external locus of control. The obvious implications of this are that people are likely to follow the orders of others (those who have power). What is the importance of being internally versus externally controlled? Were students surprised about the way in which they scored? How honest were they in their responses?

10.11 Locus Of Control Test

Directions: Read each statement and indicate whether you believe it true or false.
1. Getting good grades is due to hard work.
2. It is not important to vote in elections.
3. I earn the honors I receive
4. A person can get rich by gambling and winning.
5. I have a need to be kept informed about the world.
6. I sometimes don't know who my real friends are.
7. I can often convince friends that I am right.
8. The grades I get are due to the teacher's moods.
9. There is no such thing as luck.
10. The jobs I get are often a matter of who I know.

10.12 Attribution Of Motive

The following activity is taken from Morris, C. (1988). Psychology: An introduction, (6th ed.) Englewood Cliffs, NJ: Prentice Hall, p. I-67-68.

Objective: To demonstrate the attribution of motives.
Procedure: Prepare two sets of instructions for the class so that half of the students will receive instructions as follows:

"List, in order of importance, the five most important reasons why people work."

The other half of the class will receive the following instructions:

"List, in order of importance, the five most important factors for you in choosing a job."

Make sure the students are told that this work is to be done individually, but they are not to put their names on the papers. The work will be collected. When the students are finished, collect the papers and sort them according to instructions. Summarize the reasons for each set of instructions on the board.
Discussion: Explain that people tend to perceive the motives of others externally, while they tend to perceive their own internally. How does attribution of motivation influence other ideas we may have about people?

Discussion Questions

1. Explain why a student would be motivated to study for a test according to a behavioral viewpoint and a cognitive viewpoint. Explain why a student would be motivated not to study for a test from both viewpoints.

Motivation: Issues and Explanations

2. Can children not learn in school if they are hungry, have felt unsafe in their neighborhood? Take Maslow's hierarchy of needs into account when answering this question. What criticisms would you offer for this hierarchy?

3. If a student's attribution of failure to internal-stable causes is fairly accurate ("I'm not very smart and there's nothing I can do about that"), how can a teacher prevent the student from becoming apathetic and discouraged?

4. How can the improper use of praise have a negative impact on a student?

5. Do you think it is generally true that first-graders have more curiosity and are more motivated to learn than sixth-graders or high school students? If so, can you explain the decline? Be careful to consider the development that occurs during this time period.

6. Although research has shown that over-reliance on extrinsic motivation can reduce intrinsic motivation in students, many teachers resort to stickers, candy, and extra privileges to control students' behavior. Do you think these two systems can be used simultaneously? If so, explain how. If not, give reasons.

7. How would you teach students to set their own goals and monitor their success in accomplishing these goals?

Additional Resources for Teaching This Chapter

PRINT RESOURCES

Hahn, A. (1987). Reaching out to America's dropouts: What to do? Phi Delta Kappan, 69(4), 256-263. Hahn outlines the causes and consequences of dropping out of school and looks at what we have learned about programs that identify and assist dropouts.

Rogers, C. R. (1977). Beyond the watershed: And where now? Educational Leadership, 34, 623-629. Rogers presents a definition of person-centered education, explores the current state of humanistic education and its ramifications, the research that supports it, and the means for sustaining it. He suggests that the inner (intuitive) person is the next great frontier of education.

Test anxiety, Hot Topics Series from Phi Delta Kappa. In six chapters of this booklet, test anxiety is defined, examined from a psychological and physiological level, attributes of test anxious students are described, variables that affect anxiety are reviewed and treatments are suggested. Order from: Phi Delta Kappa, P. O. Box 789, Bloomington, IN, 47402-0789.

REFERENCES

Bandura, A. (1986). <u>Social foundations of thought and action: A social cognitive theory</u>. Englewood Cliffs, NJ: Prentice Hall.

Gottfried, A. E. (1985). Academic intrinsic motivation in elementary and junior high school students. <u>Journal of Educational Psychology, 77</u>, 631-645.

Jones, E. E., Kanouse, D. E., Kelley, H. H., Nisbett, R. E., Valins, S., & Weiner, B. (1987). Attribution: Perceiving the causes of behavior. Hillsdale, NJ: Lawrence Erlbaum.

Manning, B., & Payne, B. D. (1996). <u>Self-talk for teachers and students</u>. Needham Heights, MA: Allyn & Bacon.

Reeve, J. M. (1996). <u>Motivating others: Nurturing our inner resources</u>. Needham Heights, MA: Allyn & Bacon.

Seligman, M. E. (1992). <u>Helplessness: On development, depression, and death</u>. New York, NY: W. H. Freeman & Co.

Stipek, D. J. (1993). <u>Motivation to learn</u>. Needham Heights, MA: Allyn & Bacon.

FILMS, VIDEOTAPES, AND AUDIOCASSETTES

What I learned from not learning. An insightful examination of what really goes on in a classroom: teachers present accurate information in unintelligible ways to uninterested students; or irrelevant answers to appropriate questions. Teachers may be so intent on what they are teaching that they are unable to distinguish between students who already know what they are being taught and those who are only pretending to understand. The format used is that of an adult classroom; of course the same applies at all levels of education. (12 minutes, color) To purchase: #CC-1915. Order from: Films for the Humanities & Sciences, Inc. P. O. Box 2053, Princeton, NJ, 08543, or Telephone: (800)-257-5126.

Head of the class. This story aroused tremendous interest when it was broadcast on *60 Minutes*. It reveals the high pressure of the Japanese educational system, where the goal is to gain admission to the university. American educators must decide which elements of the Japanese educational system they should draw upon to improve their own. From Films for the Humanities. 14 minutes.

Handout Master 10.0

Lecture Outline ----- Motivation: Issues and Explanations

- What is Motivation?

- Goals and Motivation

- Needs and Motivation

- Attributions, Beliefs, and Motivation

- Anxiety and Coping in the Classroom

Copyright © 1998 by Allyn and Bacon

Handout Master 10. 1

Encouraging Motivation

From the list of <u>General Motivational Approaches</u> below, indicate which ones would be appropriate in the given situations. Then describe the exact behaviors or actions which could be applied.

1.	Arrange extrinsic rewards	7.	Structure a cooperative learning task
2.	Use student interests in lessons	8.	Set up an individualistic goal structure
3.	Give more challenging work	9.	Use individualized instruction
4.	Praise success	10.	Involve student in setting reasonable goals
5.	Provide a safer learning situation	11.	Fulfill need for affiliation and belonging
6.	Communicate your expectations	12.	Provide realistic success experiences

1. Carol is a very bright, friendly girl who has been working individually on math because she is more advanced than the rest of the class. At first she was enthusiastic about working on her own, but after three weeks she is beginning to drag and complain about doing math, and the amount of work she does is decreasing. How would you help Carol to become more motivated in math?

    General motivational approach(es):_____

    Specific action(s): _____

2. Mike seems to be interested in social studies, which is generally conducted with the entire class in an oral discussion and report format. Mike listens to whoever is speaking, nods, laughs, looks puzzled, and so on at appropriate times, so you know he's paying attention. But Mike never voluntarily contributes anything, and when you call on him, he seems so embarrassed and confused that you feel sorry for putting him on the spot. How can you encourage Mike to be motivated to participate during social studies class?

    General motivational approach(es):_____

    Specific action(s): _____

3. Jody is going to be a student in your class this fall, and you're already thinking about your first interactions with him. His two older brothers have a reputation for being smart, but disruptive. Jody has been living up to their reputation plus the other kids like to follow his lead. He seems to thoroughly enjoy their attention and admiration. How can you influence Jody so that he will be motivated to use his intelligence and leadership qualities in a more positive way?

    General motivational approach(es):_____

    Specific action(s):_____

4. Mary is truly a pitiful sight. Hair uncombed, poorly dressed, listless, shy, thumb in mouth, she sits at her desk in your second-grade class, hardly moving without your speaking directly to her. As far as you can tell she learned very little during her two years in the first grade and unless some changes occur, she's not going to learn much this year. How would you encourage Mary's motivation to engage in learning experiences?

    General motivational approach(es):_____

    Specific action(s): _____

Copyright © 1998 by Allyn and Bacon

Handout Master 10.1

Encouraging Motivation

From the list of General Motivation Approaches indicate which ones would be appropriate in the numbered cases that follow. Then describe the exact behaviors or actions that would operationalize the general approach.

General Motivation Approaches

1. Arrange extrinsic rewards
2. Use student interests in lessons
3. Give more challenging work
4. Praise success
5. Provide a safe learning environment
6. Communicate your expectations
7. Structure a cooperative learning task
8. Set up an individualistic goal structure
9. Use individualized instruction
10. Involve student in setting reasonable goals
11. Fulfill need for affiliation and belonging
12. Provide realistic success experiences

Cases

1. Carol is a very bright, friendly girl who has been working individually on math because she is more advanced than the rest of the class. At first she was enthusiastic about working on her own, but after three weeks she is beginning to drag and complain about doing math, and the amount of work she does is decreasing. How would you help Carol to become more motivated in math? ,

General Motivational Approach(es):
_____

Specific action(s):
_____

Mike seems to be interested in social studies, which is generally conducted with the entire class in an oral discussion and report format. Mike listens to whenever is speaking, nods, laughs, looks puzzled, and so on at appropriate times, so you know he's paying attention,. But Mike never voluntarily contributes anything, and when you call on hum, he seems so embarrassed add confused that you feel sorry for putting him on the spot. How can you encourage Mike to be motivated to participate during social studies class?

General Motivational Approach(es):
_____

Specific action(s):
_____

Jody is going to be a student in your class this fall, and you're already thinking about your first interactions with him. His two older brothers have a reputation for being smart, but disruptive. Jody has been living lip to their reputation plus the other kids like to follow his lead. He seems to thoroughly enjoy their attention and admiration. How can you influence Jody so that he will be motivated to we his intelligence and leadership qualities in a more positive way?

Copyright © 1998 by Allyn and Bacon

General Motivational Approach(es):
_____

Specific action(s):
_____

4. Mary is truly a pitiful sight. Hair uncombed, poorly dressed, listless, shy, thumb in mouth, she sits at her desk in your second-grade class, hardly moving without your speaking directly to her. As far as you can tell she learned very little during her two years in the first grade and unless some changes occur, she's not going to learn much this year. How would you encourage Mary's motivation to engage in learning experiences?

General Motivational Approach(es):
_____

Specific action(s):
_____

Copyright © 1998 by Allyn and Bacon

Handout Master 10.2

Achievement Motivation: Observation Chart

Record the frequency with which the teacher you are observing engages in behaviors that might increase or decrease motivation.

Behavior	Observed?
Promises reward	
Threatens punishment	
Provides goals for a task	
Provides rewards	
Provides praise	
Stimulates interest	
Uses challenging tasks	
Verbally challenges children	
Gives students choices	
Lets students set goals	
Lets students evaluate their own work	
Stimulates curiosity	
Stimulates questions	
Allows free time	

Copyright © 1998 by Allyn and Bacon

Handout Master 10.3

Maslow's Hierarchy and Motivation

Decide whether the source of each response to positive experiences is internal or external. Then write I or E in front of each item. Using Maslow's hierarchy, shown on page 383 of your text, write the name of the level of need that is the source of motivation for each response.

Maslow Level	Internal Or External	Student's Positive Experiences
_____	_____	1. "Getting good grades."
_____	_____	2. "Having a teacher who cares."
_____	_____	3. "My wanting to learn and to understand."
_____	_____	4. "Having success now that I understand."
_____	_____	5. "Teacher wanting to know every student."
_____	_____	6. "My own satisfaction from doing well."
_____	_____	7. "Teacher paying attention to me."
_____	_____	8. "Teacher never giving up on me."
_____	_____	9. "Getting on the honor roll."
_____	_____	10. "Getting a good job in the future."
_____	_____	11. "Knowing how to do the work—understanding."
_____	_____	12. "Parents caring about me."
_____	_____	13. "Not wanting to disappoint the teacher."
_____	_____	14. "Having a bright teacher who is interested in the subject."
_____	_____	15. "Teacher explaining well so I enjoy the subject."

From Bragstad, B. J. & Stumpf, S. M. (1987). A guidebook for teaching study skills and motivation, 2nd Ed. Boston: Allyn and Bacon.

Handout Master 10.4

Training Students to be Origins

Approach: Introduce a set of words describing origin behavior

<u>Origins</u> are people who:

(a)   take **personal** responsibility
(b)   **prepare** their work carefully
(c) **plan** their lives to help them achieve their goals
(d)   **practice** their skills
(e)   **persist** in their work
(f)   have **patience**—they know that they have to do certain things to reach their goals
(h)   check their **progress** (use feedback)
(i)   move toward **perfecting** their skills, paying special attention to improvement.

Activity: Students are asked to set personal goals and construct checklists to keep track of the number of times they act in accordance with their goals.

How do these characteristics reflect the social-learning theorist's ideas about motivation?

_____

How does this program relate to research on metacognitive skills?

_____

How do the behaviors and attitudes in this program relate to attribution theory?

_____

From de Charms, R. (1976). <u>Enhancing motivation: change in the classroom</u>. New York: Irvington Publishers, Inc.

Copyright © 1998 by Allyn and Bacon

Handout Master 10.5

Explain This

You have sneaked a look at your report card and are horrified to find that you have gotten two "F" grades in English and in Mathematics. You know you will be asked to explain these grades to your parents. As you are looking at your grades, your good friend from class looks over your shoulder and wants a look at your report card. Your friend hates school and thinks grades are a waste of energy. In the spaces provided below, write an explanation for these grades to your parents and to your friend.

Explaining bad grades to parent:

My grades in English and Mathematics are bad because.....

Explaining bad grades to friend

My grades in English and Mathematics are bad because.....

What kind of attribution did you make to your parent?

What kind of attribution did you make to your friend?

Was there a difference in the attribution made? What changed?

Copyright © 1998 by Allyn and Bacon

Handout Master 10.6

Locus of Control Test

Directions: Read each statement and indicate whether you believe it is true or false.

_____ 1.   Getting good grades is due to hard work.
_____ 2.   It is not important to vote in elections.
_____ 3.   I earn the honors I receive.
_____ 4.   A person can get rich by gambling and winning.
_____ 5.   I have a need to be kept informed about the world.
_____ 6.   I sometimes don't know who my real friends are.
_____ 7.   I can often convince friends that I am right.
_____ 8.   The grades I get are due to the teacher's moods.
_____ 9.   There is no such thing as luck.
_____10.   The jobs I get are often a matter of whom I know.

Now identify and circle all the statements that reflect an external locus of control. How many of these statements did you say were true? What is the significance of being internally or externally controlled? Were you surprised at the way you scored?

Copyright © 1998 by Allyn and Bacon

Handout Master 10.7: Links to Other Chapters

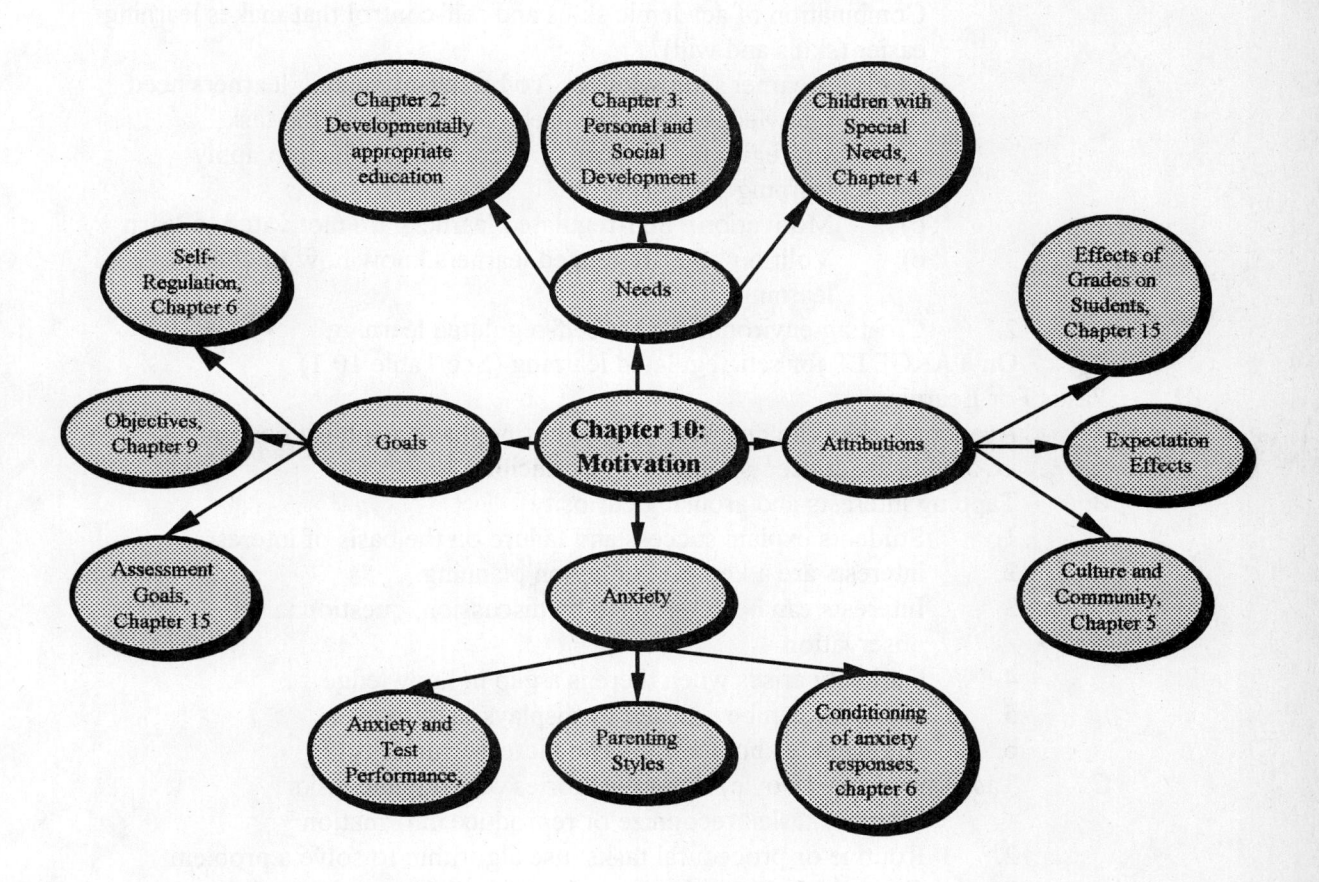

- **Chapter 10: Motivation**
  - **Needs**
    - Chapter 2: Developmentally appropriate education
    - Chapter 3: Personal and Social Development
    - Children with Special Needs, Chapter 4
  - **Goals**
    - Self-Regulation, Chapter 6
    - Objectives, Chapter 9
    - Assessment Goals, Chapter 15
  - **Attributions**
    - Effects of Grades on Students, Chapter 15
    - Expectation Effects
    - Culture and Community, Chapter 5
  - **Anxiety**
    - Anxiety and Test Performance
    - Parenting Styles
    - Conditioning of anxiety responses, chapter 6

Copyright © 1998 by Allyn and Bacon

Motivation, Teaching, and Learning

11

Motivation, Teaching, and Learning

Teaching Outline

I. What Do You Think?
II. The Ultimate Goal Of Teaching: Life-Long-Learning
    A. Self-regulated learning
        1. Combination of academic skills and self-control that makes learning easier (skills and will)
            a) Learner's knowledge: To be self-regulated, learners need knowledge about themselves, the subject, the task, strategies for learning, and context in which to apply learning
            b) Motivation: Self-regulated learners are motivated to learn
            c) Volition: Self-regulated learners know how to control learning.
        2. Creating environments for self-regulated learning
    B. On TARGETT for self-regulated learning (See Table 10.1)
III. Tasks For Learning
    A. Academic tasks can be interesting or boring; have a subject content; involve facts, concepts, opinions or principles
    B. Tapping interests and arousing curiosity
        1. Students explain success and failure on the basis of interest
        2. interests are a key part of lesson planning
        3. Interests can be determined by discussion, questionnaire, observation
        4. Curiosity arises when there is a gap in knowledge
        5. Curiosity can be aroused by displays or activities
        6. Knowledge about a topic can increase curiosity
    C. Task operations (Doyle): Four categories of academic tasks
        1. Memory tasks: recognize or reproduce information
        2. Routine or procedural tasks: use algorithm to solve a problem
        3. Comprehension tasks: transform, combine, or choose best information
        4. Opinion tasks: state a preference
    D. Risk and ambiguity
        1. Risk: Some tasks involve more likelihood of failure
            a) Few risks: memory or procedural tasks
            b) High risks: longer and more complex memory or procedural tasks
        2. Ambiguity: How straightforward the expected answer is

Motivation, Teaching, and Learning

3. Ambiguous: opinion and understanding tasks
    a) Unambiguous: memory and procedural tasks
E. Relationship with motivation
    1. Students motivated to lower risks and decrease the ambiguity in schoolwork
    2. Motivation can increase performance on low-risk, clear tasks
F. Task value
    1. Motivation in a specific situation is determined by expectations of success and the value attached to that success
    2. Attainment value: importance of doing well on the task
    3. Intrinsic or interest value: enjoyment obtained from a task
    4. Utility value: contribution of a task to meeting goals
G. Task types
    1. Authentic task is one that has some connection to real-life challenges
    2. Problem-based learning: students meet an ill-structured problem before they receive any instruction

IV. Supporting Autonomy And Recognizing Accomplishment In The Classroom
    A. Advantages of autonomy in the classroom
        1. Classroom environments that support student autonomy are associated with greater student interest, sense of competence, self-esteem, creativity, conceptual learning, and preference for challenge
        2. Students and parents seem to prefer more controlling teachers, even though students learn more when teachers support autonomy
    B. Information and control
        1. Cognitive evaluation theory explains that various events (reminders, grading,) can be controlling and informational
        2. If information is provided that increases a sense of competence, students' intrinsic motivation will be enhanced
        3. If events are controlling, intrinsic motivation is decreased
    C. Supporting autonomy
        1. Acknowledge students' points of view
        2. Encourage students' choice and initiative
        3. Provide rationale for limits, rules, and constraints
        4. Acknowledge the validity of negative reactions to teacher control
        5. Use noncontrolling, positive feedback
    D. Recognizing accomplishments

V. Grouping, Evaluation, and Time
    A. Grouping and goal structures
        1. Cooperative
        2. Competitive
        3. Individualistic
    B. Cooperative learning
        1. Increases achievement when the task involves complex problem solving

Motivation, Teaching, and Learning

        2. Well designed cooperative learning results in important social outcomes
    C. Motivating with cooperative learning
        1. Student Teams-Achievement Divisions system (STAD)
            a) Students are assigned to heterogeneous teams
            b) Students previous work used as base score or Individual Learning Expectation score (ILE) to rate improvement
            c) Improvement regardless of ability level, contributes to group score
        2. Teams-Games-Tournament (TGT)
            a) Heterogeneous groups help students to prepare for weekly tournaments
            b) Students compete across groups with students of similar ability
        3. Caution: research shows that students on unsuccessful teams were unhappy

VI. Evaluation And Time
    A. Evaluation
        1. Emphasis on competitive grading results in performance goals rather than learning goals, and ego-involvement rather than task-involvement
        2. Decrease the focus on performance goals by emphasizing the value of the tasks
    B. Time
        1. Students need time to process knowledge rather than "cover" it
        2. Students develop persistence and efficacy if they are allowed to stick with an activity

VII. Teacher Expectations
    A. Origins of the construct
        1. "Pygmalion in the classroom" effect in elementary classrooms
        2. Controversy over Rosenthal and Jacobson's research findings remains

VIII. Two Kinds Of Expectation Effects
    A. Self-fulfilling prophecy: incorrect expectation confirmed because it has been expected
    B. Sustaining expectation effect: teacher's, initially accurate, but unchanging expectation sustains student's achievement at the expected level
    C. Sources of expectations
    D. Point/Counterpoint: Can Teacher Expectations Affect Student Learning?
    E. Teacher behavior and student reaction
        1. Instructional strategies
            a) Ability grouping: have effect on students and teachers; preference for higher ability groups
            b) Pace and quantity of instruction increases as soon as students are ready

Motivation, Teaching, and Learning

                c)   Problem: teachers sometimes select inappropriate teaching methods
        2.   Teacher-student interactions that communicate expectations
                a)   Teachers ask high achieving students harder questions, give more chances, and longer time to respond, and provide more clues, prompts, and encouragement
                b)   Teachers ask lower achieving students easier questions, give less time for answering, and are less likely to give prompts and praise
        3.   The effects on students
                a)   Decreased motivation follows lowered expectations
                b)   Lowered performance because of lower motivation "confirms" teacher's expectation
                c)   Misbehavior and disruption may follow; discourages teacher's attention for academic work
    F.   Guidelines: Avoiding the Negative Effects of Teacher Expectations

IX.   Strategies To Encourage Motivation And Thoughtful Learning
    A.   Necessary conditions in the classroom
        1.   Classroom organized and free from constant interruptions
        2.   Teacher patient and supportive of mistakes
        3.   Challenging but reasonable work
        4.   Worthwhile learning tasks
    B.   Can I do it? Building confidence and positive expectations
        1.   Begin work at the students' levels, moving in small steps to assure students' understanding
        2.   Emphasize clear, specific, attainable learning goals
        3.   Stress self-comparison, not comparison with others
        4.   Communicate that academic ability can improve.
        5.   Model good problem-solving
    C.   Do I want to do it? Seeing the value of learning
        1.   Intrinsic and attainment value
        2.   Class activities tied to student needs and interests
        3.   Arouse curiosity
        4.   Make the learning task fun
        5.   Use novelty and familiarity
    D.   Instrumental value
        1.   Explain to students the connections between school and life outside of school
        2.   Provide incentives for learning when needed
        3.   Use ill-structured problems and authentic tasks
    E.   What do I need to do to succeed? Staying focused on the task
        1.   Frequent opportunities to demonstrate skills, permitting more corrective feedback
        2.   Have students create a finished product
        3.   Avoid competitive evaluation

Motivation, Teaching, and Learning

            4. Model the motivation to learn
            5. Teach particular learning tactics
     F. How do beginning teachers motivate students?
            1. Research: Over half of the motivational strategies used by new teachers were reward/punishment
            2. Teachers also tried to focus student attention
            3. Minor strategies were commenting on the importance of the material and building students' confidence
            4. Commenting on relevance was positively correlated with on-task behavior
            5. The use of rewards and punishments was negatively correlated
X. Summary
XI. Key terms and concepts
XII. Teachers' Casebook/What Would They Do?

Learning Activities and Related Research

ACTIVITIES	HANDOUTS
Chapter 11	11.0 Lecture Outline
	11.1 Concept Map: Self-regulated learning
	11.2 Flow chart: Monitoring and controlling strategies for self-management
Cooperative Activities	
11.1 Keeping them curious	11.3 Questions as Curiosity
11.2 Ambiguity and Constructivism	
11.3 What happens when our expectations are correct?	
Research Activities	
Using Technology	
Field Experience	
11.4 Teachers' Communication of Task Value	
11.5 TARGETT in the classroom	11.4 Observation guide
11.6 Motivated behavior in museums	
Other Teaching Activities	
11.7 Rewards For Cooperative Learning Groups	
11.8 Motivating High School Students to Achieve in Mathematics	
11.9 Motivating High School Girls in Mathematics	
11.10 Academic Counseling: Reflections on the Middle Grades	
	11.5 Concept Map: Necessary conditions for motivation
	11.6 Concept Map: Links to Other Chapters

Motivation, Teaching, and Learning

Cooperative Activities

11.1 Keeping Them Curious

Berylyne, D. E. (1960). Conflict, arousal, curiosity. New York: McGraw-Hill.
Lowenstein, G. (1994). The psychology of curiosity: A review and reinterpretation. Psychological Bulletin, 116, 75-98.

The references listed above provide some key sources related to curiosity. Berlyne proposed that curiosity had two dimensions: exploration and perceptual curiosity. Lowenstein suggested that curiosity reflected an information gap and questions could provoke such curiosity. Have your students in groups generate a list of questions that might provoke curiosity. Have them record their responses on **Handout Master 11.3**.

11.2 Ambiguity and Constructivism

Classrooms that are organized and conducted from a constructivist perspective will most likely include some ambiguous tasks. Have your students discuss the appropriateness of presenting such tasks to students who have a high fear of failure, cannot cope with ambiguity, and are poor risk-takers? How can a constructivist classroom serve the needs of these children?

11.3 What Happens When Our Expectations Are Correct?

Have your students discuss the question of "What happens when our expectations are correct?" in small groups. Some of the work on teacher expectations would suggest that low expectations "cause" low achievement and one is generally encouraged not to have low expectations. However, what happens if low achievement is accurately considered? What does it really mean when people encourage teachers to have "high expectations?"

Field Experience

11.4 Teachers' Communication of Task Value

Ask your students to observe in a classroom and count the number of times during a 30 minute period in which the teacher communicates to the students about the VALUE of the task in which they are engaged? In class, conduct a group summary of the frequency with which such statements have been found. Discuss the implications of the findings.

Motivation, Teaching, and Learning

11.5   TARGETT in The Classroom

TARGETT for motivation involves a number of elements:
- tasks
- support for autonomy
- recognition
- grouping
- evaluation
- time
- teacher expectations

Have your students use **Handout Master 11.4**, Observation Guide, to guide their observation of how these elements are being used in a classroom.

11.6   Motivated Behavior in Museums

Have your students develop an observation guide like that in **Handout Master 11.4** for use in observing behavior in a museum. Have them observe children at a museum and record evidence of motivated behavior or motivational strategies being employed by the adults accompanying the children. Discuss the differences in motivation observed in museums and classrooms.

Other Teaching Activities

11.7   Rewards For Cooperative Learning Groups

References:
   Dishon, D., & O'Leary, P. W. (1984). A guidebook for cooperative learning. Holmes Beach, FL: Learning Publications, Inc.
   Kagan, S. (1989). Cooperative learning: Resources for teachers, Laguna Nigel, CA: Resources for Teachers.
   Slavin, R. E. (1983). Cooperative learning. White Plains, NY: Longman.
   Whisler, N., & Williams, J. (1990). Literature and cooperative learning: Pathway to literacy. Sacramento, CA, Literature Co-op.
   Whisler and Williams (1990) suggest that cooperative learning groups differ from traditional learning groups in eight major ways: Shared leadership rather than one leader; heterogeneous rather than homogenous groups; positive interdependence (success of the group) rather than no interdependence (success of the individual); social skills directly taught) rather than group "told" to cooperate (social skills assumed, not directly taught); academic and social goals are a top priority, rather than only academic goals; teacher interacts rather than intervenes; students take responsibility for self and the group, rather than solely for self; and students are the primary resource, rather than only the teacher.

Each of these eight characteristics can be matched with appropriate rewards. Rather than apply extrinsic rewards such as the individual recognition, privileges, and tangible rewards which are suggested by Dishon and O'Leary (1984), group effort should be rewarded in ways that encourage intrinsic involvement and engagement with the goal at hand.

Rewards for shared leadership: As group members learn to work with one another on the basis of mutual interests rather than on strict grouping by ability, rewards should emphasize the development of interests rather than on interpersonal comparisons. The generation of ideas (initiative), the ability to agree upon concrete goals and make plans to accomplish these goals can be seen as separate abilities, each of which is deserving of separate encouragement and attention. In this manner, students learn that leadership is more than promoting ideas, but calls for group consensus on goals and means. The ability to attain consensus (group cohesion leadership) is thus seen as equally important to the ability to accomplish goals (task leadership).

Rewards for heterogeneous grouping: As an ice-breaker when groups are recently formed, each student might interview another member of the group and use the interview as a basis for an introduction to the group at large. The teacher may supply a list of questions suggested for use during the interview, such as "Family members," "Place of birth," or "Favorite foods." The interviewer may receive praise for a job well done, and thus the interpersonal relationships which form between heterogeneous students receive reinforcement.

Rewards for positive interdependence (success of the group): The more the students must depend upon one another, the more they will come to care for one another and share resources and effort. This positive interdependence does not come automatically. In cases in which one group member vies for individual attention and reinforcement, the teacher must ensure that the team as a whole receives verbal praise. Some kinds of cooperative grouping strategies reward group-assisted individual achievement. The Student Teams and Achievement Divisions style of cooperative learning (Slavin, 1983) pits individual students against their own previous achievement, while encouraging students to study together, so that the group as a whole achieves a team score. Other ideas for team building are featured in Kagan (1989).

Rewards for exercise of social skills: Students need instruction that includes a rationale why a certain social skill is necessary, as well as a demonstration of what the particular skill looks like and sounds like. Whisler and Williams (1990) recommend a wall chart that reminds students what to look for and listen for. During the group work time the teacher may circulate and take notes if these behaviors are practiced, and assign competence or offer group praise to groups that have been observed as incorporating these social skills as they work.

Rewards for academic and social goals: At the end of each group work period, the teacher may encourage each group to share what they have accomplished academically, as well as review to what extent the group used cooperative social skills. In this manner, reflective evaluation on the part of each group becomes a student reward.

Rewards for interaction with teacher: The teacher may wish to share pleasure when students have a good interactive discussion and share ideas, as well as caution when the group exhibits dependency behaviors. Teachers may wish to be cautious about intervening on group disputes, allowing the group to work together to achieve consensus.

Rewards for students taking responsibility for self and the group, rather than solely for self: Helping behaviors between group members or instances of observed altruism should receive verbal praise directed toward the group as a whole. Lessons need to ensure that individual students are accountable for their own learning as well as for the progress of others. Selecting a paper from the group at random to grade or a student at random to explain the group's progress will reward each group member's participation.

Rewards for students relying upon one another as resources: Students who bring resources for use in the group should be praised or assigned competence for their effort. The group that plans for a variety of resources to be used on a project should also receive positive attention for their planning. The teacher may wish to systematically decline to be used as an information source, but rather seek to be seen as a referral source. Students may also receive praise for paraphrasing what they have learned after reading new material, and for explaining it to other group members. Opportunities for discussing information among group members should be plentiful.

11.8 Motivating High School Students To Achieve In Math

Escalante, J. & Dirmann, J. (1990). The Jaime Escalante math program. Journal of Negro Education, 59(3), 407-423.

Jaime Escalante's dramatic success in preparing students at Garfield High School in East Los Angeles to pass the Advanced Placement calculus test was featured in the movie Stand and Deliver. Garfield High school prepares 27% of all the Hispanics in the United States and Puerto Rico who pass the AP calculus examination. Before Escalante began teaching at Garfield High School, only 10 advanced placement tests were administered (1979). As the number of students who are studying calculus at Garfield has dramatically increased, the total number of Advanced Placement activities at Garfield have also exploded in other technical subjects such as physics, chemistry, biology, and computer science. In 1989 the school set a record with over 450 AP tests administered in 16 different subjects.

The following are the main components of Escalante's program:

Origins: The Game Of Education. In 1952, while still an undergraduate in La Paz, Bolivia, Escalante began teaching at local high schools. He found that students learned faster when learning is a game and a challenge. In the eighties and nineties at Garfield

Motivation, Teaching, and Learning

High School, the game is to beat ETS: The Educational Testing Service. The AP calculus examination is the most difficult of all exams administered nationally to secondary school pupils and it gets tougher every year. Less than 2% of high school seniors nationally sit for the exam. For the students in calculus, the exam provides a formidable opponent that galvanizes the students and unites students and teacher in a united challenge toward an inexorable deadline: the second week of May. The students chant, "De-fense, de-fense!" In this context, it means hard work, holding up under pressure, and not giving the opponent an inch.

Recruiting Students. A growing number of junior high school students who wish to be part of the program enroll early and participate in their first math class during the summer program at East Los Angeles College (ELAC) between their ninth-grade and tenth-grade year. By the time these students enter the tenth grade, they are ready to take geometry. Escalante has established an informal recruiting program in the three feeder junior high schools to Garfield, identifying promising students who have "ganas"--the desire to learn and succeed. Sometimes these are not the obvious "gifted" students, but class "cut-ups" who may be bored by poor teaching and disillusioned by the perceived dead-end of schooling. Sometimes the deciding factor is simply if the student likes math.

The Curriculum. A student must have taken and passed the following courses to take the AP exam: Algebra I, Geometry, Algebra II, Trigonometry/Math Analysis, Calculus AB (first-year) and/or Calculus BC (second-year college calculus). Typically, geometry must be taken in an intensive eight-week summer program conducted at East Los Angeles College after the tenth grade. Trigonometry/ Math Analysis must be taken in the summer between eleventh and twelfth grade. If the student has taken Algebra I in junior high school, then the curriculum is advanced one year, allowing the student to take AP Calculus BC during the twelfth grade.

Scheduling. In effect, a student has to take six years of math in three years of high school. Students must arrive early in the morning to begin studying math. They must study at lunch, after school each afternoon, and even on Saturdays in special math classes held at ELAC. They are required to do homework every day. On random days they must recite formulae and axioms out loud at the door to the classroom just to get authorization to enter class. They do daily quizzes and frequent tests.

Textbooks. The demand for quality texts has been the cornerstone of the Escalante Math Program. Students use four calculus texts, ones that are peppered with lively examples, ingenious demonstrations of math at work, and lots of linkages between math principles and their real-world applications. The ideal textbook for the program is one that develops concepts gradually, with many practice problems.

Past Graduates As Models Of Achievement. Escalante invites former students who have well-paid, fulfilling jobs in careers achieved through higher education to return to Garfield for pep talks to students. He also takes the high school students to field trips to high-tech labs or industrial sites such as the Jet Propulsion Laboratory (JPL) in Pasadena,

Motivation, Teaching, and Learning

where math is employed daily in many different kinds of exciting jobs. Seeing that minorities can get these jobs and that higher education creates opportunities for larger financial reward is as much a lesson as seeing math being used in such settings.

Recruiting Community Resources. ARCO Foundation, the National Science Foundation, and the Foundation for Advancements in Science and Education (FASE) have become supporters of Escalante after the program's early years of success. This support has provided copiers, audiovisual aids, computers, tutor awards, transportation and lunches for students during extra study periods, tee-shirts, caps, team jackets, and scholarships. The support of FASE has made possible a series of motivational videotapes called "FUTURES," which feature real classroom scenes of Escalante's teaching.

The Team Approach. Escalante uses examples of famous professional sports stars as examples of the will to win, successful self-discipline, persistence in the practice of skills, and outstanding performance. The class members wear classy satin team jackets, caps, and tee-shirts; their practice schedule is as rigorous as any championship football team. He often uses language of team sports and competition. After school, students almost always work in teams.

Humor. Escalante believes teaching should be fun. Many students initially enroll in the course because they hear it is fun, despite little initial interest in mathematics. Usually, interest follows.

Accountability. Escalante approaches the work with the belief that he is solely responsible for the success or failure of the program. The students, parents, and school administration are also accountable for the product. Students who enter the program must sign a contract which binds them to participation in the summer programs, strict completion of homework, and attendance at Saturday morning classes. Parents and Escalante sign the contract as well. Escalante discourages the students from "goofing off" with TV, sports, or headphones playing "Heavy Metal." He does not give up on students and expects them not to give up. He demands that students perform their assigned tasks and does not accept excuses when homework is not done.

Love. A deep love and caring for students is evident as Escalante sets about changing young lives. This happens when a teacher loves to motivate and teach the difficult students as well as the good ones. The strong intention he communicates to them to succeed must be great enough to overcome the combined negativity of their previous failures, the prejudices of others who predict their likely future failures, and the lack of preparation in mathematics with which they are burdened after nine years in the educational system. A teacher must be an active listener and work hard to understand what students are thinking and saying.

Other Active Components Of The Program. Parental involvement, attention to students' nutrition, a campaign against drug use, an effort to teach respect and values-- every part of the students' lives becomes a factor in the struggle to overcome negativity

Motivation, Teaching, and Learning

and produce strong math scholars. The mathematics "pipeline" that Escalante built in East Los Angeles is not the result of a miracle, but systematic attention to instilling the values of hard work, good teaching, and community support for higher education. According to Escalante, our society depends on teachers who can cultivate young men and women to shape the future. The Escalante Math Program is a demonstration vehicle showing how this can be achieved.

11.9   Motivating High School Girls to Achieve in Mathematics

Have your students determine if girls are motivated to achieve in mathematics. How would they find out? What would they do about it?

11.10   Academic Counseling: Reflections On The Middle Grades

Fenwick, James J. (1986). The middle school years. San Diego, CA: Fenwick Associates. Reprinted in Caught in the middle, California State Department of Education, Sacramento, CA, 1987.

The significance of [academic counseling during] the middle years is found in recognizing the following:

- That adolescence is a time to experience; to explore; to ask questions; to wonder; to imagine; to believe; to doubt; to feel; to sense life in its various shapes and sizes.

- That all youth need to develop unique interest; to uncover hidden talents; to experience satisfaction in accomplishments; to talk about the meaning of these things; to pursue diligently some aptitudes, abilities, and interests; to set others aside to "mellow" for a while.

- That some youth need to press the limits of their teacher's knowledge; that the teacher's role is to provide a chart and a compass in such instances and then to step back and watch young adventurers strike out on their own.

- That other youth will need extraordinary amounts of acceptance and affirmation from their teachers; that their experiences are too often threatening and destructive; that there may be no one else to whom they can turn for mature guidance and reassurance.

- That for still others, their lives are genuinely at risk; that becoming "disconnected" is a distinct possibility; that missed opportunities will not be repeated; that for whatever dreams and ambitions might be present there is no hope unless a miracle happens; that teachers and counselors have the potential to set the stage for "miracles" even if they cannot guarantee them.

- ...that all students experience deep thoughts, feelings, or events that impact indelibly the formation of their adult values; that the sensitivity and responsiveness of teachers

Motivation, Teaching, and Learning

and counselors have the potential to make enormous differences in the value systems of their students.

- That the answers to the questions "Who am I?" and "Where am I going?" are deeply imbedded in the attitudes and values that emerge in adolescence; that without positive, mature values there can be no positive, mature answers to these questions.

Discussion: How can teachers assist in academic counseling in the middle school years? Can this be done in the large class setting in which most instruction takes place? Do the middle schools need other, smaller structures in which students can work closely with teachers to explore academic direction, values, and aspirations?

Discussion Questions

1. Given what you have experienced in school and college, what adverse affects on student motivation might be expected if grades were totally eliminated?

2. In mastery learning, teachers must break down a course or lesson into small discrete units of study. Each unit may have one or more objectives and a criterion for mastery of each. How might this procedure of reducing the learning into discrete units affect students' motivation?

3. Do you think teachers should read their students' cumulative folders at the beginning of the school year? If so, how can they keep from forming low expectations? Does the formation of low expectations imply that teachers act on these expectations?

4. What are some of the negative effects of ability grouping? (See Good and Brophy, 1984). What can be done to counteract these effects?

5. Can gifted students work effectively in mixed ability classes?

Additional Resources for Teaching This Chapter

PRINT RESOURCES

Bragstad, B.J. and Stumpf, S. M. (1987). A guidebook for teaching study skills and motivation. Boston: Allyn and Bacon, Inc. This resource book for the classroom teacher reviews the basics of motivation theory, exploring the teacher-student relationship from a foundation in human needs. Many academic skills are reviewed, such as vocabulary building, time management, note-taking, test-taking, and strategic reading.

Nielsen, L. (1982). How to motivate adolescents. New York: Prentice-Hall International. A multifaceted primer on motivation, this book is addressed to parents, teachers, and counselors of adolescents. Beginning with the physiological and emotional needs of teenagers, this book offers suggestions for improving conduct, teaching self-management skills, and using the peer group as a positive force in academic achievement.

REFERENCES

Bartz, D. E., & Maehr, M. L. (1984). Advances in motivation and achievement: Vol. 1. The effects of school desegregation on motivation and achievement. Greenwich, CT: Ablex Publishing.

Conrad, D. & Hedin, D. (1982). The impact of experiential education on adolescent development. Child and Youth Services, 4, 57-76.

Covington, M. V., & Teel, K. M. (1996). Overcoming student failure: Changing motives and incentives for learning. Washington, D. C.: American Psychological Association.

Good, T., & Brophy, J. (1984). Looking in classrooms, (3rd ed.) New York: Harper and Row.

Johnson, R., & Johnson, J. D. (1983). Effects of cooperative, competitive, and individualistic experiences on social development. Exceptional Children, 49, 323-29.

Rist, R. (1979). Student social class and teacher expectations: The self-fulfilling prophecy in ghetto education. Harvard Educational Review, 40, 411-51.

Slavin, R. (1983). **Cooperative learning**. New York: Longman, Inc.

Sharan, S. (199). Handbook of cooperative learning methods. Greenwood Publishing.

FILMS. VIDEOTAPES, AND AUDIOCASSETTES

ASCD Library of Teaching Episodes. The following is an example of a video from the ASCD Library of Teaching Episodes. Each features an actual scene from a classroom which has been selected and edited for use with pre- or in-service teachers. Developing formulas for polygons. 7th grade math, 18 min.

Head of the class, video, 14 minutes, color. Why are Japanese students so much more goal-oriented than Americans? Who motivates them? How? This story aroused tremendous interest when it was broadcast on 60 Minutes. And no wonder: it shows three- and four-year-olds doing homework for hours each day to polish their skills so that they will get into the best kindergarten, and mothers overseeing (driving, Americans would say) their children so that they will do more and better. The goal of the learning process is to gain admission to college, which assumes a job commensurate with the exclusivity of the college. Education ends with the posting of one's name on a list of the admitted. #CC-1684.

Mastery learning by Tom Guskey, audio. Find out why mastery learning is building a successful track record for improving student achievement. Get an overview of the most widely used approaches. Stock #612-20348C2.

Motivation, Teaching, and Learning

Mastery learning by James Block, audio. What is the mastery learning concept? And why can it help you boost student achievement in your district? Find out how to introduce mastery learning to your staff and use a proven model for implementing this successful approach to learning. Stock #612-20156C2. Order from: Assoc. for Supervision & Curriculum Development, 125 N. West St., Alexandria, VA 22314-2798, or Telephone: (703) 549-9110.

Motivating underachievers, video, 28 minutes, color. This program explores the problem of underachieving children and examines why so many schools fail to deal with the problem effectively. Suggestions for teachers and parents to motivate underachievers are shown. #CC-1592. Order from: Films for the Humanities and Sciences, Inc., P. O. Box 2053, Princeton, NJ 08543, or Telephone: (800) 257-5126 (8:30 am - 5:30 PM EST).

Motivation, cognition, and instruction: The dynamic interplay, audio. Invited Symposium, Division C, AERA 1987 Annual Meeting, Washington, DC. Order RA7-15.04 from: Teach'em, Inc., 160 E. Illinois St., Chicago, IL 60611, or Telephone: (800) 225-3775.

Handout Master 11.0

Lecture Outline ---- Motivation, Teaching, and Learning

- On TARGETT

- Tasks for Learning

- Supporting Autonomy

- Grouping, Evaluation, and Time

- Teacher Expectations

- Strategies for Encouraging Motivation

Handout Master 11.1: Self-Regulated Learning

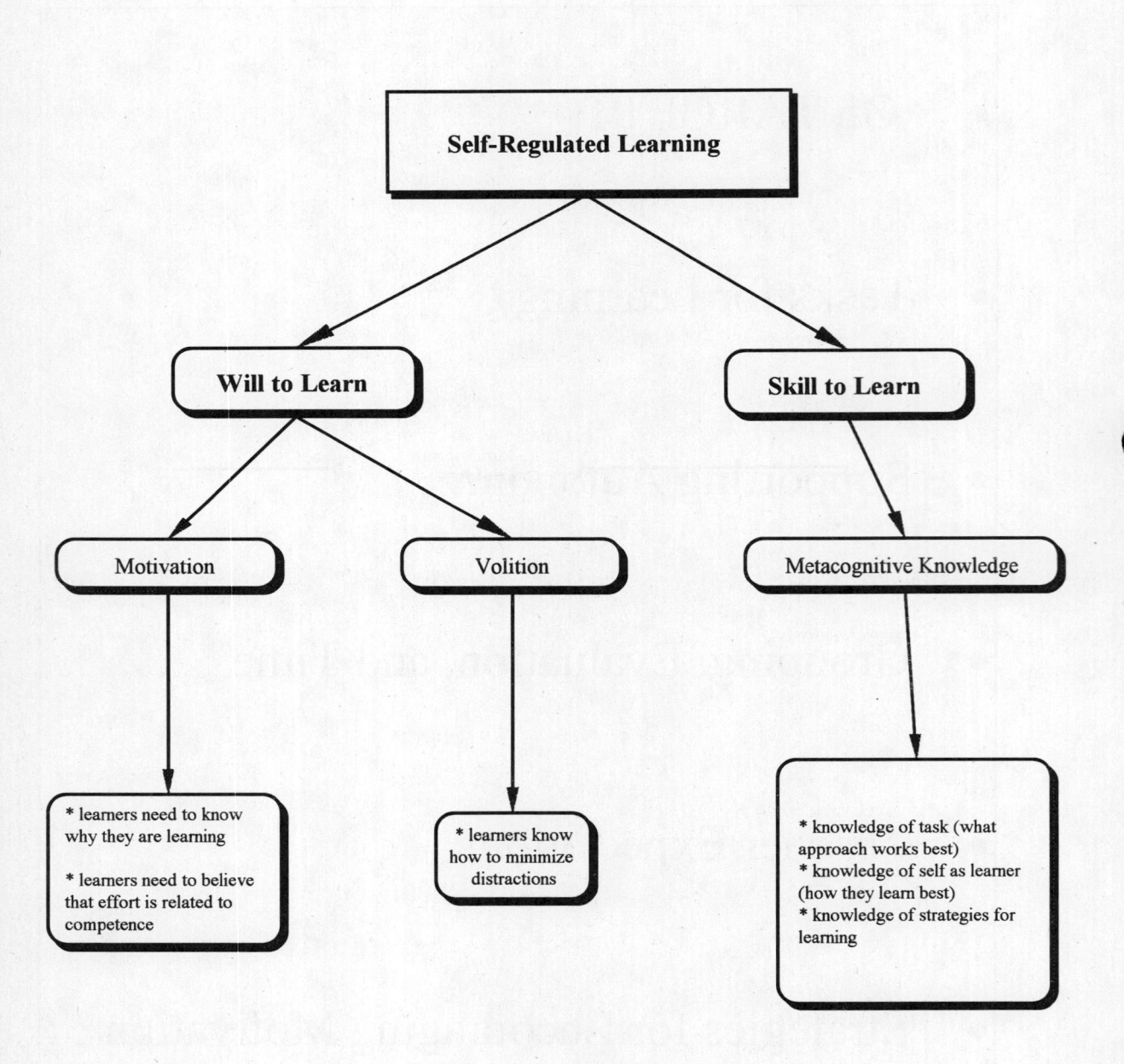

```
                    ┌─────────────────────────┐
                    │  Self-Regulated Learning │
                    └─────────────────────────┘
                         /              \
                        /                \
              ┌─────────────┐       ┌─────────────┐
              │ Will to Learn│       │ Skill to Learn│
              └─────────────┘       └─────────────┘
                /         \                │
               /           \                │
       ┌──────────┐   ┌──────────┐   ┌──────────────────────┐
       │Motivation│   │ Volition │   │Metacognitive Knowledge│
       └──────────┘   └──────────┘   └──────────────────────┘
            │              │                     │
```

Motivation:
- learners need to know why they are learning
- learners need to believe that effort is related to competence

Volition:
- learners know how to minimize distractions

Metacognitive Knowledge:
- knowledge of task (what approach works best)
- knowledge of self as learner (how they learn best)
- knowledge of strategies for learning

Copyright © 1998 by Allyn and Bacon

Handout Master 11.2: Monitoring and Controlling Strategies for Self-Management

Prepare to Learn

Set management goals: "What am I supposed to do?"
Use prior knowledge of task: "What do I already know?
Consider alternative strategies: What ways can I do this?"
Make a schedule: "What should I do first, second?
Set contingency plans: "What if I run into trouble?"

Executive Learning Plan

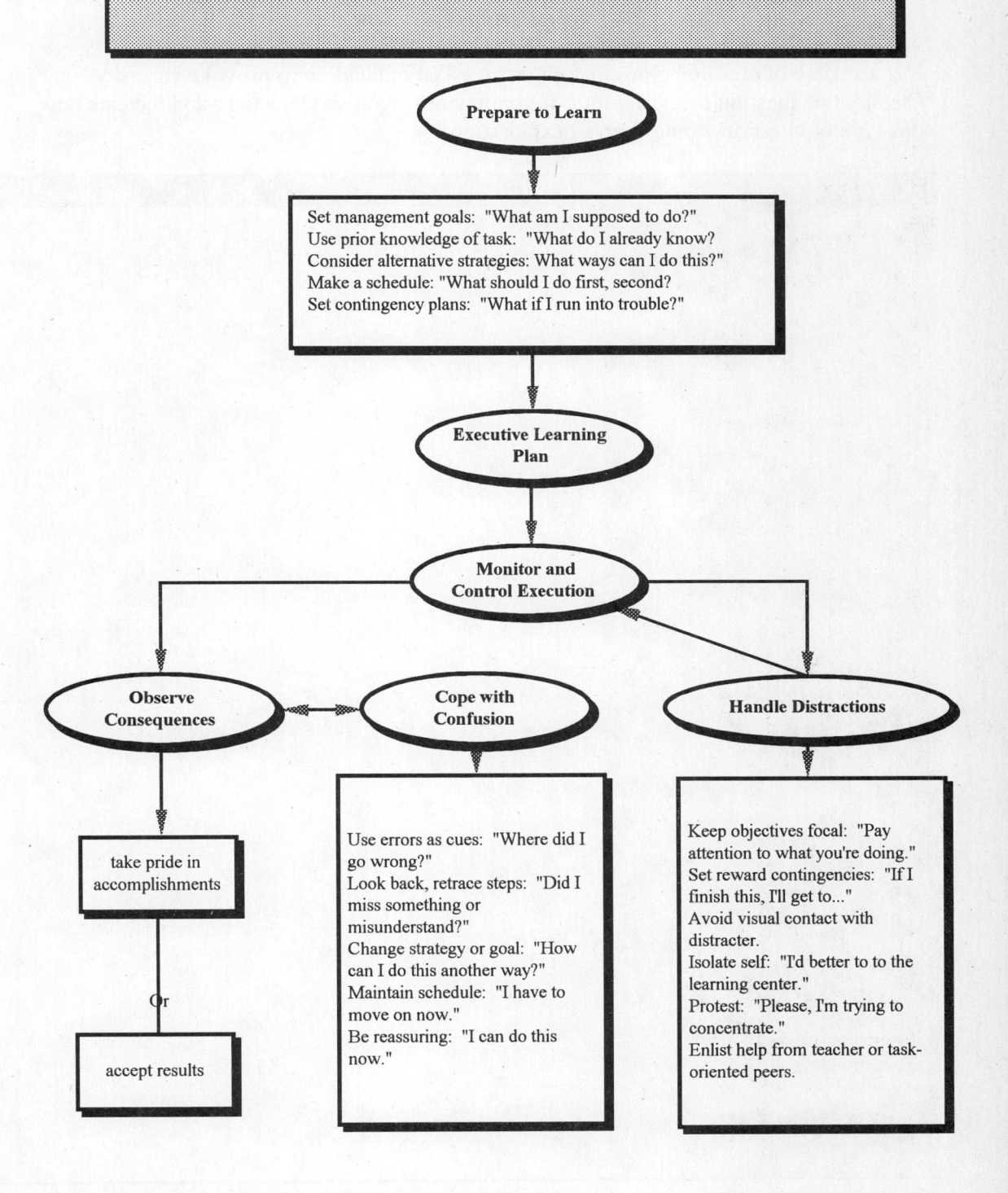

Monitor and Control Execution

Observe Consequences

- take pride in accomplishments

Or

- accept results

Cope with Confusion

Use errors as cues: "Where did I go wrong?"
Look back, retrace steps: "Did I miss something or misunderstand?"
Change strategy or goal: "How can I do this another way?"
Maintain schedule: "I have to move on now."
Be reassuring: "I can do this now."

Handle Distractions

Keep objectives focal: "Pay attention to what you're doing."
Set reward contingencies: "If I finish this, I'll get to..."
Avoid visual contact with distracter.
Isolate self: "I'd better to to the learning center."
Protest: "Please, I'm trying to concentrate."
Enlist help from teacher or task-oriented peers.

Courtesy of Corno, L. (1987), "Teaching and self-regulated learning." In D. Berliner and B. Rosenshine (Eds.), <u>Talks to teachers</u>. New York: Random House

Copyright © 1998 by Allyn and Bacon

Handout Master 11.3

Questions as Curiosity

List a variety of question types that might be asked of children to provoke curiosity. Classify the question using Bloom's Taxonomy of Cognitive Objectives and indicate how this type of question would support exploration.

Question	Classification	Support Exploration?

Copyright © 1998 by Allyn and Bacon

Handout Master 11.4

Observation Guide

Observe a classroom and complete the grid below, making comments in the right hand column as you observe events that are pertinent to the categories in the left hand column.

TARGETT	IN THE CLASSROOM
TASKS • risky? • ambiguous?	
AUTONOMY SUPPORT • how supported?	
RECOGNITION • extrinsic rewards? • praise? • focus on learning?	
GROUPING • are group used? • how?	
EVALUATION • competitive grading? • emphasis on performance or learning goals?	
TIME • are students given time to finish tasks? • are they encouraged to persist?	
TEACHER EXPECTATIONS • evidence of expectations of the teacher?	

Copyright © 1998 by Allyn and Bacon

Handout Master 11.5: Necessary Conditions for Motivation

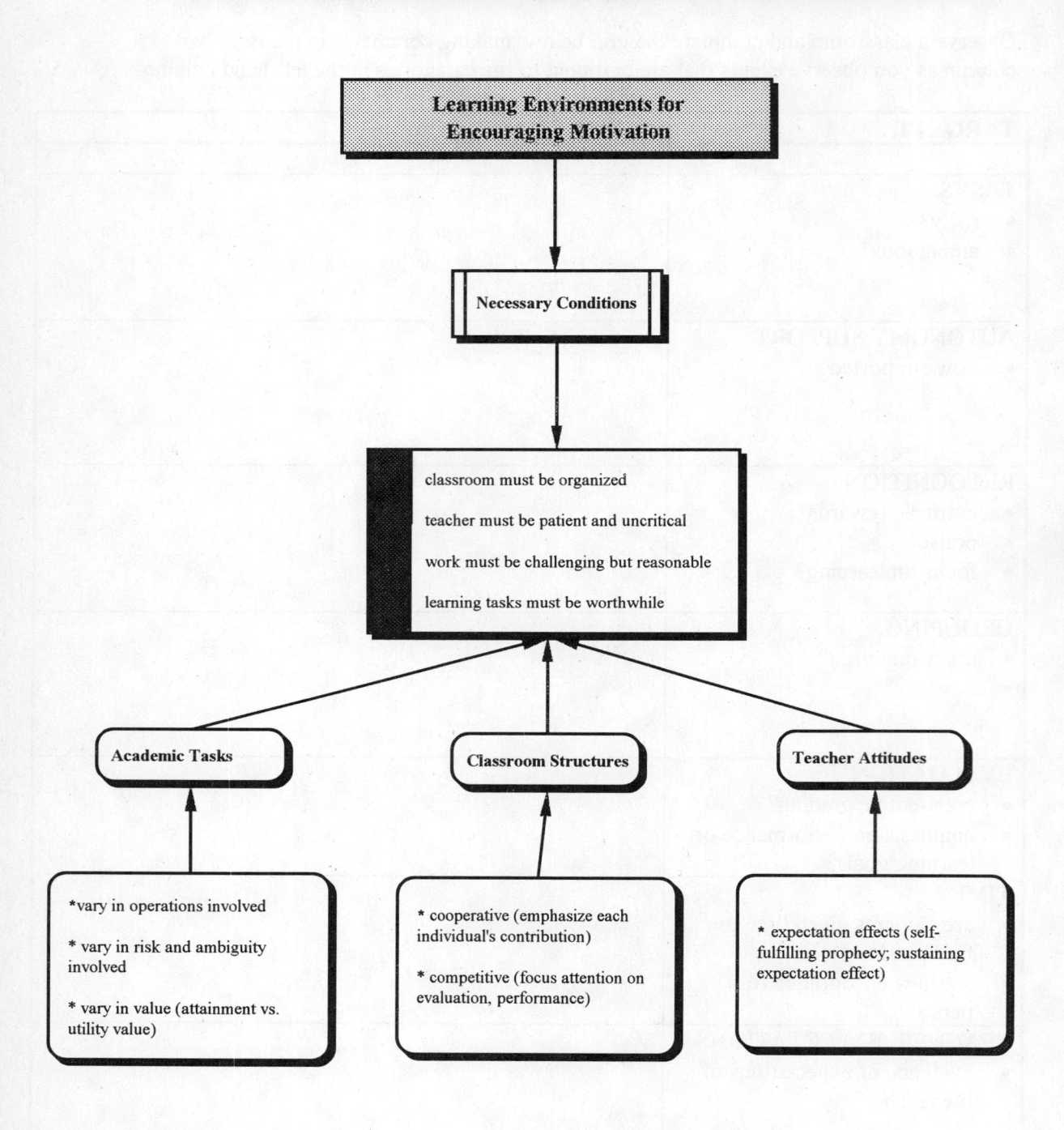

Learning Environments for Encouraging Motivation

↓

Necessary Conditions

↓

- classroom must be organized
- teacher must be patient and uncritical
- work must be challenging but reasonable
- learning tasks must be worthwhile

↑ ↑ ↑

Academic Tasks
- *vary in operations involved
- * vary in risk and ambiguity involved
- * vary in value (attainment vs. utility value)

Classroom Structures
- * cooperative (emphasize each individual's contribution)
- * competitive (focus attention on evaluation, performance)

Teacher Attitudes
- * expectation effects (self-fulfilling prophecy; sustaining expectation effect)

Copyright © 1998 by Allyn and Bacon

Handout Master 11.6: Links to Other Chapters

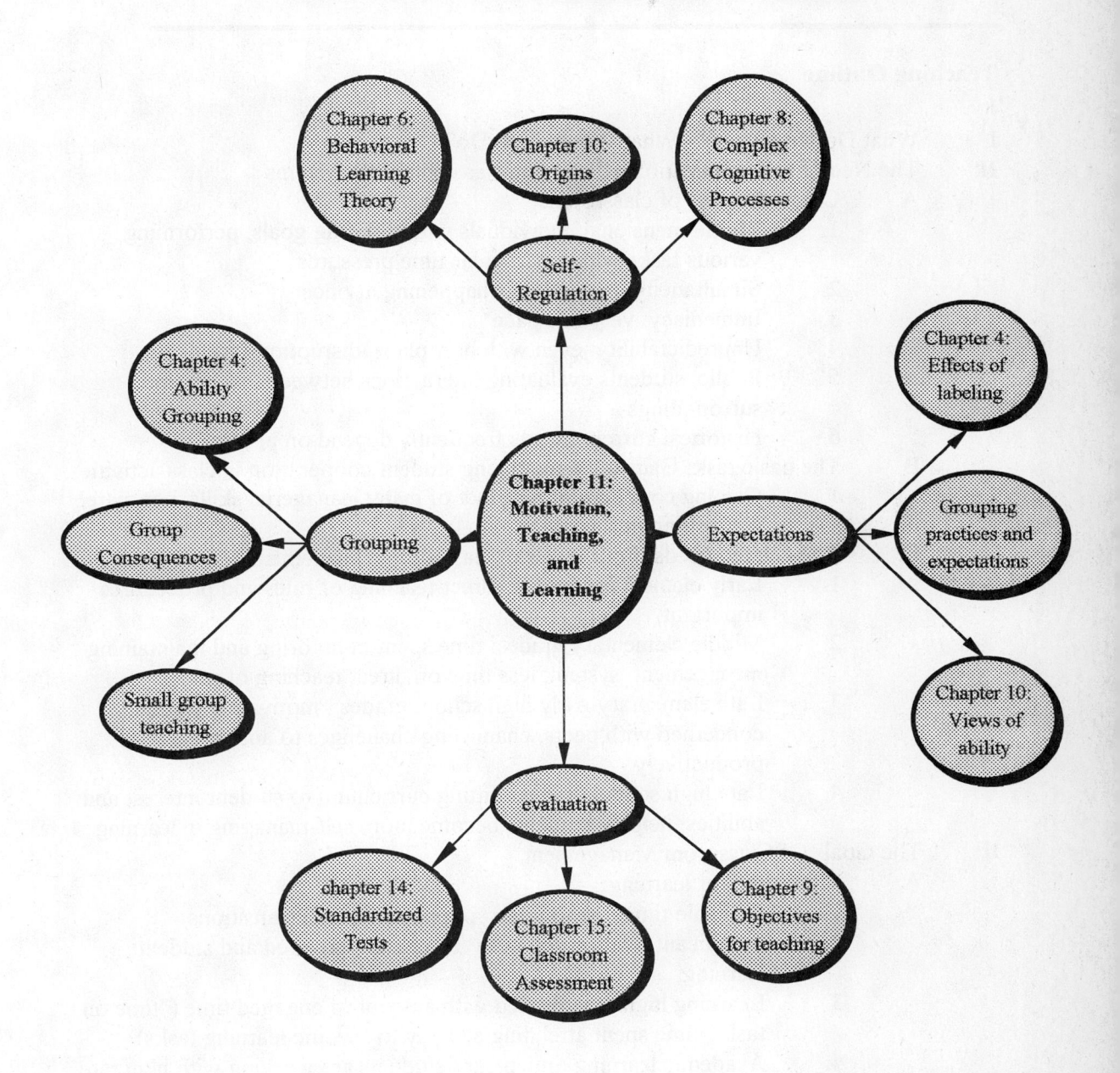

- **Chapter 11: Motivation, Teaching, and Learning**
  - Self-Regulation
    - Chapter 6: Behavioral Learning Theory
    - Chapter 10: Origins
    - Chapter 8: Complex Cognitive Processes
  - Grouping
    - Chapter 4: Ability Grouping
    - Group Consequences
    - Small group teaching
  - Expectations
    - Chapter 4: Effects of labeling
    - Grouping practices and expectations
    - Chapter 10: Views of ability
  - evaluation
    - chapter 14: Standardized Tests
    - Chapter 15: Classroom Assessment
    - Chapter 9: Objectives for teaching

Copyright © 1998 by Allyn and Bacon

12

Creating Learning Environments

Teaching Outline

I. What Do You Think?/ What Would You Do?
II. The Need For Organization: Classrooms as ecological systems
    A. Characteristics of classrooms
        1. Multidimensional: individuals with differing goals, performing various tasks within particular time pressures
        2. Simultaneity: many things happening at once
        3. Immediacy: very fast pace
        4. Unpredictability: even with best plans, disruptions are likely
        5. Public: students evaluating interactions between teacher and surroundings
        6. Histories: current events frequently depend on past
    B. The basic task: Gain and maintaining student cooperation in class activities.
        1. Gaining cooperation: product of many managerial skills, not merely controlling misbehavior
    C. Age-related needs: Four levels of classroom management
        1. Early elementary grades: direct teaching of rules and procedures important
        2. Middle elementary grades: time spent monitoring and maintaining management system; less time on direct teaching of rules
        3. Late elementary-early high school grades: motivating students concerned with peers, channeling challenges to authority productively
        4. Late high school grades: fitting curriculum to student interest and abilities, helping students become more self-managing in learning
III. The Goals Of Classroom Management
    A. More time for learning:
        1. available time lost to interruptions and rough transitions
        2. Significant relationship between content covered and student learning;
        3. Learning highly correlated with amount of engaged time ("time on task"; time spent attending actively to specific learning tasks)
        4. Academic learning time means students are working with high rate of success
    B. Access to learning
        1. Explicit participation structures: rules defining participation in various activities

2. Implicit participation structures: students ability to participate influenced by structure in home
3. Inconsistent rules: cause confusion and increased disruptions
4. Teachers need to show awareness and communication of rules
C. Management for self-management: Help students manage themselves

IV. Creating A Positive Learning Environment
A. Good instructional planning prevents many management problems
1. Assign work at students' ability level
2. Make an effort to motivate students
B. Research results
1. Effective teachers were studied as they "got started" in the first weeks of class; connections were made to management problems, and management principles were identified
2. Teachers who applied these principles had fewer problems; achievement was higher
C. Rules and procedures required
1. Procedures: describe how to accomplish activities in the classroom (see Guidelines: Establishing Class Procedures)
   a) Administrative routines: taking attendance, etc.
   b) Student movement: entering and leaving room
   c) Housekeeping: taking care of classroom and personal items
   d) Routines for accomplishing lessons: collecting and distributing papers
   e) Interactions between teacher and student
   f) Talk among students
2. Rules: Have a few general rules specifying expected and forbidden actions in the class
3. Rules for elementary school
   a) Be polite and helpful
   b) Respect other people's property
   c) Listen quietly while others are speaking
   d) Do not hit, shove, or hurt others
   e) Obey all school rules
4. Rules for secondary school
   a) Bring all needed materials to class
   b) Be in your seat and ready to work when the bell rings
   c) Respect and be polite to everyone
   d) Respect other people's property
   e) Listen and stay seated while someone else is talking
   f) Obey all school rules
5. Consequences
   a) Determine beforehand the consequences for following or breaking rules
   b) Logical consequences: have the student go back and do it right

Creating Learning Environments

                      c)   Consequences should be clear and enforceable

V.   Spaces for learning
- A. Interest-area arrangements
    1. Note the fixed features that you must deal with
    2. Have easy access to materials in a well-organized place to store them
    3. Provide students with clean, convenient surfaces on which to use equipment
    4. Make sure work areas are private and quiet
    5. Arrange that you can see the students and they can see instructional presentations
    6. Avoid dead spaces and racetracks
    7. Provide choices
    8. Provide flexibility
    9. Give students a place to keep their personal belongings
- B. Personal territories
    1. Action zones: Where participation is the greatest (not necessarily the front)
    2. Home-base formations work well for whole-class instruction and allow for cooperative work

VI.   Getting Started: The First Weeks Of Class
- A. Effective teachers for elementary students
    1. Organized from the first day
    2. Gave children interesting tasks
    3. Monitored behavior as a whole group
    4. Taught rules
    5. Provided consequences for misbehavior immediately
- B. Ineffective teachers for elementary students
    1. Gave vague or complicated rules
    2. Provided inconsistent consequences for both positive and negative behaviors.
    3. Procedures were not taught or practiced
    4. Teachers frequently left the room
- C. Effective managers for secondary students
    1. Focused on establishing rules
    2. Clearly communicated standards for academic work and class behavior
    3. Dealt with infractions of rules quickly
    4. Students in low achieving classes were given a variety of tasks
    5. Student behavior was closely monitored so students would face consequences for avoiding work

VII.   Maintaining A Good Environment For Learning
- A. Encouraging engagement
    1. Lesson format

Creating Learning Environments

    a) Increasing teacher supervision increases student engaged time
    b) Providing cues on next steps and materials for completion of task
    c) If students are interested, they will be motivated to stay on task
   2. Involvement without supervision
    a) Well-planned systems
    b) Guidelines: Encouraging Student Responsibility
 B. General characteristics of effective managers: Prevention
   1. Prevent problems
   2. Are 'withit" (aware of what is happening in the classroom)
    a) Stop minor disruptions before they become major
    b) Avoid blaming the wrong student for misbehavior (target errors)
    c) Avoid timing errors: waiting too long before intervening in misbehavior
    d) If two problems occur simultaneously, deal with the most serious one first
   3. Overlapping and group focus
    a) Overlapping: keeping track of and supervising several activities at the same time
    b) Group focus: keeping as many students as possible involved in appropriate class activities
   4. Movement management
    a) Making smooth transitions, maintaining an appropriate pace, and using variety when changes are necessary
    b) Avoid slowdown: taking too much time to start new activities
 C. Dealing with discipline problems
   1. Making sure students get back to work: eye contact, move closer, and use non-verbal signals
   2. Reminding students of procedures
   3. Calmly asking student to state correct procedure
   4. Assertively, telling student to stop misbehavior
 D. Special problems with secondary students
   1. Enforcing established consequences for incomplete work
   2. Students who continually break the same rules:
    a) Seat difficult students away from others who can be influenced
    b) Be consistent about consequences
    c) Encourage self-management techniques
    d) Remain friendly
   3. The defiant, hostile student:
    a) Get out of situation, allow cool down time

Creating Learning Environments

      b) Follow through with consequences
      c) Talk privately about outburst
VIII. Special Programs For Classroom Management
   A. Group consequences: Can build cooperation among students
     1. Team-Based Good Behavior Game
      a) Give a discipline mark if a team member transgresses a "good behavior" rule
      b) Team with the fewest marks receives a special reward or privilege
     2. Reward based on the good behavior of the whole group (e.g. listening to a radio)
     3. Reward to group if a single problem student behaves
     4. Caution in applying group behavioral consequences
      a) Negative peer pressure can be exerted
      b) Difficult students may need individual arrangements
   B. Token reinforcement programs
     1. Tokens are symbolic rewards which can later be exchanged for prizes or privileges
     2. Schedules of giving tokens
      a) When system begins, tokens are given continuously, exchanged often for reward
      b) Once system works, intermittent tokens are given and time between exchange is longer
     3. Home-based consequences: parents provide reward based on school report of tokens earned (caution: do not use if parents may punish severely for poor reports)
      a) When to use token reinforcement systems
       (1) To motivate students who are completely disinterested and unresponsive
       (2) To encourage students who have failed to make academic progress
       (3) To deal with a class that is out of control
   C. Contingency contract programs
     1. Individual contract with a student describing what behavior will earn which reward
      a) Students may participate in deciding on behaviors and rewards
      b) Students learn to set reasonable goals and abide by terms of contract
     2. Caution: extrinsic rewards may undermine intrinsic motivation
IX. The Need For Communication
   A. Message sent - message received
     1. May be different
      a) Body language, tone of voice, and word choice convey messages

Creating Learning Environments

      b) Students may hear unintended message and react to it
    2. Paraphrase rule
      a) Participants must summarize in their own words what the previous speaker said before responding
      b) Speaker explains again if misunderstood
      c) Cycle continues until the speaker agrees that the listener has heard the correct message
  B. Diagnosis: Whose problem is it?
    1. If problem is student's: respond with active or empathetic listening
    2. If problem is teacher's: solution is found through problem-solving with student
    3. Deciding problem ownership: does the student's action concretely and tangibly prevent me from fulfilling my role as a teacher?
  C. Counseling: The student's problem
    1. Empathetic listening: hearing student's intent and emotions; reflecting them back through paraphrasing
    2. Four components of empathetic listening:
      a) Blocking out external stimuli
      b) Attending to verbal and nonverbal message
      c) Differentiating between intellectual and emotional content
      d) Making inferences about speaker's feelings
  D. Confrontation and assertive discipline
    1. "I" messages
      a) Teacher owns the problem and must intervene to change the student's behavior
      b) Description of student's behavior, how it affects you as a teacher, and how you feel about it
    2. Assertive discipline
      a) Clear, firm, non hostile response style
      b) Teachers make expectations clear and follow through with established consequence
      c) Students have clear choice: follow rules or accept consequences
      d) Mistakes of the passive or non assertive response style
      e) Mistakes of the hostile response style
      f) Assertive response style: teacher's care is communicated in a calm, firm, and confident manner; expectations clearly stated;
    3. Confrontations and negotiations
      a) If I-message or assertive response fails to change behavior, a conflict situation arises
      b) Three methods of resolving conflict: teacher imposes solution, teacher gives in to student demands, or "no-lose method" used
    4. Point/Counterpoint: Does Assertive Discipline Work?

Creating Learning Environments

        5.   Student conflicts and confrontations
            a)   Conflicts between goals and needs
                (1)   accomplishing goals, fulfilling needs
                (2)   maintaining relationships
            b)   Violence in schools
                (1)   prevention is the best strategy
                    (a)   establish mentoring programs
                    (b)   establish conflict resolutions programs
                    (c)   parent community involvement
                    (d)   relevant curricula
            c)   Peer mediation programs
                (1)   Jointly define problem
                (2)   Exchange positions and interests
                (3)   Reverse perspectives
                (4)   Invent agreements that allow mutual gain
                (5)   Reach an integrative agreement
    E.   Communicating with families about classroom management
X.   Summary
XI.   Key terms and concepts
XII.   Teachers' casebook/ What would they do?

Learning Activities and Related Research

ACTIVITIES	HANDOUTS
Chapter 12	12.0 Lecture outline
Cooperative Activities	
12.1 Teacher's casebook	12.1 Teacher's Casebook
12.2 Glasser's Principles	12.2 Encouraging responsibility
12.3 Conflict and confrontation	12.3a Handling conflict/Scoring
	12.3b Assertiveness scale/Scoring
12.4 Conflict with a parent	12.4a A letter from Tommy's mommy.
	12.4b A teacher's reply
Research Activities	
Using Technology	
Field Experience	
12.5 Time on Task	
12.6 The Effective Classroom Manager	
12.7 Classroom Management	12.5 Classroom Management Observation Sheet
Other Teaching Activities	
12.8 Fostering student self-management	
12.9 Using behavior modification in classroom discipline	
12.10 Who owns the problem?	12.6 Who owns the problem?
12.11 I messages	
12.12 Student mediators	
	12.7 Contingency contracts
	12.8 Concept map: Links to other chapters

Cooperative Activities

12.1   <u>Teacher's Casebook: What Would You Do?</u>

Use **Handout 12.1** with this activity. Have your students in groups discuss the material in the beginning of Chapter 12 under the title *Teacher's casebook*. The teacher in the class described has been presented with a number of problems: 1) how to accommodate a child with cerebral palsy; 2) how to promote integration across ethnic lines; and 3) how to manage the behavior of an emotionally disturbed student. The problems posed involve challenges of instructional management and behavior management.

Having come to some conclusions of their own, students should consult the end of the chapter in which teachers provide some suggestions about how they would respond to these problems. Ask students to compare their responses with those of their more experienced counterparts. What does "experience" add to the analysis of these classroom situations?

Creating Learning Environments

12.2   Using Glasser's Principles

Divide the class into teams containing eight students each. Have the first two students in each group write a paragraph describing a middle-school-age child with a behavioral or learning problem. Read the problem aloud. Have the second two students write a description of the teacher who is involved with this student, and who reacts to the problem. They read this solution aloud, while the first two students jot down a critique and amplification of this solution. The next students describe briefly how the teacher would get the student to evaluate his/her own behavior and make a plan and get a commitment to the plan. The previous two students jot down a critique and amplification of this description. The next two students describe how the teacher would respond to the student's commitment, giving an example of not accepting excuses but not interfering with natural consequences of the student's failure-- and not giving up. The previous two students write a brief critique and amplification of this description. The group then goes back to the first two students, who discuss the teacher's involvement, while the next two discuss the plan, the next two discuss the consequences and the final two students sum up what they have gained from the exercise.

12.3   Confrontation and Conflict

This activity allows your students to practice different responses to confrontation and conflict. These exercises can be done after the class has had practice in constructing "I-messages." Divide the class into pairs and have the member of each pair sit facing one another. Allow a minute for each person to think of a situation in which another person's behavior was unacceptable to him or her. One member of the pair is to "go first." This person should briefly describe the situation to his partner, and his partner plays the role of the person whose behavior is unacceptable. The first person begins telling his partner everything he would like to say (if he had the nerve) to the person in the real situation. Encourage the use of lots of "you-message," for example "You are an inconsiderate slob," "You are unbelievably stupid," "You have got a lot of nerve," and so on. The role-player can respond in whatever ways he feels like responding.

After two or three minutes, stop the activity. Using the same situation, ask the first person to now approach the other with an "I-message" instead of a "you-message." Again the role-player should respond however he feels like responding, and the first person should continue giving "I-messages." After two or three minutes, stop the activity. Follow the same procedure with the partners reversing positions. The other member of the pair describes his situations, and so on. After both members of the pairs have experienced giving and receiving "you-messages" and "I-messages," bring the class back together as a group. Ask them their reactions to the activity. (You may notice that the "you-message" situations were much louder and more agitated than the "I-message" situations).

Using **Handout Master 12.3a** (How do you handle conflict?) students can assess themselves on their conflict resolution styles. **Handout Masters 12.3b** (Assertiveness

Scale/ Scoring) can be self-administered and scored. Students can evaluate their approaches to conflict resolution and their level of assertiveness, and discuss how it might influence their teaching..

12.4   Conflict with a Parent

Conflict can be avoided by communication. Use **Handouts 12.4a and 12.4b** for this activity. **Handout 12a** is a parent's letter to a teacher objecting to a homework assignment. Have your students write a response to this parent. Once they have completed the task, distribute **Handout 12.4b** which is the teacher's actual response to the parent. Have your students compare their response to the parent and the actual teacher's and comment on the most appropriate way to solve this issue.

Field Experience

12.5   Time on Task

There are two parts to this activity. Part A requires students to read the following article. In Part B, students observe the use of time in classrooms and discuss their observations and conclusions.

Part A

Walberg, H. (1988, March). Synthesis of research on time and learning. Educational Leadership, 76, 80.

Love, I. H.. *Getting the Most Out of the School Day.* (Principal, J. F. Chick Elementary School, 4101 E. 53rd St., Kansas City, MO 64130.)

Time Awareness Program. In many schools the amount of time lost is frightening. We spend more time getting ready to teach than teaching. In some schools, there is more movement daily than in the elevators in a public building. Several years ago achievement at J. F. Chick Elementary School was typical of inner-city schools. Today Chick School has achieved national norms at every grade level, except 3rd grade in reading and math, where we fell short by a matter of two or three months. Much of this success is the result of our Time Awareness Program. Here are a few of the problems we addressed in our effort to get the most out of our school day.

Starting the day. When the first bell sounds, students often take five minutes to get to their classrooms. Once inside, they can lose another 15 minutes hanging up coats, looking for pencils, sharpening pencils, turning in money for fund-raising, and looking for homework assignments. Ten more minutes are lost when teachers start asking for lunch money and taking attendance, usually calling the name of every child. Finally, everyone is asked to stand for the Pledge of Allegiance and the opening song. After this, directions for starting the morning activities often consume another 5 or 10 minutes. By then, 30 to 40 minutes have been spent doing what could have been done in 15 minutes or less.

313

Creating Learning Environments

Children can be trained to enter the classroom and start to work on morning practice activities immediately. They can also learn to check their presence on a chart, which the teacher can see at a glance. This is not a time to sharpen pencils or visit with other students. Teachers can schedule a special time during the day to sharpen pencils and save early morning time for concentrating on learning.

Changing subjects. When finishing one subject and starting another, a teacher can lose 10 minutes without meaning to. Often students use this time to open and close desks, disturb each other, or call the teacher's attention to some unrelated topic. Their loss of time can be reduced by giving the students something to think about to bridge the gap between subjects. Teachers can use an idea related to the objective in the next subject to capture students' attention. They can motivate the children to look forward to "coming attractions." Recess and restroom. Recess is important, but if we are not careful, this block of 20 minutes can turn into 30 or 40. Just putting away classwork and getting in line can take five minutes. Then, getting to the restroom at the end of the hall and finally arriving outside can take an additional 10 minutes. That leaves only five minutes to do organized games, line up to come inside, find a seat, take out work for the next subject, and listen for directions. There is a remedy to this situation, too. Children can be trained to take out books for the next subject when opening their desks to put away materials from the previous subject. This allows for a smooth start when the class returns from recess. Carefully taught routines are necessary, if the teacher intends to get the students to the restrooms, outside, and back into the classroom within the allotted time.

Assemblies and programs. Assemblies and programs are necessary, but only within limits. When the excitement starts building, classroom management becomes difficult; additional time is spent just settling down. Some programs become detailed and involved, including making decorations and costumes, learning speeches, and rehearsing frequently. The description can be devastating to the instructional plans of every teacher in the building. The principal must give direction as to what assemblies and programs will be held during the year. It is not wise to allow every activity proposed by every teacher; we must set limits and stand firm. It is urgent that we stress the relationship of these activities to subjects being taught in the classrooms. Other ways to lose instructional time include too many fund-raising activities, classroom visits from parents, emergency personal calls, late arrivals, intercom calls, poor attendance, and late buses; the list goes on. Even when these are not daily occurrences, together they result in the loss of substantial amounts of time.

The key to successful learning is to allow the teacher to teach all day without breaking the teaching/learning cycle. When we use time well, we see happiness in the faces of students who are learning to read their books and master their lessons.

Part B: Observing Time on Task

Discuss "on-task time" and have students give examples. Then assign your students to observe a class, bringing with them a watch with a second hand. Use **Handout 12.5** for this activity. Set a fifty-minute observation time, preferably after lunch. Instruct the observers to keep a running tally of the seconds spent in actual instruction. Do not include time spent waiting for students to become quiet, time spent reprimanding individuals or the group, or time spent in transition from one activity to the next. "Wait-time," or time spent waiting for a student to answer an academic question, is considered instructional time. At the end of the fifty-minute interval, add the seconds and divide by 60 to record the actual instructional time in minutes. After students have performed this observation, ask them to share the results they have obtained. Is the "on-task time" associated with good teaching, that is, are the teachers whom the students perceive as competent those with a high percentage of on-task time?

12.6   The Effective Classroom Manager

Looking back on the observations made to date in various classrooms, describe the teacher whose classroom is best managed. Describe the communication patterns, transitions between activities, and provisions for student behavior management that make the classroom "work."

12.7   Classroom Management

Using **Handout Master 12.5**, Classroom Management Observation Sheet, discuss with students what effective management might consist of in four categories: students' assignments, including seatwork; a teacher's sense of "withitness," teacher's organization of lessons, materials, student helpers, and transitions between activities; and teacher's use of classroom rules. Using the handout, students can rate the teachers they observe on a scale of 0-10 and makes suggestions for improvement. Students can use their rating sheets as a basis for discussion about management challenges in the classes they have observed.

Other Teaching Activities

12.8   Fostering Student Self-Management

Wayson, W. W. and Lasley, T. J. (1984, February). Climates for excellence: Schools that foster self-discipline. Phi Delta Kappan, 65, 419-421.

What are the aspects of a school in which students effectively discipline themselves? The Phi Delta Kappa (PDK) Commission on Discipline reviewed a wide variety of schools and extracted the principles which encouraged students to behave properly without direct supervision.

In schools with effective discipline, everyone tries to develop a positive culture, one in which "belongingness," service, and learning are valued. The PDK study found five factors to be necessary in order to create an environment that encourages teachers and students to feel good about themselves and to develop and maintain a culture conducive to learning.

Creating student belongingness and responsibility. The overriding goal is to have as many students as possible involved in the life of the school. Teachers and administrators alike must help students feel that the school is worth "belonging to." In her book, *Teacher's Pets, Troublemakers, and Nobodies*, Helen Gouldner found that only a favored few students receive most of the teachers' positive attention. Others develop a reputation for defiance. By far the largest group, however, are those who seldom receive recognition of any kind. They are not valued by school personnel, and the feeling becomes mutual.

One correspondent described the efforts of the Rocky River (Ohio) High School to get students to participate:

Our philosophy is to get everyone involved. We have a separate cheerleading squad for each varsity team, thus involving 56 different cheerleaders. Students who are cut from the varsity and junior varsity basketball teams form their own "B" team, which has its own coach and plays its own schedule of games. We encourage wide participation in all extracurricular activities and try to have enough to involve all the students.

The Charleston, South Carolina schools have developed a plan for dealing with students who are chronic discipline problems. "Target" pupils are given special attention, such as tutorial assistance and psychological support services, and they are strongly encouraged to participate in extracurricular activities at school. Another urban school was turned around as a result of a student leadership program. Students from a troubled urban school were asked to work with teachers to tackle the problems of absenteeism, apathy, tardiness, and low achievement. This student participation created visible and positive results.

Pursuing superordinate school goals. Teachers and administrators in schools with effective discipline believe in the importance of every individual. They share a set of core values and translate these values into qualitative statements of purpose. The PDK Commission found that the key elements for effective goal setting are participation, ownership, and responsibility. Staff members and students participate in goal setting and decision making, and consequently they exhibit more commitment to the decisions and outcomes. Frequently, leadership teams of students, teachers, parents, and administrators cooperate to identify and solve problems. Schools with excellent discipline strive to create long-term, broadly-based involvement rather then relying on one-shot, isolated practices. Achieving superordinate goals requires two fundamental conditions: 1) methods for diffusing core values and 2) leadership that fosters positive beliefs about the value system.

Creating symbols of identity and excellence. Schools often create slogans or aphorisms to reinforce and disseminate values. Such slogans serve to strengthen certain aspects of the school culture, succinctly stating values that exemplify what is expected of all. For example, the Mechanicsburg Elementary School in Liberty, New York describes the use of their slogan to foster commitment:

Principal Bill Carter and staff have emphasized that "every student has a talent." Students are taught athletic, artistic, dramatic, or musical skills. Each week features a talent assembly in which these skills are practiced and demonstrated. Success in these areas influence behavior and commitment throughout the school program. Discipline and achievement have improved markedly since the program began.

Fostering leadership to sustain positive school values. Principals are often cast in the role of "visionary" heroes. They have the greatest opportunity to shape the culture of their schools to suit collectively defined purposes. Visionary heroes take on responsibility of the success of the system; they bring out the best in others and help create and sustain values. Principals can enable teachers and students to believe in themselves.

Students are often cast in the role of "situational hero," to serve as examples of the behaviors that are necessary for success in the school environment. Some schools have set up reward systems for recognizing students who best exemplify desired behaviors. Staff members seek to recognize the efforts of students who are committed to the behavior norms of the school. Student situational heroes serve as role models for their peers, and personify behavioral value that other students are encouraged to emulate. This strengthens the school's culture and sustains desired values. One respondent to the PDK Commission's survey described a program to recognize good behavior at Meadow Elementary School in Stafford, Texas:

Our school uses a variety of activities to implement a positive discipline program. The Principal's Award for Leadership is given monthly to three students from each homeroom, and these students are featured in the monthly newsletter that goes to all parents. We use positive reinforcement and behavior contracts to teach self-disciplined behavior.

<u>Creating clear formal and informal rules</u>. Schools with effective discipline reduce behavioral problems by establishing a behavioral code for students. Expectations are explicitly delineated, and students know what is expected of them. Poorly developed rules and weak enforcement procedures cause discipline problems. Explaining rules carefully is particularly important at the beginning of the school year, when students are developing an understanding of the norms of the school. Rules must be taught; they cannot be merely announced or published.

Whenever possible, rules should be developed collectively. Rules generated by individuals or small committees are less effective in uniting students and staff members to achieve behavioral goals. Individuals who are not involved in developing the rules have neither an understanding of nor an interest in following the rules.

To supplement the formal rules, schools need informal rules, the norms of behavior that communicate tacit understanding of how individuals-- teachers and students alike-- should act. Teachers who respect students are modeling adherence to an informal rule. If modeled often enough, a particular notion of respect will become ingrained in the norm of the school. Students will understand what respect is and how they are expected to treat others.

Rather than rely on power and enforce punitive models of behavior control, effective schools share a school climate in which everyone wants to achieve self-discipline. This seems to be the most effective approach to the business of preparing self-disciplined individuals for life in a democratic society.

References: Gouldner, H. (1978). <u>Teacher's pets, troublemakers, and nobodies</u>. Westport, CT: Greenwood Press.

12.9 <u>Using Behavior Modification In Classroom Discipline</u>

Siggers, W. (1980). Changing teacher correcting behavior: Using aversive and positive contingencies. <u>Educational Research Quarterly, 5</u> (3), 25-32.

Problem: Many teachers are aware of strategies such as token economies and contracting techniques. However, when faced with planning individual behavioral management programs for disruptive students, teachers are skeptical about the use of positive reinforcement to correct disrupting behavior. The institutional climate encourages teachers to be "tough on discipline," resulting in teachers showing a preference for punishing disrupting behaviors even though the punishments as applied were not particularly effective in reducing the disruptions. Little research has been done on the use of positive and aversive contingencies in schools. If teachers were trained in the use of such procedures, would they use them effectively?

Participants and Setting: Eleven female elementary teachers from a small, suburban school district volunteered to participate in the study. The teachers ranged in grade level assignment from kindergarten to fifth grade, including one special education teacher.

Procedure: Teachers were given a questionnaire which assessed their proclivity to punish across 12 simulated situations. The responses which they could choose corresponded with the use of positive and aversive contingencies. The teachers were then taught to use contracts which included positive and aversive contingencies. Each teacher developed a behavioral management plan to use with her most disruptive student. The plan specified a given number of target behaviors, and established a treatment schedule for each behavior. Teachers were then to gather baseline data on the student's behavior before discussing the contract or the management plan. To establish reliability of the teacher's baseline data collection, the investigator simultaneously recorded target behaviors in the classroom for each student. Teachers were then to draft the actual contracts, discuss the contract with the student, and implement the treatment schedule in the classroom.

     To train in behavioral principles, the teachers attended 10 hour-and-a-half after school workshops devoted to application of the contracting technique. Seven principles were incorporated into the workshops, and the teachers trained to criterion on identifying each. Observers recorded teachers' correcting behaviors during two 25-minute sessions, at the beginning and end of an eight-week period. Teachers were given a questionnaire on the day of the last workshop on which they reported on the usefulness and applicability of the contracting procedure. The correcting behaviors are as follows:

1. Providing cognitive structure: Teacher gives an appropriate explanation why the child cannot continue the behavior.

2. Providing an alternative: Teacher explains the desired alternative behavior and indicates the positive consequences, i.e. positive reinforcement for desired behavior.

3. Correcting softly: Teacher gives correction in a lower volume than previous teacher comments.

4. Correcting privately: Teacher makes definite effort to limit audience of correction.

5. Correcting with relative intensity: Teacher informs child of a threat or consequence that will occur if student behavior were to continue; or teacher effects the consequence.

6. Correcting with inconsistency: Teacher follows an inconsistent pattern of correction, i.e. gives a reprimand and then reverts to ignoring behavior or fails to follow through with a threatened consequence.

7. Escalating of threats: Teacher corrects by overuse of threats or by improper sequence of correcting behaviors, i.e. threat, then a reprimand, then another threat.

Results: Analysis of data from the initial questionnaire showed that for 80% of all responses, punishments were chosen. The data from the experiments showing the efficacy of the contracts was encouraging: 85% of all behaviors treated by all teachers showed at least 50% reduction. The final questionnaire showed that five teachers had already used contracts on a total of 12 other children. Ten teachers reported that their correcting behavior had changed; they used more cognitive restructuring, they provided more alternatives when correcting disruptions, and they used the correcting format of the contracts "*if you do a* (disrupting behavior), *then you will get a* (contingency)" in their correcting of other children. Review of anecdotal notes showed a recurring comment that the techniques worked "better then expected."

Discussion and Conclusion: Teachers seemed to generalize the use of the techniques they were given beyond the experimental case in which they were supervised through the workshop. Some limitations of the experiment were that there was no long-term measure of the effectiveness of this training; the actual observed change in teacher behavior was modest; and the validity of the self-report measures was not tested. This study points out the need to attend to the predisposition of teachers to punish, and suggests that a change in teacher correcting behavior might be more substantial if teachers were taught how to punish rather than not to punish.

12.10 Who Owns The Problem?

This activity allows your students to analyze typical classroom situations. The class can work as a whole on this activity. In the situations depicted in **Handout Master 12.6**, first have students decide who owns the problem, and then respond appropriately with active listening or an "I-message." Active listening paraphrases the other person's message and includes the feeling communicated. An "I-message" states what the other person is doing, its effect on you, and how you feel about it. **Handout Master 11.2** can be used as an independent or class activity.

12.11 "I" Messages

(This activity can also be conducted as a cooperative activity. To use it as a group activity, assign students to groups of four, with the following roles: Reader, Responders (2), and Commentator. Reader will read the following situations that include a teacher's typical response. The second and third persons (Responders) will change the teacher's response to an I-message. Then the fourth person (Commentator) will reflect on the effectiveness of the I-message, and the group will work together to modify the response if

Creating Learning Environments

necessary. Have each Reader share the group's responses in class and so the group as a whole can comment on them.)

Individual Instructions

Read the following situations and ask students to rewrite the teacher's comments as an "I-Message." Have the students note the different effects that the two messages (the teacher's original message and the rewritten message) might have on students.

1. Cathy is the class rebel of the ninth grade. She attempts to undercut all authority figures, especially her history teacher. Today she is making sarcastic remarks to her best friend while the teacher lectures. The teacher says, "All right, Cathy, I've put up with your wisecracks for as long as I can. Even a teacher runs out of patience sooner or later. Now shut up."

2. This is a sixth grade spelling class and it is the day before Christmas holidays. The teacher is having trouble getting the students to quit giggling and study their spelling words, so she says, "If you're going to act like babies, I'm going to treat you like babies. From now on, anyone who speaks without raising his hand will stand in the corner."

3. Ralph is always coming to his third-grade class without paper or pencil in spite of the teacher's repeated reminders and punishments. Today he ambles up to the teacher's desk, opens the top drawer and takes out a pencil. The teacher says, "Is your father a thief, Ralph? Is that where you learned to take things without asking? Now bring back that pencil you just stole out of my desk."

4. The fourth-grade class tended to be rather lively with occasional horseplay and note writing. One day when the teacher was writing on the board, she was hit with a spitwad on the head. She turned around and said, "In the 20 years I've been teaching, I've never had a class as bad as this one. You deliberately start trouble whenever I turn my back, and I'm getting sick and tired of it."

5. Ray was the class clown in the 11th grade chemistry class. Most of his antics were funny, but occasionally he went too far with his practical jokes. One day he was playing around with some acid and spilled some on a girl's purse. His teacher said, "It doesn't take any brains to figure out where you're going to be when you grow up. Anyone with a talent like yours for cutting up will be lucky to make trustee in an insane asylum."

12.12 <u>Student Mediators</u>

From <u>Harvard Education Letter, (1989, January/February), 5 (1)</u>, 4-5. Talking it out: Students mediate disputes,.

Before school, a fight erupts between two seventh-grade girls in the schoolyard. "You better watch out, I'm gonna get you on the bus after school today - nobody talks about my sister that way and gets away with it!" Wanda gives Denise's hair a yank. These two girls have a history of name-calling and squabbling. Another student observes this episode and suggests to Denise that they go to peer mediation. With the help of a trained peer, Denise and Wanda discuss their conflict and come to an agreement that they and the mediator then sign.

Why have Wanda and Denise agreed? Is there a chance this time that it will work? According to teachers and administrators involved in school mediation programs, young people are much more likely to resolve their differences when they - with the help of trained peers - sit down together and work out a solution.

Discussion Questions

1. Identify aspects of your college class that exemplify the six characteristics of classrooms. Do college classes fit into these characteristics? How would elementary and secondary classrooms be different? How would they be the same?

2. Choose a particular age group and develop a set of classroom rules. How would you teach each rule to students? Is it necessary to teach the rules to these students? How does a teacher develop creditability for these rules?

3. Give some examples of disruptive school situations that you remember or have observed recently. How did the teacher handle the situation? Was the teacher effective? If confronted with a similar situation, would you deal with it in the same way?

4. What can teachers do to make the classroom participation structures fit the structures that students bring from the culture of the home?

5. What are some nonverbal behaviors that can communicate a message that is different from the verbal message?

6. What are some types of responses which tend to stop or block communication? (See Roadblocks to Communication in Gordon, 1974).

Additional Resources for Teaching This Chapter

PRINT RESOURCES

Brophy, J. (1983). Organization and management. Elementary School Journal, *83*, 265-85. Various classroom management systems are presented and critiqued.
Charles, C. M. (1989). Building classroom discipline, 3rd. ed. White Plains, NY: Longman. This book contrasts eight models of classroom discipline: The Redl and Wattenberg model, Kounin model, neo-Skinnerian discipline, Ginott's communication-

Creating Learning Environments

based model, and the Dreikurs, Canter, Glasser, and Jones models. Readers are given a structure for building a personal system of discipline.

Curwin, R. L., & Mendler, A. N. Discipline with dignity (1988), Alexandria, VA: ASDC Publications. The thesis of this book is that controlling student behavior simply is not enough; they must be helped to become decision makers and critical thinkers regarding the consequences of their behavior. The authors respect students' individuality and make an eloquent distinction between consequences and punishment. They present strategies intended to enhance student self-esteem and self-regulation to cast teachers as educators, not policemen.

Dinkmeyer, D., McKay, G. G., & Dinkmeyer, D. Jr. (1980). Systematic training for effective teaching: Teacher's handbook. Circle Pines, MN: American Guidance Service. This is the guide for the training program with the same name also available from AGS. The program promotes a democratic classroom where choices are clear, discipline is logical, and self-discipline is encouraged. It is based upon theories of behavior articulated by Alfred Adler and Rudolf Dreikurs.

Flygare, T. J. (1981). Disciplining special education students. Phi Delta Kappan, May, 670-671. In the 1977-78 school year, seven mentally retarded students were expelled from Clewiston High School in Hendry County, Florida, on charges ranging from willful defiance of authority to sexual acts against other students. The students filed suit in U.S. district court seeking an injunction requiring state and local school officials to provide them with the educational services that were their rights under P. L.. 94-142. This article follows the case through the Fifth Circuit Court of Appeals and summarizes briefly the general principles which have emerged from these proceedings regarding appropriate disciplinary procedures for special education students.

Glasser, W. (1986). Control theory in the classroom. New York: Harper and Row Publishers. According to Glasser, no more than half of the secondary school students in America's schools are willing to learn, wasting an enormous human and financial resource. Control theory teaches that students who attend school to satisfy internal needs will find that school work is satisfying and rewarding for the effort expended. Glasser's description of school learning teams draws heavily upon cooperative learning research to construct a learning approach that features positive interdependence, collaborative skills, and individual accountability.

Lee Canter's program of "Assertive Discipline" offers suggestions for classroom discipline from the behavioral school of thought. A catalog of printed materials may be obtained from Lee Canter and Associates, 1307 Colorado Avenue, Santa Monica, CA 90494-3312.

Time on task. This practical booklet about using instructional time more effectively is prepared by the American Association of School Administrators (1801 N. Moore St., Arlington, VA 22209). It reviews the research, discusses role of students, effective teaching, management procedures of teachers, and provides a step-by-step approach to assess the use of time in the classroom.

REFERENCES

Emmer, E. T., Evertson, C. M., Clements, B. S., & Worsham, M. E. (1997). Classroom management for secondar school teachers. Needham Heights, MA: Allyn and Bacon.

Evertson, C. M., Emmer, E. T., Clements, B. S., & Worsham, M. E. (1997). Classroom management for elementary school teachers. Needham Heights, MA: Allyn and Bacon.

Gordon, T. (1974). T.E.T.: Teacher effectiveness training. New York: Peter H. Wyden.

Hyman, I. A.. (1997). School discipline and school violence: The teacher variance approach. Needham Heights, MA: Allyn and Bacon.

Johnson, D.W. (1993). Reaching out: Interpersonal effectiveness and self actualization. Boston, MA: Allyn & Bacon.

FILMS, VIDEOTAPES, AND AUDIOCASSETTES

Boot camp for troubled teens. Some parents who have come to the end of their rope are sending their kids to Challenger Foundation, an Utah summer camp which specializes in strict and harsh treatment for rebellious kids. Does this "toughlove" boot camp actually turn these kids around, or is it a brutally harsh answer to parents' prayers? Both sides of the argument are covered in this specially adapted Phil Donahue program. From Films for the Humanities and Sciences, Inc., 28 min.

Classroom management by E. Emmer, audio. Learn how to identify which skills areas are most characteristic of effective classroom managers. (ASCD) Stock #612-20324C2. Assoc. for Supervision and Curriculum Development, 125 N. West St., Alexandria, VA 22314-2798.

Classroom management: A proactive approach to creating an effective learning environment, video. This one-hour video shows how teachers can minimize student behavior problems - and maximize learning - with a three-stage management plan: Planning: How to arrange a classroom, direct students' attention, and present rules. Implementing: How to provide time for practicing classroom rules and procedures - including homework assignments. Maintaining: How teachers can evaluate their own management systems. (to members of ASCD), #614-160ER. Assoc. for Supervision and Curriculum Development, 125 N. West St., Alexandria, VA 22314-2798.

Classroom management: Setting the tone. Teachers model specific techniques for creating a positive learning environment. 40 minutes, 1988. Available from Insight Media, 2162, Broadway, New York, NY: 10024

Conducting effective conferences with parents. This program suggests strategies for preparing and conducting conferences with parents. 22 min. 1988. Available from Insight Media, 2162, Broadway, New York, NY: 10024

Creating Learning Environments

Conflict resolution strategies in schools. Presents strategies for resolving conflict and provides a model for student mediation. 1994. 98 minutes. Available from Insight Media, 2162, Broadway, New York, NY: 10024

Good old-fashioned discipline, video, 28 minutes, color. Are schools to be the repository for everyone below a certain age, or should those who disrupt classes and prevent others from learning be barred? This Phil Donahue program features a heated discussion between Deputy Undersecretary of Education Gary Bauer, author of a government report on the issue of escalating school violence; Joe Clark, outspoken principal who expelled one-tenth of his high school student body in an anti-violence campaign; proponents of other, innovative solutions, and critics of the expulsion policy. #CC-1584. Order from: Films for the Humanities & Sciences, Inc., P. O. Box 2053, Princeton, NJ 08543, Telephone: (800) 257-5126.

Discipline and the law. Addresses legal questions about teachers' rights to discipline children. 29 minutes. Available from Insight Media, 2162, Broadway, New York, NY: 10024

Kids out of control. This program discusses normal adolescence and today's too-frequent scenarios: an 8th grader whose drug use altered his personality; a girl who became severely depressed; a teenage rape victim who ran away from home, attempted suicide, and became addicted to drugs. It presents a quiz to help others determine whether a child is only being troublesome or is actually in need of help; discusses how society is attempting to deal with troubled kids; and offers an inside look at a group therapy session for parents and kids. From Films for the Humanities and Sciences, Inc., 25 min.

Organizing classrooms. This program considers different forms of classroom organization. 1987. 30 minutes. Available from Insight Media, 2162, Broadway, New York, NY: 10024

Taking charge in the classroom: Humanistic discipline methods that work, by Richard Curwin, audio. Discover proven ways to manage student behavior. (ASCD) Stock #612-20495C2. Assoc. for Supervision and Curriculum Development, 125 N. West St., Alexandria, VA 22314-2798.

Handout Master 12.0

Lecture Outline: Creating Learning Environments

- **Need for Organization**

- **Creating a Positive Learning Environment**

- **Maintaining a Positive Environment**

- **Classroom Management Programs**

- **Need for Communication**

Copyright © 1998 by Allyn and Bacon

Handout Master 12.1

Analyzing the Teacher's Casebook

What are the key problems in the classroom? Rank them in order of urgency (i.e., the problem must be solved first, etc.).

Why did you select the problem as the "most urgent?" Can you solve all problems at once?

List the steps you will take to solve the problem and provide a reason for why you would perform these actions?

Compare your solutions to those provided by experienced teachers (see the end of the chapter). How does your solution differ? How is it the same? What role does experience play in problem solving as evidenced by your reading of experienced teachers' responses to the same questions you addressed?

Copyright © 1998 by Allyn and Bacon

Handout 12.2

Encouraging Responsibility

The following is taken from Cornell, N. (1989). Encouraging responsibility: A discipline plan that works. Learning 86 (1986, September). Springhouse, PA: Springhouse Publishers.

The Educator Training Center, which gives workshops on William Glasser's theories, suggests eight steps to help teachers implement effective programs in their classrooms. Each one includes questions you can ask yourself to make sure you're helping students.

1. Stay involved with students.
   Do I spend time having fun with students?
   Have I stopped threatening, using sarcasm, and other failure-breeding habits that break down relationships?
   Can I tell when a student is testing me to see if I'll give up or get angry?
   Do I try to work with students when they're upset? When I'm upset?
   Do I get involved with a child only when I'm upset with his behavior?

2. React only to current behavior.
   Do I avoid using past failures to "put down" a student?
   Am I careful to ask "What," not "Why"?

3. Get students to evaluate themselves.
   Am I guiding the student to evaluate his own behavior instead of just telling him the behavior is wrong and he must change it?

4. Help students make plans to change behavior.
   Is the plan specific?
   Is it reasonable?
   Is it short?
   Does it help build feelings of confidence and self-worth?
   Does it avoid resentment?

5. Respond to student commitment.
   Do I check up on the student's commitment and give him a word or sign of encouragement?
   Do I respond regularly - not only when the child has failed?

6. Accept no excuses.
   Do I ask "What are you going to do now?" instead of "Why did (or didn't) you do that?"

7. Avoid punishments.
   Am I careful to ensure that plans focus on changing behavior and on improvement - not on retribution?
   Am I careful not to interfere with natural consequences of the student's failure?
   When a student doesn't meet his plan, do I focus on "recycling" that plan into one that works, instead of abandoning it in exasperation?

8. Don't give up.
   Am I willing to go back to step one and start again, if a child isn't ready to make a plan to change?
   Am I willing to keep trying just a little longer than the child thinks I will?

Copyright © 1998 by Allyn and Bacon

Handout Master 12.3 a

How Do you Handle Conflict?

Purpose: It can be stated with confidence that people will face conflict throughout their lives. Dealing with conflict effectively is an important factor in human dynamics. There are different ways of dealing with conflict. This exercise will help you identify methods to use.

Directions: The following statements describe possible responses to various conflict situations. Read each statement carefully, and write the number that most closely describes your behavior in the space provided.

Response Scale:

1	2	3	4	5
never	rarely	sometimes	often	always

Response

____ 1. When strong conflict occurs, I prefer to leave the situation.
____ 2. I feel very comfortable about taking a conflict between a friend and me to a third person.
____ 3. I try to find a compromise when a conflict occurs.
____ 4. I find conflict exciting and challenging.
____ 5. I tend to concentrate on the problem and the issues in a conflict rather than the other person.
____ 6. When conflict occurs, I act as though there is no real problem and try to "get along."
____ 7. I prefer to have a third person help solve a conflict between a friend and me.
____ 8. I'm willing to give a little if the other person in a dispute is also willing to give on some things.
____ 9. It's important that I win, even if the problem or issue in a disagreement is not really important to me.
____ 10. I search for a solution to a conflict that both the other person and I can find acceptable.
____ 11. I would quit a job if many conflicts occurred daily.
____ 12. It's easier to have an outsider settle a dispute than to argue it out alone with another person.
____ 13. I like to find what each person wants most strongly, then work for a point in the middle.
____ 14. I hate to lose or not get my own way.
____ 15. I like to look at lots of possibilities and options before trying to find a solution to a conflict.
____ 16. When a conflict occurs, I prefer to get out of the situation rather than work to resolve the conflict.
____ 17. I like to take disagreements to someone who has authority and have that person make a ruling.
____ 18. I believe resolving conflict requires that each person give up something.
____ 19. When someone tries to get me to back down or give in during a conflict, that makes me hold my position more strongly.
____ 20. When I especially need to have my plan accepted or when an issue is very important to me, I tell the person with whom I am in conflict.
____ 21. I prefer to walk away from conflict if there is strong personal disagreement.
____ 22. I prefer to have a counselor decide for two people in conflict, not just ask the two people to listen to each other.
____ 23. I believe working out a middle-of-the-road agreement is best, even if both people are still somewhat unhappy about not getting their way completely.
____ 24. When I work to resolve a conflict, I work to win.
____ 25. I consider the other person's preference as well as my own and work to find a solution both of us can live with.
____ 26. I prefer to let conflicts "work themselves out."
____ 27. I believe it is important to get the opinion of a friend when I am in conflict with someone.
____ 28. It's okay to give up some things if the other person gives up something too.
____ 29. I believe settling a conflict with another person is not different from competing in sports, the goal is to win.
____ 30. I believe a conflict is really a problem, not a contest; therefore the goal is to find a solution both people can live with,, not to "beat" the other person.

Copyright © 1998 by Allyn and Bacon

Handout Master 12.3 a (continued)

How Do you Handle Conflict? Scoring

Scoring: The numbers listed below refer to the statements that you have just responded to. Write down the number you circled on the scale for each statement.

	1.	2.	3.	4.	5.
	6.	7.	8.	9.	10.
	11.	12.	13.	14.	15.
	16.	17.	18.	19.	20.
	21.	22.	23.	24.	25.
Total Scores	A:	B:	C:	D:	E:
	withdrawing avoiding	going to a third person	compromise	win-lose	win-win or problem solving

List the letters and total scores from the highest down to the lowest.

Letter	Total Score		*If you total score is*	*You tend to use this method*
____	____	Highest	26-30	a great deal
____	____		21-25	often
____	____		16-20	sometimes
____	____		11-15	occasionally
____	____	Lowest	6-10	infrequently

Interpretation: *The total scores indicate which ways of handling conflict you use most. If two or more scores are close together (for example, compromise 30 and withdrawing-avoiding 28), you tend to use those methods about the same amount of time.*

- **A. Withdrawing-Avoiding.** Handling conflict by getting away from it or ignoring it. This includes giving in quickly, to avoid unpleasantness, pretending there is no conflict, moving out of the situation by quitting, breaking the relationship, or physically moving. Withdrawing may be helpful if the problem is not important to you, or if it not a good time to discuss the disagreement. Withdrawing usually means the other person wins.
- **B. Going to Third Person.** Having a third person listen to both sides of a conflict and then help settle it. A third person can be useful if he or she helps the two people in conflict see each other's points of view. Many times, however, third person are not fair. The success of this method depends on an unbiased third person and whether the two people in conflict will follow what the third person recommends.
- **C. Compromise.** Finding a solution that allows each person to win something. Both persons may be somewhat disappointed and yet, each has the satisfaction of getting part of what he or she waned. Most conflicts have more than two solutions, and many possibilities should be discussed before a compromise is made.
- **D. Win-Lose.** Holding out for your point of view or working to get the other person to give in. This is a high risk method because you tend to win completely or lose completely. If the other person insists on trying to win totally, you have little choice but to use win-lose, unless you can get the other person to change methods.
- **E. Win-Win or Problem-Solving.** Looking at conflict as a problem and searching for a solution or plan that both persons feel good about. This method may end in a compromise, but usually not until after many solutions are discussed. The spotlight is on the problem, not on the personalities of the people in conflict. If personalities are the problem, then they are discussed openly, along with how each person needs to behave differently to resolve or reduce the conflict.

Kammerman et al., *Wellness, RSVP,* Menlo Park, CA: Benjamin Cummings, 1983; pp. 51-54.

Copyright © 1998 by Allyn and Bacon

Handout Master 12.3 b

Assertiveness Scale

Purpose: This inventory is designed to give you an indication of your own degree of assertiveness.
Directions: Respond to each statement by circling the letter that best represents how you would generally respond to the given situation. If the situation does not apply to you, respond according to what you think would best characterize your behavior. Keep in mind that your responses should be your honest opinion of what you actually do or would do in these situations, not what you wish you could do.

		Never	Rarely	Sometimes	Usually	Always
1.	In conversations, I find it difficult to maintain eye contact.	A	B	C	D	E
2.	When I meet new people in social situations, I initiate introductions and start conversations.	A	B	C	D	E
3.	My close friends dominate decisions about how we spend our leisure time together.	A	B	C	D	E
4.	If I am angry with friends/parents/roommates, I find it difficult to directly communicate my feelings to them.	A	B	C	D	E
5.	I ignore it when someone cuts in line in front of me.	A	B	C	D	E
6.	When a friend or roommate is overdue in returning something valuable, I mention it.	A	B	C	D	E
7.	If someone were tapping my chair in class or constantly talking at the movies, I would ask them to stop.	A	B	C	D	E
8.	I feel comfortable asking reasonable favors of other people.	A	B	C	D	E
9.	With family or friends, I find it difficult to break into or even initiate a conversation.	A	B	C	D	E
10.	If someone's cigarette smoke were bothering me in a public building, I would politely ask them to stop.	A	B	C	D	E
11.	In regard to necessary chores, I insist that a roommate or partner take on a fair share.	A	B	C	D	E
12.	I avoid asking questions in class fearing that they just won't sound right.	A	B	C	D	E
13.	If my instructor mad, in my opinion, an unfair request, I would express my feelings to him or her.	A	B	C	D	E
14.	I will buy things I really don't need if a salesman applies pressure.	A	B	C	D	E
15.	If my dinner in a restaurant were not to my liking, I would demand that it be corrected.	A	B	C	D	E
16.	I feel uncomfortable when someone gives me a compliment.	A	B	C	D	E
17.	I would freely offer information or my opinion in group discussions, even if I didn't know the other people very well.	A	B	C	D	E
18.	I have difficulty communicating with an attractive person of the opposite sex.	A	B	C	D	E
19.	I feel uncomfortable about returning a defective piece of merchandise.	A	B	C	D	E
20.	I would be reluctant to invite someone of the opposite sex out on a date.	A	B	C	D	E
21.	I would feel uncomfortable explaining to a friend/boss/instructor a better way in my opinion of completing a specific task.	A	B	C	D	E
		Never	Rarely	Sometimes	Usually	Always

Copyright © 1998 by Allyn and Bacon

Handout Master 12.3 b (continued)

Assertiveness Scale: Scoring

Scoring: Use the following table to determine the number of points to assign to each of your responses. To determine you total score, add all the numbers that match the letter (A, B, C, D, or E) you circled for each statement.

Statement	A	B	C	D	E
1.	4	3	2	1	0
2.	0	1	2	3	4
3.	4	3	2	1	0
4.	4	3	2	1	0
5.	4	3	2	1	0
6.	0	1	2	3	4
7.	0	1	2	3	4
8.	0	1	2	3	4
9.	4	3	2	1	0
10.	0	1	2	3	4
11.	0	1	2	3	4
12.	4	3	2	1	0
13.	0	1	2	3	4
14.	4	3	2	1	0
15.	0	1	2	3	4
16.	0	1	2	3	4
17.	0	1	2	3	4
18.	4	3	2	1	0
19.	4	3	2	1	0
20.	4	3	2	1	0
21.	4	3	2	1	0
Statement	A	B	C	D	E

Total Score _____ This is your assertiveness score. Classify your score in the appropriate level.

66-84   Very Assertive
44-65   Somewhat Assertive
22-43   Somewhat Unassertive
0-21   Very Unassertive

Interpretation. Assertiveness is different from both passiveness and aggressiveness. It is not, as some people might think, halfway between these, it is quite different. Passiveness refers to acquiescing to another person's demands regardless of the consequences to yourself. Aggressiveness means attempting to force your desires on another in order to satisfy your own needs, regardless of the other person's rights. Assertiveness is characterized by a degree of confidence in your pursuits combined with respect for your fellow human beings - respect that you would expect in a reciprocating manner. With each of the situations listed, an aggressive statement or an assertive statement could be made. Kind in mind that assertiveness is determined not only by the words stated, but also in the tone of voice and body language. In addition, the individual on the receiving end of a statement may perceive the circumstances or statement differently and therefore view what was intended to be assertive act an aggressive act.

Kammerman et al., *Wellness, RSVP*, Menlo Park, CA: Benjamin Cummings, 1983; pp. 47-49

Copyright © 1998 by Allyn and Bacon

Handout Master 12.4 a

A letter from Tommy's Mommy

Tommy is a 5 year old child in kindergarten. He is doing well in kindergarten. His teacher has been working on number problems and measurement. In the particular assignment in question, children are given a picture with what look like footprints between different objects. In some places, the "footprints" are replaced with a cluster of leaves. The child is asked to figure out how far it is between two objects. The child can use a paper ruler that accompanies the task or the child can count the "footprints" and guess the distance under the leaves. Children are given paper rulers and asked to use the ruler to measure how many "steps" the hiker in the picture takes. *Children have practiced these kinds of problems at school and according to their teacher, they are comfortable with the activity.*

Parent's Letter

Dear Mr. Xxx,

I would like to contest the math homework Tommy brought home from school yesterday, i.e, Problem Solving: Using a Drawing. The instructions are very misleading, in that, to write the amount of steps "the hiker: takes between each place (which is hardly definitive at that), the instructions then say, "some of the steps are hidden." Alright then.. The example given for the "hidden step" is a leaf formation in the amount of three leaves. As the steps progress, the next lapse is a four leaf cluster. Is this then a hidden step as well. Not as per example! So, s our "hiker" progresses, we then see an altogether different leaf shape and formation, one which bears no resemblance to the EXAMPLE of the hidden step, also we see again the cluster of four. At the end, (or what I am assuming to be the end of the problem), we have the different cluster of three and lo and behold, a leaf formation which matches the EXAMPLE exactly.

Okay.. I am confused. What then is the solution? As for checking this with a ruler…who is out of their mind!! Please don't think me simple, I assure you I am not. I presented this problem to a fired of mine who happens to be a math major at AnyPlace State College, and her summation was the same as mine, for a child (make that a five year old child) to follow. Therefore, I am submitting to you , as Tommy's Mommy, my response to this homework: I am not going to try and explain the obviously unexplainable. Forgive the absence of Tommy's math homework today if you please and perhaps we can all redeem ourselves on the next assignment.

Sincerely,

Tommy's Mommy.

Copyright © 1998 by Allyn and Bacon

Handout Master 12.4 a

A Reply to Tommy's Mommy (actual teacher's response)

Dear xxx,

We'll have to have a friendly disagreement on this one. I think the homework sheet was appropriate for kindergarten. The number of leaves in each cluster is irrelevant to the problem. If you see a trail with four steps and two clusters of leaves, you can reason that two steps are hidden beneath the leaves, thus yielding six steps in all. The purpose of the ruler is simply to check the answers. Each step is approximately, one unit (inch) long. A trail of approximately six inches would have 6 steps.

Sincerely,

Teacher A

Copyright © 1998 by Allyn and Bacon

Handout Master 12.5

Classroom Management Observation Sheet

Use the following scale to rate the degree to which the aspect of the classroom you observe matches the descriptions provided below.

        1   totally different
        2   a little like the description
        3   somewhat similar
        4   mostly like what is described
        5   exactly as described

Seatwork: Varied, interesting, on student's ability level

Rating: _____   *Observation:*
_____
_____

Organization: Use of student helpers, smooth transitions between activities, lessons well organized and well paced, materials are readily available, quickly takes care of routine activities

Rating: _____   *Observation:*
_____
_____

Withitness: Teacher monitors class, spots potentially disruptive situations, reacts calmly in problem situations, moves around the classroom

Rating: _____   *Observation:*
_____
_____

Assignments: Clearly presented, procedure for getting help, work is checked, student knows what to do when finished

Rating: _____   *Observation:*
_____
_____

Rules: Few and general, reasons for rules explained by teacher, flexible and may change as class develops

Rating: _____   *Observation:*
_____
_____

What overall changes would you suggest that the teacher make?
_____
_____
_____

Copyright © 1998 by Allyn and Bacon

Handout Master 12.6

Who Owns the Problem

In each of the following situations, decide whose problem it is and them respond appropriately with active listening or an "I message." Active listening paraphrases the other person's message and implied feelings. An "I message" states what is happening, its effect on you, and how you feel about it.

A. Student: "You always blame me everytime something goes wrong in the classroom. I know that you don't like me and I don't like you either."
Who owns the problem? _____
Response: _____
_____

B. Student: "My dog got run over by a car last night and is in the hospital."
Who owns the problem? _____
Response: _____
_____

C. An A student suddenly starts making bad grades on his tests and assignments.
Who owns the problem? _____
Response: _____
_____

D. A teacher continually complains about a certain students when he's in the teacher's lounge.
Who owns the problem? _____
Response: _____
_____

E. A student persists in daydreaming and being uninterested in class, and your efforts to motivate him seem to have no effect.
Who owns the problem? _____
Response: _____
_____

F. Several pages are torn from the books at the Reading Center.
Who owns the problem? _____
Response: _____
_____

G. Student: "I can't get my homework done at night because I have to babysit my brothers and sisters when my parents work."
Who owns the problem? _____
Response: _____
_____

Copyright © 1998 by Allyn and Bacon

Handout Master 12.7

Contingency Contracts

Social Studies Class Contract

I, _____, understand that my assignments for my fourth quarter social studies class include the following:
1. Read Chapters 25 through 30 in the text.
2. Complete the exercises at the end of each of the six chapters.
3. Write two papers, one on the executive branch of government and one on the legislative branch.

When I complete each individual task card, I may engage in the reinforcing activity listed on the card. I understand the following grading criteria will be used to determine my class grade.

Grade		% of Assignments Complete	% of Accuracy
A	=	100%	90% to 100%
B	=	100%	89% to 89%
C	=	100%	70% to 79%
D	=	100%	60% to 69%
F	=	100%	less than 60%

_____ _____ _____
Student   Teacher   Date

Contract specifying the assignments and contingencies for a fourth-quarter social studies class. The contract is used with task cards.

Science Project Contract

I, _____, agree to complete each step of my science projects by the following due dates:

Task	Due Date
1. Select a project	Oct. 10
2. Find the necessary resource	Oct. 14
3. Outline the project	Oct. 17
4. Collect the needed equipment	Oct. 20
5. Develop the project	Oct. 27
6. Try to out	Oct. 28
7. Make the necessary modifications	Oct. 30
8. Prepare project in class	Nov. 10-14 (day to be assigned)
9. Write rough draft of paper	Nov. 19
10. Rewrite paper	Nov. 24
11. Final paper	Dec. 3

I will turn in each task card when the task is completed and pick up the next card. The task cards will list the reinforcing activity that I will earn if the task is completed on time.

_____ _____ _____
Student   Teacher   Date

Contract designed to help a student who procrastinates when working on assignments. The teacher assists the student by contracting for task completion leading to punctual assignment completion.

Copyright © 1998 by Allyn and Bacon

Handout Master 12.8: Links to Other Chapters

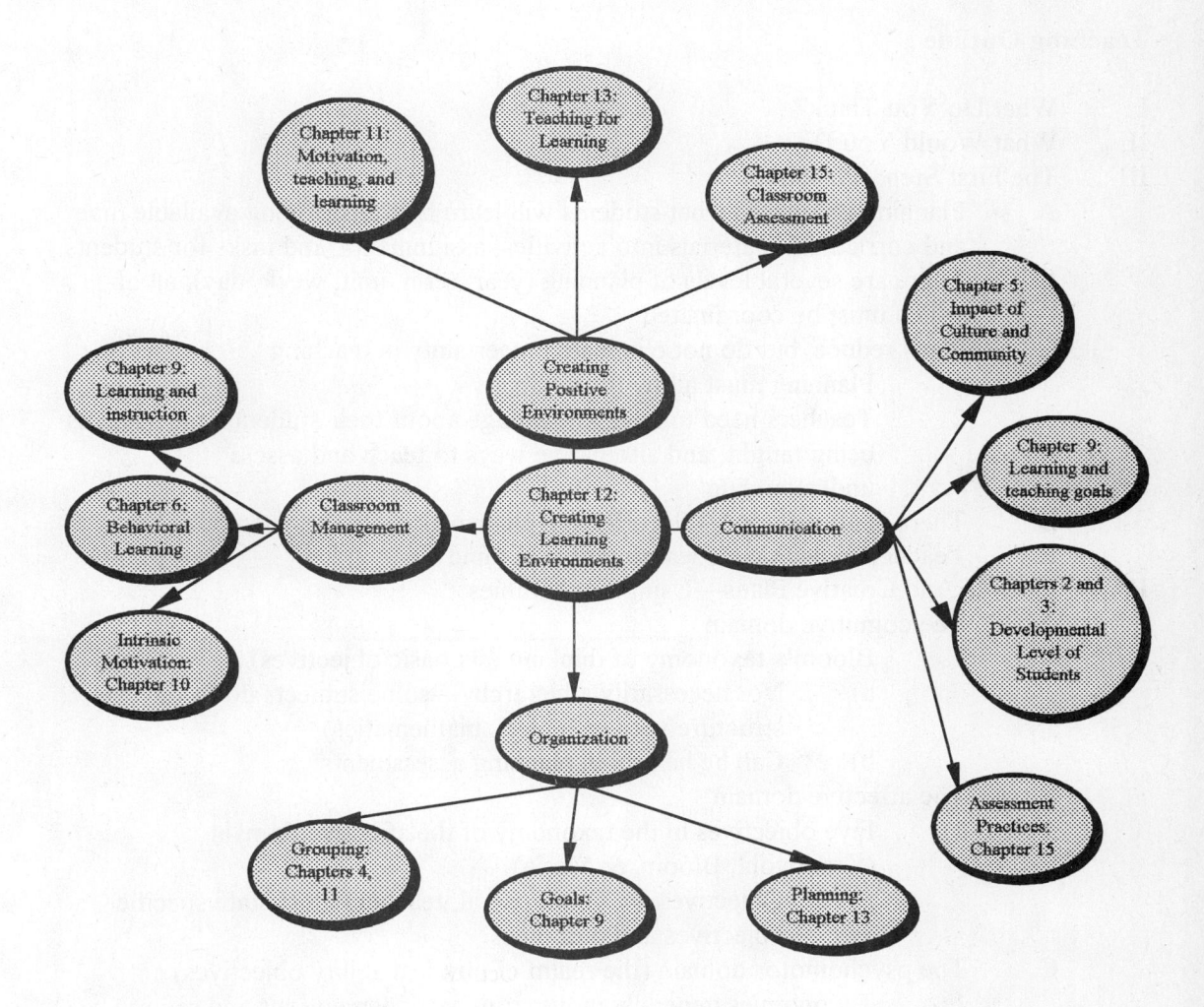

- Chapter 12: Creating Learning Environments
  - Creating Positive Environments
    - Chapter 11: Motivation, teaching, and learning
    - Chapter 13: Teaching for Learning
    - Chapter 15: Classroom Assessment
  - Classroom Management
    - Chapter 9: Learning and instruction
    - Chapter 6: Behavioral Learning
    - Intrinsic Motivation: Chapter 10
  - Communication
    - Chapter 5: Impact of Culture and Community
    - Chapter 9: Learning and teaching goals
    - Chapters 2 and 3: Developmental Level of Students
    - Assessment Practices: Chapter 15
  - Organization
    - Grouping: Chapters 4, 11
    - Goals: Chapter 9
    - Planning: Chapter 13

Copyright © 1998 by Allyn and Bacon

Teaching for Learning

13

Teaching for Learning

Teaching Outline

I. What Do You Think?
II. What Would You Do?
III. The First Step: Planning
   A. Planning influences what students will learn by transforming available time and curriculum materials into activities, assignments, and tasks for students
   B. There are several levels of planning (year, term, unit, week, day), all of which must be coordinated
   C. Plans reduce, but do not eliminate, uncertainty in teaching
      1. Planning must allow for flexibility
      2. Teachers need to have knowledge about their students, the subjects being taught, and alternative ways to teach and assess understanding
   D. There is no one model for effective planning
   E. Teachers must have a learning goal in mind
IV. Flexible And Creative Plans—Using Taxonomies
   A. The cognitive domain
      1. Bloom's taxonomy of thinking (six basic objectives)
         a) Not necessarily a hierarchy—some subjects do fit the structure very well (e.g., mathematics)
         b) Can be helpful in planning assessments
   B. The affective domain
      1. Five objectives in the taxonomy of the affective domain (Krathwohl, Bloom, & Masia)
         a) Objectives are very general, teachers must state specific objectives and outcomes
   C. The psychomotor domain (the realm of physical ability objectives)
      1. Taxonomies generally move from basic perceptions and reflex actions to skilled, creative movements
      2. Of interest to educators in fine arts, vocational-technical education, and special education. Other subjects also require specialized movements and well-developed hand and eye coordination
      3. Learning in the psychomotor area means developing a performance ability
         a) Assessment—ask student to demonstrate skill and observe student's proficiency
         b) Need a checklist or rating scale to focus on the skill being evaluated

V. Planning From A Constructivist Perspective
   A. In constructivist approaches, planning is shared and negotiated between the teacher and students
      1. Overarching goals guide planning rather than specific student behaviors and skills as objectives
      2. Create a learning environment that respects students' individual interests and abilities (Figure 13.1)
   B. Focus in on the processes of learning and the thinking behind the products rather than the students' products themselves
   C. Integrated and thematic plans used from kindergarten through high school to design integrated content units (Table 13.1)
   D. Assessment
      1. Use of authentic assessment (exhibitions, portfolios, and performances)
      2. Teachers and students share authority to evaluate work (Table 13.3)
VI. Teaching: Whole Group And Directive
   A. Lecturing and explaining
      1. Advantages
         a) Appropriate for communicating large amounts of material to many students in a short period
         b) Teachers can integrate information in less time than it would take the students
         c) Good way to introduce a new topic, giving background information, and motivating students
         d) Helps students learn to listen accurately and critically
         e) Teachers can make immediate changes to help students understand
      2. Active learning
         a) Scripted cooperation (Chapter 11) can be used to incorporate active learning into lectures
            (1) Teacher asks students to work in pairs; one student is summarizer and the other critiques the summary
            (2) Gives students a chance to organize thinking and check understanding
         b) Other ways to incorporate active learning (Table 13.5)
      3. Disadvantages
         a) Students may tune out the teacher
         b) Puts students in a passive position
         c) Does much of the cognitive work for student
         d) Pace of lecture may not match the pace of students' learning

- B. Recitation and Questioning
    1. Pattern consists of structure, solicitation, and reaction
    2. Questioning
        a) Kinds of questions—those found in Bloom's taxonomy; convergent (only one right answer) or divergent questions (many possible answers)
        b) Fitting the questions to the students. Younger and lower-ability students benefit from simple questions allowing for a high percentage of correct answers; high-ability students benefit from harder questions at both higher and lower levels and from more critical feedback
        c) Wait time—need to wait 3 to 5 seconds before calling on a student to answer (may not affect learning in university classes)
        d) Selecting students—call on all students
    3. Responding to student answers
        a) Fifty percent of the time, a teacher's response is simple acceptance, "OK" or "uh-huh"
        b) Tailor response to answer given
- C. Seatwork and homework
    1. Seatwork
        a) Little research on seatwork, but clearly often overused in classrooms
        b) Should follow up a lesson and give supervised practice
        c) Requires careful monitoring
    2. Homework
        a) 1980s research reported strong correlations between amount of homework and students' grades
        b) Must be meaningful extension of class lessons, not just busywork
        c) Make sure students understand assignments
    3. Guidelines

VII. Teaching: Small Group And Student-Centered
- A. An example of constructivist teaching (Table 13.6)
- B. Individualized instruction
    1. Each student works with learning plans designed to fit needs, interests, and abilities
        a) Modifying lessons to fit individual needs
            (1) Pace
            (2) Learning objectives
            (3) Learning activity
            (4) Reading level
            (5) Demonstration of new learning
        b) Research on individualized instruction

Teaching for Learning

      (1) Not superior to traditional methods when used as only form of instruction
      (2) Students must be motivated and self-directed
      (3) Can use team-assisted individualization (variation of cooperative learning) to incorporate individualized learning into regular class lessons

 C. Group Discussion
   1. Advantages
    a) Students are directly involved, have opportunity to participate
    b) Gives students change to clarify questions, examine interests, assume responsibility
    c) Useful when discussing concepts that go against common sense
   2. Disadvantages
    a) Unpredictable, students may not have enough knowledge to direct the discussion
    b) Some students may become anxious by having to speak
    c) Requires a great deal of preparation to ensure sufficient background information
    d) Large groups are often unwieldy
    e) Some students will dominate the discussion in many cases
   3. Guidelines: Humanistic education
    a) Carl Rogers, Abraham Maslow, Art Combs
    b) Stresses the importance of feelings, open communication, and the value of every student—a philosophy, not a collection of strategies
    c) Open schools—students grouped by project or activity; individualized instruction; negotiated objectives and activities; "hands-on" learning. Encourages creativity, cooperation, self-esteem, and social adjustment; academic learning no greater than in traditional classrooms
   4. Guidelines: Leading class discussions
   5. Inviting school success (Table 13.7)
 D. Computers, videodiscs, and beyond
   1. Computers as learning environments
    a) Computers games encourage learning and problem solving (e.g., "Where in the World is Carmen San Diego?")
    b) Computer simulations are simplified versions of situations that the student would encounter in real life
    c) Microworlds encourage discovery through exploration
    d) Computers and learning
     (1) Computer-assisted instruction may be moderately more effective than conventional methods
     (2) Provide back-up or extended instruction

Teaching for Learning

        2. Guidelines
           a) Videodiscs such as *The Adventures of Jasper Woodbury* (Vanderbilt University) present complex situations that require the application of mathematics, science, history, and literature to solve problems. Data required to solve the problems are embedded in the stories presented. Students are highly motivated
           b) Using Computers and Other Technology

VIII. Successful Teaching: Focus On The Teacher
    A. Characteristics of effective teachers
        1. Teachers' knowledge
        2. Organization and clarity
        3. Planning for clarity—try to anticipate problems that students may have; have definitions ready for new terms
        4. Clarity during the lesson—explanatory links; signal transitions; use familiar words; be precise
        5. Warmth and enthusiasm are the teacher traits most strongly related to student attitudes

        B.   Guidelines:
              1.   Putting it all together: The effective teacher
                    a)   Direct instruction Cannot ensure that students understand
              2.   Teaching effectively

IX.   Successful Understanding: Focus On The Student
        A.   The New Zealand studies
              1.   Graham Nuthall and Adrienne Alton-Lee conducted studies focusing on how and what students learn
              2.   Conditions for learning from teaching
                    a)   Students must have resources to learn
                    b)   Students must have many opportunities to learn
                    c)   Students must take advantage of these resources and opportunities
        B.   Learning functions: The effective student—expectations, motivation, prior knowledge activation, attention, encoding, comparison, hypothesis generation, repetition, feedback, evaluation, monitoring, and integration are necessary for learning (Table 13.8)

X.   Integrations: Beyond Models To Outstanding Teaching
        A.   Point-Counterpoint: What is the best way to help students at risk of failing
        B.   Matching methods to learning goals
              1.   Teacher-centered direct instruction leads to better performance on achievement tests
              2.   Open, informal methods are associated with better performance on tests of creativity, abstract thinking, and problem solving. They are also better for improving attitudes toward school; stimulating curiosity; cooperation among students; and lower absence rates
        C.   APA's learner-centered psychological principles

XI.   Summary
        A.   The first step: planning
        B.   Teaching: Whole group and directive
        C.   Teaching: Small group and student-centered
        D.   Successful teaching: Focus on the teacher
        E.   Successful understanding: Focus on the student
        F.   Integrations

XII.   Teachers' Casebook: What Would They Do?

XIII.   Key Terms And Concepts

Teaching for Learning

Learning Activities and Related Research

ACTIVITIES	HANDOUTS
Chapter 13	13.0 Lecture outline
Cooperative Activities	
13.1 Critique and support of objectives	13.1 Objectives in the cognitive domain
13.2 When plans fail	
Research Activities	
13.3 Whole language or code-oriented approaches?	
Using Technology	
13.4 Lesson plans on the Internet	13.2 What changes?
Field Experience	
13.5 How active are your lectures?	13.3 Active and inactive learning in lectures.
Other Teaching Activities	
13.6 Scripted cooperation	
13.7 Meeting the needs of low achievers	
13.8 Effective teaching with different students	13.4 A story about assigning competence
	13.5 Analysis of teacher's explanation
	13.6 Concept map: Links to other chapters

Cooperative Activities

13.1 <u>Critique and Support of Objectives</u>

Assign every other group the task of developing an argument in favor or against the use of objectives. Allow 15 minutes to prepare their argument. When they have finished, inform the students that they will be asked to defend <u>the opposite</u> point of view than the one they spent the fifteen minutes preparing. Allow an additional 10 minutes for this redirected preparation. Conduct a classwide debate on the topic. Use **Handout Master 13.1** for this activity.

13.2 <u>When Plans Fail</u>

Have your students discuss a situation in which they had a plan that didn't work out. Ask them to discuss *why* the plan didn't work out. Was it because of insufficient preparation or inappropriate assumptions? What did they do in response to the failed plan? Now ask them to consider what they would if a plan they had for teaching did not work out. Ask them to give specific examples of what might go wrong and what they might do about it.

Teaching for Learning

Research Activities

13.3   Whole Language or Code-Oriented Approaches?

Have your students locate 3-4 research articles on the topic of how to teach reading. They should use articles from some of the journals listed in **Handout Master 1.8**. In groups, they should organize the materials collected in terms of which method is the most appropriate method for teaching reading. They should list the evidence for and against the use of whole language and code oriented approaches. They should then determine which evidence can be relied upon and why.

Using Technology

13.4   Lesson Plans On The Internet

Have your students do the following activity. It is available on **Handout Master 13.2**. They should locate 4 different lesson plans on the Internet and print them. The four lesson plans should be as follows:

Lesson Plan # 1   Science Topic for early elementary grades
Lesson Plan # 2   Science Topic for late elementary grades
Lesson Plan # 3   Language Arts topic for early elementary grades
Lesson Plan # 4   Language Arts topic for late elementary grades

The topic for the early and late elementary grades should be the same. For example, if you find a lesson on the "Butterfly" for first graders, you should find a lesson the same topic for 5th graders. You should follow the same procedure for the language arts topic.

Required

You should compare and contrast the lesson plans you found using the following questions to guide your written analysis.

1. What model of instruction underlies the lesson plans (e.g., discovery, constructivist, direct instruction, etc.). Explain how you know.
2. What changes in lesson plans as a function of the age of the child? You can use the comparison of early/late elementary grades for both language arts and science to answer this.
3. What changes in lesson plans as a function of the content area being taught? You can use the comparison of language arts and science to answer this.
4. Select the lesson plan you like best of the four you include here. Explain why you like and why you think it is an example of good instruction.

Teaching for Learning

Field Experience

13.5   How Active Are Your Lectures?

Have your students use **Handout Master 13.3** to note the kinds of strategies used by college faculty to produce activity learning. In this context, "active learning" is defined as any strategy for learning that suggests active engagement on the part of the learner. Students should monitor "active learning" strategies in two lectures from different disciplines. Are there differences across disciplines? This question might be addressed by pooling the responses of all students in the class.

Other Teaching Activities

13.6   Scripted Cooperation

About 20 minutes into one of your classes, ask students to pair off. Tell the students that you are going to have them review the material from the class in a particular way. One student will summarize the content of the class to that point to his or her partner while the partner listens and tries to detect errors. Both students do these activities without their notes. At the end of the summarization, the listening partner provides feedback on what was missing from the summary. Both partners should then discuss how the material covered up to that point in the class connects to other things they know.

13.7   Meeting the Needs of Low Achievers

Have your students read the article summarized below and discuss the implications of this research for classrooms.

Lumpkins, B., Parker, F., Hall, H. (1991). Instructional equity for low achievers in elementary school mathematics. Journal of Educational Research, Jan./Feb., 84 (3), 135-139.

Problem: Low achievers in the elementary grades are often placed in less demanding curricula with lower teacher expectations. Once a child is assigned to a particular ability group, a strong probability exists that he or she will never be reassigned to a higher ability group for the remainder of the years at school. This study tested an innovative program designed to help low-achieving fourth- and fifth-grade students to increase their achievement in mathematics.

Sample And Setting: Approximately 120 fourth- and fifth-grade students and four full-time teachers were organized as a community of learners.

Procedure: An intensive faculty inservice effort preceded the year of implementation of the program. A seminar room equipped with current professional journals, videotapes, and books was made available to the team of teachers, who spent one hour together reading and discussing the materials daily. The teachers were able to come to consensus on several important points during this pre-implementation period: 1) All parts of the instructional program are interrelated and must be in harmony, including the curriculum content, the instructional grouping schemes, and teaching methods; 2) Teachers must be empowered to make decisions about scheduling, use of resources, organizing students for learning, and instructional delivery; 3) Student assignment to groups must be short-term, so students can have the opportunity to advance; 4) A scheduled time must be set aside for collaborative teacher planning; 5) Children learn more if they can work together, particularly across ages; 6) Student mathematics achievement will increase if math instructional time increases.

During the instructional phase of the program, math was taught in an 80-minute block. One teacher led a homogenous group of 40 students while the other three teachers worked with three small groups of 12 to 13 pupils. The other 40 pupils were involved in independent study under the general supervision of the three teachers directing the three small-group sessions. The curriculum was organized into major units of study around concepts, skills, and operations, with units of about 4-6 weeks in length. The unit proceeded in the following manner: first, an overview of the skills to be covered was presented to the 120 students and a pretest administered to assess understanding of the material. Using these data, the teachers met to organize the 120 students into homogenous instructional groups of approximately 40 pupils per group. These groups were instructed in 40-minute sessions using didactic methods. Students then went to one of three teachers for follow-up in a 40-minute small-group session. Another 40 minutes was allocated for independent practice and follow-up, with students receiving two of the three 40-minute sessions daily on a rotating basis. The daily 80-minute session was 25 minutes longer than the traditionally allotted time. Each unit culminated in an assessment process that involved large-group testing, small-group oral questioning, and optional reteaching.

Results: The fourth-grade students classified as low-achievers made significant gains in mathematics concept development as well as in computational skills, with normal curve equivalency scores in computation increasing from 28.2 to 51.8 between fall and spring of the academic year. The fifth grade low-achievers' scores in mathematics concept development increased from 30.6 in the fall to 44.9 in the spring, with computational skills increasing from 21.4 to 53.6.

Discussion And Implications: The finding of this study supports the conclusion that this program was effective with low achievers. The authors attribute the success to such factors as non-discriminatory grouping factors, effective instructional methodologies, extended class periods for mathematics, and non-limiting teacher expectations. The authors offer this as an alternative to traditional tracking practices in sustaining student achievement and motivation.

Teaching for Learning

13.8   Effective Teaching with Different Students

Have the students reflect on their experiences when in elementary school. Was there a particular competence which they discovered due to the attention paid to them by a teacher? Have the students recall their extracurricular activities in elementary and middle school, such as plays, musicals, choral events, or service projects. What skills did they develop because of these experiences? Use **Handout Master 13.4** with this activity. Now read the following excerpt to your students.

From Arends, R. I. (1991) Learning to teach. (2nd Ed.) New York: McGraw-Hill.

There are a number of instructional strategies that teachers can develop in classrooms that are multicultural. For instance, teachers can apply a variety of techniques in any particular lesson that will help students of diverse cultures be more successful in mastering the curriculum and in navigating the mainstream culture. Teachers can anchor instruction in students' prior knowledge and help them to construct links between what they know and what they are to learn. By so doing, teachers will help students see commonalties and differences between cultures and will assist them in becoming bicultural.

A related consideration in planning and presenting lessons is to capitalize on students' existing abilities. This is particularly crucial for exceptional or culturally different children, who may be ascribed low status by their mainstream peers. Teachers can use a technique called "assigning competence" with these low-status children. To assign competence, teachers first carefully observe their students as they work at a variety of tasks, focusing on the low-status children, and then identifying the special abilities these children have. Teachers then publicly and specifically draw the class's attention to the low-status student's special competence. Children that have been troubled by lack of motivation and low achievement often bloom after teachers assign them competence.

Ask your students to read the story about assigning competence in **Handout Master 13.4** taken from Lotan, R. A., and Benton, J. (1989). Finding out about complex instruction: Teaching math and science in heterogeneous classrooms. In N. Davidson (Ed.), Cooperative learning in mathematics: A handbook for teachers. Menlo Park, CA: Addison-Wesley, pp. 60-62. In this story, a teacher discovers the special abilities of a bilingual child. Use the story as a basis for discussion.

Discussion Questions

1. Planning takes a great deal of time. Justify the use of time in this fashion.
2. Describe four different instructional delivery strategies that could be incorporated into a direct teaching lesson whose objective is that students will be able to describe the land forms of Australia. Example: Using a large classroom map as a visual aid.
3. Using the lesson objective in question 2 above, describe four instructional strategies in which students are actively involved.

4. While teaching the direct instruction lesson in question 3, describe how a teacher could monitor student response and adjust instructional delivery accordingly.
5. What does it mean to have a learning goal? Explain.

Additional Resources for Teaching This Chapter

PRINT RESOURCES

Rosenshine, B. (1986). Synthesis of research on explicit teaching. Educational Leadership, 43 (7), 60-69. Rosenshine summarizes in a very readable article ten years of research on teaching which establishes the effectiveness of systematic, step-by-step instruction. This issue has several other good articles on direct instruction and teaching basic skills.

REFERENCES

Brophy, J. (1982). Reply to Stodolsky's review. Elementary School Journal, 83,(1), 80-83.

Stodolsky, S. (1982). Book review of student characteristics and teaching. Elementary School Journal, 83(1), 76-79.

Wyne, M., & Stuck, G. (1982). Time and learning: Implications for the classroom teacher. Elementary School Journal, 83(1), 67-75.

** See D. Berliner and R. Calfee (Eds.), Handbook of educational psychology, 1996, New York: Macmillan, for extensive resources on subject matter teaching.

FILMS, VIDEOTAPES, AND AUDIOCASSETTES

ASCD library of teaching episodes. Each of the following videos is an actual scene from a classroom which was selected, taped, and edited for use with pre- or in-service teachers. Each counts as one video library selection.
    2nd grade math (Ways to make 10) 18 min.
    3rd grade math (Symmetry) 16 min.
    5th grade science (The solar system) 15 min.

Effective teaching for higher achievement, video. The following effective teaching strategies are demonstrated in 2 hours of videotape: (1) Increasing academic learning time; (2) Managing student behavior; (3) Six functions of effective teaching, daily review, structure presentation, guided practice, feedback, periodic review. To purchase: Stock #614-120C2. To rent: Stock #614-120C2, $100. To preview: Stock #614-123C2. Order from ASCD.

Instructional decisions for long-term learning, Video. The program's three hours of videotape and 80-page Leader's Guide help teachers plan lessons and make sound decisions in the classroom. Use the second 1-hour tape to show teachers how to structure lesson plans that get the students' attention, hold it, and deliver the new knowledge in

Teaching for Learning

ways that build retention. Videotaped sequences give the following tips for effective lesson planning:
> When - and when not - to tell the objectives of a lesson.
> Why not to ask, "Does everyone understand?"
> What kind of homework assignments produce the most learning.

Tape #3 in this program demonstrates how teachers use active participation in the classroom to boost test scores and increase student retention of knowledge. The 30-minute video introduces teaching pairs, choral responses, and five other techniques for increasing student participation. To purchase: Tape #2 - *Guidelines for Decisions,* Stock #614-148V2; Tape #3 - *Student Participation,* Stock #614-149V2; To preview: Stock #614-152V2. Order from: ASCD, 125 N. West St., Alexandria, VA 22314-2798.

Teacher and school effectiveness (video). Featured educators: Ronald Edmonds, Michigan State University; Barak Rosenshine, University of Illinois; Peter Mortimer, London Schools. Spark discussion and sharing about the fundamentals of effective teaching with this 21-minute video. Interviews with expert educators examine the following topics:
> Why student groupings improve learning.
> How the demonstration-practice-feedback model is effective teaching.
> Why to emphasize mastery of learning.
> What are the 5 ingredients of effective schools?

To purchase: Stock #614-116V2; To rent: Stock #614-116V2, $50. To preview: Stock #614-116V2. ASCD.

Teaching mathematics effectively (video). Eight actual classroom episodes in this 30 minute videotape demonstrate the most effective way to structure a math lesson. Beginning activities: To get students to review and check homework or to conduct mental computation exercises. Development: To introduce students to the new problems, give them controlled practice, and then assess their comprehension with appropriate questions. Seatwork: To increase and sustain involvement and make students accountable for their work through well-timed alerts. Homework: To help students retain the new skills. Purchase: Stock #614-117C2 1 voucher (HRDP members). Order from ASCD.

Video library of teaching episodes, a set of 10 videos.
> Episode #1: *Kindergarten math* (readiness skills)
> Episode #2: *3rd grade math* (symmetry)
> Episode #3: *2nd grade math* (ways to make 10)
> Episode #4: *3rd grade classroom art* (rules and procedures)
> Episode #5: *4th-6th grade general studies* (rules and procedures)
> Episode #6: *7th grade social studies* (crimes of commission and omission)
> Episode #7: *8th grade social studies* (4th and 6th Amendments)
> Episode #8: *9th grade English* (rules and procedures through letter writing)
> Episode #9: *10th grade biology* (RNA/DNA transfer)
> Episode #10: *12th grade history* (student debate of Malthus essay)

Handout Master 13.0

Lecture Outline: Teaching for Learning

- **Planning**

- Directive and Whole Group Teaching

- Student-Centered, Small Group Teaching

- Successful Teaching: Role of the Teacher

- Successful Understanding: Role of the Student

- Outstanding Teaching

Handout Master 13.1

Objectives in the Cognitive Domain

Operationalizing the Taxonomy of Objectives in the Cognitive Domain

Taxonomic Categories and Subcategories	Verbs to Use in Objectives	Examples of Appropriate Content in Objectives
1.0 Knowledge 1.1 Knowledge of specifics 1.2 Knowledge of ways and means of dealing with specifics 1.3 Knowledge of universals and abstractions	Define Distinguish Acquire Identify Recall Recognize	Vocabulary words Definitions Facts Examples Causes Relationships Principles Theories
2.0 Comprehension 2.1 Translation 2.2 Interpretation 2.3 Extrapolation	Translate Give in one's own words Illustrate Change Restate Explain Demonstrate Estimate Conclude	Meanings Samples Conclusions Consequences Implications Effects Different views Definitions Theories Methods
3.0 Application	Apply Generalize Relate Choose Develop Organize Use Restructure	Principles Laws Conclusions Methods Theories Abstractions Generalizations Procedures
4.0 Analysis 4.1 Analysis of elements 4.2 Analysis of relationships 4.3 Analysis of organizational principles	Categorize Distinguish Identify Recognize Deduce Analyze Compare	Statements Hypotheses Assumptions Arguments Themes Patterns Biases
5.0 Synthesis 5.1 Production of a unique idea 5.2 Production of a plan 5.3 Derivation of a set of abstract relations	Document Write Tell Produce Originate Modify Plan Develop Formulate	Positions Products Designs Plans Objectives Solutions Concepts Hypotheses Discoveries
6.0 Evaluation 6.1 Judgments in terms of internal evidence 6.2 Judgments in terms of external evidence	Justify Judge Argue Assess Decide Appraise	Opinions Accuracies Consistencies Precisions Courses of action Standards

Copyright © 1998 by Allyn and Bacon

Adapted from N. S. Metfessel, W. Michael, and D. Kirsner. (1969). Instrumentation of Bloom's and Krathwohl's taxonomies for writing educational objectives. Psychology in the Schools, 6, 227-231.

Handout Master 13.2

What Changes?

Your task is to locate 4 different lesson plans on the Internet and print them so that you can refer to them. The four lesson plans should be as follows:

Lesson Plan # 1   Science Topic for early elementary grades
Lesson Plan # 2   Science Topic for late elementary grades
Lesson Plan # 3   Language Arts topic for early elementary grades
Lesson Plan # 4   Language Arts topic for late elementary grades

The topic for the early and late elementary grades should be the same. For example, if you find a lesson on the "Butterfly" for first graders, you should find a lesson the same topic for 5th graders. You should follow the same procedure for the language arts topic.

Required
You should compare and contrast the lesson plans you found using the following questions to guide your written analysis.

1. What model of instruction underlies the lesson plans (e.g., discovery, constructivist, direct instruction, etc.). Explain how you know.
2. What changes in lesson plans as a function of the age of the child? You can use the comparison of early/late elementary grades for both language arts and science to answer this.
3. What changes in lesson plans as a function of the content area being taught? You can use the comparison of language arts and science to answer this.
4. Select the lesson plan you like best of the four you include here. Explain why you like and why you think it is an example of good instruction.

Try These Links for Starters

1.   http://www.classroo.net/classroom/search.htm/

This site provides you with some hints about searching the World Wide Web.

2.   http://www.kn.pacbell.com/wired/bluewebn/

Lesson plan ideas.

5.   http://www.cea.berkeley.edu./~edsci/lessons/lessons_teacherdeveloped.html

Teacher developed earth science lesson plans.

7.   http://www.teachnet.com/lesson.html

Lesson plan ideas.

Copyright © 1998 by Allyn and Bacon

Handout Master 13.3

Active and Inactive Learning in Lectures

For each of two lectures in different disciplines, note what strategies are used by the teachers to promote active learning on the part of the students. Also note what strategies are used to limit active learning.

LECTURE	STRATEGIES FOR PROMOTING ACTIVE LEARNING	STRATEGIES FOR LIMITING ACTIVE LEARNING
CLASS 1		
CLASS 2		

Copyright © 1998 by Allyn and Bacon

Handout Master 13.4

A Story About Assigning Competence

Alicia, a rather tall, bilingual Spanish-English-speaking second grader was the type of youngster whom people barely noticed. She was not a discipline problem; she did not make demands on the teacher or the other students, nor did she actively participate in interactions. Alicia seldom raised her hand to answer questions, and she rarely voiced her opinions.

One day in April, while videotaping group interactions in Alicia's classroom, we focused on students who frequently exhibited low-status behavior. While working on the coordinates and measurement Unit, Alicia had teamed up with another child in her group, Aneke. Their task was to draw lifesized representations of their bodies. The girls took turns, lying on large sheets of butcher paper and them outlining each others' bodies with a thick, felt-tipped pen. After making the outlines, the children had to cut out the replicas and then color in their features and clothing. Aneke had possibly the highest academic status in dais second grade classroom. She was petite, precocious, and popular. She knew the answer to almost every question the teacher asked. She was a delightful, outgoing child, who seemed to be skilled at everything she was asked to do. Among the important skills needed by students in the second grade is the ability to use scissors and to cut accurately. However, it became apparent that Aneke did not know how to use scissors properly, nor did she know how to cut the outline of the body. Aneke was distressed. Patiently and expertly, Alicia guided Aneke through the procedure, coaching her partner on how to use the scissors and follow the outline.

When Alicia's teacher viewed the videotape of this incident with one of the authors, the teacher commented on the fact this was the first time since school started that she had seen Alicia show real mastery on a skill relevant to a classroom task. During the next period, the teacher shared her observation with the class. She wanted all the children to realize that Alicia was particularly skilled at using scissors and that if ever they needed help cutting, they could turn to Alicia as a resource.

Coincidentally, the school was getting ready to present a musical called "Let George Do It." This colonial play required that each class be responsible for making a number of three cornered hats. The teacher decided to put Alicia in charge of making these hats for her class. Alicia was to pick children to be on the committee, decide on what materials was needed, get the pattern from the teacher in charge of costumes, and to see to it that the hats were made to specification.

Alicia took to the making of three cornered hats with tremendous enthusiasm. Again, it was the first time since September that her teacher had seen Alicia talking and wowing with other children in such an animated and empowered way. Alicia was now raising her hand more often, answering questions frequently and accurately. During the same period of time, the teachers also discovered that Alicia had good spatial reasoning and visual thinking skills. For example, when the task for her group was to draw a map for the classroom to scale, Alicia drew the map and then created an impressive three dimensional model of the room. The teacher made sure that Alicia was assigned competence for this accomplishment also.

After the beginning of the next academic year, the opportunity arose to talk with Alicia's third grade teacher. This teachers said she never would have guessed that Alicia had been a low-status student for a large part of her second grade. Alicia interacted frequency and effectively with her classmates, raised her hand and answered questions correctly and expressed her opinions readily. Children listened to Alicia were often observed going along with her suggestions. Alicia was greatly valued by her teachers and her classmates for her artistic and organizational skills. It appeared dial Alicia was also performing better academically in almost every subject

Source: Lotan, R.A., and Benton, J. (1989). Finding out about complex instruction: Teaching math and science in heterogeneous classrooms. In N. Davidson (Ed.), <u>Cooperative learning in mathematics: A handbook for teachers</u>. *Memo* Park, CA: Addison-Wesley, pp. 60-62.)

Copyright © 1998 by Allyn and Bacon

Handout Master 13.5

Analysis of Teachers' Explanation

Teacher D

The discourse	Analysis
T: Okay, let's take a look at the first sentence. Mr., Mr. Perez, would you read that first sentence, please? S: "We ground up the meat into hamburger with our new grinder." T: All right, the underlined word would be . . ?	**Focuses attention:** (on the appropriate sentence) **Assesses:** (elicits data about Perez's understanding of which word it unknown)
S: (in chorus) Ground T: Now, this it for Sergio. We're letting him show us what he can do with the strategy. Okay, you did the first thing, S: Read the sentence T: Now, what Use do you do? What would be the next step? S: Reread the sentence. S: No, you look for the underlined word. T: And the underlined word is?	**Management:** (attempts to stop "call-outs") **Focuses attention :** (back on the task at hand) **Assesses:** (elicits data about Sergio's understanding of what the unknown word is)
S: Ground. T: All right And now what do you do?	**Reinforces** **Assesses:** (elicits data about Sergio's understanding of what the next step is)
S: Reread the sentence. T: Well, do it. S: "We ground up the meat into hamburger with our new meat grinder." T: Okay. Is [sic] there any other steps in our little strategy"?	**Directs** **Reinforces** **Assesses:** (elicits data about Sergio's understanding of what the next step is)
S: Look for clue words. T: Are there any clue words?	**Assesses:** (elicits data about whether the students know the next step)
S: Ya. T: Well, what are they? S: Meat, hamburger, grinder. T: I'm assuming that you know all the words in the sentence. Because if you don't know what a grinder is, then you wouldn't be able to help him. S: 'cause it says "meat"	**Directs** **Presents information:** (that you need to know what the words mean to figure out the unknown word)
T: All right So you put all the club together. Can you figure out the word? S: (in chorus) Ground, ground.	**Reinforces** **Assesses:** (elicits data about whether students know the meaning of the word)

Courtesy of Duffy, G. G., Roehler, L. R., Meloth, M. S., and Varus, L. G. (1986). Conceptualizing instructional explanation. Teaching and Teacher Education, 2, 197-214.

Copyright © 1998 by Allyn and Bacon

Handout Master 13.6: Teaching for Learning

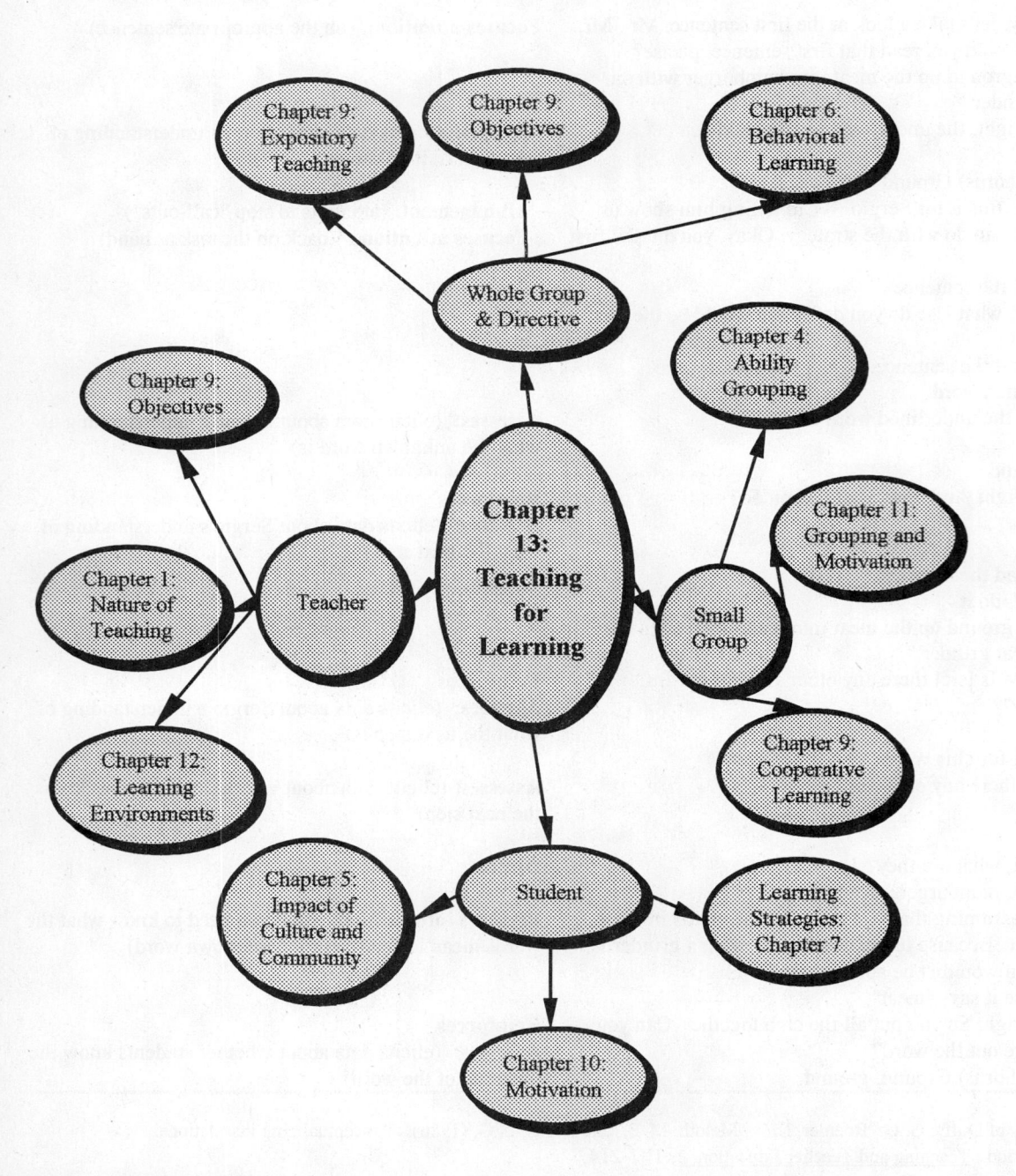

- **Chapter 13: Teaching for Learning**
  - **Teacher**
    - Chapter 9: Objectives
    - Chapter 1: Nature of Teaching
    - Chapter 12: Learning Environments
  - **Whole Group & Directive**
    - Chapter 9: Expository Teaching
    - Chapter 9: Objectives
    - Chapter 6: Behavioral Learning
  - **Small Group**
    - Chapter 4: Ability Grouping
    - Chapter 11: Grouping and Motivation
    - Chapter 9: Cooperative Learning
  - **Student**
    - Chapter 5: Impact of Culture and Community
    - Learning Strategies: Chapter 7
    - Chapter 10: Motivation

Copyright © 1998 by Allyn and Bacon

14

Standardized Testing

Teaching Outline

I. What Do You Think?
II. Measurement And Evaluation
    A. Evaluation: Comparing information to criteria and then making judgments: always involved in teaching
    B. Measurement
        1. Applying a set of rules to describe events or characteristics with numbers
        2. Allows comparison of one student's performance with a standard or with the performance of other students
        3. Evaluation may involve more than measurement, but measurement can be a source of unbiased data
    C. Norm-referenced tests
        1. Performance of others as basis for interpreting a person's raw score (actual number of correct test items)
        2. Three types of norm groups (comparison groups): Class, school district, national
        3. Score: Reflects general knowledge of subject rather than mastery of specific skills and information
        4. Uses of norm-referenced tests: measuring overall achievement and choosing a few top candidates
        5. Limitations:
            a) Do not indicate if prerequisite knowledge for more advanced material has been mastered
            b) Less appropriate for measuring affective and psychomotor objectives
            c) Tend to encourage competition and comparison scores
    D. Criterion-referenced tests: Comparison with fixed standard
        1. Example: Driver's license
        2. Uses: Measuring the mastery of very specific objectives when goal is to achieve set standard
        3. Limitations:
            a) Absolute standards difficult to set in some areas
            b) Standards tend to be arbitrary
            c) Not appropriate comparison when others is valuable
III. What Do Test Scores Mean?
    A. Basic concepts

Standardized Testing

        1. Standardized tests
            a) Standard methods of administration, scoring, and reporting
            b) Test items and instructions have been tried out; final version has been administered to a norming sample (a comparison group)
        2. Frequency distributions: Listings of the number of people who obtain
        3. Measurements of central tendency and standard deviation
            a) Measures of central tendency: Mean (arithmetical average groups of scores); median (middle score); and mode (score that occurs the most often)
            b) Bimodal distribution: Two modes
            c) Standard deviation: Measure of how wide the scores carry from the mean (degree of variability among scores)
            d) Knowing the mean and standard deviation gives meaning to the individual score (Figure 14.2)
        4. The normal distribution: The bell-shaped curve (Figure 14.3)

    B. Types of scores
        1. Percentile rank scores
            a) Shows the percentage of students in the norming sample who scored at or below a particular raw score
            b) Interpretation problem: Greater difference in raw score points to make difference in percentile rank at the extreme ends of the scale
        2. Grade-equivalent scores
            a) Averages obtained from different norming samples for each grade
            b) Interpretation problem: Different forms of test often used for different grades
            c) High score indicates superior mastery of material at that grade level rather than capacity for doing advanced work
            d) Often misleading; should not be used
        3. Standard Scores
            a) Differences in raw scores are the same at every point on the scale
            b) Based on the standard deviation: Z-score has mean of 50 and SD of 10 (eliminates negative numbers)
            c) Stanine scores combine some of the properties of percentile ranks and standard scores; nine possible units (1 through 9) have a mean of 5 and a SD of 2; each unit contains a specific range of percentile scores

    C. Interpreting test scores
        1. No test provides a perfect picture of a person's abilities
        2. Reliability

a) Test-retest reliability: Consistency of scores on two separate administrations of the same test
b) Alternate-form reliability: Consistency of scores on two equivalent versions of a test
c) Split-half reliability: Degree to which all the test items measure the same abilities

3. True score
a) Hypothetical mean of all scores if test were repeated many times
b) Standard error of measurement: Standard deviation of scores from hypothetical true score; the smaller the standard error the more reliable the test

4. Confidence interval or "standard error band": Raw score plus or minus the standard error; provides a range within which true scores might be found

5. Validity:
a) A test is valid if it measures what it is supposed to specifically measure
b) Ways to determine validity: Content, criterion, and construct evidence
c) Factors which interfere with validity: Lack of relation to curriculum; mismatch with students' test-taking skills
d) To be valid, a test must be reliable
e) Guidelines: Increasing Test Reliability and Validity

IV. Types Of Standardized Tests
A. Achievement tests: What has the student learned?
1. Intention: Measure how much the student has learned in specific content areas
2. Frequently used achievement tests
a) Group tests for identifying students who need more testing or for grouping students
b) Individual tests for determination of academic level of diagnosis of learning problems
3. Using information from a norm-referenced achievement test: Individual profiles (Figure 14.6)
4. Interpreting achievement test scores: Norm-referenced and criterion-referenced interpretations

B. Diagnostic tests: What are the student's strengths and weaknesses?
1. Given individually by a trained professional, usually to elementary students
2. Intention: Identify students' specific problems and weaknesses

C. Aptitude tests: How well will the student do in the future?
1. Intention: Measures abilities developed over years, predicts how well a student will do in learning new material in the future
2. Scholastic aptitude (SAT, ACT, etc.): Achievement or aptitude?

Standardized Testing

      a) SATs used as predictors of future achievement (less subject to teacher bias and grade inflation than grades)
      b) Controversy continues over fairness and validity
    3. IQ and scholastic aptitude tests: Small differences in scores not important
    4. Vocational aptitude and interest
      a) Vocational aptitude: Differential Aptitude Test (DAT) matches student's aptitude to average scores for people in different occupations
      b) Vocational interest tests: Ask students to rate activities and identify interests
      c) Tests should be used to motivate, not to close off career options

V. Issues In Standardized Testing
  A. Uses of testing in American society
    1. Readiness testing: Used to determine if a child is ready for first grade or developmental kindergarten
    2. National testing: Same test administered across the United States
    3. Minimal competency testing: Proposed as solution to adult literacy; still controversial
    4. Point/Counterpoint: To Test or Not To Test?
    5. Testing teachers: Teacher assessment designed to test basic skills, professional skills and academic knowledge
  B. Advantage in taking tests—fair and unfair
    1. Bias in testing: Factors that put low SES and minority students at a disadvantage
      a) Most standardized tests predict school achievement equally well for all groups
      b) Caution; some tests' content and procedures believed to put minorities at a disadvantage (e.g., language, achievement orientation)
    2. Culture-fair tests: Making assessment more appropriate for minorities
  C. Coaching and test-taking skills: Popular test preparation technique
    1. Special training courses usually result in only a ten to fifty point gain
    2. Familiarity with the procedures of standardized tests appear to help
    3. Instruction in general cognitive skills (metacognitive and study skills) appears to be helpful
    4. Guidelines: Taking a Test

VI. New Directions In Standardized Testing
  A. Assessing learning potential: Learning Potential Assessment Device looks at process of learning, rather than product, to gauge potential for future learning

Standardized Testing

- B. Authentic assessment: Problem of how to assess complex, important, real life outcomes
  1. Some states developing authentic assessment procedures
  2. "Constructed-response formats" have students create, rather than select responses; demand more thoughtful scoring
- C. Changes in the SAT: New SATs will have tests of verbal and mathematical reasoning and subject matter; will use constructed-response format and essay questions

VII. Summary
- A. Measurement and evaluation
- B. What do test scores mean?
- C. Types of standardized tests
- D. Issues in standardized testing
- E. New directions in standardized testing

VIII. Key Terms and Concepts

IX. Teachers' casebook/What Would They Do?

Learning Activities and Related Research

ACTIVITIES	HANDOUTS
Chapter 14	14.0 Lecture outline
Cooperative Activities	
14.1 Legal Issues in Testing	14.1 Key Legal Decisions
14.2 How should teachers be graded?	
Research Activities	
14.3 School Reports	
14.4 Readiness Tests	
Using Technology	
14.5 Video Portfolio	14.2 Considerations in Making a Teaching Portfolio
Field Experience	
14.6 Preparing for the standardized test	
Other Teaching Activities	
14.7 If you didn't have a test score	
14.8 What else do you need to know?	
14.9 Central Tendency	
14.10 Types of tests and the interpretation of test scores	14.3 Types of tests and interpretations of test scores
	14.4 Relationship of tests scores to the normal curve
	14.5 Concept map: Types of test scores
14.11 Problems with Grade Equivalent Scores	
14.12 Test score interpretation	
14.13 Minimum Competency tests	
14.14 Accountability: As a Reform Strategy	
	14.6 Concept map: Links to other chapters

363

Standardized Testing

Cooperative Activities

14.1   Legal Issues In Testing

Read the following to your students. Have them locate information about recent problems in relation to the use of classifying children (e.g., New York City schools in 1997 were ordered to reduce the number of students assigned to special education classes). Use **Handout Master 14.1** for this activity. Have them discuss how one can be certain about "best placement."

Testing on Trial. The question of bias in IQ testing found its way into the courts. In the early 1970s, the issue in Diana v. State Board of Education was the overrepresentation of Mexican-American children in California's public school classes for the mildly mentally retarded. The plaintiff charged that the percentage of Mexican-American children in these classes was higher than the percentage in the school population because IQ tests, given in English, were biased against these children. The court ordered the schools to correct the disproportionate placement and to administer placement tests in a student's native language. The native language requirement for testing later became a part of federal law, PL 94-142, the Education for All Handicapped Children Act.

In 1971, also in California, Larry P. v. Riles, was initiated on behalf of minority children placed in classes for the mildly retarded. The issue again was overrepresentation of certain groups of students in these classes and bias in the IQ tests. In 1979, the court ruled that no intelligence tests could be used to place minority students in special classes for the retarded unless the tests met these standards.

1.   The scores from the tests had to predict academic achievement and classroom performance fairly well.

2.   All groups of students (Blacks, Mexican-Americans, Whites) had to have the same pattern of scores on the tests and the same mean scores.

The second requirement meant that standard individual IQ tests could not be a part of the evaluation and placement process for minority students. In making the decision, the judge assumed that any test yielding different mean scores for different groups of students was automatically biased. This rejects the possibility that some groups of students, for whatever reason, might be less able in the particular school-related skills measured by the tests. In 1984, the Ninth Circuit Court of Appeals upheld the 1979 ruling. As of this writing, no further appeals were pending, but the case could still go to the Supreme Court.

In the years since the schools in California stopped including IQ tests with the placement procedures, the actual number of students enrolled in classes for the mildly retarded has decreased substantially, but the percentage of minority students remains almost the same, around 50 percent. The IQ testing was only one of many elements in the decision to place a student in a special class. First, the child had to fail in the regular class. Then other test results and teacher recommendations were examined. Simply eliminating IQ testing cannot be expected to help children who are failing in school. The real question is how to give these students an appropriate education.

14.2   How Should Teachers Be Graded?

Give students this assignment: In your groups, reflect on whether you would rather be assessed in your teaching effectiveness through a standardized test or an authentic test, such as a portfolio. What should the evaluator want to know? What is the best way to know this? Justify your responses. Try to convince another group of your decisions.

Research Activities

14.3   School Reports

Have your students locate information on local schools' reports. These reports (e.g., average test scores) are often printed in local papers or may be available through the Internet. Compare a set of elementary or secondary schools using the information presented in these reports. Critique the interpretations made.

14.4   Readiness Tests

Divide your class into cooperative learning groups. Then have your groups come up with a pro and con defense for the use of readiness tests for promoting children to first grade based on research in the library. Your students should locate and synthesize research material on the utility and accuracy of readiness tests in predicting school performance. Students might want to refer back to chapter 2 to remind themselves of developmental changes for young children.

Using Technology

14.5   Video Portfolio

Have your students consider what would be important to consider in developing a video portfolio of their teaching performance. Use **Handout Master 14.2** to assist with this task.

Field Experience

14.6   Preparing For A Standardized Test

Have your students interview a teacher about changes to normal classroom practices before a standardized tests? Is it "business as usual" in the classroom? If not,

Standardized Testing

why not? Your students will most likely interview teachers at different grade levels. Discuss with your students how classroom practices are changes as a consequence of the standardized test. Are there differences across the grades?

Other Teaching Activities

14.7   If You Didn't Have a Test Score?

Ask your students to consider the following:

Supposing you needed to select 50 applicants for college scholarships and 1,000 students have applied. You do not have any scores from standardized tests on any of the applicants. How would you select students? How would you ensure you were being fair? What could be unfair about the way you decided to make your selections? Would you like standardized test scores to assist you? Why?

Discuss these issues with the class.

14.8   What Else Do You Need to Know?

You learn that a student in your class is at the 95th percentile rank on a group administered intelligence test. What other information would you need to know about this child in order to maximize her learning potential?

14.9   Central Tendency

Give this scenario to students:

A superintendent administered a standardized math test to all seventh-grade pupils in the system. He found that the median score of the pupils in one of the classes was seriously below the norm and criticized the teacher for this fact. The teacher wants to raise the median on the next test. She feel (correctly) that the best chance of doing so rests upon her concentrating her efforts on just a few students.

On which students of the students should she concentrate her efforts and why?

Standardized Testing

14.10 Types Of Tests And The Interpretation Of Test Scores

Using **Handout Master 14.3 and 14.4,** have your students respond as directed:

Answers:

A	B	C
1. a	1. b	1. mean = 11, median = 6, mode = 3
2. b	2. a	2. Better in reading (over 1 standard deviation.)
3. c	3. d	3. Class A, they have less variability
4. d	4. c	4. About 30
5. a		
6. a and b		
7. e		

14.11 Problems With Grade-Equivalent Scores

From Lyman, H. B. (1986). Test scores and what they mean. Boston, MA: Allyn & Bacon, 106:

   Grade-placement scores are usually stated in tenths of a school year; for example, 8.2 refers to the second month of grade eight. (This system gives a value of 1.0 to the beginning of the first grade - which presumably should be the true zero point in school grade placement.)

   A basic assumption seems to be that children learn more or less uniformly throughout the school year (but that no learning occurs during the summer vacation).

   Grade-placement scores are intrinsically appealing. It seems reasonable at first glance to think of children who stand high in comparison with others in their school grade as doing the same quality of work as youngsters more advanced in school. And in a sense they are. But that does not mean that these children should be promoted immediately to a higher grade. These grade-placement scores are based on the average performance of pupils having that actual placement in school. In obtaining that average, we had some better scores and some poorer scores.

   Furthermore, regardless of how high a child's grade-placement score is, the child has had only a given amount of time in school. And there are probably breadths and depths of understanding and competency that are closely related to the experiences and to the length on one's exposure to school. A child's higher score is more likely to mean a more complete mastery of (and therefore fewer errors on) material taught at his/her grade.

Standardized Testing

When this fact is considered, we see that the direct meaning of grade-placement scores is more apparent than real.

Grade-placement scores resulting from tests produced by different publishers are likely to give conflicting results. Not only is there the always-present possibility of their selecting different normative samples, but the tests of different publishers are likely to place slightly different emphases on the same subject matter at the same level. For example, among grammar tests, one may include many more questions on adjectives than another test does. Such differences inevitably alter the grade-placement scores of individual pupils and of entire classes of pupils.

Standard deviations are bound to differ for various subject matters - even when the tests are included in the same standardized achievement test battery and based on the same normative groups. Students are much more likely, for example, to have grade-placement scores several grades higher than their actual grade placement in reading and in English than in arithmetic and in science. The latter subjects depend much more on specific, school-taught skills. The result is that standard deviations are almost certain to be larger for English and reading than for arithmetic and science; similar, less extreme, differences exist for other subjects.

Test manuals of all major publishers of achievement tests carefully point out these differences in standard deviations. Many test users, though, do not understand the critical importance of these differences in any interpretation of scores. Among many other points, these different standard deviations reflect the greater possible range in grade-placement scores on some tests of an achievement battery than on others. Grade-placement scores on one test may extend up 4.5 grade equivalents, as compared with only 2.5 grade equivalents for another test in the same coordinated achievement battery.

Grade-placement scores are so confusing that a lower score on one test may indicate relatively higher performance than does a higher score on another test. Because of the difference in size of standard deviations, the following might easily happen: A grade-placement score of 8.5 in reading may be equal to a percentile rank of 60, but a grade-placement score of 8.2 in arithmetic fundamentals may be equal to a percentile rank of 98. Especially for higher elementary grades and beyond, grade-placement scores cannot meaningfully be compared from test to test - even within the same battery!

Test publishers know the limitation of grade-placement scores and point them out carefully in their manuals. But not all tests users have a Ph.D. in educational measurement. The more lengthy the documentation from the publisher, the more likely the test user will not read it carefully.

14.12   Test Score Interpretation

Pose this situation to students:

In October of the school year, a third-grade boy has an IQ score (from a group intelligence test) of 83 and a grade-equivalent score in reading of 4.7

- Is the student an "overachiever" or an "underachiever"?
- Do you think his IQ score is valid?
- Does it make any difference whether the score is valid or not?
- What may be the effect of his IQ score being recorded in his cumulative folder?

Use **Handout Master 14.4.**

14.13   Minimum Competency Testing

Many local school districts are writing and administering minimum competency tests for high school graduation. Have students debate the current movement toward a national competency exam. What are some of the advantages, disadvantages, and potential effects on the high school drop-out rate?

14.14   Accountability As A Reform Strategy

From Lieberman, A. (1991, November). Accountability: As a reform strategy. Phi Delta Kappan, 73 (3), 219-220.

Mandated, standardized national testing is now being discussed as a means of improving education by holding schools accountable. On 5 June 1991 a group of well-known researchers with expertise in testing, measurement, and policy -- all members of the American Educational Research Association (AERA) -- met with members of the education policy community in Washington, D. C. (This was the first meeting called by the AERA to build bridges between the research community and those responsible for framing and implementing national education policy.) The researchers presented evidence that raised serious questions about the President's plan to establish national testing and about his timetable for doing so. They also offered recommendations for alternative means of assessment and accountability that hold the promise of improving teaching and learning in the nation's schools.

Underlying the proposal for national testing are the assumptions that uniform tests will improve the education system as a whole, that instruction will necessarily improve as a result, and that teachers and students will benefit. The tests are supposed to measure the most important outcomes of schooling --those for which the education system should be held accountable -- while providing direction and motivation for teachers and students. They will become the standard by which the public can measure success or failure.

Questions about standardized testing

So far, most policy discussions have not dealt seriously with the harm that standardized testing may already have done. For example, ample evidence shows that, while the low-level skills of U.S. students have increased, higher-order skills have declined.

The reasons why standardized testing has been implicated in these findings are complex and interrelated: teachers learn to postpone efforts to teach thinking and reasoning until after basic skills have been mastered; those students already in lower tracks are exposed to a limited curriculum oriented toward rote learning. Consequently, less successful students receive a disproportionate share of dull and largely meaningless instruction because they never do well enough to get "the good stuff." Rarely are low-achieving students given opportunities to talk about what they know, to read books, to write, or to identify and solve real problems. Instruction is narrowed to match the content of the tests, and students are damaged by adherence to the limits that the tests impose. This model of learning -- delaying the teaching of "thinking skills" until the higher grades -- has been refuted by the last 20 years of research in cognitive psychology.

Testing further limits students' opportunities to learn because it is used as a means to track and retain students -- practices that have been shown to produce lower achievement, lower self-esteem, and higher dropout rates. Thus, testing has been used to widen the achievement gap between white students and minority students and between students from high-income families and students from low-income families. Rather than finding in these tests an aid to good teaching and a means to be held accountable for it, teachers find that their professional judgment and their ability to provide good instruction are inhibited by the need to teach students to succeed on multiple-choice tests.

Assessment for learning and accountability

Making schools genuinely accountable for student learning will require involving teachers in the development of methods and modes of assessment that measure what students know and are able to do. In this way assessment can be tied to instruction, improvement of practice, and the creation of greater knowledge and shared standards across the educational enterprise as a whole. Many schools, districts, and states have already begun to develop alternative forms of assessment based on essays, research projects, exhibitions, and portfolios of students' work.

We need high standards, but those standards must be adapted to local needs. They must be flexible, situational, and multicultural, rather than national, mandated, and standardized. They must be tied to instructional decisions that teachers have helped to make and for which they can be held accountable.

Discussion Questions

1. What academic purposes do standardized tests serve? Can each purpose be met by "portfolio" evaluations?

2. A teacher says to you "These statistics like percentile ranks and stanines get me all confused. Why don't they just report percent correct scores and leave it at that?" What would you reply?

4. Define and distinguish between validity and reliability. Is it necessary for a test to be valid to be reliable? Is it necessary for a test to reliable to be valid? Explain.

5. Explain why you as a teacher should be more concerned about the reliability of a test of attitude and/or creativity than the reliability of an academic aptitude test.

6. Use the concepts of validity, reliability, and test bias to explain two reasons why they should not be used to evaluate the effectiveness of teachers and schools.

7. What is the major inherent construct bias of test standardization and norming?

8. How do norming populations for norm-referenced aptitude tests for intelligence, home construction, and law differ from norming populations of criterion-referenced tests for the same aptitudes?

9. What interpretations of academic skill and grade placement would you offer for a ninth grader who scored 12.6 on a ninth-grade achievement? (b) 3.4?

10. What are minimum competency tests and how are they used for students and teachers?

Additional Resources for Teaching This Chapter

REFERENCES

Allen, M. J., and Yen, W. M. (1979). Introduction to measurement theory. Belmont, CA: Wadsworth, Inc.

American Educational Research Association. (1985). Standards for educational and psychological testing. Washington, D. C.: Author.

Cameron, R. (1989). Issues in testing bias. College and University, 64 (3), 68-279.

Darling-Hammond, L. (1991, November). The implications of testing policy for quality and equality. Phi Delta Kappan, 73 (3), 220-225.

Dreher, M. J. and Singer, H. (1984). Making standardized tests work for you. Principal, 63, 20-24.

Standardized Testing

Green, D. (1987). A guide for interpreting standardized test scores. <u>NASSP Bulletin</u>, *71*, (496), 23-24, 26-30, 32-35.

Jaeger, R. M. (1991, November). Legislative perspectives on statewide testing: Goals hopes, and desires. <u>Phi Delta Kappan, 73 (3)</u>, 239-243.

Johnson, S. T. (1988). Test fairness and bias: Measuring academic achievement among black youth. <u>Urban League Review, 11</u>, 76-92.

Koretz, D. (1988). Arriving in Lake Woebegone: Are standardized tests exaggerating achievement and distorting instruction? <u>American Educator, 12</u>, 8-15.

Maddaus, G. F. (1991, November). The effects of important tests on students: Implications for a National Examination System. <u>Phi Delta Kappan, 73 (3)</u>, 226-231.

McLaughlin, M. W. (1991, November). Test-based accountability as a reform strategy. <u>Phi Delta Kappan, 73 (3)</u>, 248-250.

Neil, D., and Medina, N. (1989). Standardized testing: Harmful to educational health. <u>Phi Delta Kappan, 70 (9)</u>, 688-697.

Shepard, L. A. (1991, November). Will national tests improve student learning. <u>Phi Delta Kappan, 73 (3)</u>, 232-238.

FILMS, VIDEOTAPES, AND AUDIOCASSETTES

Criterion-referenced measurement: Today's alternative to traditional testing, video, 30 minutes. Viewers learn what they are, how they are constructed and how they are used.

Failures before kindergarten, video, 28 minutes. There is intense debate going on over the screening of preschool children to determine whether they are ready for admission to kindergarten. This specially adapted Phil Donahue program discusses the pros and cons of assessing the educational readiness of such young children. Panelists on the program include the director of the National Association for the Education of Young Children, and a teacher who kept back the entire first grade. (From Films for the Humanities & Sciences, Inc.)

Making sense out of standardized test scores, video, 30 minutes. Interpretation of test scores that students earn on standardized tests: Percentiles, grade-equivalents and scale scores.

Norm-referenced tests: Uses and misuses, video, 30 minutes. Origins and nature of norm-referenced standardized achievement tests are discussed. Inappropriate uses of tests are shown how they can lead to unsound educational decisions.

Handout Master 14.0

Lecture Outline: Standardized Testing

- **Measurement and Evaluation**

- **What do Test Scores Mean?**

- **Types of Standardized Tests?**

- **Issues in Standardized Tests?**

- **New Directions in Standardized Testing**

Copyright © 1998 by Allyn and Bacon

Handout Master 14.1

Key Legal Decisions

Find out what are the key legal decisions that influence the use of tests and test scores. List the decisions below and their implications for classroom testing.

LEGAL DECISION	IMPLICATION FOR TESTING

Copyright © 1998 by Allyn and Bacon

Handout Master 14.2

Considerations in Making a Teaching Portfolio

1. What am I trying to demonstrate?

2. What do I think effective teaching is?

3. Should I show a number of lessons that demonstrated improvement or should I show my best one?

4. What teaching behaviors can I demonstrate?

5. How can I demonstrate I am a good teacher?

6. Do I show students' work?

7. Do I include comments from parents?

8. If I videotape a class, should I teach the lesson beforehand as a warmup?

9. What other questions should I ask myself?

Copyright © 1998 by Allyn and Bacon

Handout Master 14.3

Types of Tests and The Interpretation of Test Scores

A. Match the specific test with its type:
      a.   IQ test d aptitude test   d.   aptitude test
      b.   achievement test answers   e.   interest test
      c.   diagnostic test

___ 1. WISC-R
___ 2. Iowa Test of Basic Skills
___ 3. Detroit Test of Learning Aptitude
___ 4. SAT
___ 5. Stanford-Binet
___ 6. Woodcock-Johnson Psycho-Educational Battery
___ 7. Kuder Preference Record

B. Match the type of test that would be most appropriate in the following situations.
   a.   individual IQ test   c.   diagnostic test
   b.   achievement test   d   aptitude test

___ 1. The teacher wants to know how her biology class performs in comparison with the classes in other high schools.

___ 2. A student is being evaluated to determine if he should be placed in a class for mentally retarded.

___ 3. A teacher needs to predict which eighth grade students would be likely to succeed in freshman algebra class and which should take ninth grade math.

___ 4. A third grade student is having difficulty in reading and the teachers wants to know the specific skills in which he needs remedial help.

C. The following questions pertain to the interpretation of test scores. Respond as indicated.

1. Find the mean, median, and mode for the following group of scores: 3, 3, 4, 6, 21, 30. Which is more representative of central tendency?

   Mean =   Median =   Mode =

2. A reading test has a mean of 30 and a standard deviation of 5. A math has a mean of 50 and a standard deviation of 8. Johnny made a raw score of 37 on the reading test and 56 on the math test. Did he perform better in math or reading? (Hint: Draw a normal distribution curve for the reading test and for the math test and locate Johnny's scores on the curves.)

3. Two English classes took the same test. Class A had a mean of 50 and a standard deviation of 4. Class B had a mean of 50 and a standard deviation of 8. Which class is probably grouped according to ability?

4. A high school with 1200 students is placing students with an IQ score of 130 and above and above in an accelerated class. Assuming a normal population, approximately how many students will be assigned to the accelerated class?

Copyright © 1998 by Allyn and Bacon

Handout Master 14.4

Relationship of Test Scores to the Normal Curve

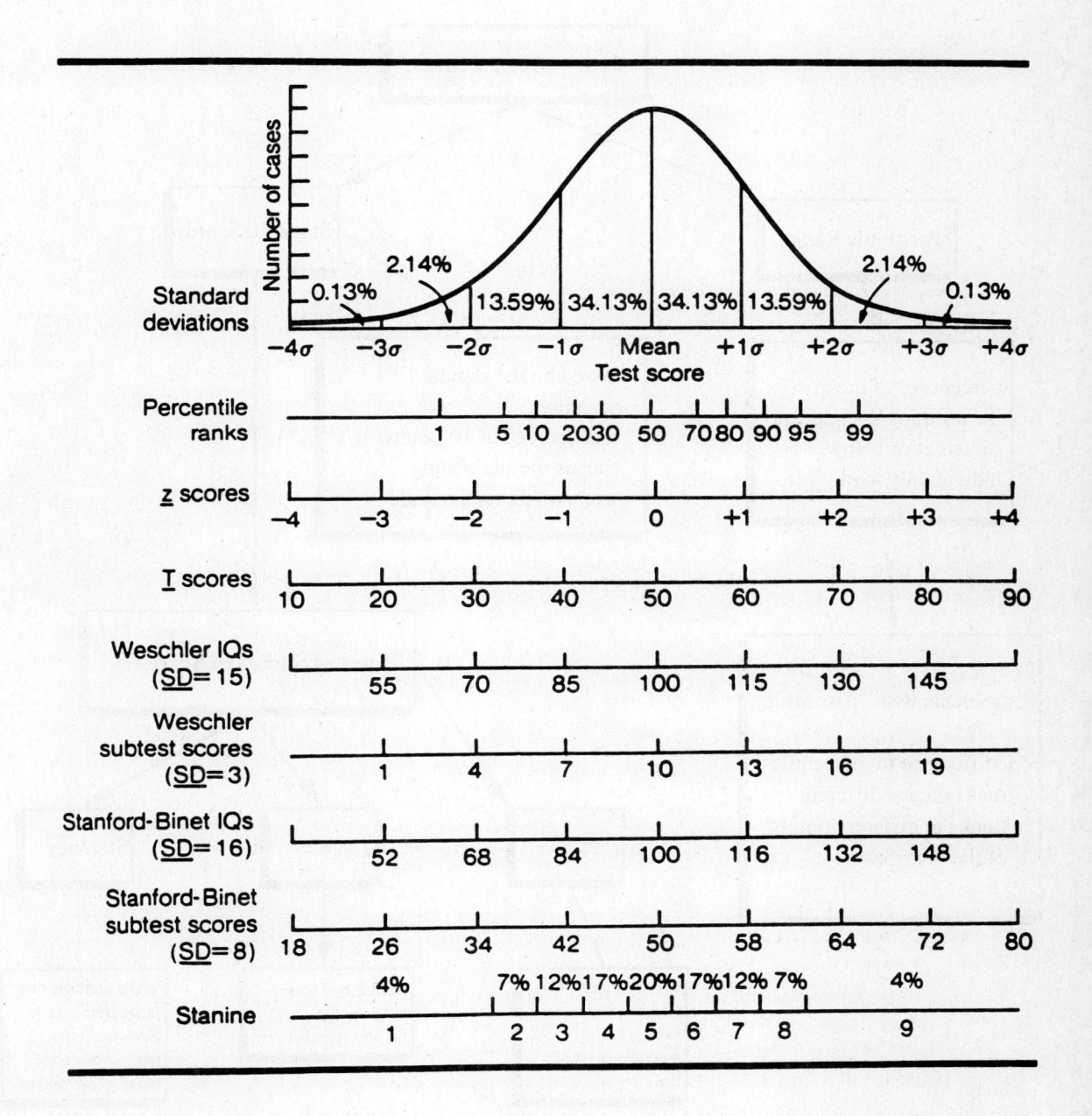

Copyright © 1998 by Allyn and Bacon

Handout Master 14.5: Types of Test Scores

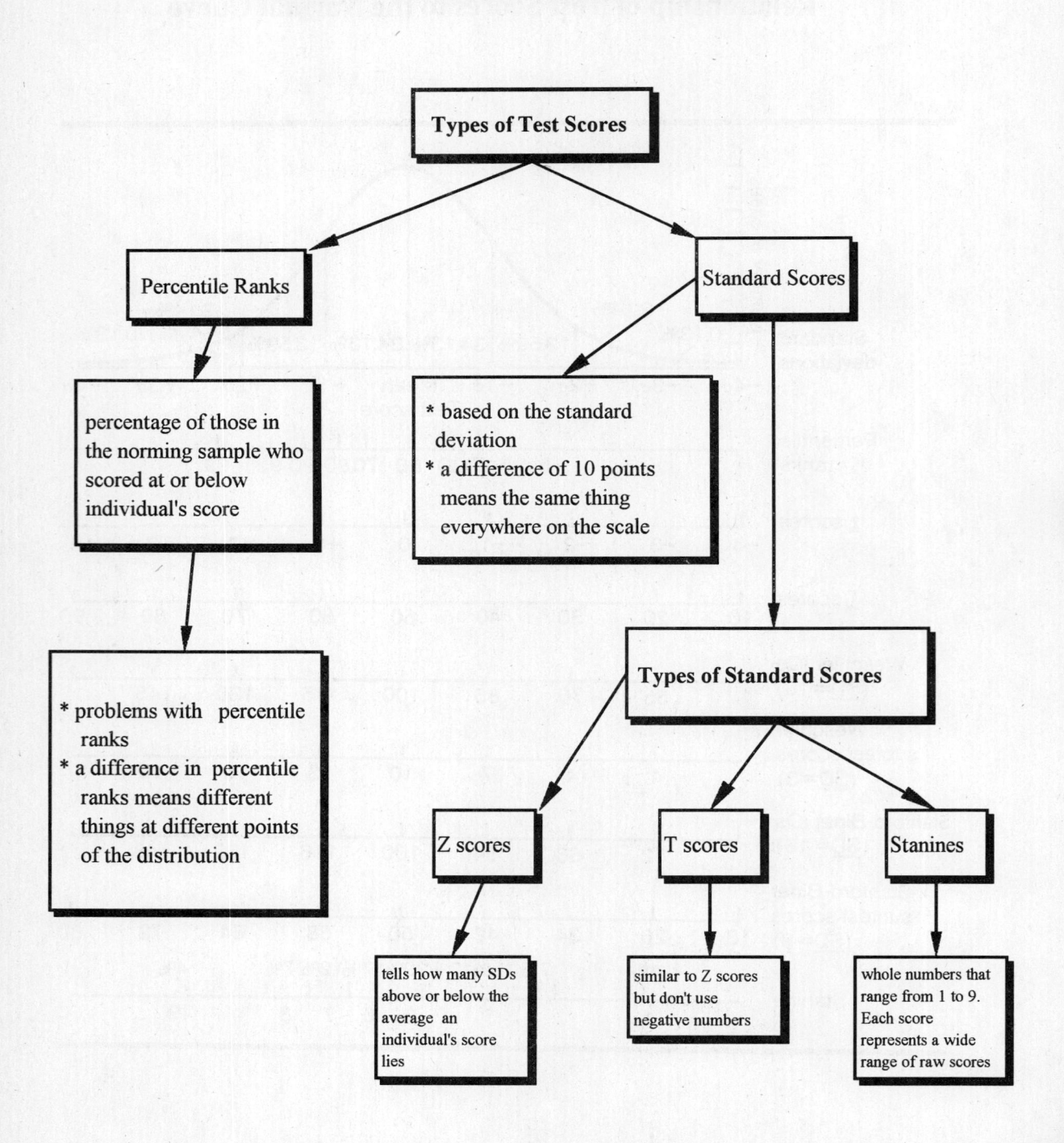

Types of Test Scores
- **Percentile Ranks**
  - percentage of those in the norming sample who scored at or below individual's score
  - * problems with percentile ranks
  - * a difference in percentile ranks means different things at different points of the distribution
- **Standard Scores**
  - * based on the standard deviation
  - * a difference of 10 points means the same thing everywhere on the scale
  - **Types of Standard Scores**
    - **Z scores**: tells how many SDs above or below the average an individual's score lies
    - **T scores**: similar to Z scores but don't use negative numbers
    - **Stanines**: whole numbers that range from 1 to 9. Each score represents a wide range of raw scores

Copyright © 1998 by Allyn and Bacon

Handout Master 14.6: Links to Other Chapters

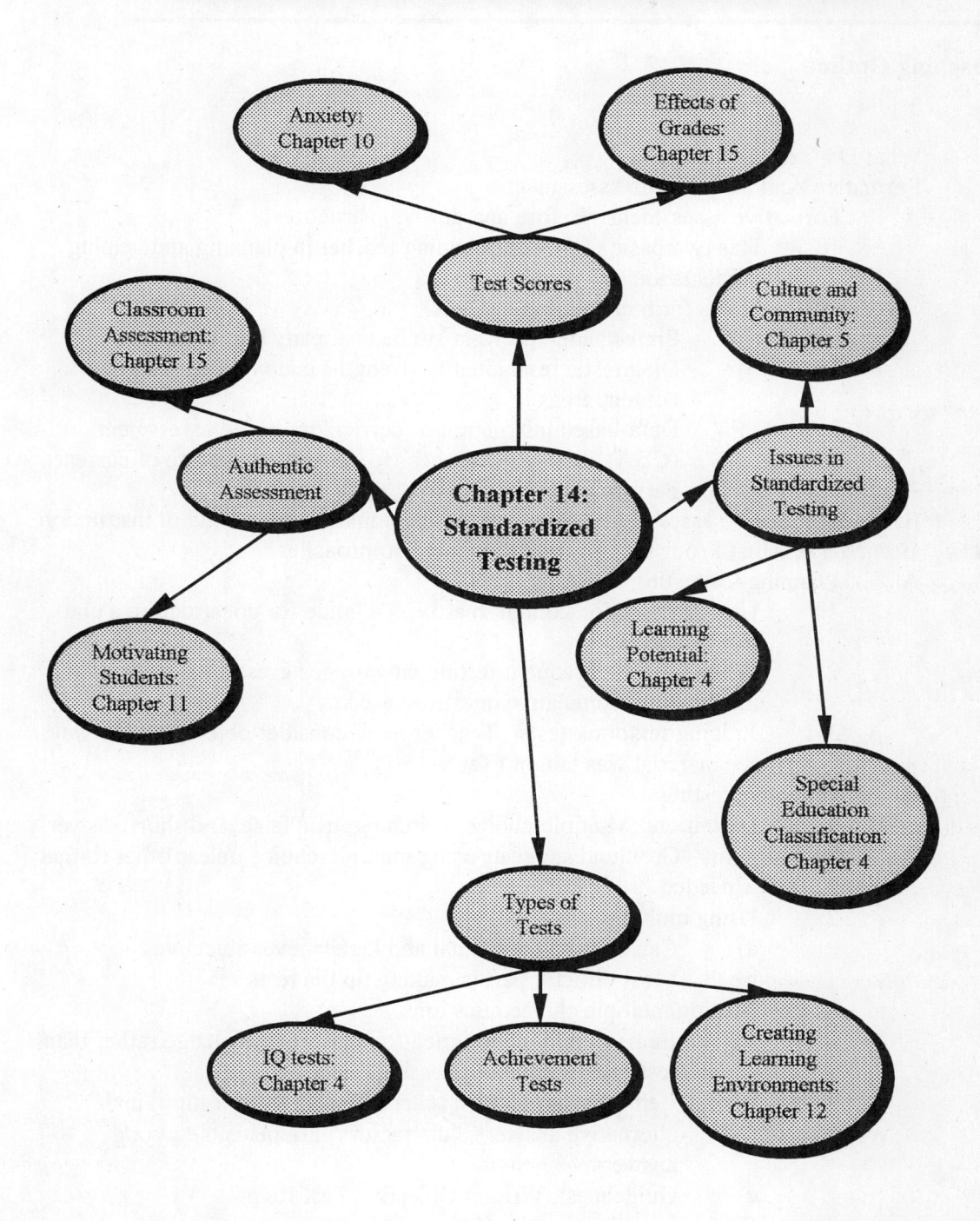

- Anxiety: Chapter 10
- Effects of Grades: Chapter 15
- Test Scores
- Classroom Assessment: Chapter 15
- Culture and Community: Chapter 5
- Authentic Assessment
- Issues in Standardized Testing
- **Chapter 14: Standardized Testing**
- Motivating Students: Chapter 11
- Learning Potential: Chapter 4
- Special Education Classification: Chapter 4
- Types of Tests
  - IQ tests: Chapter 4
  - Achievement Tests
  - Creating Learning Environments: Chapter 12

Copyright © 1998 by Allyn and Bacon

15

Classroom Assessment and Grading

Teaching Outline

I. What Do You Think?
II. Formative And Summative Assessment
    A. Formative assessment: Before and during instruction
        1. Has two basic purposes: Guiding teacher in planning and helping students identify problem areas
        2. Helps form instruction
            a) Pretests identify what students already know
            b) Diagnostic tests identify strengths and weaknesses in content areas
            c) Data-based instruction or curriculum-based assessment (CBA) uses daily "probes" to get precise picture of current performance
    B. Summative assessment: Summary of accomplishments at end of instruction
III. Getting The Most From Traditional Assessment Approaches
    A. Planning for testing
        1. Using a behavior-content matrix as a guide for constructing a unit test (Figure 15.1)
        2. When to test? Frequent testing encourages greater retention of information; cumulative questions are key
        3. Judging textbook tests: Teacher must consider objectives, the way the material was taught (Table 15.1)
    B. Objective testing
        1. Definition: Multiple-choice, matching, true/false, and short answer items: Gronlund suggests using multiple-choice unless other format is needed
        2. Using multiple-choice tests
            a) Can be used for factual and higher-level objectives
            b) Most difficult part is making up the tests
        3. Writing multiple choice questions
            a) Items should be designed to measure knowledge rather than test-taking skills or guessing'
            b) Items consist of stem (part that asks the question) and alternative answers; "distractors" are plausible wrong answers
            c) Guidelines: Writing Objective Test Items
        4. Evaluating objective test items

Classroom Assessment and Grading

    C.   Essay testing
        1.   Constructing essay tests
            a)   Essay tests sample a small number of learning outcomes; require more time to answer; use should be limited to complex learning objectives
            b)   Present a clear and precise task
            c)   Ample time for answering should be provided
            d)   Should include only a few questions
        2.   Evaluating essays: Dangers
            a)   Graders' individual standards and unreliable scoring procedures produce wide variability of scores
            b)   Research: Jargon-filled verbose essays that are neatly written with few grammatical errors seem to be given better grades
        3.   Evaluating essays: Methods
            a)   Construct model and assign points
            b)   Assign grades and sort
            c)   Skim pile for consistency within grades
            d)   Grade all answers to one question before going to the next
            e)   Consider having another teacher grade tests as a cross-check

IV.   Innovations In Assessment
    A.   Authentic classroom tests: Tests that ask students to write, speak, create, think, solve, and apply (Table 15.5)
    B.   Performance in context: Portfolios and exhibitions
        1.   Portfolio
            a)   Purposeful collection of student work that exhibits effort, progress, and achievement in one or more areas
            b)   Guidelines: Creating Portfolios
        2.   Exhibition: Performance tests that are public and require hours of preparation because that are culminating experiences of a whole program of study
    C.   Evaluating portfolios and performances:
        1.   Scoring rubrics
        2.   Reliability, validity, and equity
        3.   Point/Counterpoint: To Test or Not To Test, Part II

V.   Effects Of Grades And Grading On Students
    A.   There are many different aspect of grades on students
        1.   High standards and competitive atmosphere associated with increased absenteeism, dropout rates; hard on anxious or low self-confidence students
        2.   Failure can have both negative and positive results
            a)   Helpful if students can see connections between hard work and improvement
            b)   May help students to learn to take risks, cope with failure

Classroom Assessment and Grading

     c)   Being held back results in lowered self-esteem; positive effects unclear
  B.   Effects of feedback
    1.   Helpful if reason for mistake is explained so same mistake is not repeated
    2.   For older students, encouraging personalized written comments appropriate to improved performance
    3.   For younger students, oral feedback and brief written comments appropriate
  C.   Grades and motivation
    1.   Grades can motivate real learning; appropriate objectives are key
    2.   Grades should reflect meaningful learning so working for a grade and working to learn can be the same
    3.   Guidelines: Minimizing the Detrimental Effects of Grading
VI.   Grading And Reporting: Nuts And Bolts
  A.   Criterion-references versus norm-referenced grading
    1.   Criterion-referenced systems reflect achievement according to preset criteria for each grade
     a)   Motivation to succeed and academic improvement can be enhanced
     b)   Clearly defined instructional objectives govern judgments about students
    2.   Norm-referenced system reflects student's standing in comparison with others who tool the same course
     a)   "Grading on a curve": Grading relative to "average grade" assigned to group's average level of performance
     b)   Flexible use of curve is usually more appropriate: Depends on actual distributions of scores and characteristics of particular group
  B.   Preparing report cards
    1.   Criterion-referenced grading: Report level or proficiency for objectives listed on the report card
    2.   Norm-referenced grading: Merge all scores based on a common scale
  C.   The point system
    1.   System for combining grades from many assignments
    2.   Points assigned according to assignment's importance and student's performance
    3.   Grades are influenced by level of difficulty of the test and concerns of individual teacher
  D.   Percentage grading
    1.   Grading symbols A to F commonly used to represent some percentage categories
    2.   System assumes we can accurately measure what percentage of a body of knowledge each student should attain

3. Grades are influenced by the level of difficulty of the test and concerns of individual teacher
E. The contract system
1. Specifies types, quantity, and quality of work required for each grade; students "contract" to work for a grade
2. Can overemphasize quantity of work at expense of quality
3. The revise option: Revise and improve work
F. Grading on effort and improvement
1. Question underlying many grading systems: Should grades be based on how much a student improves or on the final level of learning
2. Using improvement as a standard penalizes the best students, who naturally improve the least
3. Individual learning expectations (ILE) system allows everyone to earn improvement points based on personal average score
4. Dual marking system is a way to include effort in grade

Classroom Assessment and Grading

    G. Cautions: Being fair
      1. The halo effect: Tendency for a general impression of a person to influence perception of any aspect of that person
      2. Guidelines: Using Any Grading System
VII. Beyond Grading: Communication
    A. Conference with students and parents
      1. Individual student conferences can make judgments of nonacademic achievement and attitudes more accurate and valuable
      2. Teachers need skill in interpersonal communication, especially listening and problem-solving skills
      3. Guidelines: Conducting a Successful Parent-Teacher Conference
    B. The Buckley Amendment
      1. Information in student's records available to students and/or parents
      2. Information in cumulative folders must be based on firm, defensible evidence
VIII. Summary
    A. Formative and summative assessment
    B. Getting the most from traditional assessment approaches
    C. Innovations in assessment
    D. Effects of grades and grading on students
    E. Grading and reporting: Nuts and bolts
    F. Beyond grading: Communication
IX. Key Terms And Concepts
X. Teachers' Casebook: What Would They Do?

Learning Activities and Related Research

ACTIVITIES	HANDOUTS
Chapter	15.0 Lecture Outline
	15.1 Different kinds of test items
Cooperative Activities	
15.1 How to evaluate test items	15.2 Checklist for evaluating test items
15.2 Writing multiple choice items	15.3 Analyzing multiple choice items
15.3 Portfolio content	
15.4 Difficulties in self-evaluation	
15.5 Grading multiple pieces of work	15.4 Eddie's writing
Research Activities	
15.6 Computerized testing	
Using Technology	
Field Experience	
15.7 Students' views of grades	
15.8 Comparing report cards	
Other Teaching Activities	

Classroom Assessment and Grading

15.9 Teaching to the authentic test	15.5 Characteristics of authentic tests
15.10 Grading students	15.6 Grading systems
15.11 Classroom standard setting	
15.12 Dealing with a student who refuses to work	15.7 A student who refuses to work
15.13 Norm referenced grading	
15.14 Determining grades	
15.15 Evaluation decisions	15.8 Beliefs about grades
15.16 Contracting	
	15.9 Concept Map: Alternative assessments
	15.10 Concept Map: Links to other chapters

Cooperative Activities

15.1   Evaluating Test Items

   From Gronlund, N. E. (1988). How to construct an achievement test (4th edition). Englewood Cliffs, NJ: Prentice Hall, pp. 153-155.

   Distribute and discuss **Handout Master 15.2**, *Checklist for Evaluating Test Items* based on Gronlund's work. Then in small groups or cooperative groups, give students an achievement test to analyze. Have them use Gronlund's checklist for evaluating test items as criterion. You may want to give each group one kind of test to focus on. After students finish their analysis, have them share the results with the whole class.

15.2   Writing Multiple Choice Items

   Divide your class into cooperative learning groups. Using **Handout Master 15.3**, have students identify the faults in the multiple-choice items. They should rewrite each item so that it is satisfactory.

15.3   Portfolio Content

   In cooperative groups, have students identify at least five documents that should be in a pupil's portfolio. Students should discuss the content of the documents and how they will go about obtaining them; for instance, what time of year to obtain them, what format to require, and so on. Have students consider the statement " An artist's portfolio contains the work he feels exemplifies his best performance." Should students decide what goes into his or her portfolio or should the teacher? What are some problems with either practice?

Classroom Assessment and Grading

15.4   Difficulties in Self-Evaluation

Eddie was asked to comment on a writing sample he considered to be good and a writing sample that he felt was not as good. He wrote the following about writing he said was good:

"My good sheet. On my good sheet I made a lot of marks and I made it more scarey."

He described his weaker piece as follows:

"My bad sheet. On my bad sheet I forgot to put marks on it. I forgot to put capital letters."

Have your students in groups discuss what Eddie thought good writing was about. Have them design a plan to assist him with evaluating his own writing.

15.5   Grading Multiple Pieces of Work

Use **Handout Masters 15.4 a and b** for this task. Three samples of a child's writing are presented. Ask you students to evaluate Eddie's writing as described in **Handout Master 15.4 a**.

Research Activities

15.6   Computerized Testing

How does taking a test on a computer influence one's test scores if at all? Have your students find an answer to this question by finding out what is known about this issue.

Field Experience

15.7   Comparing Report Cards

Have students visit classroom and collect examples of the kinds of report cards that teachers use (they can be blank). Compare and contrast the different types of report cards in terms of what changes as children become older, what kind of information is conveyed, and the degree to which the report card is communicative.

15.8   Students' Views of Grades

Have students interview 2 students of different ages about what they believe grades represent or communicate. Have a class discussion on this topic.

Other Teaching Activities

15.9   Teaching To The Authentic Test

From Wiggins, G. Teaching to the (authentic) test. Educational Leadership, 46(7), April 1989, 41-47.

Practical alternatives and sound arguments now exist to make testing once again serve teaching and learning. Ironically, we should "teach to the test." The catch is to design and then teach to standard-setting tests so that practicing for and taking the tests actually enhances rather than impedes education, and so that a criterion- referenced diploma makes externally mandated tests unobtrusive -even unnecessary.

Setting Standards

If tests determine what teachers actually teach and what students will study -- then the road to reform is a straight but steep one: Test those capacities and habits we think are essential, and test them in context. Make them replicate, within reason, the challenges at the heart of each academic discipline. Let them be -- authentic.

What are the actual performances that we want students to be good at, that represent model challenges? Design them by department, by school, and by district -- and worry about a fair, efficient, and objective method of grading them as a secondary problem. Do we judge our students to be deficient in writing, speaking, listening, artistic creation, research, thoughtful analysis, problem posing, and problem solving? Let the tests ask them to write, speak, listen, create, do original research, analyze, pose and solve problems.

Rather than seeing tests as after-the-fact devices for checking up on what students have learned, we should see them as instructional: The central vehicle for clarifying and setting intellectual standards. The recital, debate, play, or game (and the criteria by which they are judged) -- the "performance" -- is not a checkup, it is the heart of the matter; all coaches happily teach to it. We should design academic tests to be similarly standard setting, not merely standardized.

Reform of testing depends, however, on teachers' recognizing that standardized testing evolved and proliferated because the school transcript became untrustworthy. An "AH in "English" means only that some adult thought the student's work was excellent. Compared to what or whom? As determined by what criteria? In reference to what specific subject matter? The high school diploma, by remaining tied to no standard other than credit accrual and seat time, provides no useful information about what students have studied or what they can actually do with what was studied.

To regain control over both testing and instruction, schools need to rethink their diploma requirements and grades. They need a clear set of appropriate and objective criteria, enabling both students and outsiders to know what counts, what is essential -- what a school's standards really are. Until we specify what students must directly demonstrate to earn a diploma, they will continue to pass by meeting the de facto "standard" of being dutiful and persistent --irrespective of the quality of their work.

And standardized testmakers will continue to succeed in hawking simplistic norm-referenced tests to districts and states resigned to using them for lack of a better accountability scheme.

Exhibitions of Mastery

The diploma should be awarded upon a successful final demonstration of mastery for graduation -- an "Exhibition" ...As the diploma is awarded when earned, the chool's program proceeds with no strict age grading and with no system of "credits earned" by time spent in class. The emphasis is on the students' demonstration that they can do important things. (From the Prospectus of the Coalition of Essential Schools.)

The "exhibition of mastery," proposed by Ted Sizer in Horace's Compromise (1984) and a cornerstone of the "Essential School," is one attempt to grapple with these issues. The intent of the exhibitions project is to help schools and districts design more authentic, engaging, revealing, and trustworthy "tests" of a student's intellectual ability.

The reference to engagement is not incidental. The exhibition of mastery was initially proposed as an antidote to student passivity and boredom, not merely as a more valid form of assessment. The idea is to capture the interest value of an authentic test of one's ability, such as is often provided in schools by literary magazines, portfolios, recitals, games, or debates. Thus, "any exhibition of mastery should be the students' opportunity to show off what they know and are able to do rather than a trial by question . . . "

The exhibition of mastery, as the name implies, is meant to be more than a better test. Like the thesis and oral exam in graduate school, it indicates whether a student has earned a diploma, is ready to leave high school. The school is designed "backwards" around these standard-setting tests to ensure that teachers and students alike understand their obligations and how their own efforts fit in a larger context. Teachers "teach to the test" because the test is essential --and teacher designed.

But why institute a radically new form of assessment? Why not just improve conventional teaching and course-related tests? As the "Study of High Schools" documented, a major cause of the high school's inadequacies is the absence of direct teaching of the essential skills of inquiry and expression. Even in "demanding" schools, students often fail to learn how to learn. The culprit is discipline-based curriculums that lead to content-based teaching and testing: The essential (cross-disciplinary) habits and skills of reading, writing, questioning, speaking, and listening fall through the cracks of typical content- focused syllabi and course credits; as indicated, for example, when teachers say "I teach English, not reading."

Classroom Assessment and Grading

A required final public exhibition of know-how ensures that those essentials are taught and learned. The final exit-level exhibition reveals whether a would-be graduate can demonstrate control over the skills of inquiry and expression and control over an intellectual topic that approximates the expert's ability to use knowledge effectively and imaginatively. A final exhibition provides students with an occasion to make clear, if only perhaps symbolically, that they are ready to graduate.

An exhibition challenges students to show off not merely their knowledge but their initiative; not merely their problem solving but their problem posing; not just their learning on cue, but their ability to judge and learn how to learn on an open-ended problem, often of their own design. The experience thus typically focuses on the essential skills of "inquiry and expression" -- a synthesis that requires questioning, problem posing, problem solving, independent research, the creation of a product or performance, and a public demonstration of mastery. Significantly, there is often a component calling for self-reflection and analysis of what one has undergone and learned.

Thus, a final exhibition is a misnomer in an important sense. Many Coalition schools provide a semester- or yearlong course, an adult adviser, and a committee to ensure that a student has adequate guidance, evaluation, and incentive. The exhibition of mastery is as much a process as a final product, if not more so. The process of choosing topics, advisers, and committees and refining one's ideas and skills is a yearlong exercise in understanding and internalizing standards.

A similar approach to a diploma at the college level has been used successfully at Alveno College, Milwaukee, Wisconsin, for over a decade. Assessment is a central experience, with coursework a means to a set of known ends: Students must achieve mastery in the following eight general areas, with their progress in each area being charted on a multistaged scale:

1. Effective communication ability
2. Analytic capability
3. Problem-solving ability,
4. Valuing in a decision-making context
5. Effective social interaction
6. Taking responsibility for the global environment
7. Effective citizenship
8. Aesthetic responsiveness

15.10 <u>Grading Students</u>

Using **Handout Master 15.6,** have students consider if the grading systems can provide answers to the following questions.

1. How do you know that students have learned?

Classroom Assessment and Grading

    2. What is the most informative aspect of the grades?
    3. What is the most difficult aspect of the grading system?

15.11 Classroom Standard Setting And Grading Practices

From Terwilliger, J. (1989) Classroom standard setting and grading practices. Educational measurement: Issues in measurement, 8 (2), 15-19.

Terwilliger believes there are six propositions concerning the grading process which are self-evident truths:

1. Grading should be directly linked to an explicitly defined set of instructional goals that takes into account both the content of instruction and the cognitive complexity of outcomes. In principle, grades should reflect the level of the outcomes with the highest grades being assigned to those who achieve the most advanced outcomes.

2. All data collected for purposes of judging student achievement should be expressed in quantitative form. This implies that (a) Results on quizzes, tests, exams, and so forth, should be reported as points earned based upon an explicit scoring scheme; (b) Homework, assigned projects, term papers, and so forth, should be scored using a clearly defined quantitative rating system; and (c) Classroom performances, demonstrations, exhibitions, and so forth, should be evaluated using a well-defined system of numeric ratings or check lists.

3. The process of judging the quality of student performance (evaluation) should be distinguished from the process of collecting data about student performance (measurement). In particular, a valid judgment typically requires that (a) Data be collected over a period of time, and (b) An explicit frame of reference be formulated as the basis for the judgment (evaluation).

4. From an educational viewpoint, the assignment of a grade of failure, unsatisfactory, no credit, and so forth, has a special significance to students in terms of their future educational options. A failing grade should reflect a categorical judgment that the student does not possess a minimal level of competence independent of the student's performance relative to other students.

5. An evaluation plan should be prepared for distribution to students. This plan should be explicit about (a) Timing for data collection (e.g., dates for quizzes, exams, class presentations, etc.; due dates for assignments, projects, etc.), (b) Conditions under which data collection takes place (e.g., format of items/questions in quizzes and exams, time limits for quizzes and exams, availability of reference materials, computational aids, etc., during quizzes and exams, penalties for late assignments, etc.), and (c) How the data are to be employed in making summative judgments about students (e.g., the relative weight to be given to each item of data in arriving at evaluations).

6. Teachers need time to establish an approach to grading that is both practical and consistent with the particular classroom setting in which they work. Realistic expectations concerning student performance can best be arrived at through trial and error.

15.12 Dealing With A Student Who Refuses To Work

Teachers often have trouble coping with a student who does not put much effort into his work. Using **Handout Master 15.7** as a basis for information, have students create and act out role-plays of a teacher and student discussing the reasons the student is not working up to potential. After they act out their plays, the whole class could address the two following questions:

- How would you explain to a pupil the factors that entered into a grade you gave him for "effort"?

- In giving special attention to a student, what should the teacher keep in mind regarding the needs of the class?

15.13 Norm-Referenced Grading

On an overhead projector, display the following test scores and have the students respond to the questions below.

Test 1:   56 50 48 48 45 40 39 37 35 33 31 30 30 28 27 25 23 22 20 17 15

Test 2:   95 91 88 86 84 79 77 75 74 71 70 67 66 65 63 62 59 56 50 49 45

Assuming that the course grade is based on these two tests, what grades should Jan and Judy receive?

Student	Test 1	Test 2	Grade
Jay	30	79	?
Judy	39	70	?

How can you justify your assignments of grades?

15.14 Determining Grades

Pose the following problem to students:

You have a pupil who made poor grades last year but so far this year he seems to be trying to do better. You are grading one of his written reports and are trying to decide whether he deserves a C+ or a B-.

Classroom Assessment and Grading

What factors might influence you to give the lower grade? What factors would influence you to give the higher grade? If you gave the lower grade, how could you offset its discouraging effect?

15.15 <u>Evaluating Decisions</u>

Adapted from Harris, B. M., Bessent, E W., & McIntyre, K. E.(1969). <u>Inservice education: A guide to better practice.</u>, Englewood Cliffs, NJ: Prentice-Hall.

Distribute **Handout Master 15.8**, which gives brief descriptions of seven boys, each of whom went home last month with a "D" on his report card in English on his report card.

Students should read the description of each child and then indicate whether or not they think the child should receive a "D" for the reasons given: Circle YES if they think the child should receive a "D" and circle NO if they think he should not receive a "D." Students should explain their rationales and the actions they would take to try to increase performance the following term. Have students compare and interpret their responses.

15.16 <u>Contracting</u>

Have students consider the following situation:

You are using a contract system in one of your classes. One of the requirements for an A is "to write book report." Some students, however, are reporting on books that you think they read last year and some are handing in short, superficial reports. How can you structure the contract system to improve the quality of students' work?

Discussion Questions

1. Differentiate between formative and summative measurement and give examples of how each might be used in your own expected teaching situation.

2. Discuss the consideration involved in selecting between objective and essay test items. Suggest key guidelines involving the construction of each.

3. How do grades serve to increase or decrease motivation to learn? What are the implications of these effects for the adoption of ungraded versus graded assignments?

4. Identify the basic orientation and procedures involved in each of the following grading system: norm-referenced, criterion-referenced, point, percentage, and contract.

Classroom Assessment and Grading

5. Evaluate the implications of the Buckley Amendment for teachers' testing and grading practices. Will it be a likely influence the way you prepare tests, provide feedback, and determine final grades? Explain.

6. Discuss some of the advantages and disadvantages of true-false, matching, and short-answer objective test items.

7. Some educators think we should get rid of grades because they are educationally unimportant, unnecessary and harmful. What are some alternatives to grades in educational evaluation?

8. Why is it that many courses, especially on the secondary level, seem to require a "regurgitation of the facts" rather than a thoughtful understanding of the material?

9. How much authority should a student teacher have in determining a student's grade?

10. What are the advantages and disadvantages of "no failures" grading policy?

11. In what ways may "portfolio" evaluations minimize/maximize teachers' attention to individualized assessments? How will "portfolio" evaluation satisfy society's need to maintain "standards"?

12. What criteria would you use to evaluate student "portfolios"? Are these criteria different from those used to determine grades?

13. Would grades or "portfolios" be better measures of academic achievement in the classes you expect to teach? Are they mutually exclusive? Why?

Additional Resources for Teaching This Chapter

REFERENCES

American Educational Research Association. (1985). Standards for educational and psychological testing. (5th ed.) Washington, DC: American Educational Research Association. The standards for all persons involved in educational testing. A very basic and necessary reference.

Gable, R. A., & Hendrickson, J. M. (1990). Assessing students with special needs. White Plains, NY: Longman.

Kubiszyn, T., and Borich, G. (1987). Educational measurement. 2nd ed. Glenview, Ill.: Scott, Foresman, & Co.

Maeroff, G. I. (1991). Assessing alternative assessment. Phi Delta Kappan, 73 (4), 272-281.

Noll, V., Scannell, D., Craig, R. (1989). <u>Introduction to educational measurement</u>. University Press of America

Popham, W. J. (1995). <u>Classroom assessment: What teachers need to know</u>. Needham Heights, MA: Allyn and Bacon.

Stiggins, R. (1988). Make sure teachers understand student assessment. <u>Executive Educator, 10(8)</u>, 24-26.

Stiggins, R. J. (1994). <u>Student-centered assessment</u>. New York, NY: Macmillan.

Terwilliger, J. (1989). Classroom standard setting and grading practices. <u>Educational Measurement: Issues and Practices. 8 (2),</u> 1-19.

Tierney, R. J., Carter, M. A., & Desai, L. E. (1991). <u>Portfolio assessment in the reading-writing classroom</u>. Norwood, MA: Christopher Gordin Publishers.

Watson, D. and Rangel, L (1989). Can cooperative learning be evaluated? <u>School Administrator, 46(6),</u> 8-10.

FILMS, VIDEOTAPES, AND AUDIOCASSETTES

Four keys to classroom testing, This audio-visual instructional package (approx. $300) that covers planning, constructing, assembling, and scoring teacher-made tests. It is well organized and can be used as a basis for a course, several class meetings, independent or small group work. The package contains a guide for each of the four major sections, transparency masters, filmstrips, and accompanying audiocassettes. (From ETS, 1984)

Test interpretation, filmstrip, cassette. Introduction to the language of testing. Designed for the person who has had little training in tests and measurements and who needs some knowledge. (From CAR)

Using test results, b &w, 15 minutes. Shows what can be done with data obtained from standardized tests in guiding students. (ETS, 1965)

Handout Master 15.0

Lecture Outline: Classroom Assessment and Grading

- **Formative and Summative Assessment**

- **Traditional Assessment**

- **Innovations in Assessment**

- **Effects of Grades and Grading**

- **Grading and Reporting**

- **Communication about Assessment**

Copyright © 1998 by Allyn and Bacon

Handout Master 15.1

Different Kinds of Test Items

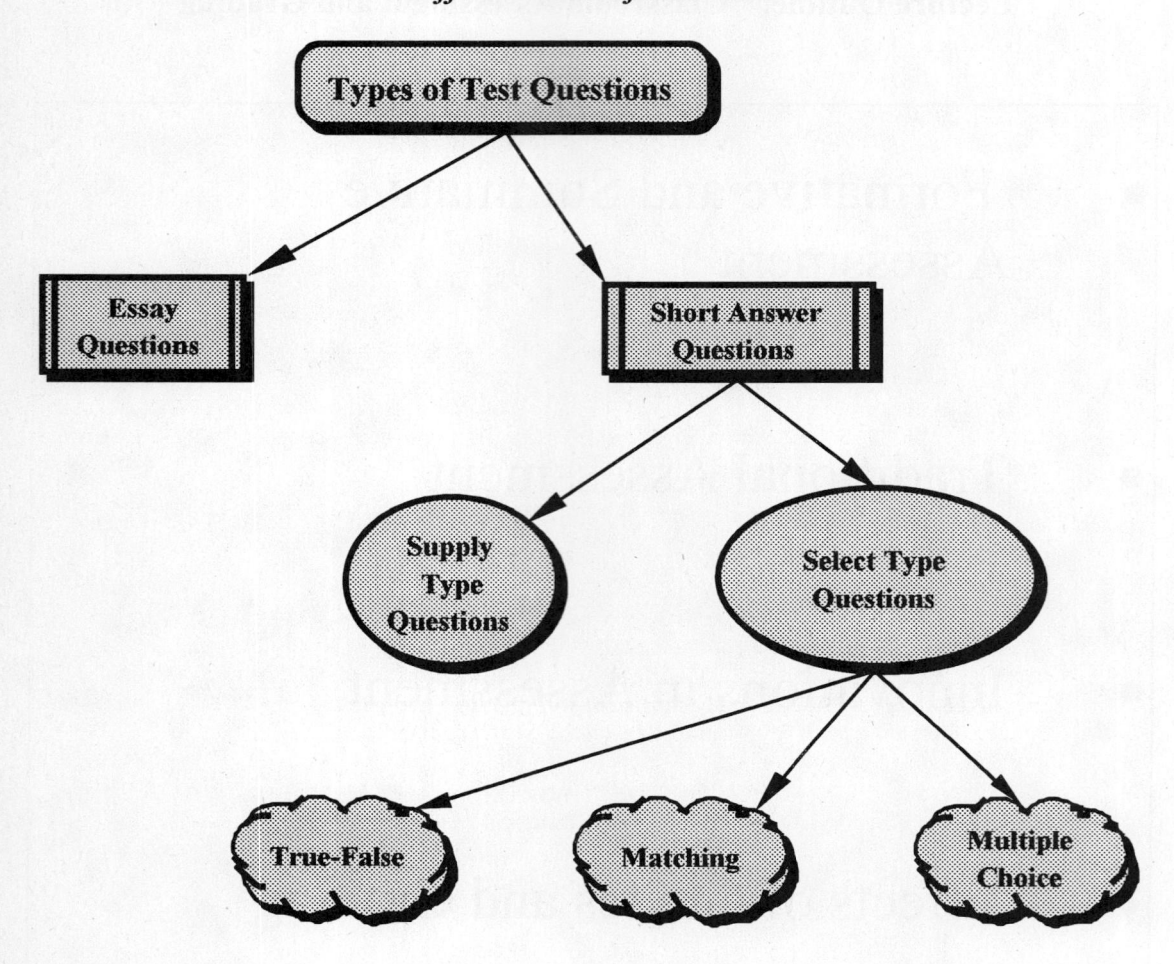

- Types of Test Questions
  - Essay Questions
  - Short Answer Questions
    - Supply Type Questions
    - Select Type Questions
      - True-False
      - Matching
      - Multiple Choice

Copyright © 1998 by Allyn and Bacon

Handout Master 15.2

Checklist for Evaluating Test Items

A. General
1. Is the purpose of the test clear? :
2. Have the intended learning outcomes been identified and defined?
3. Are the intended learning outcomes stated in performance (measurable) terms?
4. Have test specifications been prepared that indicate the nature and distribution of items to be included in the test?
5. Does the specified set of items provide a representative sample of the tasks contained in the achievement domain?
6. Are the types of items appropriate for the learning outcomes to be measured?
7. Is the difficulty of the items appropriate for the students to be tested and the nature of measurement (e.g., mastery or survey)?
8. Is the number of items appropriate for the students to be tested, the time available for testing, and the interpretations to be made?
9. Does the test plan include "built-in" features that contribute to valid and reliable scores?
10. Have plans been made for arranging the items in the test, writing directions, scoring, and using results?

B. Multiple-Choice Items
1. Does the stem of the item present a single, clearly formulated problem?
2. Is the stem stated in simple, clear language?
3. Is the stem worded so that there is no repetition of material in the alternatives?
4. If negative wording is used in the stem, is it emphasized (by underlining or caps)?
5. Is the intended answer correct or clearly best?
6. Are all alternatives grammatically consistent with the stem and parallel in form?
7. Are the alternatives free from verbal clues to the correct answer?
8. Are the distracters plausible and attractive to the uninformed?
9. To eliminate length as a clue, is the relative length of the correct answer varied?
10. Has the alternative "all of the above" been avoided and "none of the above" used only when appropriate?
11. Is the position of the correct answer varied so that there is no detectable pattern?

C. True-False Items
1. Does each statement contain one central, significant idea?
2. Can each statement be unequivocally judged true or false?
3. Are the statements brief and stated in simple language?
4. Are negative statements used sparingly and double negatives avoided?
5. Are statements of opinion attributed to some source?
6. Have specific determiners (such as, always, sometimes, may) and other clues (such as length) been avoided?
7. Is there approximately an even number of true and false statements?
8. When arranged in the test, are the true and false items put in random order?

D. Matching Items
1. Does each matching item contain only homogeneous material?
2. Is the list of items short with brief responses on the right?
3. Is the list of responses longer or shorter than the list of premises, to provide an uneven match?
4. Do the directions clearly state the basis for matching and that the responses can be used once, more than once, or not at all?

Copyright © 1998 by Allyn and Bacon

Handout 15.2 b

Checklist for Evaluating Test Items

E   Interpretive Exercises

1. Is the introductory material relevant to the learning outcomes to be measured?
2. Is the introductory material new to the examinees?
3. Is the introductory material as brief as possible and at the appropriate reading level?
4. Do the test items call forth the performance specified in the learning outcomes?
5. Do the test items call for interpretation (rather than recognition or recall)?
6. Do the test items meet the criteria of effective item writing that apply to the item type used?
7. Is the interpretive exercise free of extraneous clues?

F.   Short-Answer Items
1. Is the item stated so that a single, brief answer is possible?
2. Has the item been stated as a direct question whenever feasible? Does the desired response relate to the main point of the item?
3. Is the blank placed at the end of the statement? Have clues to the answer been avoided such as "a" or "and length of the blank)? Are the units and degree of precision indicated for numerical answers?

G.   Essay Test
1. Is the question designed to measure complex learning outcomes? Is each question relevant to the learning outcome being measured? Does the question make clear what is being measured and how the answer will be evaluated?
2. Has terminology been used that clarifies and limits the task (e.g., "describe," not "discuss")?
3. Are all students required to answer the same question?
4. Has ample time been allowed for answering, and has a time limit been suggest for each?
5. Have adequate provisions been made for scoring the essay answers (e.g., model answers or criteria for evaluating)?

From: Gronlund, N. E. (1993). <u>How to make achievement tests and assessments</u>. (5th Ed.).   Needham Heights, MA: Allyn and Bacon, pp. 33, 60, 69, 72, 76, 82, 91.

Handout Master 15.3

Analyzing Multiple Choice Items

Identify the faults in the following multiple choice items. Rewrite the item so that it is satisfactory.

1. The word "gordo" in Spanish means:
a.   thin   b.   underweight   c.   skinny   d.   fat
Fault: _____
_____

Rewrite: _____
_____

2. The spider is an
a.   marsupial   b.   arachnid   c.   vertebrate   d.   chordate

Fault: _____
_____

Rewrite: _____
_____

3. Tennis courts that will require the least maintenance than any other tennis court is the tennis court which;
a.   is made of grass   b.   made of clay   c.   made of lakold   d.   made of Rubico
Fault: _____
_____

Rewrite: _____
_____

4. The development of the self-concept is not principally influenced by:
a.   parents   b.   peers   c.   growth rate   d.   physical appearance
Fault: _____
_____

Rewrite: _____
_____

5. "Culture-fair" tests are always
a.   reliable   b.   always valid   c.   power tests   d.   usually nonverbal in order to offset cultural differences in language

Fault: _____
_____

Rewrite: _____
_____

Copyright © 1998 by Allyn and Bacon

Handout Master 15.4

Eddie's Writing

Eddie is a fourth grade student and he has collected samples of his writing for one month (October/November, 1992). Students were given "starter" lines for a story such as "Some boys and girls were at a party one night.." They were asked to finish the story. At the end of a period of time, children were asked to pick their best work and their worst work

1. Read the writing samples from "Eddie." Decide on how you will grade his work. How will you explain your grading system to Eddie? What are the advantages, disadvantages of your grading system? This is vague. You have 3 pieces of writing and Eddie's comments on his writing to evaluate in some fashion. The information in Chapter 15 should be helpful here.

2. Describe the child's strengths and weaknesses in language arts as represented in his or her writing. You will need to take into account the time element. Does he improve, should you grade improvement? You should use concepts you have learned in this course to describe these strengths and weaknesses. You might want to first develop a list of characteristics of the child's writing you might wish to comment upon.

3. Based on your reading of the child's work and the child's efforts to comment on his own work, what concept of "writing" do you think the child held? What concept of "writing" would you like the child to have? How would you get the child to share your concept of "writing?"

4. What are the factors that make it difficult to grade Eddie's work? Are there other things you would like to know? List those things that you would like to know. Why are they important? What effect would they have on your grading?

5. What is your overall assessment of Eddie as a student? Good, poor, average student? Would you expect him to do well in other subjects? Why/Why not?

Copyright © 1998 by Allyn and Bacon

Handout Master 15.4 b

Eddie's Writing

1   10/26/96

My uncle was walking down a lonely dirt road one day. He is there because he had a fight with his wife because he killed her wifes mother. At the dirt road he saw a girl just like the one he killed. He ran as fast as he can then he ran into the woods. At the end he tried to get out but he was surrounded by all dead people. Then he went back home and said to his wife he will never kill anyone again.

2   10/28/96

Some boys and girls were at a party one night. There was a graveyard down the street and they were talking about how scarey it was. When the boys and girls went to the graveyard they saw a person just like a dead person and they ran back in the house, and the mother said what happen and they said they saw a dead person walking. When her mom reached to her face, she riped her face off and her face had blood and worms crawling out of her face. They ran out of the house and they both found a rope to kill themself so they cannot see anymore monsters.

3   2/18/97

When I got glasses I was about five years old. Before I wasn't able to see the chalkboard and the teacher had to move me of the front of the room. On Saturday, we went to Lens Crafters and they that I need glasses. When I got glasses it was sort of weird because it felt like I was walking it felt like I was sideways and when I went to school I said to my teacher: "Miss Rugg can I go back where I sat" and then I began getting good grades.

** Note: The spelling and grammatical errors are those made by the child.

Copyright © 1998 by Allyn and Bacon

Handout Master 15.5

Characteristics of Authentic Tests

A. Structure and Logistics

1. Are more appropriately public; involve an audience, a panel, and so on.
2. Do not rely on unrealistic and arbitrary time constraints.
3. Offer known, not secret, questions or tasks.
4. Are more like portfolios or a *season* of games (not one-shot).
5. Require some collaboration with others.
6. Recur-and are *worth* practicing for, rehearsing, and retaking.
7. Make assessment and feedback to students so central that school schedules, structures, and policies are modified to support them.

B. Intellectual Design Features

1. Are "essential"-not needlessly intrusive, arbitrary, or contrived to "shake out" a grade.
2. Are "enabling"- constructed to point the student toward more sophisticated use of the skills or knowledge.
3. Are contextualized, complex intellectual challenges, not "atomized" tasks, corresponding to isolated "outcomes."
4. Involve the student's own research or use of knowledge, for which "content" IS a means.
5. Assess student habits and repertoires, not mere recall or plug-in skills.
6. Are *representative* challenges-designed to emphasize *depth* more than breadth.
7. Are engaging and educational.
8. Involve somewhat ambiguous ("ill-structured") tasks or problems.

C. Grading and Scoring Standards

1. Involve criteria that assess essentials, not easily counted (but relatively unimportant) errors.
2. Are not graded on a "curve" but in reference to performance standards (criterion referenced, not norm-referenced).
3. Involve demystified criteria of success that appear to *students* as inherent in successful activity.
4. Make self-assessment a part of the assessment.
5. Use a multifaceted scoring system instead of one aggregate grade.
6. Exhibit harmony with shared schoolwide aims-a *standard*.

D. Fairness and Equity

1. Ferret out and identify (perhaps hidden) strengths.
2. Strike a *constantly* examined balance between honoring achievement and native skill or fortunate prior training.
3. Minimize needless, unfair, and demoralizing comparisons.
4. Allow appropriate room for student learning styles, aptitudes, and interests.
5. Can be-should be-attempted by *all* students, with the test "scaffolded up," not "dumbed down," as necessary.

Adapted from G. Wiggins (1989). Teaching to the (Authentic) test. Educational Leadership, 46(7), p. 44.

Copyright © 1998 by Allyn and Bacon

Handout Master 15.6

Grading Systems

Listed below are the test scores received (percent correct) by students in Ms. Wohl's algebra class. Assign different sets of grades to each using these percentage grading standards and norm-referenced grading standards:

Percentage: 90-100 (A); 80-89 (B); 70-79 (C); 60-69 (D); below 60 (F)

Norm-referenced: A = 10% of students; B = 25%; C = 30%; D = 25%; F = 10%

Then answer the questions that appear below the test scores.

Student	Test Score
Frank	80
Marcos	93
Jamie	85
Will	98
Robin	82
Lorna	75
Corsica	85
Larry	97
Willis	87
Maureen	99
Elsa	100
Burt	100
Boris	98
Trevor	81
Sandra	84
Laurie	86
Anna	90
Francis	92
Alice	94
Ranjita	95

A. Which distribution yielded the higher grades?
B. Assuming the test was void and sufficiently challenging, which system would you prefer? Why?
C. The Honors Program at Ms. Wohl's school has limited places for the best students. Which grading system might provide the best basis for nominations of that program? Explain.
D. Compare Frank's grades under both system. What information does the grade provided by each convey to him regarding his performance.

Copyright © 1998 by Allyn and Bacon

Handout Master 15.7

A Student Who Refuses to Work

I first noticed Carl at the time I was making an assignment in my History class. As I explained the assignment, his face went through some of the most amazing contortions ever witnessed by man. His facial expressions alternately portrayed agony, disgust, and despair. Each day as the assignment was made, he would act as if it were a personal punishment for him. I ignored these antics because no matter how much he complained or made faces, he was always prepared.

At the end of the first marking period, I gave Carl a C, but wrote on his report card that his effort was only fair. The day after the cards were distributed, he came up to my desk and bluntly told me, "If you say I don't try, then I won't" He turned and walked back to his seat before I could say anything.
I had a quiz scheduled for that day, and gave it as usual. When I collected the papers, I noticed that Carl's paper had only one printed statement on it: "I don't try, so I won't try." When I asked Carl about his statement, he shouted: "Why should I do any work when I don't get credit for it?" I directed him to leave the room. "Go to the principal, and tell him that you do not want to do any work."

After class I went to see the principal. He told me that Carl was one of the problems that the school had learned to live with. Carl and his whole family, it seems, were rebellious against authority and the suggestions of others. Homework was considered by Carl as a means of harassment. The next day, I asked Carl to remain after class. Our conversation went something like this:

"All right, Carl, why did you act as you did yesterday?"
"Because you said I wasn't trying, and I was."
"What grade did you get?" I asked.
"I got a C," he replied disdainfully.
"Is that the best you can do?"
"No, I can do at least B work."
"Why don't you then?"
"I will."
"How?" I asked.
"I'll work harder."
"And how will you do that?" I persisted.
"By trying harder, I suppose," he replied uncomfortably.

After his own admission that he was not trying hard enough, I tried to help Carl get over his belligerent attitude by giving him special attention in class. I went over his papers with him carefully. I gave him special little jobs around the classroom. I tried to give him recognition when I was explaining material, by asking him, "Is that right, Carl?" He would usually smile, and nod his head in approval.

I would like to be able to report that he became a good student, and that he got over his resentful attitude, but such was not the case. He still makes faces when assignments are given out, and he is still not trying as hard as he should. Worst of all, since I started treating him as someone special, he expects attention all the time and becomes extremely upset if he does not get it. When his attention wanders, I make a comment such as, "You're not here, are you Carl?" The class laughs, and Carl smiles. So I have the feeling that Carl is at least learning to live with the world, and that soon his attitude and work will improve.

Points for Discussion

- How would you explain to a pupil the factors that entered into a grade that you gave him for "effort?"
- In giving special attention to a student, what should the teacher keep in mind regarding the needs of the class?

Copyright © 1998 by Allyn and Bacon

Copyright @ 1993 by Allyn and Bacon

Handout Master 15.8

Beliefs About Grading

*These are brief descriptions of seven children, each of whom went home last month with a "D" on his report card in English. Read the description of each child and then indicate whether or not you think this child should receive a D for the reasons given. Circle YES if you think the child should receive a D' and circle NO if you think he should not receive a "D". Compare your responses with those of others in your class.

A	YES	NO	John is just not very bright. He tries hard but barely has enough ability to get by in school
B	YES	NO	Fred is bright enough, but he is lazy. He knows when he has done enough to earn a "D." and then he quits working.
C	YES	NO	Walter is bright, but he has a language handicap because he comes from home in which the English language is not spoken. He barely earns a "D" but should do much better when he learns the language.
D	YES	NO	John is probably a "C" student in English, but he is such a discipline problem that his teacher is not inclined to give him the benefit of any doubt, so he receives a "D."
E	YES	NO	Mac does "A" or "B" work when he is in school, but he is absent so much of the time that he barely makes a "D."
F	YES	NO	Steve does "B" or "C" work in the English literature part of the course, but his composition, is atrocious, so his marks average out at a "D."
G	YES	NO	Ben is doing far below passing work in English, but he flunked the course last year, and we see no point in failing him more than once in the same thing.

Adapted from Hams, B. M., Bessent. E. W., and McIntyre, K. E., <u>Inservice education: A guide to better practice</u>. Prentice-Hall. 1969.

Handout Master 15.9: Alternative Assessments

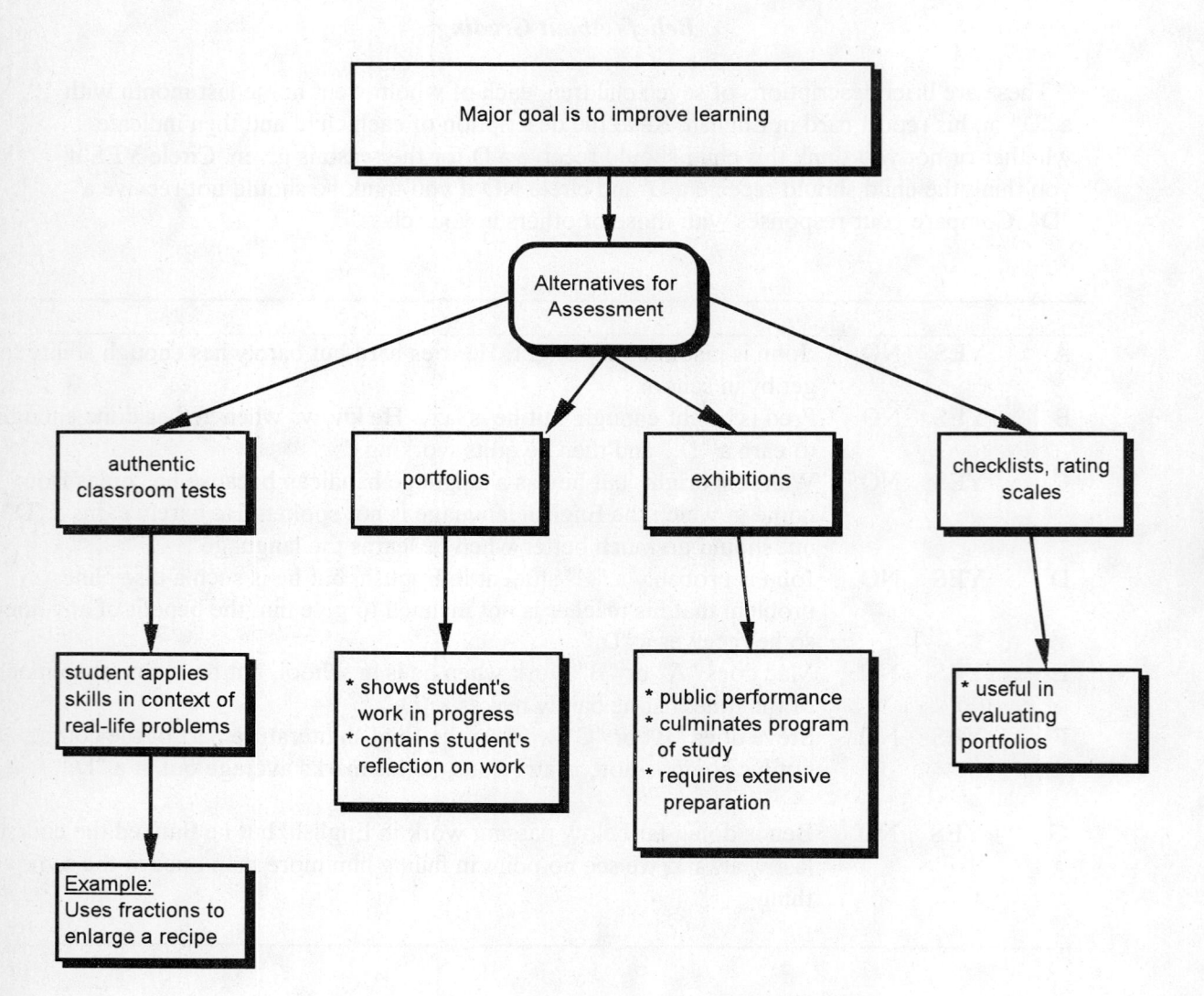

```
                    ┌─────────────────────────────┐
                    │ Major goal is to improve learning │
                    └─────────────────────────────┘
                                   │
                                   ▼
                        ┌──────────────────┐
                        │  Alternatives for │
                        │    Assessment     │
                        └──────────────────┘
```

- **authentic classroom tests**
  - student applies skills in context of real-life problems
  - Example: Uses fractions to enlarge a recipe

- **portfolios**
  - * shows student's work in progress
  - * contains student's reflection on work

- **exhibitions**
  - * public performance
  - * culminates program of study
  - * requires extensive preparation

- **checklists, rating scales**
  - * useful in evaluating portfolios

Copyright © 1998 by Allyn and Bacon

Handout Master 15. 10: Links to Other Chapters

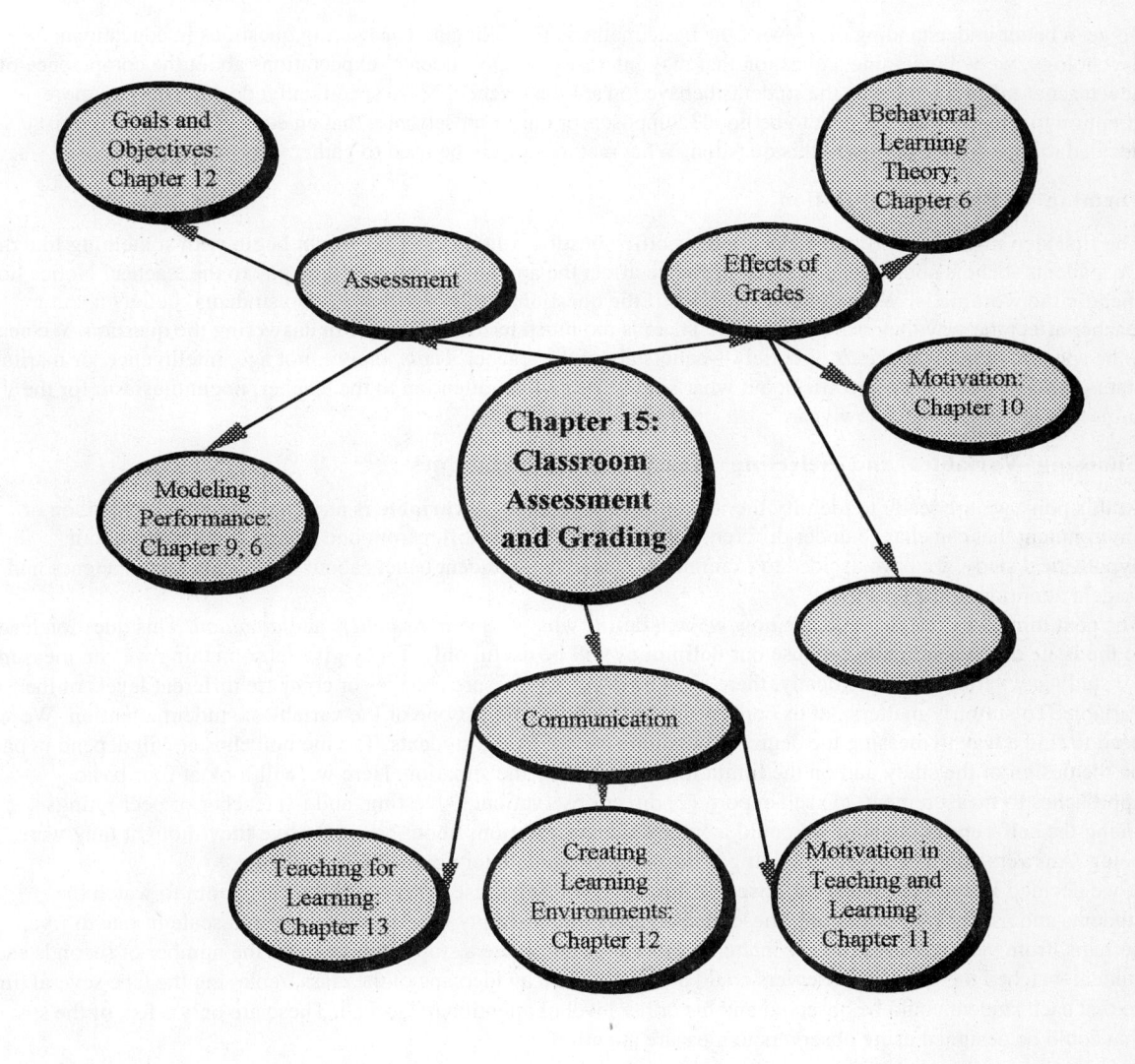

- Goals and Objectives: Chapter 12
- Assessment
- Behavioral Learning Theory: Chapter 6
- Effects of Grades
- Motivation: Chapter 10
- Modeling Performance: Chapter 9, 6
- **Chapter 15: Classroom Assessment and Grading**
- Communication
- Teaching for Learning: Chapter 13
- Creating Learning Environments: Chapter 12
- Motivation in Teaching and Learning Chapter 11

Copyright © 1998 by Allyn and Bacon

RESEARCH IN EDUCATIONAL PSYCHOLOGY
APPENDIX TO EDUCATIONAL PSYCHOLOGY, SEVENTH EDITION
BY ANITA E. WOOLFOLK

In order to achieve a better understanding of educational psychology, you must know how information in the field is created and how to judge the information you encounter. In this appendix we will explore the value and limitations of research, the major road to knowledge in educational psychology. Then we will examine a specific problem to determine how research might answer questions posed by teachers. Finally, we will describe how to judge a research study by evaluating a real experiment.

Asking and Answering Questions

To get a better understanding of a few of the basic methods for asking and answering questions in educational psychology, we will examine a question that may interest you: Do students' expectations about the competence of a new teacher influence the way the students behave toward the teacher? More specifically, do students pay more attention to a teacher they expect to be good? Suppose, for our purposes here, that an educational psychologist decided to look for an answer to this question. What methods might be used to gather information?

Forming a Research Question

The first step might be to frame a clear and specific question. In this case, we might begin with something like this: Do students' beliefs about a teacher's competence affect the amount of attention they pay to the teacher? Notice how specific the wording is. We will have problems if the question is too vague, as in: Do students' beliefs about a teacher affect the way they behave in class? There is too much territory to cover in answering the question. We need to be specific about what *kinds* of beliefs—beliefs about the teacher's *competence,* not age, intelligence, or marital status. And we need to be specific about what kind of behavior—attention to the teacher, not enthusiasm for the subject or anxiety about a new year.

Choosing Variables and Selecting Measurement Techniques

At this point we are ready to identify the variables to be studied. A **variable** is any characteristic of a person or environment that can change under different conditions or that can differ from one person to the next. In our hypothetical study, we have decided to examine two variables—student beliefs about the teacher's competence and student attention to the teacher.

The next thing we must do is decide how we will define what we mean by *beliefs* and *attention.* This question leads to the issue of measurement, because our definitions will be useful only if they give us something we can measure. To study any variable systematically, there must be a way to measure changes or compare different levels of the variable. To simplify matters, let us concentrate at this point on just one of the variables: student attention. We will need to find a way to measure the degree of attention shown by the students. The method chosen will depend in part on the design of the study and on the limitations imposed by the situation. Here we will look at four basic approaches to measurement: (1) self-report, (2) direct observation, (3) testing, and (4) teacher or peer ratings.

Using the **self-report** method, we could ask the students questions about how attentive they thought they were being. Answers could be given in writing or face to face, in an interview with the students.

If we decided instead to use **direct observation,** we could send researchers into the classroom to watch the students and assess their attention. These investigators might simply rate the students (on a scale of one to five, perhaps, from very attentive to very inattentive), or they could use a stopwatch to count the number of seconds each student watched the teacher. Observers could also work from a videotape of the class, replaying the tape several times so that each student could be observed and his or her level of attention rechecked. These are only a few of the systems that could be designed using observers to measure attention.

A **test** would be a little more difficult to construct in this case. Many variables are measured with tests, especially those involving learning or achievement. But since attention is a process rather than a product, it is difficult to design a test to measure it. One approach, however, would be to use a "vigilance task." We could see if the students were paying attention by having the teacher give an unpredictable signal, such as saying "Stand up," during the lesson. The measure of attention in this case would be the number of people who stood up immediately (Woolfolk & Woolfolk, 1974).

Finally, we might decide to use **teacher ratings** or **peer ratings.** We could measure attention by asking the teacher or the students to rate the attention of every student in the class.

Clearly, each of these approaches has advantages and disadvantages. Using self-reports or ratings of teachers or peers means relying on the judgments of the participants themselves. Using observers or tests can be disruptive to the class, at least initially. Videotaping is difficult and expensive. Let us assume, however, that we have chosen direct observation from videotapes. We will train the observers to time student attention with a stopwatch to determine how many seconds each student looks at the teacher during a 10-minute lesson. Note that our system of measurement has given us our definition of *attention:* the number of seconds each student looks at the teacher during a 10-minute lesson. This seems to offer a reasonably good definition. If the measurement system did not offer a good definition, we would need to find another way of measuring.

To define and measure our first variable—students' beliefs about the teacher's competence—we could also choose from a number of methods. Let us assume, at least for the time being, that we have selected a rating system. Students' answers to the question "How competent do you think this teacher is?" should give us a good idea of student opinion.

One other definition may be in order here, although in this particular study it seems rather obvious. Since we will be studying student beliefs and student attentiveness, the subjects in our investigation will be students. As you probably know, **subjects** is the term for the people (or animals) whose behavior is being measured. We would want to specify the grade, sex, and type of student to be studied. For our hypothetical study, we will select male and female sixth graders in a predominantly middle-class school.

Stating a Hypothesis and Choosing an Approach

At this point we have our research question, the variables to be studied, the definition of these variables, the system for measuring them, and the subjects to be studied. We are now ready to add two new details: a **hypothesis** or guess about the relationship between the two variables, and a decision about what kind of approach we will use in our study. To some extent, the hypothesis will dictate the approach.

At the most general level, there are two approaches to answering research questions. The first is to describe the events and relationships in a particular situation as they take place in real life. The second approach is to change one aspect of a situation and note the effects of the change. These two approaches are generally called descriptive and experimental.

A Descriptive Approach. One hypothesis we might establish in our study of student beliefs and attention is that students pay more attention to a teacher they believe to be competent. To test this hypothesis, we could go into several sixth-grade classrooms and ask students to rate their teachers on competence. Ideally, we would conduct the study in a middle school where sixth graders usually have more than one teacher each day. We could then observe the students and measure their level of attention to each teacher. At this point we could get some idea about whether the two variables—believing that a teacher is competent and paying attention to that teacher—go together.

Let's assume, for the sake of the argument, that the two variables do go together. What we have now is a **correlation.** If two variables tend to occur together, they are correlated. We have just assumed such a correlation between beliefs and attention. Other variables that are often correlated are height and weight, income and education, and colder temperatures and falling leaves. A taller person, for example, is likely to weigh more than a shorter person. A richer person is likely to have completed more years of education than a poorer person. And, for the sake of the argument, we are now assuming that a student who believes a teacher to be competent is more likely to pay attention to that teacher.

But what does this correlation give us? If educational psychologists know that two variables are correlated, they can then make predictions about one of the variables based on knowledge of the other variable. For example, because the IQ scores of parents and children are correlated, educators can predict a child's IQ based on that of the mother or father. The prediction may not be correct every time, because the correlation between parents' IQs and children's IQs is not perfect. But the prediction is likely to be correct or nearly correct much more than a prediction based on no information at all. Several studies have found a correlation between a teacher's enthusiasm and student learning. If we have information about a teacher's enthusiasm, we can make a prediction about the achievement level of the students in his or her class.

This last example brings us to a very important point about correlation and prediction, mentioned briefly in chapter 1. Knowing that two variables tend to occur together does not tell us that one variable is actually causing the other. Although enthusiastic teachers may tend to have students who achieve more than the students of unenthusiastic teachers, we cannot say that teacher enthusiasm leads to or causes student achievement. We know only that teacher enthusiasm and student achievement tend to occur together. Perhaps teaching students who are achieving more makes a teacher more enthusiastic. Perhaps a third factor—the interesting materials a teacher has chosen to work with, for example—causes both the teacher enthusiasm and student achievement.

Although being able to predict levels of one variable from information about levels of another is useful, teachers are often interested in finding out what factors actually will cause a desired change in behavior. For this, they would need a different kind of research—research based on experimental manipulation.

An Experimental Approach. Returning to our original question about student beliefs and attention, suppose we made a different hypothesis. Rather than just hypothesizing that student attention and beliefs about teacher competence go together, we could hypothesize that one of the factors actually causing students to pay attention is the belief that a teacher is competent. In this case, the hypothesis states a causal relationship. To test this hypothesis, we must change one of the variables to see if this change actually causes changes in the other variable. In our study, this assumed cause, known as the **independent variable,** is the belief that the teacher is competent. The purpose of our experiment will be to see if changes in this variable really cause changes in the other variable—the **dependent variable** of student attention to the teacher.

Assume that we create three comparable groups of students by randomly assigning the students to the groups. Since the selection and assignment of students to groups is totally **random**—by chance, based on no particular plan—the three groups should be very similar.

We then tell one group of students that the teacher they are about to meet is a "very good" teacher; we tell the second group that the teacher they will have is "not a very good" teacher; and we tell the third group nothing about the teacher they are going to have. This final group serves as the **control group.** It will give us information about what happens when there is no experimental manipulation. At some point in the experiment we would ask the students what they believed about the teacher to make sure they had accepted the description they were given.

Next, the teacher, actually the same person in all three cases, teaches the same lesson to each group. Of course the teacher should not be told about the experimental manipulation. We videotape the students in each group as they listen to the teacher. Later, raters viewing the tapes measure the number of seconds each student in the three groups has looked at the teacher. (You may have noticed that although the definition and measurement of the attention variable remain the same as they were in the descriptive study, the definition and measurement of the belief variable have changed. As you can see, such a change is necessary to turn the study into an experiment.)

What kind of results can we expect? If we find that students who believed the teacher was competent paid attention most of the time, students who believed the teacher was not very good paid very little attention, and students who were given no information paid a moderate amount of attention, have we proved our hypothesis? No! In psychology and in educational psychology it is assumed that hypotheses are never really proven by one study, because each study tests the hypothesis in only one specific situation. Hypotheses are "supported" but never proven by the positive results of a single study. Have we supported the hypothesis that student beliefs affect student attention? The answer to this question depends on how well we designed and carried out the study.

Since this is just a hypothetical study, we can assume, once again for the sake of argument, that we did everything just right. If you read the following list of requirements for a "true experiment," set forth by Van Mondrans, Black, Keysor, Olsen, Shelley, and Williams (1977), you will see that we were indeed on the right track:

The "true experiment" is usually defined as one in which the investigator can (a) manipulate at least one independent variable; (b) randomly select and assign subjects to experimental treatments; and (c) compare the treatment group(s) with one or more control groups on at least one dependent variable. (p. 51)

With a real experiment, however, we would need to know more about exactly how every step of the investigation was conducted. And we would also want to know whether other researchers could come up with the same results if they did the same experiment.

Is the Research Valid?

Being able to evaluate research studies has a dual payoff. The kind of thinking needed is in and of itself valuable. It is the same kind of thinking required to evaluate any complex idea, plan, argument, or project. In all these cases, you need to search for errors, oversights, inconsistencies, or alternative explanations. The analytical ability necessary to evaluate research is useful in any occupation, from law to business to motorcycle maintenance. The second payoff is more specifically valuable for teachers. As an educator, you will have to evaluate research done in your school district or reported in professional journals to determine if the findings are relevant to your own situation.
To be valid, the results of an experiment must pass several tests. Changes in the dependent variable must be due solely to the manipulation of the independent variable. In the following pages, we will look at eight questions that can be asked in an evaluation of a research experiment.

1. *Were the groups to be studied reasonably equal before the experiment began?* If the subjects vary greatly from group to group, any changes found at the end of the experiment may be the results of the original differences in the groups and not of changes in the independent variable. Random assignment of subjects to groups usually takes care of this problem. If instead of randomly selecting the subjects in our own study we had used three different sixth-grade classes, our results would be questionable. Maybe one class already had more generally attentive students. Had they been given the teacher labeled "very good" in the experiment, their high degree of attention would have been relatively meaningless. With random selection from a number of sixth-grade classes, however, each group is likely to have gotten an equal share of the generally attentive and generally inattentive students.

2. *Were all the variables except the independent variable controlled so that the only real difference in the treatment of each group was the change in the independent variable?* We have just seen that the subjects in each group must be equivalent. This principle is equally true of everything else in the experiment. If different procedures were used with each group, it would be difficult to determine which of the differences caused the results. In our study, for example, if we had used different teachers or different lessons in each group, we would have run into this problem in evaluating the results. The students' attention to the teacher could have been based on many things other than the initial statement given by the experimenter about the teacher's competence (the independent variable).

3. *Were the measurement procedures applied consistently to each group?* Unreliable results may at times be caused by an inconsistent measurement system. In our study, if we had used a different videotape rater for each group, we could not have trusted our results. Perhaps one rater would give credit for student attention when students had their faces pointed toward the teacher even if their bodies were turned away. Perhaps another rater would give credit only if the students' entire bodies were directed toward the teacher. Ideally, one rater should make all the measurements. If more are used, there must be some test of the raters' ability to agree on the results. One way to check this would be to see if they agreed when measuring the same students' behaviors.

4. *Are the results of the study due to the experimental procedures rather than to the novelty of the situation?* It is always possible that subjects will respond in some special way to any change, at least temporarily. This possibility was pointed out dramatically by studies conducted at the Western Electric Plant in Hawthorne, Illinois. Investigators were trying to determine which changes in the plant environment would lead to greater worker productivity. As it turned out, everything they tried, every change in the working conditions, seemed to lead to greater productivity, at least for a while (Roethlisberger & Dickson, 1939). In other words, the workers were reacting not to the actual changes but to something new happening. Because the experiment took place in Hawthorne, Illinois, such results are now said to be examples of the **Hawthorne effect.** Our control group helped us avoid this problem. Although the independent variable of a "good" or "bad" teacher label was not applied to the control group, these students were given the special treatment of being in an experiment. If their attention ratings had been particularly high, we might have suspected the Hawthorne effect for all three groups.

5. *Has the investigator who designed the study biased the results in any way?* There are numerous obvious and subtle ways in which an investigator can influence the participants in an experiment. The investigator may have no intention of doing so but may still communicate to the subjects what he or she expects them to do in a given situation (Rosenthal, 1976). In our study, for example, if the investigator had told the teacher involved what the purpose of the experiment was, the teacher might have expected less attention from one of the groups and unintentionally done something to increase or decrease the attention actually given. If the investigator had told the videotape raters the purpose of the experiment, the same thing might have happened. Without meaning to, they might have looked harder for attention in one of the groups. In order to eliminate these problems, both teacher and raters would have to be unaware of the independent variable that was being studied.

6. *Is it reasonably certain that the results did not occur simply by chance?* To answer this question, researchers use statistics. The general agreement is that differences among the groups can be considered "significant" if these differences could have occurred by chance only 5 times out of 100. In reading a research report, you might see the results stated in the following manner: "The difference between the groups was significant ($p < .05$)." Unless you are planning to do your own scientific research, the most important part of this is probably the word *significant*. The mathematical statement means that the probability (p) of such a difference occurring by chance factors alone is less than ($<$) 5 in 100 (.05).

7. *Will the findings in this particular study be likely to fit other, similar situations?* This is really a question of generalization. How similar to the research situation does a new situation have to be to get the same results? Consider our own experiment. Would we get similar results (a) with much older or younger students? (b) with students who are more or less intelligent? (c) with students who already know the teacher? (d) with different teachers or different lessons? (e) with the removal of videotape cameras? (f) with a lesson that lasts more than 10 minutes? We cannot answer these questions until the study has been repeated with many different subjects in many different situations. This brings us to the question of **replication.**

8. *Has the study been replicated?* A study has been replicated if it has been repeated and the same results are found. Replication may involve exactly the same study conditions, or it may involve changes in conditions that will give us a better idea of the extent to which the findings can be applied to other situations. If results have been replicated in well-designed studies, the findings form the basis for principles and laws.

Since our own study was only hypothetical, we cannot get a replication of it. But we can look at a similar study done by Feldman and Prohaska (1979). Analyzing this study should be useful to you in two ways. First, it will provide a model for considering other research articles you will find in textbooks and in professional journals. Second, the results of the study itself will probably be of interest because they suggest ways in which student expectations may cause teachers to be more or less effective.

A Sample Study: The Effect of Student Expectations

Feldman and Prohaska's 1979 study concerns student expectations about a teacher's competence and the effect of these expectations on the students' and the teacher's behavior. (Remember that we are looking only at student behavior in our hypothetical study.) You may want to read the study in *Journal of Educational Psychology* (vol. 71, no. 4, 1979). At the beginning of the article you will find specific information: the names of the authors, the university where they work, the name of the article, the name of the journal, and the basic facts about the study. The basic facts describing the design and results of the study are usually included in a brief summary called an **abstract,** found at the beginning of such an article.

Essential Data

The subjects in Feldman and Prohaska's first experiment were undergraduate female volunteers from an introductory psychology class. Each subject was randomly assigned to a positive-expectation group or a negative-expectation group, but was not told which group she was in.

Each subject arrived separately at the experimental center and was told she would have to wait a few minutes before she could see the teacher. While she waited, she met another student who had supposedly just been working with the teacher and was now completing a questionnaire evaluating the teacher. Actually, this student, a male, was a **confederate** of the experimenter—an assistant pretending to be one of the subjects. The confederate played one of two roles, depending on whether he was meeting a subject from the positive-expectation group or the negative-expectation group. (The subjects, of course, did not know what group they were in.) When the confederate met a subject from the positive group, he told her the teacher had been really good, effective, and friendly. He then gave her a completed questionnaire (which also said good things about the teacher) and asked her to turn it in for him, since he had to leave. When the confederate met a subject from the negative group, he said very uncomplimentary things about the teacher and gave the subject a questionnaire with very negative comments on it.

The subject then went into a room and met the teacher, who was the same person for both groups. The teacher did not know the subject had been given any expectations at all. While she was teaching two minilessons, she and the subject were secretly videotaped. After the two lessons, the subject took a short quiz on the material and filled out a questionnaire just like the one she had seen the confederate completing. The same procedure was repeated for each subject.

Finally, the videotapes of all the subjects were shown to trained coders who were unaware of the actual experimental conditions. These coders measured three things: (1) percentage of time each subject looked at the teacher, (2) each subject's forward body lean toward the teacher, and (3) each subject's general body orientation toward the teacher. Taken together, these student behaviors could be called *paying attention*. When the coders rated the same subject's videotape, their ratings of the three behaviors were highly correlated. Thus we can assume that the coders agreed about how to use the measurement technique.

Results showed that the subjects who expected the teacher to be "bad" rated the lesson as significantly more difficult, less interesting, and less effective than the subjects who expected the teacher to be "good." They also found the teacher to be less competent, less intelligent, less likable, and less enthusiastic than the other subjects did. Furthermore, the subjects who expected the teacher to be "bad" learned significantly less as measured by the short quiz. They also leaned forward less often and looked at the teacher less frequently than the subjects who expected the teacher to be good.

How would you evaluate this study? The full report (Feldman & Prohaska, 1979) gives many more details, but based on our summary alone, what can you tell about the validity of the findings?

Judging Validity

If you look back at the eight questions for evaluating a research study, it appears that numbers 1, 3, 5, and 6 have been met. (Do you agree?) We cannot yet be certain about question 2—equal treatment of the subjects—because in this first experiment we have no detailed information about the way the teacher behaved toward the subjects. We know only that the teacher was instructed to give the same lesson, in the same way, to each subject. But what if the differences in the subjects' behavior toward the teacher—the differences that were found in the study—caused the teacher to give the lesson in different ways to different students? Perhaps after the first minute or so, subjects were reacting to real differences in the way the teacher delivered the lesson.

Feldman and Prohaska looked at this very real possibility in their second experiment. They found that students' nonverbal behavior (leaning forward or looking at the teacher) actually could affect how well the teacher taught the lesson. Although this may, to some extent, lessen the validity of their first experiment, it is a worthy finding in and of itself.

You may have noticed that we have not yet discussed conditions 4, 7, and 8. Feldman and Prohaska did not include a control group. The fact that the two experimental groups reacted in significantly different ways, however, shows that they were not simply reacting to the novelty of the situation. If both groups had been particularly eager or bored, we might have had good reason to expect the Hawthorne effect.

We can't know anything about conditions 7 and 8, or course, until further research has been conducted. We can say, however, that two respected educational psychologists have reported findings that seem to support our initial hypothesis. In some cases, at least, student expectations about a teacher's competence do have an effect, not only on the students' behavior but also on the teacher's behavior.

The last two questions are equally difficult to answer. It is almost always possible to offer alternative explanations for the findings of any study. In a well-controlled study, an attempt is made to eliminate as many of these alternative explanations as possible. The question of educational versus statistical significance is also one on which reasonable people might easily differ. How large a difference between the test scores of the two groups is large enough to warrant a change in educational practice? This question must be answered in part by the individual teacher. Do the potential gains offered by the findings seem worthwhile enough to make whatever change is called for?

Closer to Home: Action Research

Thus far we have considered how to evaluate and apply research conducted by other people. But in teaching today there is another type of research--action research. **Action research** is conducted by teachers to examine their own practice and the impact of their teaching on students.

> Teachers throughout the world are developing professionally by becoming teacher-researchers, a wonderful new breed of artists-in-residence. Using our own classrooms as laboratories and our students as collaborators, we are changing the way we work with students as we look at our classrooms systematically thorough research. (Hubbard and Power, 1993, p. xiii)

The idea of action research--of teachers systematically studying and improving their own practice--is not new. It is based, in part, on Kurt Lewin's theory of social science research. Lewin (1948) believed that social science should focus on real situations, not laboratory situations. Stephen Corey (1953) applied Lewin's idea of action research to education. By planning and implementing changes, carefully noting effects, evaluating outcomes, and then revising based on results, teachers can understand and improve their teaching. Corey noted, "The value of action research...is determined primarily by the extent to which findings lead to improvement in the practices of the people engaged in the research" (p. 9).

There are many approaches to action research (Calhoun, 1993; McCutcheon & Jung, 1990; McKniff, 1993; McKernan, 1991; Richardson, 1996), but most include five phases that define a cycle of planning, action, and reflection:
- Reflecting on current practice to identify a problem or goal
- Planning a response (what will be done, what data will be collected, what observations made or records kept)
- Acting--implementing the plan
- Evaluating the evidence to determine the effects of the actions
- Reflection--revising plans based on the evaluation and continuing the cycle

This cycle is similar to the systematic approach to behavior change described in Chapter 6, Thomas Gordon's no-lose problem solving method explained in Chapter 12, and to many other approaches to planning. This cycle can be applied to a simple problem related to one student or to a school-wide project to revise the curriculum. The critical feature is that actions are planned and evaluated in light of carefully gathered and meaningful evidence. Very often action research in schools is collaborative--teachers working with each other, with university professors, with students, or even with parents to study and improve teaching and learning.

Calhoun, E. F. (1993). Action research: Three approaches. <u>Educational Leadership, 51</u>(2), 55-60.
Corey, S. M. (1993). <u>Action research to improve school practices</u>. New York: Teachers College Press.
Hubbard, R. S., & Power, B. M. (1993). <u>The art of classroom inquiry: A handbook for teacher-researchers</u>. Portsmouth, NH: Heinemann.
Lewin, K. (1948). <u>Resolving social conflict.</u> New York: Harper and Brothers.
McCutcheon, G., & Jung, B. (1990). Alternative perspectives on action research. <u>Theory Into Practice, 29</u>(3), 144-151.
McKernan, J. (1991). <u>Curriculum action research: A handbook of methods and resources for the reflective practitioner</u>. London: Kogan Page Limited.
McNiff, J. (1993). <u>Teaching as learning: An action research approach</u>. London: Routledge.
Richardson, V. (1996). The case for formal research and practical inquiry in teacher education. In F. B. Murray (Ed.), <u>The teacher educator's handbook: Building a knowledge base for the preparation of teachers</u> (pp. 715-737). San Francisco: Jossey-Bass.